Christian Social Witness and Teaching

Volume I

To His Holiness Pope John Paul II
in boundless admiration and deepest gratitude
for his work for the Church and the world.
'Fearless in unshakable hope
deeply in love with God'
[Mother Teresa]

Christian Social Witness
and
Teaching

The Catholic Tradition from
Genesis to Centesimus Annus

Volume I

From Biblical Times to the Late Nineteenth Century

Rodger Charles SJ

First published in 1998

Gracewing
Fowler Wright Books
2 Southern Avenue, Leominster
Herefordshire HR6 0QF

Published with ecclesiastical approval

Vol I paperback ISBN 0 85244 460 5
Vol II paperback ISBN 0 85244 461 3

Typesetting by Action Typesetting Ltd,
Gloucester, GL1 1SP

Printed by Cromwell Press,
Trowbridge, Wiltshire, BA14 0XB

General Contents

Analytical Contents

Part 1: The Scriptures and the early Church

Chapter 11 The medieval Church: some social attitudes

Part 3 The marginalization of the Church in the modern world (c 1500–1878): Absolutism, imperialism and revolutions

Chapter 12 The Church, absolutism and imperialism

Chapter 13 The age of revolutions: the seventeenth to the nineteenth centuries

Foreword

As the Introduction to this first volume shows, by the late 1980s, with the increasing interest in liberation theology, the collapse of real Communism and the lead given by John Paul II in the revitalization of the social teaching of the Church, our understanding of the nature of that teaching and what is required for a properly balanced study and knowledge of it has been deepened and clarified, and this work is based on these developments. They tell us that the sources of the teaching are fourfold, forming an integrated whole.

1 The teaching of the scriptures on social ethics.
2 The apostolic tradition, that is the relevant teaching of the Fathers and Doctors of the Church, the decisions and directives of Councils and Popes, especially the Popes since 1878, the witness of the Saints and martyrs, and the writings of approved theologians and philosophers on social ethics.
3 The experience of the Church and her members throughout her history, in different cultures and social, political and economic systems.
4 The relevant findings of the human and social sciences.

The work then is in four parts based on this structure:

Part One   The Scriptures and the Early Church.
Part Two   Western Christendom c604–1500; the social role of the Church.
Part Three The marginalization of the Church in the modern world [c1500–1878]: absolutisms, imperialism and revolutions.
Part Four   The modern teaching: contexts, summaries, analysis.

The first three parts constitute the first volume. Though the Church has no direct mandate in social, political and economic affairs – the secular order having its own legitimate autonomy under the natural law – yet she is the first budding forth of the kingdom of God on this earth, and the good of the secular order must be of concern to her for that reason; when we pray that 'thy will be done on earth', we are praying for true charity and justice in human society, and through her moral and spiritual guidance the Church makes her contribution to it. Through considering the Christian social witness and teaching from the scriptures and the Church's experience in history, we understand the influence she has had on the development of ideas, organizations and institutions which have contributed to human advancement, to works of charity and justice, and the evolution of the social, political, and economic forms which serve the needs of mankind. We also see what problems have arisen for her in her efforts to influence, for the good, secular developments in these areas, her successes and her failures, and the lessons to be learned from both. We then understand the foundations of the modern teaching and are better able to judge its application to society in the modern world.

The fourth part, the modern teaching, constitutes the second volume; that modern teaching is contained in the Papal social encyclicals from 1878, and other Papal pronouncements which deal with social issues, the teaching of the Second Vatican Council, the documents that have emerged from the meetings of the Council of Latin American Bishops [CELAM II–IV 1968–1994], and those of the Congregation for the Doctrine of the Faith on Liberation theology [CDF 1984–86]. Though they were all issued within the last 100 years, and most of them in the last forty or so, examination of them forms fifty per cent of this study which deals with the development of a tradition over some two thousand years. We remember, however, that it was out of that tradition that the teaching they contain grew; they represent its maturing. These documents are the basis on which further developments of the teaching that new circumstances may require will take place. They therefore deserve and require their prominence in such a study as this.

The main problem with the presentation of the social teaching of the Church is that it is too easy for those presenting it, consciously or unconsciously, to impose their own social, political and economic agenda on it, either only dealing with these aspects which suit that agenda, or being biased in favour of those elements, so that the balance of the teaching is destroyed and other valid options for Christian commitment are down played. Since they are citizens of a free society, those who teach Catholic social doctrine will as responsible citizens have their own political opinions and they will range across the whole right, left and centre perspectives within the limits of that doctrine, but they must avoid the temptation to let their own opinions colour the way in which they approach the subject. They must make clear that they respect all the political options a Christian in good conscience can take, not only that which they have espoused. The Church's social teaching is not to be used to support the personal beliefs or options of a person or group, any expert or any school of thought, any race, culture or political and economic system or party, or particular interest. It must be allowed to speak for itself and tolerate or encourage all that it tolerates or encourages. Some of its ethical judgements on particular matters will favour one school of thought, or one party or interest on specifics, but except in extreme cases where the good of souls and fundamental human rights demand, this should not be stressed. Where those goods do require it then the decision is for the Bishops, in union with Rome. Where the majority of the people are Catholics it is difficult for her to maintain this freedom but she must strive to do so, as her experience in such cultures teaches. So the titanic struggles she engaged in with the German Emperors and the other Catholic crowned heads of Europe in medieval times and then against the Bourbons in the eighteenth century. All centred on the question of giving Caesar his due while also giving God the same.

In summary, the presenter of the modern teaching must deal with the whole of it, and must do so in a balanced way so that the left, right and centre can see where their responsibilities lie. This means expounding the texts in such a way that their overall message is clear. The defects of the literature in the field, including my own previous contributions, were apparent to me as I grappled with the problems of teaching the subject in the late 1980s and I decided that I would make a study of the whole Catholic tradition with the hope of providing an exhaustive and balanced treatment of it and providing a coherent analysis which the reader could see was tied to the texts, allowing that teaching to speak for itself so that the reader could make up his or her own mind as to whether I had interpreted it correctly or not.

Given the vast mass of material that has to be so expounded, the only practical way to do this was to provide a summary paragraph by paragraph, or page by page where relevant, of each document – with each page or paragraph numbered to facilitate exact reference to the full text, and direct quotes from the texts on key points in the summaries. This is the method that has been adopted in the second volume of this study. There remains no substitute for the reading of the full documents themselves but this compromise in the face of necessity will, I think, give the essential teaching in

outline and make easy the reference to the originals where particular problems or ideas arise on cases in point. An analysis of the
teaching of each group of documents, showing its coherence
under the headings of civil, political and economic society, is also
provided so that the essential theory is evident. The final chapter
of volume two gives a summary of the teaching and its theory
overall in some forty pages.

The study will also, I hope, provide a methodology, the syllabus
which will encourage the study of Catholic social doctrine as an
academic sub discipline in its own right, and to the standard of any
other serious academic subject, because unless this is done it
cannot be put properly at the service of the Church. Her social
doctrine is part of her moral theological patrimony, but it has
always been difficult to deal with that teaching within the confines
of a purely theological/philosophical academic approach because
the understanding of it, of its evolution, its relevance to the problems of human society and the value of its application to the
modern world, requires a range of historical knowledge and a
familiarity with the main problems of social, political and
economic theory and practice which goes well beyond any purely
theological or philosophical syllabus as traditionally understood.
Though therefore in essence it is theological and philosophic, it is
also essentially interdisciplinary, demanding a coherent, well
ordered and integrated knowledge from the other fields indicated
in order to achieve its purpose. I hope I have shown this. My experience of presenting a postgraduate course on the subject,
following a syllabus similar to this tells me it can be done, and the
one that these volumes contain is a considerable improvement on
the one I have previously taught because of the clarifications the
documents and the experience of the Church over the last decades
have given us. From among the graduates studying the subject as
structured on the fourfold approach here suggested, would come
those who wish to do further research on aspects of it, and publish
their results so that we can build up a properly integrated, scholarly and popular literature on it. Now that the book is published, I
will be devoting myself to that task of establishing a post graduate
degree on the subject, and developing the needed doctoral
programme.

In its writing over many years, and bringing it to publication, I
find myself in debt to many for their help, advice and encouragement. Thanks first to the British Province of the Society of Jesus for
giving me the freedom, and the means, to conduct the study and
particularly for financial help in preparing it for publication, and

to my colleagues at Campion Hall where the obsession with getting the book finished and published, in the face of a series of happenings which seemed determined to prevent that actuality, has not made me the best of companions over the years. I am grateful to the Directors of the Ignatius Institute at the University of San Francisco, Fr. Bob Maloney SJ and Mr John Galten, and to my students there, who in the Fall Semesters 1986–91 gave me the opportunity to begin to clarify my ideas through teaching. Thanks are due also to the Moral and Pastoral theology group on the Theological Faculty of the University of Oxford for accepting me among their number and requiring minimal teaching duties of me while it was being researched and written here in Oxford 1991–97.

In the last stages of its preparation for publication I owe a very special debt of gratitude to Fr. Alfred Buttigieg SJ, one of my colleagues at Campion Hall, among whose many talents is an understanding of the mysteries of computer technology and all that, of which I was totally ignorant at the outset and remain not much wiser at the end. I would have had great difficulty in bringing the book to be without his help. Likewise I am indebted to Fr. Edward Yarnold SJ, who guided it through one of the more delicate later stages of preparation for publication. Mr. Stratford Caldecott of Westminster College was also generously supportive, as were the Rev. Dr. Frank McHugh of St. Edmund's College Cambridge and Fr. Jock Earle SJ, former Provincial, on sabbatical at Campion Hall from South Africa in 1995, both of whom read the whole text and helped me with their comments. It helps also to have an understanding publisher, and I have one in Tom Longford, and an efficient and long suffering Production Manager in Jo Ashworth – and her team – who put up with more than the normal annoyances during its progress to the press and publication. My grateful thanks to them all.

Rodger Charles SJ
Campion Hall
3rd February 1998

Introduction

The relationship between Christian social witness and teaching is one which has been highlighted by liberation theology; its view has been that praxis comes before theory in the sense that theology is only valid when it is 'done' by those involved in work for the liberation of the poor. In fact Christian praxis and theory, though they can be distinguished, cannot be opposed; the two have always gone hand in hand, with orthodoxy of doctrine having the logical precedence. It is because there was an embryo social doctrine[1] in the Scriptures and in the tradition, that in the early Church Christians were able to give witness to their beliefs in social action before theology as a science, of which social doctrine is part, evolved. Christian social witness developed on sound theoretical lines because it was faithful to the guidance given by the revealed word of God. Orthodoxy preceded orthopraxis, as it must. This orthodoxy, and the orthopraxis based on it, were reflected on by the Fathers and theologians of the Church and formed the heart of the social teaching they elaborated. Once elaborated, it was subject to development, as all doctrine is, through the evolution of Christian moral philosophy and theology over the centuries. The Scriptures, the living tradition and the magisterium provide the Catholic theological tradition with its methodology. Though the phrase 'social doctrine' or teaching is a modern one, the reality it refers to is not; it has in essence been there since the beginning and has developed throughout the Church's history.

The shock of the Protestant Reformation in the sixteenth century, the result of the corruption in the Church which popes and bishops were too slow to check, did much to put that theology and theologians on the defensive. Establishment of theology on a firmer basis took precedence of all else as the Catholic Counter-

Reformation got under way. In its turn that Counter-Reformation Church had to struggle to make the reforms effective in a Christian world, still European in its orientation, in which the Catholic crowned heads of Europe were almost at one in seeking to limit as much as possible the influence of the reforming international Church, personified in the Papacy. They wished to control the Church in their own realms according to their own ideas without interference from Rome.

This was the background to the eighteenth century, the Enlightenment and the Industrial Revolution, which made the modern world. The Catholic kings and princes were on the point of achieving their ambition to neutralize the Papacy in the period immediately before the French Revolution as Gallicanism, Febronianism and Josephism flourished. The revolutionary forces which swept away the absolute monarchies threatening the international Church thereby saved her, but the Revolution itself was not her friend. Meanwhile the Enlightenment, which also saw the Church as its enemy, had provided Europe with a self-confident ideology which dispensed with the God of revelation and salvation, an ideology which exactly suited the ambitions of the new industrial capitalist class and its friends who were in process of developing the Western economies in accordance with the principles of liberal capitalism. Those principles denied the right of God or man to limit the industrialist's pursuit of the maximum profit regardless of the personal or social rights of others. The result was that the social problems of industrialization combined with theories let loose by the French Revolution, to produce the labour unrest, socialism, Marxism and anarchism which in the nineteenth century seemed likely to tear Western society apart.

The situation facing the Church in the early part of that century seemed at first a bleak one. She was still predominantly European but her basis in European society looked more uncertain than ever. The Papacy itself had been humiliated and its territory seized. Pius VI died as Napoleon's prisoner in 1799, and his successor Pius VII was also imprisoned by him. The central organization in Rome, and all the necessary services for the international Church, were for a time abandoned or in chaos. But appearances were deceptive. Pius VII regained the Papal States and lived to see his former jailor himself exiled and imprisoned for life. Rome and the international Church lived again and the spiritual and moral fervour of the Catholic communities throughout Europe increased, supporting missionary endeavours worldwide. One new problem faced her, however, and that was the social question, the labour problem presented by industrialization now affecting the mainland of Europe as the century went on. Until the 1830s no country with a sizeable Catholic population had been deeply affected by it but thereafter Belgium, France and Germany were, and the local churches were divided on how to respond. Since the problem was international, that meant a response from Rome and the Papacy. It came with the publication in 1891 of Leo XII's *Rerum Novarum*, the first of the modern social encyclicals. Since then there have been a series of such encyclicals and other authoritative documents issued by the Church, and we now have a corpus of writings which add to and update the patrimony of her social doctrine which has built up through the centuries. Particularly since the 1960s have conditions demanded that this teaching be presented in greater depth, and the number and comprehensiveness of the Church's documents on it since then enable us to see how study needs to be structured in order to give that depth.

1 The basis of the teaching and its purpose

That teaching rests on one principle, namely that 'individual human beings are the foundation, the cause and the end of every social institution'.[2] This stems from the 'primordial assertion' of Christian anthropology, 'that man is made in the image and likeness of God'[3] who, by the Incarnation, by God's becoming man in Christ, was 'raised to a dignity beyond compare' so that 'the Son of Man is in a certain way united with each man'.[4] Man then 'cannot be reduced to a mere fragment of nature or to an anonymous element in the human city'.[5] It is a contradiction of the dignity that is implied in man's being made in the image of his maker, if those who control social organizations make him a mere instrument in their hands. The purpose of the Church's social teaching is to give guidance on rights and responsibilities in the light of this dignity.

This social teaching is of 'permanent validity' and is an 'integral part of the Christian conception of life'[6] because man is a social animal; by his nature he congregates with others in private societies which form civil and ultimately political society. The teaching therefore is not something added as an optional extra to Christian belief: it is an integral part of it. In particular, it is not 'a third way between liberal capitalism and Marxist collectivism ... it constitutes a category of its own'. Nor is it an ideology, but the result of 'careful reflection on ... the complexities of human existence ... in the light of faith and the Church's tradition'[7] and its modern development since *Rerum Novarum* constitutes an 'updated doctrinal corpus'.[8]

2 Sources of the teaching and its nature

Its origins therefore are in the Scriptures 'beginning with the book of Genesis ... the Gospel and the writings of the Apostles'. It is 'born of the encounter of the Gospel message and of its demands, summarized in the supreme commandment of love of God and neighbour in justice'. It develops as the Church faces 'problems emanating from life in society' and establishes itself 'as a doctrine by using the resources of human wisdom and the sciences'.[9] It has built up gradually, the Church reading the signs of the times 'even as they unfold in the course of history ... to lead people to respond, with the support ... of rational reflection and of the human sciences, to their vocation as responsible builders of earthly society'.[10]

It is then concerned with the ethical aspects of social problems, taking into account 'the technical aspects ... but always in order to judge them from the moral point of view'.[11] It belongs therefore to theology ... 'and particularly moral theology'.[12] In particular it is concerned with the demands of love/charity and justice. The two go together. A social ethic that lacks one or the other, or overemphasizes one at the expense of the other, is from the Christian point of view fundamentally unsound. 'Justice alone can, if faithfully observed, remove the causes of social conflict, but it can never bring about the union of minds and hearts.' This will be achieved when 'the constituent parts of society feel themselves children of the same heavenly father'.[13]

This ethical, moral teaching is concerned to help Christians form their consciences on social, political and economic issues. Since Christ did not bequeath to the Church a mission in the social, political or economic order, but one which was religious,[14] that Church can claim no special competence in sociology, politics or economics; these are human sciences and have their own legitimate autonomy, their own purpose and methodology. It is not for the Church to determine the form of society, the State or government; nor is for her to decide who should wield political power or determine the policies pursued. The people and their chosen leaders must decide this. 'The Church, by reason of her role and competence, is not identified with any political community nor bound by ties to any political system.' It must be first and foremost both a sign and a guarantee that the person transcends the secular and political order.[15]

One implication of this is that the clergy, from the highest to the lowest, have no mandate in these matters. They have the right to their own political views provided they are compatible with the Church's social teaching, and provided also they do not let them colour the public responsibilities they possess as preachers of the Gospel. In dealing with political, social and economic issues when it is part of their task, the clergy must only concern themselves with the moral issues involved and must avoid political partisanship. By contrast the laity have to take their full part in the affairs of the earthly city according to their respective vocations and abilities, and so contribute to the common good, and they are entitled to declare their loyalties. They cannot 'shirk their earthly responsibilities'; rather, Christian belief demands that in these matters they should be 'even more ready to fulfil their responsibilities according to the vocation of each'.[16] For clergy and laity alike, the social doctrine of the Church should be their guide. The doctrine is dynamic, not static; it offers principles for reflection, criteria for judgement and directives for action.[17] 'Far from constituting a closed system, it remains constantly open to new questions which continually arise; it requires the contribution of all charisms, experiences and skills'.[18] The principles it teaches are no substitute for, bur rather should stimulate the 'acquisition of the essential technical and scientific skills' needed for practical social action. It does not 'dispense from education in the political prudence needed for guiding and running human affairs'.[19] In their commitment, lay Christians should respect legitimate differences of opinion regarding the management of secular affairs and respect those who have different political affiliations, all of which, however, must put the common good first.[20]

3 The development of the teaching and the structure of this study

In summary then the origins of the teaching are fourfold. It is derived from (i) the Scriptures, (ii) the tradition of the Church, that is, the teaching of its Fathers and Doctors, the decisions of councils and popes, the witness of the saints, and the writings of approved theologians and philosophers, (iii) the experience of the Church and her members throughout her history among peoples of all cultures and social, political and economic systems, and (iv) in the relevant findings of non-Christian and thinkers and writers on the social, political and economic life of man. It also draws on the lessons to be learned from the experience of different non-Christian social, political and economic systems.

In the Old and New Testaments, the history of the people of God reveals a pattern of response to the needs of the world around it, guided by the sacred writers. In the witness of the early Church in the first and second centuries we see her putting those scriptural principles into practice, when theology was in its infancy. The early Church refused in any way to seek direct influence on social, political and economic affairs as such, but she had a slow permeative effect on them through example and practice, and where the choice between loyalty to the Church and loyalty to the State had to be faced, her martyrs, by their refusal to bow to the almighty State, made a statement with political implications which profoundly affected the development of Western ideas of personal freedom. Her organized works of charity were also new in their scale, their comprehensiveness and the soundness of the theory that lay behind them. The Fathers of the Church drew on this experience in giving us the main elements of a Christian social ethic; in so doing they also drew on the classical authors, Cicero and Seneca in particular, where their reasoning possessed insights which helped clarify those of the Christian tradition.

Under the Christian Roman Empire after AD 313 the Church had the first experience of reconciling her rights with those of the State in a society where she was no longer in danger of persecution, but positively accepted. Her moral stature and the strength of her social organization made it inevitable that the disintegrating State would make use of her in many ways. This close alliance posed problems, to which answers were only partially found before the collapse of the Roman power in the West in the fifth and sixth centuries. On this too the Fathers of the Church reflected in developing her social teaching.

With the Papacy of Gregory I 'the Great' (590–604), the historical period which has come to be known as the Middle Ages can be accounted to have had its beginning, and the context of the Church's work of evangelization changed completely once more. With the Roman civilization and culture in the West finally disintegrating around her, she found herself the only social organization which retained its structures and vitality. Since she existed throughout the extent of the former Roman world, it was only she who kept alive what survived of the Graeco-Roman tradition of order, government and civilization. It was on the Church's

personnel, organization and spiritual and moral resources that the
Franks drew in establishing once more in Europe, however briefly,
a civilized State in the eighth and ninth centuries. The kingdom
and Empire of the Franks, the Papacy, the monasteries and the
Church's organization were the mainsprings of medieval civilization.

In the early Middle Ages, agriculture was the basis of the
economy and the Church was at home in it. She was also equally at
home in the urbanizing central period; the towns fostered the new
universities which sprang up primarily to meet the needs of clerical education; they were the centres of the apostolic work of the
new religious orders, and in them too flourished the hospitals and
her other works of charity. In providing these educational and
social welfare services, as well as being the effective registrar of
births and deaths, she possessed functions which were later
regarded as proper to the State. European society was the first to
have religious uniformity for a very large population as a whole; at
the same time the Church insisted that she was autonomous in all
that concerned her spiritual mission, and these factors enabled her
to have an unparalleled influence on social developments. Society
and Church were, for many practical purposes, one during a
period of some eight hundred years. It was the time when the mind
of European society was slowly moulded and its institutions were
framed. These modern Europe inherited and developed, and
through them they have had influence on the nations of the world.

The Church's experience in the exercise of her secular influence in the medieval period raises the question of her
identification with a political system, and we will have to examine
the implications of this at some length, so important are the
lessons it has for us. It was one of the reasons why, in the late
Middle Ages (c. 1300–1500), her spiritual and moral influence,
which had been the reason for the Church's wide acceptance and
influence in medieval society, was in decline. Later, with the
Renaissance and the Reformation, and the ages of absolutism,
reason and the Enlightenment, she was increasingly marginalized
in European affairs.

With the advent of the Industrial Revolution in the England of
the eighteenth and nineteenth centuries, which for the first time
produced a major civilization based on an industrial economy and
an urbanized people, 'the social problem' emerged: the problem,
that is, of providing fair working and living conditions, and financial rewards, for the non-property owning majority of wage earners
in the towns and cities, whose labour contributed so much to the

new wealth-creation process. This was the context in which the modern social magisterium began to develop, and *Rerum Novarum* was its founding document.

This outline of the contexts in which the Church's social teaching developed provides the framework of this study, which is in four parts. The first deals with the Scriptures and the early Church, the second with Western Christendom in the Middle Ages, and the third with the situation which faced an increasingly marginalized Church as the modern world emerged in the sixteenth to the nineteenth centuries. These three parts constitute this the first of the two volumes. The fourth part constitutes the second: it examines the documents of the modern social teaching from 1891 down to today, looking at the background of the successive popes who were mainly responsible for that development, and also at the contexts in which their teaching was elaborated. It concludes with a summary of teaching as we have it today.

Part 1
The Scriptures and the early Church

1

The Old Testament

1 Introduction

The Old Testament, which we think of as one book, is in fact a compilation of books; some of which are concerned with the history of a people, formed under the guidance of the Holy Spirit, and reminded throughout that history of God's great mercy to them. The Israelites were very much aware of their special destiny, of their being God's chosen people and of their place in God's plan. But the message of the Scriptures was not for the Israelites only. They give us an account of God's self-revelation to all mankind and his instructions for its right living. They are valid for all men and women and all time. From the Scriptures we get the essential guidance we need on all aspects of man's life before God. That does not mean that they constitute a theological textbook, still less a complete guide to social ethics, its teaching on which subject is our particular concern, but unless we take their teaching into account, our theology or social ethics will not be Christian.

What the Old Testament has to tell us, then, is very much tied up with the history of a people God had chosen for himself.[1] In the first stage, the age of the patriarchs (c. 2000 to 1700 BC) Abraham and his successors were semi-nomads who led their people from Mesopotamia to Canaan. Emigrating to Egypt under the leadership of Jacob in a time of famine, they so flourished there that their hosts, fearful of them, oppressed them until, in about 1300 BC, Moses was inspired by God to free them from their bondage and to form them into a nation, through some 40 years of wandering in the desert.

The years of hardship encouraged a strong sense of community and racial unity, and the decisive religious experience of Mount

* The notes and references for Chapter 1 are to be found on p. 375

Sinai and the Covenant sealed the bond with their God; it was his
power that was at work, not their genius. During a period of some
150 years they then, again by his power, won a foothold and then
dominance in the promised land of Canaan. At this time they were
a loose confederation of tribes, with judges, who were prophetic,
political and sometimes military leaders, raised up at crucial times
to guide them.[2] Samuel was the last of the judges, Saul the first
king. David ruled c. 1000 to 961 BC, and then his son Solomon from
961 to 922. Thereafter the kingdom divided into two, the northern
state, Israel, surviving until 721 and the southern, Judah, until 587.
It was in the period preceding Israel's fall that the written prophets
inveighed against the idolatries and injustices that were common-
place among the people of God as they became increasingly
affluent; the failure to heed the prophetic warnings of the
inevitable result of their infidelity in time led to their fulfilment.
The exile in Babylon lasted until 539. Thereafter they were subject
to other races until, in 63 BC, Rome intervened and Palestine
became part of the Roman Province of Syria.

2 The God of love, holiness and justice

The law given at Sinai outlines a social order, primitive by modern
reckoning, but one sound in ethical essentials: worship of Yahweh
is its focal point, justice its basis and love its inspiration. His people
were to love and worship him, and in return his care for them was
to be total.[3] The gods of other nations were personifications of
natural forces or of the nation's power. But Yahweh was the creator
of heaven and earth and all they contain, who held all things in
being, the only true God, eternal, all-powerful and all-holy. He had
chosen his people not because they were the largest of the nations:
they were the smallest. They were chosen because the Lord loved
them (Deut. 7:7).

God's tender and undying love for his people is reflected in the
imagery used by the Bible to describe it. A woman does not forget
the baby at the breast, the child to which she has given birth. Nor
will God forget his people (Isa. 49:15). He had chosen them but,
since he wanted them to come to him in freedom, his choice
implied his acceptance of their capacity for wrong choices, for sin,
and from their infidelity flowed terrible consequences. But his will
for them, his command to them, was to be holy as he was holy (Lev.
19:2). Etymologically the word 'holiness'[4] indicates that which is
other, marked off from the ordinary; it suggests something

removed from common experience, beyond it. They were to be holy as God is holy – which in human terms meant leading an upright personal moral life. The Baals of the Canaanite peoples among whom the Israelites lived in their promised land were as local and arbitrary as they were immoral. The religion their devotees practised was immoral of its nature: they worshipped the god of fertility, and sexual rites were part of that worship. Human sacrifice was sometimes offered also.[5] The gods of classical Greece and Rome were little better. They were 'never predominantly ethical and sometimes definitely immoral'.[6] Such deities merely reflected the sinfulness of man and man's world and could give him no confidence in an abiding and just moral order. But to love Yahweh was to love goodness and truth and to accept the obligation of obeying his absolute moral law.

There are similarities between the Covenant and the law of contemporaneous cultures, but several things distinguish the former from them. Most importantly, in the Code of Hammurabi for example, while God is mentioned at the beginning of the law and at the end, 'in the law itself the deity is silent and the human lawgiver takes the centre of the stage; the Code is expressly described as the king's own work throughout'.[7] In Israel by contrast, God, religion, law and morality are powerfully linked. There is also absent from the Law the gross brutality found in other codes; it has a greater respect for human dignity, a nobler ideal, shown in its treatment of strangers. The Hebrews were strangers in Egypt and had known harsh treatment (Exod. 22:21). They were to love strangers, the exiles among their neighbours, as themselves, not to reflect in their attitude to them the same injustice they had suffered.

In that the law bound them to God and to one another they possessed a profound social solidarity.[8] Yet though the law was for the people in general, the Decalogue especially speaks to the individual; the community, important though it was, did not dominate. The law demanded a personal response, the acceptance of personal moral responsibility for one's choices, which was the key to social solidarity. All were bound by the same law of love and its exact requirements; there was a real basis for social coherence and mutual trust. None was above the law, even the most powerful.

Their God was a God of justice (Deut. 32:4–5). The idea of righteousness or justice[9] was a key concept in the Old Testament. Obeying the law was effectively maintaining righteousness: to do the right, justice, was to restore it when it had been abandoned as a result of human weakness.[10]

Given that justice is for us primarily a legal concept, the giving to others what they have a legal claim to, charity is that virtue which disposes me to to give to others what is mine, out of compassion and for the love of God, and I give according to my means and generosity. Here the Old Testament has much to teach us. Its understanding of charity, social charity, or solidarity, makes it the dominant social virtue; it implies love and justice, and indeed this should be the perspective. But justice alone is not enough. It must proceed from love based on the knowledge that we are all children of the same Father.

3 Ethics and civil society

Civil society is prior to political society, and in complex political cultures we distinguish the two; in this way we understand the human rights of which political society may not deprive man. Israelite social organization was simple by modern standards. At its most numerous and powerful in the time of David and Solomon, it was numbered in tens and hundreds of thousands rather than millions. Yahweh and his Covenant were the focal point of their social order at all times. He had created them and all mankind in his own image, as intelligent social beings with free will, and he wanted them to serve him in freedom and love. All were bound to live in accordance with to God's objective moral law, and this would secure that solidarity in the stress of daily living as a people. The Ten Commandments bound them to love God above all and to respect their parents, marriage and sexual purity, life itself, the truth, justice and private property. There was to be no poor or oppressed class among them; the family property was to provide for all its members, and they had a particular responsibility to see that widows, orphans and strangers, all those whom misfortune had deprived of the close social support of the extended family, were cared for in their need.

4 Political ethics

(i) The development of Hebrew polity

Moses found the burden of leadership of the whole people too great and he needed assistance. He therefore instructed them to gather together wise men, men whose wisdom had been tested and proved, from each of the tribes and he would put them in charge, make them their leaders of the thousands, hundreds, fifties and tens (Deut. 1:13). They were told to give their brothers a fair hearing and to see justice done (Deut. 1:14–17). The desert wanderings and conquest subordinated the needs of the tribe to those of the whole people. During and after the settlement, the tribe remained the most significant unit of social organization. Until the time of the monarchy there was no State as we would understand it.

The settlement brought with it moral problems. The prophets contrast the fidelity to Yahweh that was a characteristic of the nomadic period (Jer. 2:2) with the moral and religious perversions that had accompanied the transition to urban life (Jer. 2:7). The sons and daughters of Israel did what displeased Yahweh and served the Baals, and for their surer guidance God appointed judges over them (Judg. 2:11–18) and then later allowed them kings. The first Book of Samuel gives us an account of the transition of Israel to monarchy, which it was hoped would make it easier for the Israelites to overcome their enemies. Samuel had been called by God to be his prophet, a judge of his people (1 Sam. 3); he kept them united, but his two sons were too corrupt to succeed him and the elders asked instead for a king (1 Sam. 8:1–5). They were warned by Samuel that the king would take their sons for his armies, their daughters for his servants and their lands for his officials (1 Sam. 8:10–18), but they insisted. Saul was the first king, and he embodied the ambiguities of the institution at the outset. The account of the origins of the monarchy shows it was not in itself divine, as it was considered to be in other cultures. The human failings of the kings kept the man and the institution in proportion.

God then gave to his people the right to choose the political system they would live under (1 Sam. 10:1). Yahweh was prepared to grant them their king with his blessing and approval, and in time to use the monarchy for his purposes.[11] On Solomon's death, Judah and Israel parted company, sometimes allies, sometimes enemies, always independent, although their peoples felt they were one. The federation of tribes was remembered and the prophets looked forward to reunion.

(ii) Theocracy and monarchy

Despite the acceptance by Yahweh of the desire of the people for a monarchy, a tradition of hostility to the institution remained in Israel (Hos. 7:3–7). By contrast it was regarded highly by another strand in that tradition which glorified David and his dynasty (Pss. 20, 21) but at all times it is stressed that the Kings ruled as chosen, accepted or tolerated by God, remaining subject to him and being judged by their degree of fidelity to the Covenant.[12] As under Moses, it is God's intervention and law which is paramount: political events serve them, not vice versa. Hence the exodus had not been primarily a political event, and it is regarded by the inspired word of God in the Old Testament not as an escape by a people, but as a deliverance of slaves, God setting them free to become a nation, to become his people. It is a demonstration of his mighty power.[13]

Solomon (962–922 BC) consolidated his power by political alliances with Egypt and Tyre, and made his into a great trading nation. His building projects were on a magnificent scale, and he was renowned for his wisdom and his patronage of the arts. The policies of David and Solomon transformed Israel, with its probable population of some 800,000 people,[14] from a tribal confederation with its in-built protection for all, into an increasingly urbanized society in which social injustices flourished. Nor was Solomon faithful to the law in his private life. In response to the pleas of the women of his harem he also allowed the worship of false gods (1 Kings 11:1–8). There was an unsuccessful revolt by Jeroboam and an increasing discontent among the people because of the forced labour imposed on them. Rehoboam (922–915) destroyed his chances of being chosen king when he threatened to increase the impositions of Solomon rather than to decrease them.

The northern kingdom, Israel, became independent under Jeroboam I. Ahab (869–850) allowed Baal-worship for which Elijah took him to task. Jehu's ruthlessness brought forth the prophet Hosea's condemnation (Hos. 1:4). Jeroboam II (786–746) gave his people general peace and prosperity, marred by religious abuses which roused the prophets Amos and Hosea. Hosea deplores the lack of tenderness, the perjury, the lies, theft, adultery and murder (4:1), the fraud, the amassing of fortunes which would not be kept because of the guilt of the owners (12:8). Amos, a near-contemporary of Hosea, condemned the effects of luxury in Israel, the corrupt city life, the social injustice, during the rule of Jeroboam II. 'They sell the virtuous man for silver and the poor for a pair of sandals; they trample on the heads of ordinary people and push the poor out of their path' (Amos 2:6–7). Yahweh wants no more of their sacrifices; instead, 'justice is to flow like water, and integrity like an unfailing stream' (5:24).

In the reign of Ahaz (735–715) in Judah, Isaiah and Micah

prophesied. Isaiah warned that Yahweh calls to judgement the elders and the princes of the people, asking by what right they grind the faces of his poor (Isa. 3:13–15). He denounced those who add house to house and join field to field until all the world goes wanting (Isa. 5:8–9). They were told to cease doing evil and learn to do good, search for justice, help the oppressed, be just to the orphan, plead for the widow (1:16–17). Micah also denounced those who seize the fields and houses they covet, who snatch the cloak from an innocent man's shoulders, drive women out of their homes and exact extortionate pledges (Mic. 2:2 and 8–10). Yahweh condemns those who do violence, and the liars. The devout have fled the land, each man is against his brother, the judge is bribed, a man's enemies are those of his own household (Mic. 7:2–6). Yahweh asks of his people that they abandon such ways of behaving and 'act justly, love tenderly and walk humbly' with him, their God (Mic. 6:8).

After the fall of Israel in 721, Judah became a satellite of Assyria and the disregard of the law went on. King Hezekiah (715–687), ignored Isaiah's warnings that he remain clear of political entanglements, and his conflict with Assyria led to defeat. Manasseh (687–642) undermined the reforms of his predecessor. Josiah (640–609) was faithful to the Covenant and restored the reforms, but Jehoiakim (609–598) was weak and irreligious and the evil practices returned once more. When he led a rebellion against Babylon, now the power in the region, Judah was defeated and surrendered in 597, Zedekiah (597–587) being the last king, and Nebuchadnezzar taking Jerusalem in 587. Jeremiah prophesied during the last years of Judah, denouncing a people who were stubborn and unresponsive. They ignored his demands that they lead upright lives – practise honesty and integrity, rescue the man who has been wronged by the oppressor, avoid exploiting the stranger, the orphan or the widow, doing no violence, and shedding no innocent blood (Jer. 22:3–4). He condemned those who made others work for them for nothing, without paying wages (Jer. 22:13).

With the exile, the period of the monarchy ended and the Israelite experiment with a formal political system ended also. Their choice of a monarchy had been approved by Yahweh. In the Middle East generally monarchy was seen as the political order ordained by God for the maintenance of Empire, but for the Israelites, with their awareness of the power and immediacy of the Covenant, and of the one true and jealous God who brooked no equal, the idea of the king as the Lord's anointed meant much more, and much less.

Above all, it avoided any suggestion that the king himself might
be a god; it made the king the agent of the Covenant, binding him
especially to give justice to his people (Ps. 72). The king himself
was subject to that justice. Kings could be challenged for their
misdeeds: David was called to account by the prophet Nathan for
his abuse of his power in arranging for the death of Uriah the
Hittite, whose wife he coveted (2 Sam. 12:1, 14) and King Ahab was
also brought to book by Elijah for allowing himself to be persuaded
by his wife that, in order to have Naboth's vineyard, she should
arrange the latter's judicial murder (1 Kings 21). In this Israel
made one high contribution to political ethics – that all those who
wield worldly power do so subject to God's laws by which they will
be judged; God is the source of social order and justice.[15]

5 Economic ethics

(i) Land and the economy

The basis of the economy of the people of God was land, and so
it is the ethics of land distribution and use which is at the heart
of their economic ethic. From the first chapter of Genesis, it is
stressed that the land is God's gift, providing from its agricultural
and other riches the means needed for man's support. It was a
gift to all mankind. God planted a garden and settled man to
cultivate it (Gen. 2:8, 15). He was to fill the earth and conquer it
(Gen. 1:28), being given all the plants (Gen. 1:29) and animals
for his use (Gen. 1:30), a gift which implied that that use must
be such as would please the giver. The particular land the
Israelites were to have for themselves was rich, a land of streams
and springs, of wheat and barley, of vines and fig trees, of olives,
oil and honey, and in it they would want for nothing – a generous gift indeed (Deut. 8:7–10). They were not to forget his gift,
making the mistake of thinking that it was their own strength,
their own efforts, that they had to thank for their good fortune.
It was the Lord who gave it to them, so confirming his Covenant
(Deut. 8:17).

There were to be no poor among them (Deut. 15:4). Each family
was to have its own land so that there was no economically
oppressed class as such. All should be able to get a decent living
through the extended family, the clan, the tribe with its endow-
ment of land distributed among individual families. The norm was
to be that every man should live under his own vine and fig tree (1

Kings 5:5, Mic. 4:4). There would always be the unfortunate, however, who fell on hard times (Deut. 14:11). These – the widows and orphans, and the strangers with no family connections which would give them a claim on the land – were to have a just share of its riches. The third-year tithe was for them (Deut. 14:28) and the gleanings of the harvests (Lev. 19:9–10). It was also always permissible to pick from the growing crops what was necessary to eat, providing nothing was carried away (Deut. 23:24–25). In the sabbatical (seventh) year the poor were to be allowed to take what grew untended in field, vine and olive grove (Exod. 23:10–11). All were to be released from their debts in the sabbatical years and all Israelite slaves freed (Deut. 15:1, 12). Wages were to be paid promptly and the taking of articles in pledge was not to lead to injustice or deprivation, nor to the humiliation of those pledging them (Deut. 24:6, 10, 14–15, 17).

The organization of the bounty given to them was through individual property right. Unlike the Canaanite kingdoms around them, where the king owned all the land and the people held it as his tenants, the Israelites had their own holdings which they knew were Yahweh's gift to them. Hence Naboth's indignant protest when King Ahab sought to take his plot from him (1 Kings 21:1–3). The law gave him the ground for resistance. Finally, being aware of the importance of God's gift of the land to all as a sign of his care and love for them, its misuse roused the ire of the prophets. Injustice here struck at the heart of the covenant relationship. Those who were oppressing the poor were doing so by perverting the gift which Yahweh had intended should unite his people in love and justice. The land was his (Lev. 25:23).

They were to pay tithes and first fruits of what they owned: they were not to trade in the family property; there was to be no market in that commodity. Property and land could, however, be held in the towns and bought and sold. Social obligations were to be met, damage to property, or negligence in its regard, was to be made good, respect for boundary rights should be maintained and the laws about leaving harvest gleanings, fallow years, and the right of passers-by to pick for immediate use what is growing on the land should be observed. The treatment of farm workers was to be just. All this required self-discipline and trust in God's providence. The temptation to glean thoroughly after the harvest, to prevent passers-by taking away the produce, to ignore the injunction to leave the land fallow for a year when it could have been profitably worked – all had to be resisted. Letting a slave go after six years, cancelling debts, and redeeming family property entailed self-restraint. The prophets reminded them that if they did not exercise it they could not claim the advantages of the covenant relationship (Jer. 7:1–11).

The Covenant also implied the duty to work. It is in man's nature to work; it is his duty and his right as a human being. Idleness is sinful, as is preventing others from working: it goes against the original injunction of Genesis to till the earth and make it fruitful. The social idea given by the Law was that every man should live under his own vine and under his own fig tree as we have noted; each was to work his own land. If he lost that land, his nearest relatives had to reclaim it; Leviticus 25 proclaimed that in the fiftieth year of jubilee all land should be returned to its original owners, but this seems not to have happened in practice.[16]

(ii) Social divisions related to property and wealth

In the first stages of settlement, differences in economic prospects among Israelites were not great. The sharing of land by lot did not mean absolute equality between tribes and families, it is true, but because wealth initially came from working the land, and trade, commerce and the buying and selling of land were minimal, there was in general little chance of great variations of fortune. There were exceptions: Job possessed 7000 sheep and 3000 camels, and after the recovery of his fortunes was even wealthier (Job 1:3 and 42:10–13). Nabal, a 'man of means' in the time of David, had 3000 sheep and 1000 goats (1 Sam. 25:2). But by contrast David's family, like Saul's, was of moderate means.

Under the Omri dynasty in Israel (876–842) prosperity went along with increasing signs of social disunity.[17] In the southern kingdom the pattern was the same. The monarchy had bred a class of wealthy officials. Others had prospered by their efforts or good fortune and made great profits. The prophets condemn luxurious building (Hos. 8:14 and Am. 3:15). By contrast there were the poor, the weak, those men who owned little and struggled to hold on even to that. These were championed by the prophets. The poor however did not form a class. They were isolated and therefore defenceless. 'Rich' and 'poor' only implied conflict as time went on. In some contexts riches were seen as a reward for virtue (Ps. 112:1). In others not so: riches deprive man of his reason; he becomes like the beasts who are destroyed (Ps. 49:20). The condemnation of the injustices of the rich by the prophets we have examined. In Zephaniah the vocabulary changes as is it spiritualized; the poor are all those who are humble before God, for what ever reason, including, though not exclusively, the materially poor (Zeph. 2:3 and 3:12f.). The second Isaiah and the post-exilic psalter developed the theme;

'the terms for poverty had lost their sociological associations: neither before nor after the exile were the poor a religious party or a social class'.[18]

Apart from the free citizens of Israel, there were also within its borders travellers and strangers who needed protection (Deut. 15:3). At first they were usually poor, and the Israelites were to remember they too were once poor and strangers in Egypt (Deut. 15:1 and 16:12) and to treat them with love and justice (Deut. 14:28 and 15:11). Eventually some of them could prosper exceed-ingly (Lev. 25:47 and Deut. 28:43).

(iii) Wage workers, commerce, trade and finance

Wage workers could be hired for the day, for a season or by the year, and the law protected them.[19] Day workers were to be paid by the day (Lev. 19:13); there was to be no exploitation (Deut. 24:14–15); there was specific condemnation of those who make others work for nothing (Jer. 22:13). Urbanization and economic development meant the growth of the crafts: the family workshop with the trade handed on from father to son was the norm, though during the monarchy there were major enterprises under royal control. Large-scale commerce[20] and foreign trade were a royal monopoly. Citizens could only provide for the local market in town or village. There was no merchant class concerned with long-distance trade: the Phoenicians fulfilled this role in the region. Not until the exile in Babylon do the Jews appear as merchants, acting as clients or agents of the trading companies. Ben Sirach thought it 'difficult for a merchant to avoid doing wrong and for a salesman not to commit sin' (Sir. 26:29), yet he allowed that one should not be afraid of 'profits ... and gaining from commercial transactions' (Sir. 42:5). Good men could trade honestly.

Interest-free loans, or loans in kind, were the only ones recog-nized by the Covenant (Exod. 22:24). They envisaged the subsistence needs of those in desperate straits; these clearly had a strong claim on both justice and charity (Sir. 29:1). However, it was permissible to take interest from a loan to a non-Israelite (Deut. 23:21 and 15:6); the annual rate for such loans was anything from 12 to 33 per cent. In Hebrew, interest was 'a bite' or 'an increase'. The 'bite' could be applied by the borrower agreeing to sign a statement that 100 shekels had been lent when in fact only 80 had. Taking interest on money loans is one of the sins the prophets complained about (Ezek. 22:12) and, after the exile, Nehemiah lists the debt problem as pressing (Neh. 5:1–5). For a rich lender to charge interest on a loan to the poor man in desperate need was an abomination.[21]

(iv) The attitude to work, property and wealth[22]

The title to livelihood, when the people of God came into their promised land, was readiness to work that land. God himself is depicted as a worker in creating the world, and he gave the world to man who was made in his image, male and female (Gen. 1:27) to fill it and conquer it (Gen. 1:28). Adam was to 'cultivate the land and take care of it' (Gen. 2:15) before the Fall; work was part of the original plan, though it would have been without the element of suffering that became attached to it as a result of that Fall (Gen. 3:17). None the less, after it the original goodness and humanity of work itself remains from God's initial plan, since the Fall did not entirely corrupt mankind, but rather left it faced with the tendency to evil within. Manual work was honoured in Israel; God blessed Isaac, who sowed his land and reaped a hundred-fold (Gen. 26:12). Hard work was held in respect (Prov. 10:4–5); the craftsman and the careful housewife earned praise, the lazy being chided (Prov. 6:6). Idleness was a curse (Sir. 10:18) and labour commended (Exod. 34:21). The ideal was that of working for self and family on one's own property, but the law gave protection to those who supported themselves by wage work. Honest labour of any kind was to be respected; wages were to be paid in full (Lev. 19:13) and cheating the labourer of his wages forbidden (Jer. 22:13 and Isa. 58:3) – conditions frequently ignored from the time of Solomon, as the complaints of the prophets remind us.

Work then in general was blessed, and about the goodness of wealth in itself there were no reservations. Yahweh had given his people a prosperous land and wanted them to enjoy it, asking only that there be no poor class among them, that all be given access to an adequate livelihood and that the unfortunate, who would always be with them, also be provided for out of the wealth given to all. Though the covenant people were not egalitarian, they were constantly warned to be aware of the dangers to which the wealthy were exposed. They were warned that when they had fine houses and their flocks had increased, when they had gold and silver a-plenty and their possessions were great, they were not to become proud, telling themselves that they had done it all by their own efforts. It was Yahweh who brought them out of the land of Egypt and enriched them (Deut. 8:12–17).

Some social attitudes

The dignity of man

God created man in his own image and likeness 'male and female he created them' (Gen 1:27). When we speak of the dignity of man therefore we speak also of the dignity of woman. The priority that the Scriptures and the tradition based on them give to the male in certain respects is a functional one, not one that implies any personal inferiority. Genesis tells us how man becomes a living being, his life a divine gift bestowed directly by his maker; among God's creatures, only he is given life by a direct transfer of divine breath. When he does not find an equal, God provides him with one; the imagery used, of woman being created out of man's side, stresses her oneness with him, her full personal equality. The vision of man as the noblest of God's creation[23] is a vision of woman too.

The reality of human dignity is seen in the Covenant in the laws regarding property, the treatment of slaves, in the recognition that human life is of immeasurably greater value than material things, there is a new idea at work.

> 'The dominant feature throughout is respect for the rights of everything that has a human face ... because of the ... hitherto undreamt-of ... nobility of man, now recognized as a binding consideration for moral conduct.'[24]

In Israel the humblest foreigner is placed under the protection of God; and if he is without legal rights, to oppress him is like oppressing the orphan and the widow, a sin which calls forth divine retribution. The moral will of God holds good for all mankind as a whole. It constitutes an order of human life which transcends national and racial boundaries. All mankind is one, male and female, of whatever race, creed or culture – all are given the unique dignity of creation in the image and likeness of God, and by that common origin are, destined to be bound together in love and justice.

Women, marriage and the family

The male from the beginning recognizes woman as his equal, 'this is at last flesh of my flesh' (Gen. 2:23), a complementarity summed up in the coming together in one flesh in marriage. (Matt. 19:5–9). Sexuality was created by God for humanity. Though he refers to himself as masculine in his revelation, there is no sexuality in God: in this there is a 'radical break with the ideological and ritual background. Yahweh is unique ... he has no consort Goddess at his side'.[25] The sexual division in mankind became relevant in a particular way after the Fall, when as result of the consequent disorder in human nature, woman was told man would lord it over her (Gen. 3:16). In so far as men have done, and do, unjustly dominate women, God can in no way be seen as conniving with that evil simply because he is referred to in human language as masculine. The human sinfulness reflected in this evil can be overcome by grace; the original harmony can be found again in Christian marriage.

Monogamy was the norm laid down by Genesis (Gen. 2:21–24), as Christ's exegesis (Matt. 19:5–9) reminds us: polygamy and concubinage were excluded. Their adoption by the Israelites was a result of cultural pressures, but the most usual form of marriage in Israel was monogamy. There was also praise for lifelong fidelity: the book of Tobit speaks only of monogamy; the picture of a perfect wife (Prov. 31:10–31) is that of an equal partner, and 'there is no doubt that this was the normal picture ... a faithful reflection of the teaching enshrined in Genesis'.[26] Nor were women entirely excluded from public roles. Deborah and Jael were celebrated as national heroines (Judg. 4), the books of Judith and Esther relate the story of two women of great courage and powers of leadership, while the prophetess Huldah did not go unheeded (2 Kings 22:14).

These were the ideals; in practice women were a depressed class in Semitic society.[27] A woman was a man's property; a man could take one wife or several, and expect them to work as hard as any man; a wife could be punished by mutilation or death for her sexual infidelity while her husband's was treated lightly; she could also be divorced at will.

> In the rich valley of Mesopotamia, where women were less of a drudge and more generally endowed with legal rights, the highest eminence which woman could attain was that of temple prostitute.[28]

Genesis, however, stresses the importance of the sexual union as a union of equals, in the context of monogamy, family and perpetual fidelity. Sex was not seen as a value itself. Woman was meant to share man's whole life in that context, not only his sexual life. In so far as the Hebrews then followed their own cultural traditions they treated

women as inferior to men. In so far as they were faithful to the law
and to its teaching on marriage, as the best among them were, they
testified to the equality of personal dignity of man and woman in
their most important human relationship, that of marriage.

(iii) Slavery

Our awareness of the importance of personal freedom makes it
difficult to understand the phenomenon of slavery in times past.
Firstly, we forget that in ancient simpler societies freedom was not
the obvious or desirable goal.[29] Security was more important –
membership of a clan or tribe, which offered a recognized place
according to some customary law in return for observing the
conventions. Secondly, all cultures accepted that those taken in
war, or who were guilty of certain crimes, should be enslaved. They
provided the pool of labour to do the hard or unpleasant work that
free men were reluctant to do, or simply provided cheap labour.
No-one could imagine any other way to order human affairs.

Domestic slavery, where the unfree were employed in the home
of their masters or in small workshops, was generally recognized to
have been less cruel than industrial slavery – that of the mine, the
large factory or the fields. But the latter only developed in Israel in
the royal service. Strictly, the law forbade Israelites to do slave
work: they were to be treated like hired men or guests, and freed
in the seventh year (Lev. 25:39), when generous provision was to
be made for them; they must remember they were slaves once in
Egypt. They were not to be bought or sold, although slaves from
other nations could be (Lev. 25:44).

Yet alien slaves must not be oppressed; the Israelites were to
remember they were once strangers in Egypt (Exod. 23:9). These
slaves were to take their place in the religious life of the community; they were to be included in the weekly sabbath rest (Exod.
23:12); they were protected from excessive punishment by the law,
and if serious bodily harm was inflicted, manumission was to be
granted (Exod. 21:26). The possibility that slaves would not want to
be freed was foreseen also (Exod. 21:6). Finally, a runaway slave
was not to be returned to the master but allowed to settle in the
village of choice (Deut. 23:16). In wars between Hebrews, some
captives were enslaved, although this practice was condemned, and
the prisoners were, on occasion at least, freed on this account (2
Chron. 28:8–4). The only reason Hebrews could be enslaved under
the law was for defaulting on debt, or as a security for a repayment
of debt (Neh. 5:2). Free men could sell themselves or their chil-

dren into slavery when destitute. The Law only envisaged domestic slavery[30] but it is evident there were state slaves in the time of David and Solomon (2 Sam. 12:31 and 1 Kings 9:21).

The treatment of slaves was determined by the character of the master. As with other aspects of the law, the Israelites were not exact in their observance of its provisions regarding slavery, and tended to follow the cultural customs of the people around them when it suited them. Yet since most of the slavery was domestic it was more natural, given the traditional hospitality of the East, to treat them as members of the family. It was in a master's interest to have contented workers, and a firmly but fairly treated worker was the best worker. Had the law been kept, there is no reason why slaves should have not have been fairly treated. But this is the lie at the heart of any slave system. The history of slavery showed beyond doubt that human beings cannot be trusted to use justly the total power over others that the system gave them. It was impossible to prevent human ingenuity, for perversity or profit's sake, destroying the best attempts of good men to make such laws work.

(iv) War

The countries of the ancient Near East were constantly at war, and its cruelty and barbarism was unashamed. Prisoners were at the captors' mercy; entire populations could be enslaved, or, if there was thought to be danger to the victor, the male population could be killed or maimed. Destruction of captured towns was the usual procedure. For the Israelites war was a sacred action, as was every function of the people of God; Israel's wars were the wars of Yahweh; but there was no Holy War in the sense of Israel fighting to spread its faith: it fought for its existence as a nation, but its army was the army of God (1 Sam. 17:26) and had the assurance of victory because he fought with them (Judg. 7:2–22). Hence, even if theirs were not wars of religious expansionism they could not help being religious wars, fought as they were at God's command to fulfil a destiny which he had given them.

However, with the coming of the monarchy and the establishment of a professional army, the sacred character of war faded. It was no longer Yahweh who led his people but the king, no longer the people who fought, but professional soldiers and mercenaries. War was secularized, profaned. Yet the idea still lingered. Isaiah assured Jerusalem that God would save it (Isa. 37:33). But Jeremiah did not mention the Holy War. Yahweh had deserted, and would punish his people. The Maccabees were not directly inspired by

God or led by him and he did not intervene in any way; they fought a war for religious freedom and for preservation of the Covenant and the Law (1 Macc. 2:27), but it was a war which set Jews faithful to the Covenant against Jews who had become Hellenized; this led to conflict with the foreign supporters of Hellenization, the consequent politicization of the struggle and its increasing secularization.

The Israelites had to fight for their promised land, but most of the bloodshed that was visited upon Yahweh's people was the result of their own refusal to do things his way. It followed on their disobedience. It in no way represents the ideal of the Scriptures: where they tell us what, ideally, God's wish for his people was.

> I know the plans I have in mind for you ... plans for peace, not disaster ... a future full of hope for you. Then when you call to me and come to plead with me, I will listen to you. When you seek me you shall find me, when you seek me with all your heart

(Jer. 29:11–13). Obedience to God's law brought peace; so the kingdom of Asa, 'who did what is right in God's sight ... was at peace and free of war ... Yahweh having granted him peace' (2 Chron. 14:1–6).

2

The New Testament

1 Ethics and social ethics in the New Testament

The New Testament contains the account of the life and teaching of Jesus Christ who announced the coming of a kingdom, and inaugurated it with his preaching: when Christ had gone from them after the Ascension, the apostles and their companions announced that the kingdom had come, and they spread the Gospel, the good news of salvation. In time their teaching, received either orally or in writing, formed the New Testament, arranged or explained in the light of the situation in local churches as they experienced it after the resurrection; in this way, under the guidance of the Holy Spirit, they presented the truth of Christ. They were either witnesses to what they preached about, or relied on trustworthy testimony concerning it: they handed on their message in order that that truth should be made known (Luke 1:2–4), the New Testament books which record their testimony all dating from the first century of the Church's life.[1]

Given its nature therefore, the New Testament does not deal so extensively with questions of social ethics as did the Old; Christ's mission was religious, his kingdom spiritual. The kingdom of God that Christ preached was concerned primarily with the personal spiritual and moral life of man, the way to holiness for its members, but paradoxically it is this orientation which in the long run has the most profound implications for social life. Man is communitarian by nature, a social animal, and the moral law provides guidance for social life too. Elements of a social ethic, and those the most fundamental, are therefore to be found in Christ's teaching.[2]

The Sermon on the Mount[3] promises the kingdom to the humble good people who suffered for their goodness (Matt. 5–7). A proper internal disposition rather than a legalistic attitude to morality was what the Sermon was intended to inculcate. We must not offer resistance to wrong done to us; we must turn the other cheek. We must love our enemies, not only our friends (Matt. 5:43–44); we must forgive others their failings or our Father in heaven will not forgive us (Matt. 6:14–15). Nor can we serve both God and mammon: we must choose between them; we must be like the plants and the animals in our dependence on God's providence (Matt. 6:24–34); we must not judge or we will be judged ourselves, and we must always treat others as we would like to be treated ourselves, (Matt. 7:12). It is not those who claim to be Christ's friends who will be saved, but those who keep his commandments and demonstrate they are his friends (Matt. 7:21–27).

There is hyperbole in the address, it is evident. The injunction to pluck out the eye, or amputate the limb which leads us into sin is clearly not meant literally (Matt. 5:30), but there could be no more powerful way of convincing us that sins of the flesh can lead to damnation for those unrepentant of them than by using such language. Interiority reinforces moral law; it does not replace it. On divorce, on forgiveness, on loving our neighbour, on oaths, the Sermon was most explicit on adherence to the law – but adherence must stem from the right interior attitude, the proper disposition of mind and heart. The abiding reality is the will of God and the acceptance of the command to love, to love God above all things and our neighbour as ourselves for God's sake. This is the law and the prophets (Matt. 22:40).

The beatitudes have always caused problems in both theory and practice. Can they, for example, provide moral guidance for those in public life as well as private? As we shall see when we look at Christ's own attitude to defence of what is right and just, he does not deny the right of resistance where justice is concerned – and those who deal with matters of public order must pursue justice. But they must always temper justice with mercy lest it become hard and destructive. Where my own self-love is concerned, therefore, I must not be aggressive or combative, but be prepared to concede even where right is on my side rather than cause futile confrontation or nurse bitterness if justice cannot be done; and when it can I must pursue it with justice, not vengeance, in mind. However, those responsible for public order must be stringent in trying to see that justice is done in society, because without it the common good cannot be maintained.

The beatitudes demand much of us. On the question of the

marriage laws the demands were so emphatic that they provoked
the response from Christ's hearers that it was better not to marry
(Matt. 19:10), or, where riches were concerned, to despair of
salvation (Matt. 19:26). Christ's response was: to God all things
are possible; to dispense with marriage was for those who choose
to live without it for the kingdom's sake (Matt. 19:11–12), while
he left hope for the rich if they were true servants of God. It
is this demand for a change in personal attitude which was the
revolutionary element in Christ's teaching, peaceable and gradual
yet seismic none the less; in time it would change the world for
good.

2 The kingdom of God, ethics and civil society

Announcing the coming of the kingdom was the starting point of
the mission of Jesus Christ, and this mission, his proclamation of
his kingdom, was the fulfilment of all the hopes of his people
(Luke 4:16–30). He was the bearer of the Spirit in the full sense, he
was the anointed of God, the Messiah. Yet the Messiahship to
which he laid claim (Luke 10:24, Matt. 13:16, Mark 14:61–64) was
a rather different one from that which his people were expecting.
The hope and belief was that Yahweh would send a Messiah-king,
son of David, to restore the kingdom of Israel politically as well as
bringing the people back to the true observance of the law (Luke
1:74–75).[4] But Christ did not offer this sort of liberation. He
brought salvation in the spiritual and religious sense, and it had no
immediate earthly impact. The kingdom was not as had been
expected. The kingdom of God in glory, its completion, would
only come at the last day, at the end of time, eschatologically.[5]
There is an intrinsic dynamism in the kingdom announced,
linking it to that fulfilment as a period of preparation, of making
oneself worthy to share fully. Yet the kingdom is very important for
this life too. If the kingdom of God and his justice is sought first,
everything else necessary will follow (Luke 12:31).

Such a vision of the kingdom did not meet the expectations of
the time. In 63 BC, the Jews had been deprived of political freedom
once more, coming under the control of Rome's representative in
Syria. In 40 BC Herod, Antipater's son, was named king of Judea
and Samaria by the Romans, but most of the Jews despised him for
his non-Jewish background and resented his rule. The division of
the country into four kingdoms on his death in 4 BC was no more
pleasing to them. Herod Antipas (AD 4 to 39) ruled Galilee and

Perea, and Archelaus, Judea (AD 4 to 6); with the latter proving incapable of his task, Judea and Jerusalem were ruled directly by Rome thereafter. The Roman procurators were mainly incompetent, and their problems were compounded by the discontent of the Jews. More and more therefore they turned their thoughts to rebellion.

Roman rule was through the Great Sanhedrin, meeting twice weekly in the Temple; it combined religious and political functions and on it sat the High Priest, who was its President, and elders. The latter were members of the main families, priestly Sadducees, scribes, doctors of the law, and Pharisees – some 71 members in all. The Pharisees were the other main party among the Jews: the Essenes and the Zealots were of lesser importance.[6] The Sadducees were aristocrats; they co-operated with the Romans and were contemptuous of the ordinary people. They favoured Hellenism, did not await the Messiah, and gradually put the survival of the nation before faithfulness to the Law. Yet they sank their differences with the Pharisees in opposing Christ.

The Pharisees were the dominant party, upholders of the Law and supporters of political nationalism while putting adherence to the Law first, multiplying the oral traditions. The scribes and the lawyers supported them, the latter undertaking the task of seeing the Law applied throughout the land and enjoying the respect and affection of the people. Their support of nationalism was peripheral to their religious interests, but they shared the messianic hopes of the people and awaited eagerly the political liberation the Messiah would bring. The Essenes were a religious brotherhood and their way of life was very ascetic; it is possible that the way of life of John the Baptist bears some affinity to theirs. The Zealots were an extreme sect in sympathy with the Pharisees, and their faith moved them to militant nationalism, but the connection between them and the second Simon among the Apostles is not clear. They attacked not only the Romans when they could, but also those of their co-religionists whom they thought were too lacking in zeal. They may have had connections with Judas the Galilean and his uprising (Acts 5:37).

There were great differences between the two main social classes among the Jews, the rich and the poor. The king and his court, the wealthier merchants and landowners, the chief tax collectors and the priestly aristocracy lived a life of great luxury. The mass of the people were very poor, and their way of life excluded them from official involvement in a national religion which had become obsessively concerned with externals. Most of the population lived in small towns and villages, the peasants nominally independent, but usually deeply in debt to wealthy landowners. The latter had concentrated most of the land in their possession and their stewards managed their property for them, as was the pattern throughout most of the Empire. Taxes were also heavy and added to the impoverishment of the poor.[7] There was no middle class in the sense of a large and influential minority (still less a majority) of businessmen, professional people, bureaucrats and managers. The skilled craftsmen and the priests formed what there was of such a class. Those who had no land were day labourers; those unable to work were supported by the Jewish tradition of almsgiving. Along with prayer and fasting, it was a work pleasing to God.[8]

Like the Old Testament, the New spoke of man made in God's image, but now he was in a new relationship with God, taken up into Christ and therefore into the life of God himself. The parable of the vine and the branches (John 15:5–6) brings this out. St Paul extended this parallel using the example of the human body. It is made up of many different parts but is none the less one body; so it is with Christ's mystical body, the Church. 'In one spirit we were baptized, Jews as well as Greeks, slaves as well as citizens' (1 Cor. 12:12–30, Rom. 12:4–8, Eph. 4:11–13).

The kingdom, then, is vivified by the life of Christ, and his Church is its first budding forth on earth, though potentially it embraces all mankind. The Gospel which united man to his God therefore was also a Gospel of solidarity and brotherhood. It encourages its citizens toward mutual association and these characteristics of its history are not accidental. There is a natural instinct which draws mankind to mutual co-operation; he is a social being. But membership of the Church raises the social connection of human beings from the sphere of convention to that of moral obligation.[9]

Charity among men, as a duty stemming from love of God, follows; the parable of the Good Samaritan and its practical implications demonstrate this most fully (Luke 10:29–37). Christ was talking about solidarity with his suffering brethren whoever they are, not only those of the Jews. 'I was hungry and you gave me food, thirsty and you gave me drink, I was a stranger and you made me welcome, naked and you clothed me, sick and you visited me ...' (Matt. 25:35–46). This new aspect of the theology of benevolence has been the basis of Christian works of charity in which the Church has been outstanding from the earliest times. In the long term, and peacefully, this kingdom, purely spiritual and moral though it was, was to exercise immense influence on earth, precisely because it did not seek access to direct political power. This is the paradox of the kingdom of God in terms of the social order, of ethics and civil society. There was in the Gospel a message of solidarity and brotherhood, an impulse to mutual association which was not accidental or peripheral to it. It spiritualized all that was best in man's social nature, the impulse that draws us to one another and endows what had been simple social convention with the character of moral obligation.

It does this through the grace of Christ. He is the vine, we are the branches. The human race, human society, is bound up into his mystical body – which is not only the Church, though it is the Church primarily; secondarily but no less really it is all mankind, whether mankind knows it or not. There is in us a supernatural life, and through us as social beings that life permeates human society also. This bond between men is capable of being stronger than any merely human bond. It should bind us together from the time we come into human society through the most basic of its forms, the family. It should teach us that man is more to be valued for what he is than for what he has, to protect the poor and defend their rights and dignity. It should enable the rich to use their riches for God's glory and the service of others as well as for their own honest enjoyment, and warns of the spiritual dangers wealth can bring.

If we let it, it provides in sum the principles and ideals on which a healthy human society can be based; it exhorts us to pray that the kingdom will come on earth and that the Father's will be done here as it is in heaven, and through grace it gives us the power to do this. Fulfilled as it will be only in eternity, the kingdom none the less begins on earth and helps inspire human society to charity and justice. It secures for us the means to self-giving because the Christ in whose life we live gave himself for us. It bases human rights on man's dignity as made in God's image and likeness, and it establishes human freedom in the context of the divine and natural laws which alone can ensure the true happiness and fulfilment which men and women seek.

3 The New Testament and political ethics[10]

(i) Christ and politics

Christ's mission therefore was from the first, and of its nature, one which precluded any direct involvement with secular power or with the political issues of the day which agitated his fellow countrymen.

Although his enemies sought to depict him as a political agitator and to get him to oppose the Roman rule in some way, he dealt decisively with attempts to embroil him in such conflict, and in so doing he gives us guidance on political ethics.

The temptation to pervert his mission in the pursuit of worldly power was one that was put to him before his public ministry began: the devil offered him all the kingdoms of the world if he would worship him (Matt. 4:8–10) but he rejected them. The question put to Christ by his enemies concerning the paying of tribute to Caesar provides us with the clearest indication of his refusal during his ministry to allow himself a secular involvement in politics. Agents of the scribes and chief priests were sent to lure him into saying something which might enable them to hand him over to the jurisdiction and authority of the governor. All Christ's enemies were interested in using this test case against him – the Herodians and Sadducees, the scribes and the Pharisees.

'They put to him this question. Master, we know you say and teach what is right; you favour no one, but teach the way of God in all honesty. Is it permissible for us to pay taxes to Caesar or not?' (Luke 20:21). The question was a particularly dangerous one because it was the conflict over the poll tax which was threatening rebellion against Rome. The Zealots particularly resented the tax, and it led to the rising of AD 66 which was to end in total disaster for the people. It was a tribute of one silver denarius per head payable to Rome, and was a way of making all those who lived within the boundaries of the Empire contribute to the cost of Roman rule. It was a tribute to Roman power.[11] Putting the question as they did, his enemies thought that any answer he gave would harm him. The answer 'yes' would antagonize those, the Pharisees and Zealots, who resented the tax as recognition of Roman authority. The answer 'no' would antagonize the Sadducees and the Herodians, and more so the Roman authorities, by encouraging those who were prepared to disturb the peace and challenge the Roman order.

Christ however answered enigmatically, and yet clearly enough. He asked them to show him a denarius and asked whose head was on it. When they responded that it was Caesar's, they were told 'give back to Caesar what belongs to Caesar and to God what belongs to God'. His answer took them by surprise and they were silenced. That answer foretold the tensions that would remain in the Church's relations with the State throughout the centuries. He respects Caesar and accepts his rights, but he balances this by saying that God has his rights also. He leaves the listener to ponder the matter. It is apparent that Christ thought a balance was possible.

Experience has taught us that there are indeed occasions when the rights of Church and State conflict, but with prudence and good judgement on both sides, such conflicts can be resolved. The spirit of the beatitudes has its relevance in the political sphere: those who seek God's justice must seek a way of reconciling the rights and interests of the two authorities upon which man relies for that good order in this world which best assures his salvation in the next.

The refusal of Christ to have anything to do with violence is shown for example in his rebuking Peter for using his sword in an attempt to protect him. Did Peter not know that he could call on legions of angels for help if he chose? (Matt. 26:53). When he was appearing before Pilate he specifically repudiated any claim to a worldly kingdom: if he had such a claim his men would have fought to protect it. He did not deny he was a king and therefore possessed a kingdom, but it was a kingdom of all those who were seeking the truth. All those who are on the side of truth listen to him (John 18:33–38). Pilate was losing patience. He had no cause to condemn him under Roman law, but he wanted Christ's co-operation in saving him, pointing out he had power to release or crucify him. But Christ merely replied that the power Pilate possessed was from above, and that the one who had handed him over had the greater guilt (John 19:8–11). Christ, Son of God, is fully in control of the situation; if he has been handed over to Pilate it is because his Father has willed it, and he himself has accepted it.

Why Pilate could find no reason to condemn Christ under Roman law is very clear from St Luke's account. The only grounds on which he could have done this would have been that Christ had opposed that power in a way which was a serious threat to public order. But this he had not done. His enemies said they had found him inciting revolt, opposing the tribute and claiming to be Christ, a king (Luke 23:2), but Pilate had examined the matter and found no cause in him. Nor had Herod either, because he sent him back without taking action (Luke 23:15). The rest we know. It was not then on political grounds that his enemies wanted him killed. It was 'because you are only a man and claim to be God' (John 10:33). For this and its implications, which undermined the whole of their world, his enemies wanted him out of the way.

Against this cumulative evidence of Christ's total rejection of any political involvement and violence, such evidence as there is that would suggest that he is in favour of it is limited indeed, resting on isolated passages taken out of context. His words about coming not to bring peace but a sword (Matt. 10:34) cannot be interpreted as referring to political and social revolution. The saying in verses 35

to 36 is a quotation from Micah 7:6 referring to dissension within
Israel. It was prophecy about the inevitable result of his teaching,
and he wanted to remove any illusions that the peace he offered
was one that avoided suffering of this kind. It did not refer to any
matter of State, but to the confusion in family and society, and the
likelihood of persecution resulting from it, that discipleship might
involve.

Similar is his remark in response to his disciple's misunderstanding of his warning to those who do not have a sword to buy
one (Luke 22:36). The context is the threatening time before the
Passion: he would be arrested, he told them – and they would face
their enemies. They told him they had two swords and he replied,
'It is enough'. The words are clearly figurative rather than direc-
tive. They were a formula of dismissal as in Deuteronomy 3:6. But
the disciples, under the stress of the situation, took the remark
literally. They over-reacted; in their fear their natural aggressive
instincts took over and they imagined that some form of violence
might be intended – although their master had specifically
rejected violence. Nor is it possible to make any assumption
concerning the presence among his disciples of Simon the Zealot.
(Luke 6:15). We know nothing more than the fact; certainly no
follower of Christ could have been a true Zealot; they were bent on
violence, which Christ had rejected.

He had rejected politics and above all political violence. At the
same time, in saying that God had to be given his due as well as
Caesar, he asserted the independence of the spiritual authority
from the political in all affairs of the spirit, of faith, worship and
morals. This was a new departure in the world's experience of religion in society. In the pagan world, the State had controlled religion
in all its aspects. The kingdom of God that Christ announced was
spiritual, but it was to have independence as a social organization so
that the things of God could be given at least equal seriousness to
those of Caesar. As the work of the Spirit in the Church made its
influence felt after Pentecost, the shape of this religious organization and its principles of operation were revealed. The Church, the
initial embodiment of the kingdom of Christ on earth, developed
peacefully as a social organization in her own right, with whose legitimate ends and means she insisted the State could not interfere.
When events led to conflict with the State on this issue, and the
Christians faced martyrdom, the political effects in theory and in
practice did much to determine the shape of European political
culture and through it that of the modern world.

(ii) Christ's teaching on pacifism

Christ's refusal to use violence had political implications. All states claim the right to defend themselves by force against aggressors, but it seems that Christ's teaching requires of his followers the duty of refusing to use violence in any cause. The wicked had to be offered no resistance; the cheek should be turned to the blow (Matt. 5:38–40). Christ's words to Peter when he tried to defend him from arrest on the eve of his passion (Matt. 26:52) and his refusal to offer any resistance to his enemies, his meek acceptance of the terrible death that awaited him, all point to the conclusion that his is the only Christian way.

But a consideration of the total evidence of the Gospels on this matter shows that this is too extreme a statement of the case. Christ himself did not turn the other cheek when the High Priest's servant offered him violence during his trial. He asked him to justify his action. (John 18:23). He was also ready to use violence to defend the sanctity of the Temple and did so, driving out the buyers and sellers (Matt. 21:11–12). And the words he frequently used to condemn the hypocrisy of his enemies were terrible in their violent finality; they were not the words of one who confused meekness with weakness. To take but one example, 'Alas for you, scribes and Pharisees', he intones through 23 verses of one chapter (Matt. 23: 13–36) condemning them as hypocrites, and bringing seven counts in all against them. This is not a pale and wilting figure who avoids conflict or is afraid to take its consequences. On occasion he so angered his listeners that they would have seized and killed him had his time come. For example, on his first return to Nazareth during his ministry, his fellow townsmen were enraged by his condemnation of their spiritual blindness in their dismissing him as Joseph's son who had got above himself. They tried to lynch him by throwing him over a cliff but he escaped them (Luke 4:28–30). His whole public ministry was surrounded with the threat of violence and death, but he never minced his words in order to placate those in error. This was the behaviour of a man who was fearless in the face of danger, a man who knew what his final fate would be and scorned to try to avert it. Christ was a fighter, but one who fought with moral courage and contempt of all the earthly power of his enemies, one who refused to use violence in his own defence but would use it in defending the honour of God's house; he was also prepared to suffer it, so giving an example to his followers.

That he showed particular respect for the Roman centurion at

Capernaum (Matt. 8:5–13) is also not without its relevance in this
context (Luke 7:5–10). His faith in Christ indicates that his profession was no bar to his being a true servant of God. John the Baptist's
words when he was asked by the soldiers what they must do if they
wished to be baptized are also relevant (Luke 3:14). They were not
told that they must abandon their profession; it appears that he did
not regard it as a danger to their salvation. The frequency with
which, in the rest of the New Testament, examples taken from the
military life are used to illustrate aspects of Christian life and belief
must surely have suggested to the early Christian community that
service of the State in this manner was not alien to their faith. St
Paul speaks of the breastplate of faith and love, and the helmet of
salvation (1 Thess. 5:8) in depicting the demands of life in Christ,
and Timothy is to fight like a good soldier with faith and a good
conscience (1 Tim. 1:19). Such literary usages must not be taken as
direct recommendations of the military life, but when that life and
its obligations are so readily used in such a way, it is clear that the life
itself is not regarded as an unworthy model.

The strong recommendation to pacifism present in Christ's own
example in refusing to use force to protect himself from the injustice of his passion and death, remains a distinctive mark of the
Gospel. The conscientious objection to the use of violence is a
form of witness which must always be open to the believer, but
where circumstances require it a Christian may choose the other
way; it is not an imperative binding on all.

(iii) The rest of the New Testament on politics

Paul, in his Epistle to the Romans, has a famous passage. He tells
them to obey all governing authorities. Since all government
comes from God, the civil authorities were appointed by God, and
so anyone who resists authority is rebelling against God's decision,
... only criminals have anything to fear from them. The authorities
are there to serve God by punishing wrongdoers.

> You must obey therefore ... for conscience' sake. This is the
> reason why you must also pay taxes ... pay every government
> official what he has the right to ask (Rom. 13:1ff.).

These words must be read in their context, one in which the possibilities of conflict with the Roman authority over rights of
conscience had not yet arisen. The proviso 'what he has a right to
ask' perhaps introduces a note of reservation on the paying of
taxes in some cases.

The methods of taxation in Roman times were anything but just; but the instruction is that, generally at least, taxes must be paid. Paul was, however, prescinding from all the questions which in time Christians would have to face concerning, for example, the misuse of political authority and how to correct it, and how to face disputes over who should wield that authority and in what manner. He was not saying that we automatically obey all those who at a particular moment have political power. A fuller understanding of the exact duties of Christians in this matter had to await the development of theology; it tells us they must be legitimate wielders of that power in the first instance, and that what they ask must be in conformity with justice and the common good. Should either of these conditions not be fulfilled then the position is changed and other aspects of political ethics come into play. St Paul at the time he wrote was not contemplating such developments but was dealing with a specific case where he saw obedience to be justified and necessary. The First Letter of Peter shows the same respect for the current political authorities.

> For the sake of the Lord accept the authority of every social institution, the emperor as the supreme authority, governors as commissioned by him ... God wants you to be good citizens so as to silence what fools are saying ... never use your freedom as an excuse for wickedness. Have respect for everyone and love for our community; fear God and honour the Emperor (1 Peter 2:13ff.).

The motives are rather different from those given by Paul, the desire to give honour to Christ's name by being good citizens. He makes no clear reference to the divine institution of political authority, but the acceptance of Roman power as worthy of obedience is based on the same assumptions as was Paul's – that at the time the advice was given Christians should respect the ruling authorities and the use they made of their power in dealing with criminals.

Political authority therefore is based on God's plan, comes from God in a very general sense, and in its proper care for the common good it can bind us to obedience in conscience; the Christian people of the time were told that Caesar's power was legitimate within these limits; they were to show that Christians were not antisocial but good citizens. In this way they would silence what fools were saying, presumably that Christians were antisocial and therefore dangerous to the State. But changes in the circumstances would produce the need for another response. In the Book of Revelation,[12] written after the first great persecutions, the Roman

State was the scarlet woman, in which was contained all manner of corruption (Rev. 17); in these circumstances a different response was needed, and the martyrs were to show they knew the limits of obedience to Caesar.

4 The New Testament and economic ethics[13]

(i) Christ's teaching on work and wealth

In reasserting the Ten Commandments (Matt. 19:18–19) Christ affirmed the morality of private ownership, which we know from the Old Testament to have included capital goods. The qualification for being a follower of his was not economic or social; the rich as well as the poor were among them; the essential requirement was to be humble of heart, charitable and just. Although, by his own manner of life, and by his teaching, he implied that these virtues were more likely to be fostered among those who were not rich in the things of this world, he did not condemn riches or the rich in themselves.

He himself chose a life supported not by the luxuries of wealth but by manual work; he was poor in that sense but clearly not destitute; he earned his daily bread, and the social stratum to which he belonged was ordinary and humble. 'This is the carpenter surely, the son of Mary' (Mark 6:3); it was among those who supported themselves and their families by manual work that he grew up. They were his people, and the majority of the Twelve were of the same background, mainly fishermen; Matthew, the tax collector, was the exception (Matt. 9:9). However, they seem to have been men of some substance among their kind: James and John were Peter's partners (Luke 5:9–10 and Matt. 4:18–22) and they hired men to work with them. When James and John were called, they 'left their father in the boat with the men he employed' (Mark 1:20). Thus they were independent and possessed of some small capital. It would also appear that the fishing industry in Galilee was a thriving one; there was a centre of the fish-pickling business at Taricheae [Magdala] on the Sea of Galilee and there was a strong demand for its products not only in Jerusalem but beyond the boundaries of Palestine.[14]

Such men still had to work hard for what they earned. That they were manual workers would have been no drawback among the Jews. There was no 'class' division implication in this. Among the Jews, working with one's hands, on the land, as a fisherman or in the workshop, was not regarded as in any way demeaning as it was in the classical societies of Greece and Rome.[15] The ordinary

Jewish manual worker from a pious family would be well instructed in his religion and its practices and this tie of blood and religion secured him his status in society; he was as welcome to take full part in the life of the synagogue and to expound the Scriptures as others, though we know that some of the Pharisees had a contempt for the mass of the people, whom they regarded as effectively incapable of practising their religion (John 7:48).

Jesus was therefore born of, lived and found his largest following among the ordinary people. Yet he did not despise or cut himself off from the wealthy – they were among his followers too. Nicodemus (John 3:1) was a leading Jew and Zaccheus was a wealthy tax collector (Luke 19:1), who on his conversion gave half his property to the poor and vowed to compensate four-fold all whom he had cheated. Joseph of Arimathea was a rich man (Matt. 27:57). Mary Magdalene, Joanna, the wife of Herod's steward, Susanna 'and several others' provided for Christ and his followers 'out of their resources' (Luke 8:3). When his mission required it he so mixed with the ordinary ruck of men and women, irrespective of their moral standing, that he was taunted by some as a glutton and drunkard, a friend of tax collectors and sinners (Matt. 11:19). He did not make the virtue and ascetism which shone out of him because of his holiness a barrier to his hearers; rather it attracted them to him.

Christ therefore called all, rich and poor, to salvation. Though the majority of his followers were poor, none were excluded. However, he emphasized the warnings of the corrupting effect of riches which were so strong in the Old Testament, repeating them with great force and insistence. The riches in themselves are not evil, but they all too easily tempt us to think they are an end in themselves: possessing them, it is too easy to forget God, goodness, justice and mercy, in the illusion of total self-sufficiency.

Luke recounts the parable of the rich man who contemplated building larger barns to accommodate his healthy crops so that he could then live prosperously for years to come. But God had other ideas and he died an early death – a punishment for not making himself rich in the eyes of God (Luke 12:16–21). Luke recounts too the parable of Dives and Lazarus. Dives had enjoyed a prosperous life on earth while Lazarus the beggar who had sat at his gate was neglected, but it was Lazarus who after death was received into Abraham's bosom, and Dives who languished amid the flames. Nor would Abraham answer appeals to warn Dives' brothers against making the same mistake and heading for the same fate. They have Moses and the prophets; they should have listened to them (Luke

16:19–31). The parable is not meant to suggest that the poor should be left to suffer because they will have happiness in heaven, nor that all the rich are corrupted by riches and will suffer endless torment. Its lesson is that the duty of charity and justice to the poor was laid down by the Law and the prophets, and the wealthy who neglected to obey them will suffer torment. The message could not be fairer or clearer.

In Matthew, Christ's teaching on the impossibility of serving both God and riches is put very succinctly: 'you cannot be the slave of both God and money' (Matt. 6:24). Matthew also deals with the subtler temptations of wealth. In the parable of the sower 'the cares and riches of this world' are the thorns which 'choke the word' (Matt. 13:22), and he shows in another place that for some the threat is a more particular one. The rich young man who asked Christ what he must do to attain eternal life was told that the way was the observance of the commandments. Wanting to do more, he was further told that he should sell all he had, give the proceeds to the poor, and follow Christ. This he found was impossible to do and he went away sad, for he was a man of great wealth (Matt. 19:22).

It was this response in these circumstances which led Christ to say that it would be easier for a camel to pass through the eye of a needle than for a rich man to enter the kingdom of heaven. Those whom God invited to give up their riches in order that they might satisfy their deeper longing to serve him more perfectly were being warned that the temptation not to let go could make it impossible for them to gain eternal life. 'Who then can be saved?' asked the disciples. Christ's answer was that for God all things are possible (Matt. 19:26). Such challenges can be met by God's help; his grace is always there for those willing to rely on it.

(ii) The rest of the New Testament on work and wealth

St Paul stressed the importance of manual work as a title for livelihood, quoting his own example. He worked with his hands so as not to be a burden to others and gave them a rule: let not anyone have any food if he refused to do any work (2 Thess. 3:7–12). Having some such useful work to do enables a Christian to have the means to help others and it also reforms thieves (Eph. 4:28). Such exhortations reveal the simplicity and practical charity of early Christian communities; they consisted of hardworking individuals who believed that such work was, among other things, an obligation placed on them by their religious belief.

The early Christians in Jerusalem sold their goods and shared out the proceeds according to need (Acts 2:44 and 4:32). They may have been touched by the contrast between their prosperity and the strict interpretation of the Gospel, but theirs does not seem to have been the common practice among the faithful and it does not seem that such a course was of precept. What was of precept was the obligation to share one's possessions as generously as possible. Paul instructs Timothy to warn the rich that they are not to look down on other people, and not to set their hopes on money – which is untrustworthy – but on God (1 Tim. 6:17). He also asked the Corinthians to show their generosity in aid of the poor of the church in Jerusalem, pointing out that those in Macedonia had already done so. This help for other churches became a mark of Christian practice. A system was developing: the churches in Galatia were told that each Sunday everyone was to set aside what they could (1 Cor. 16:2) as an earnest of their desire to imitate the generosity of their master Christ, though they were never to give beyond their means (2 Cor. 8:13). It was a pattern that reflected the Gospel values.

St James warns against the tendency to be over-respectful of the rich because of their wealth. It was the poor according to the world whom Christ chose, and it is the rich of the world who are opposed to Christ, his teaching and his Church. Since the Law says 'love your neighbour as yourself', as soon as you make distinctions between classes of people you are under condemnation for breaking the Law (James 2:1–9). Faith, he points out, is of little use if it is not evidenced in works of charity. If one of the brothers is in need and help is not given then what good is that? (James 2:15). And to cheat the labourer of his wages is specifically denounced (James 5:4).

5 Some social attitudes

(i) Christ's example of respect for others

The Old Testament ennobled mankind with the knowledge that men and women were made in God's image and likeness, and the New Testament added a further lustre to that nobility because through the Incarnation we are the brothers and sisters of God made man in Jesus Christ. Since he has now returned to heaven and reigns for ever, we also, through Jesus Christ our brother, are taken up into the life of God. Man has been restored to God. These truths enhance our awareness of our dignity; they have immeasurably strengthened the idea of human rights. Each man and woman is to be respected because they too are brothers and sisters of God incarnate, God made man, who now lives in glory for all eternity with the Father and the Holy Spirit.

The Gospel is a true liberation theology because it is based on love. It fulfils the Old Law, it does not destroy it. It lays the foundation for all liberation from evil of any kind. It strikes then at the true heart of injustice, and therefore points to the true liberation of man, the liberation from sin, from selfishness, enabling us to love others as they deserve to be loved because we are not caught up so much in love for ourselves or other false gods that we fail them. It secures human rights in God and his law, not in the transitory whims of human legislators.

Christ's attitude to his people shows what it means truly to love others: it is to respect ordinary humanity. We know most about the key moments in his dealings with Peter, the leader he had chosen for them. Peter, the natural man, had the qualities which make leaders, but he had a lot to learn about himself before he could be trusted with his mission, before the grace to be offered him could be effective. From the first, the gospels show Simon Peter as the key figure of his chosen few. His name occurs first in all the lists of the twelve apostles: his name is mentioned some two hundred times in the New Testament, more frequently than all the other apostles put together. He was present at all the crucial incidents related in the gospels. Most notably he was spokesman at Caesarea Philippi in proclaiming Christ as the Messiah, the Son of God (Matt. 16:16–18): he was here given the name Peter, the Rock on which Christ's Church was to be built. It was Peter who was given the task at the Last Supper of confirming the faith of his brethren (Luke 22:32), and later, after the resurrection, of feeding Christ's lambs and sheep (John 21:15–17).

Peter, however, was by nature impetuous, too ready to trust his own snap judgements and to ignore the advice and warnings given him by Christ. He had to learn that if he trusted in his own pride and strength, he could not do what Christ wanted him to do. So Peter's faith failed in attempting to walk across the water and he was made to look foolish before all (Matt. 14:28–32); he also refused to accept that his master would be rejected and put to death and was crushingly rebuked (Mark 8:33). He denied his master three times during the Passion (Matt. 26:30–35). The three attestations of his love evoked from him after the resurrection and recorded by St John showed he had learned his lesson: he no longer felt the need to boast but simply left it to his master to judge. 'Lord, you know all things, you know that I love you' (John 21:17). There could be no greater tribute to the dignity of man paid by the eternal Son of God, than that he should be prepared to found his Church on those who, from all we know of them, were men of faith and good life certainly, but beyond that not marked by signs of greatness, possessing only the ordinary talents of the honest everyman. Yet they did not, with one sad exception, let him down. We note also that he showed, most touchingly, a particular respect and love for young children. He held them up as an example to us of what our attitude towards the kingdom of heaven should be (Matt. 19:13–15); those who do not welcome the kingdom like little children, will not enter it. (Mark 10:15f.)

(ii) His particular respect for women

His dealings with women revealed a deep bond of personal sympathy and spiritual friendship. Mary of Magdala (a town in Galilee), the woman from whom Christ expelled seven devils, was among those closest to him, one of the women who had ministered to him (Luke 8:2); she was a witness to his crucifixion (Matt. 27:56) and it was she who was the first to visit the tomb and find it empty. The exchange between her and the risen Christ, whom she did not at first recognize, is one that reveals the extreme tenderness of their relationship (John 20:11–18). Mary Magdalen as the penitent sinner we owe to the tradition of identifying her with the woman brought before Christ after being accused of adultery (Luke 7:36–50) and also with the woman who anointed Jesus (Matt. 26:6–15) when he was invited to dine in the house of Simon the Leper. But there is no basis for the identification with the former, and the latter was a different Mary, one of the sisters at Bethany: Martha busy about her work looking after him, Mary more content to sit and listen to him (Luke 10:38–42). John identifies the latter Mary with the one who anointed Christ's head and wiped his feet with her hair (John 11:2). So close were these sisters to Christ that they could gently chide him, pointing out that his presence would have prevented the death of the brother that both he and they loved (John 11:21, 33).

The whole of the circumstances in which Christ spoke at such length to the Samaritan woman at Jacob's well were, though in a different way, revealing. No ordinary Jew would ask a Samaritan for water: Samaritans were unclean, and even their drinking vessels were tainted. Still less would a Rabbi speak familiarly with a woman in public: but to Christ these scruples meant nothing, and in the course of his conversation with this woman he so far reveals himself that she recognizes him as a prophet and then Messiah (John 4:7–42).

(iii) Christ's teaching on marriage and the family

There is no human institution on which Christ's teaching was as full as it was on marriage and the family, and to none did his own life give such strong testimony. He was known as the son of Mary and his foster-father Joseph, the just man, the carpenter, head of the holy family of Nazareth. Though he never let his obligations to his parents interfere with his mission as the Son of God, as the incident when he was found in the Temple with the teachers demonstrated (Luke 2:41–50), his love and respect for them is shown in that he was subject to them and lived with them for all but the few years of his public ministry: it was under their authority that he began to 'increase in wisdom, stature and in favour with God and men' (Luke 2:52).

His presence at the marriage feast of Cana and his choice of it as the occasion of his first miracle (John 2:1–12) reveals him as a man of his time and people, enjoying the celebration of the happiness of the young couple. Throughout the New Testament his love and respect for young children is evident, as we have already seen. Marriage, human love, family, were close to his heart therefore, but he warned that family ties – like all good things – also could come between man and God. His own extended family saw him as an embarrassment (Mark 3:21). He warned that his teaching would set members of families against one another (Matt. 10:35). When someone from the crowd blessed the mother who bore and suckled him (Luke 11:27–28), he reminded them that to obey the word of God and keep it was more blessed still – and this was supremely his own mother's virtue: with her 'be it done unto me according to thy word' she accepted the sacred charge that God had given her (Luke 1:38).

His teaching on the indissolubility of marriage was quite clear. Moses allowed divorce because of the hardness of heart of his people, but it was not so in the beginning (Matt. 19:8). That his proviso concerning fornication did not mean any relaxation in the Law is shown by the response of the disciples who said that if this was the case it is better not to marry (Matt. 19:11). Christ did not demur, pointing out that there are some who renounce marriage for the sake of the kingdom, and that those who have this gift should accept it. If Christ was in fact teaching that he was prepared to allow divorce for a compelling reason he would only have been repeating what the stricter school of rabbis, that of Shammai, taught; they only permitted it on the grounds of adultery. But given the startled reply of the disciples, he was going far beyond that. He was denying the acceptability of divorce under any circumstances. 'What God has joined together, let no man divide' (Matt. 19:6)[16] meant precisely that.

(ii) St Paul's attitude to women and marriage

St Paul's attitude to women has been frequently criticized, and to understand it correctly it is necessary to see it in its context.[17] This is particularly true of the first letter to the Corinthians where he speaks of man as 'the image of God and reflects God's glory, but woman reflects man's glory' (1 Cor. 11:7). Corinth was a wealthy two-port city, a cosmopolitan, commercial, shipping, shipbuilding and industrial centre, as well as a centre of government and of the arts; it also was host to the Isthmian games. It was a vital place, with a population from many backgrounds and cultures which were not always in harmony.

Peter Brown[18] describes the Church there as a sociological beargarden; differences between rich and poor, masters and slaves, men and women had polarized it. In reaction against profligacy, for example, some were suggesting that Christians should renounce marriage and encourage their children to do the same. The idea of a new creation had also bred some unusual ideas among them, and there were those who were prepared to dissolve all social bonds in view of it. The behaviour of some women, and also of some men with regard to them, was also causing problems, and in the year 54 Paul, responding to complaints made to him, intervened (1 Cor. 1:10–16 and 5:1–13).

The community was divided over the charismatic utterances of some women at its meetings, since they seem to have had affinity with the actions of prophetesses in some of the mystery cults. Also, it had always been customary for mature women in Greece and Rome, as well as among Jews, to cover their heads on public occasions – only young women and maidens went bareheaded; so also did mature women who were public sinners. Some mature Christian women were rejecting this convention and went bareheaded, which could be misleading.[19]

Paul reasons that 'woman came from man' and that they should cover their heads in church 'as a symbol of the authority over them out of respect for the angels' (1 Cor. 11:10). The sexes are indeed equal, and man can no more do without women than women without men, but none the less, given the circumstances 'women are to remain quiet at meetings' (1 Cor. 14:34). Generally women will be saved by childbearing, provided they live modest lives and are constant in the religious beliefs and practice which lead to holiness (1 Tim. 2:15). It does not read well today, but taking Paul's views as a whole they give a more positive view of women.

To Timothy he wrote of the sincere faith he had inherited from his grandmother Lois and his mother Eunice (2 Tim. 1:5). Paul had great hopes of Timothy as son and grandson of two such outstanding Christians, and he was not disappointed. His words in his letter to the Ephesians show how greatly he respected the sacrament of matrimony, and how it was intended to secure both parties in their personal dignity. If women should obey their husbands, he insisted husbands should love their wives just as Christ loved the Church (Eph. 5:25). There can be no talk of greater and less in such a relationship. And if there can be no talk of greater or less in this, the most important of relationships between man and woman, there can be no talk of it among the unmarried either.

Paul accepted women as full co-workers in his mission. Chloe was one of his closest contacts in the Corinthian church, someone he trusted absolutely (1 Cor. 1:11). Prisca, or Priscilla, and her husband Aquila, were Paul's hosts in Corinth (Acts 18:10) and were commended by him as his helpers (Rom. 16:3; 1 Cor. 16:19). Phoebe, a deaconess from another port near Corinth, (Rom. 16:1) and Tryphaena and Tryphosa in Rome (Rom. 16:12) are equally commended. Mary, mother of John Mark, and her servant Rhoda, were active in the Church from its first days (Acts 12:12–17). Lydia, a dealer in purple dye in Philippi, was baptized by Paul and became a trusted supporter of the mission, putting her house at the disposal of the apostles (Acts 16:14, 38).

(v) Mary, Mother of Christ

We cannot leave this question of the attitude to women in the New Testament as a basis for judging its respect for persons without briefly referring to the dignities given to Mary, Mother of Christ, dignities which bestow particular respect on all women.[20] First, she was referred to by the angel as 'full of grace' (Luke 1:28), who had been conceived immaculate, free of the sin of our first parents, the only human being ever to be so graced. In this then she stands out among all the sons and daughters of Eve, as the solitary boast of our fallen nature. Her 'behold all generations shall call me blessed' (Luke 1:48) was a prophecy; because the Almighty had done great things for her she would be venerated for all generations. For the sorrows her motherhood brought her, from the predictions of Simeon's prophecy (Luke 2:34–35) to her witnessing her son's passion and death, she is entitled to be seen as the Queen of Martyrs.

Because she 'kept all these words, pondering them in her heart' (Luke 2:19, 51) and became the source of our knowledge of the infancy of Christ, she is Queen of Evangelists, first among those who brought the Good News to mankind. She gave life to the Word made Flesh and was able to tell of him through that most intimate experience. Throughout her life, from prompting her Son's first miracle at Cana (John 2:1) and the first manifestation of his glory, to at the last in being a witness at Pentecost (Acts 1:14 and 2:3) she showed she had learned better than any other the mystery of her Son: 'blessed are they who hear the word of God and keep it' (Luke 11:28).

(vi) Labour and slavery

We have seen that in the Old Testament there was none of the prejudice against free labour, earning one's living by manual work, and that the New Testament also reflects this attitude. Christ himself worked as a carpenter for most of his adult life. It was a life spent among the poor, those who worked hard for a simple living, peasants, fishermen, artisans, housewives, servants and household slaves. The parables show how much their world was his: he drew upon their daily experience for his examples, examples which would be the more meaningful for their simplicity – the sower who saw that some seeds sown took root and produced fruit while others did not (Matt. 13:4–8), the housewife who used yeast to leaven the flour (Matt. 13:33), the merchant who found the pearl of great value and sold all to obtain it (Matt. 13:45–46) and the fishermen who hauled the full net ashore and sorted out the good from the useless among their catch (Matt. 13:47–48). St Paul earned his living as a tentmaker (Acts 18:3) and positively recommended that all should have some useful manual work to do.

Such being the ethos of the Gospel, Christians could not share that contempt for bodily labour which sprang from the belief that it so coarsened a man that he was of less worth as a human being.[21] That belief that supported much of the sentiment in favour of slavery, since it coincided with Aristotle's argument about natural slavery. The Christian ethic helped to undermine slavery but made no open attack on the institution. Slavery is only mentioned in the gospels in passing or as a means of illustrating some point: for example, that the disciple is not superior to his teacher, nor is this slave to his master (Matt. 10:24), or that the slave's place in the house is not assured whereas the son's is (John 8:34). Christ tells those who want to be first to become a slave of all (Mark 10:44) and adds that he himself had come to serve, likening himself to a slave in this context. The rights and wrongs of the institution are not considered: the institution was a part of life and none could imagine life without it.

This attitude reflects Christ's refusal to be cast in any way as an open opponent of the existing social order, which any condemnation of the institution of slavery would have made him. It is clear however that the first and great commandment – and its implication of our all being one in Christ, the whole concept of the vine and the branches – was incompatible with the doctrine of slavery, the idea that a section of humanity could be things, property, owned, used and disposed of like other property. But it was so ingrained in human society that not until minds and hearts were changed on this matter could it be effectively undermined. In the meantime the right to own slaves was not denied, but the way it was intended to be exercised involved respecting the human dignity of slaves, because they too were human beings redeemed by Christ. In return, slaves were to respect and obey their masters.

What St Paul has to say on this matter is addressed only to slave-owners and slaves who are Christians. Slaves were to be obedient to their masters for love of the Lord, and the latter were to treat slaves in the same spirit. They have the same master in heaven (Eph. 6:5–9, see Col. 3:22); slaves are to be treated justly (Col. 4:1). They are to be content to remain so unless a chance of manumission presents itself (1 Cor. 7:20). To Philemon, a friend to whom he returns Onesimus, an errant slave, he uses words which would indicate that though technically he does return a slave, it is as a free man he wished him to be received. (Phm. 1:15). The reason why slavery and Christianity were ultimately in conflict was stated by St Paul. All – Jew and Greek, slave and free, male and female – are one in Jesus Christ (Gal. 3:28). The institution remained, however, because it did not occur to the generality of men that it could be dispensed with; it was too necessary to the maintenance of life as they understood it.

3

The social witness of the early Church

1 Introduction

In this, the early Church period down to AD 604, the year 313, when the Church was recognized by the Roman Empire as a lawful organization, was a turning point because from then onwards Christianity could organize openly and had the full backing of the State. Until then it had been officially outlawed. Rome was tolerant of beliefs, religious practices, and organizations generally, provided they were open to public view, their charters were approved by it and they were not in conflict with the State, actually or potentially. Christianity, however, grew as a clandestine organization because it did not fit into this pattern. It claimed to be the one true religion. It held its meetings at night and also indulged in what were regarded as secret and immoral rites; it was therefore regarded as subversive, although initially there was no policy of persecution. The first recorded was that set on foot by the Emperor Nero who chose to blame Christians for the fire that devastated Rome in 64. Thereafter they were generally tolerated, though they could be sought out and punished unless they were ready to offer prayers to the gods; they were, in other words, illegal but not regarded as a real danger to the State.[1]

Meanwhile Christianity spread remarkably quickly. The Greek-speaking Jewish synagogues in Jerusalem were soon attracted to the new religion, and through them contact with those in the other cities of Palestine was established.[2] The speed with which Christianity spread in the first thirty to fifty years after Christ's death was a phenomenon that has no parallel in human history and it defies explanation on social and historical grounds alone. It clearly met an immense need in the world of its time, a fundamental social, psychological and spiritual need, in so varied and vast an Empire.[3] Clearly there was a force at work in it which was more than human.

Hellenistic Jewish Christians who had fled from Jerusalem after the death of St Stephen (c. AD 36) settled in Antioch, and there many of the citizens were converted (Acts 11:19–21) as a result of their influence; the Hellenistic world was opened to the Gospel and it was at Antioch that the followers of Christ were first known as Christians. The persecution of the Church in Jerusalem after Stephen's death (Acts 8:1) also scattered the leadership throughout Judea and Samaria and gave the mission there a boost. Meanwhile Paul with his missionary journeys from 46 to 58 shifted the Church's vision away from Palestine to Asia Minor and the European mainland through the Hellenistic Jewish centres established there. Paul was martyred in Rome under Nero, probably in 67.

By 135 Ephesus and Asia Minor were evangelized, Syria and Egypt had their growing communities, while the original missions of Aegean islands, Crete and Greece had been consolidated. New churches in Italy outside Rome had appeared by 80 to 90; there were new communities in Greece and also in Gaul by 170 while the expansion east to the Persian border continued; North Africa too had been evangelized, as the martyrdoms near Carthage in 180 reveal. By the time of Septimius Severus (193–211) the Church was already a challenge to all the other major religions and philosophies. Christianity was emerging as a world mission.

It had therefore been through the established Jewish communities and the synagogues that the Church first spread, just as Christianity had its roots in the Jewish tradition into which Christ had been born. In being incorporated into Christ, the convert was also being incorporated into an enlarged Israel, though now it was faith in Christ that saved, not the Law. The Jewish tradition, the Old Testament, gave Christianity a history which reached back beyond any that Rome or Greece could claim. It revealed a world created by God, evil as an abuse of the freedom he had given man, the origins of the human family and the beginnings of the key institutions of human culture. It was a simple but powerful, rational and coherent world-view. At the centre of everything and present at all times was the figure and the personality of Christ, truly man and yet truly God. The implications of this belief had yet to be set out in a satisfactory theology, but from the beginning believers were certain of the fact of God made man in Christ, as they were certain that God was three in one, Father, Son and Holy Spirit: the presence of the Holy Spirit was vividly part of their lives.

Nurtured initially in the Jewish tradition, they gradually became aware of all that separated them from that tradition.[4] They were increasingly aware also of all that separated them from normal civil life in Roman society, much though they tried not to challenge the existing order, but simply to get on with loving God and neighbour. But theatres and public games, the decadent luxury, the indulgence in the sins of the flesh, were not for them. The celebrations of an idolatrous society were not for them either; marriage, birth, the time of sowing the fields and harvesting, the inaugurations of magistrates, family festivals, all were attended by oblations, incense, banquets, sacrifices. Unable to participate in such functions because of the danger of idolatry, they were increasingly seen as a third race, a race apart.

Though bound by the laws of pagan society, paying their taxes like everyone else and stressing that they were good citizens, they did not take their legal disputes to the courts but settled them within the Church. They intermarried. If a pagan partner would not live peaceably with his or her converted mate, the marriage could be dissolved. Divorce was absolutely prohibited, and virginity was praised. In daily life Christians were expected to be peaceable, obeying the authorities, and if slaves, obeying their masters, pagan or Christian. Idleness was a disgrace; uprightness, courtesy, cheerfulness and charity were expected, as was hospitality. The Christians were expected to be pure in their sexual lives, detached from their possessions, truthful and brave.[5]

Local churches had an intense and vibrant life, founded on a faith and hope which transcended the bounds of gender, social class, nation and race: women were from the first prominent in them, and foreigners and slaves were welcome. They offered a complete social life to their members, having their own courts of justice and system of social welfare. It was the strength of these Christian cells, centred round the Eucharist and the presiding bishop, which was the secret of the growth of the expansion of the Church. They kept closely in touch with one another through a pattern of synods or councils which deliberated on matters of common concern, and one life throbbed through all.

2 Christianity and the pagan Roman Empire

The Roman Republic had proved incapable of standing up to the strains of the empire that it had won, and from 31 BC to 14 AD Augustus ruled as Emperor.[6] Thereafter Rome was an imperial

monarchy and its ruler was deified.[7] Religion and the Republic had
always been intertwined, and the political always controlled the
religious powers, but with the deification of the Emperor the identification of the two became complete, and the acceptance of the
divinity of the Emperor became important for social unity. After
Augustus's death, Tiberius (14–37), the first of the Julio-Claudian
line of emperors ruled. They were followed by the Flavians,
Vespasian (69–79) and his successors. The adoptive emperors
(96–180), those chosen for their ability and not for their bloodline,
presided over the second-century Empire when its glory was at its
height – Nerva (96–8), Trajan (98–117), Hadrian (117–38),
Antoninus Pius (138–61) and Marcus Aurelius (161–80). The latter
broke with the adoptive principle, and his incompetent son
Commodus (180–92) succeeded. The treaty which he concluded
to end the second Marcomannic War (178–84) was not in the
Empire's best interests; it was symptomatic of its increasing weakness in face of its enemies.

Commodus was overthrown in a palace revolt and Septimius
Severus (193–211) took his place. With the Severans the habit of
assassination and violent overthrow of emperors became established; the last of the line was killed by his mutinous troops at
Mainz in 235. There followed fifty years of anarchy during which
there were twenty-three Emperors, most of them nominees of the
soldiers, who reigned for a few months or years and died violently.
Meanwhile the pressures on the Empire's frontiers increased and
they were frequently pierced. Not until Diocletian (284–305) was
stability restored.

After Nero persecutions were sporadic; there was one under
Domitian (81–96), for example, but in 112 Trajan made it plain
that Christians were not to be sought out and anonymous accusers
were to be ignored; only those persisting in their error after examination were to be punished.[8] There were persecutions under
Antoninus Pius in Smyrna in 155, Marcus Aurelius at Lyons in 177
and at Carthage in 180 under Commodus.

Fearing the influence of the growing numbers of Christians
upon an already deeply troubled Empire, Commodus was led to
make the persecution systematic, and Maximinius (235–38) and
Decius (249–51) followed the same policy. Gallienus (260–68) was
by contrast tolerant, and toleration continued until in 303–13
came the last and most systematic persecution under Diocletian
and Galerius. This, however, failed, and in 311 the latter issued an
edict of toleration. Constantine, the Western emperor since 305,
invoked the God of the Christians during his successful struggle to

win supreme power in the West in 312, and he and Licinius, the
Eastern emperor, then adopted a policy of religious freedom for
all with the Edict of Milan in 313.

3 The strengths and weaknesses of the Empire

The Empire was built on conquest, with all that that entailed in
bloodshed, disruption and human suffering, but after that came
civilization. Soldiers built roads and aqueducts, towns were
founded, with their amphitheatres, public baths and municipal
buildings, their leisured, cultured life, and their function as the
self-governing centres of the local Roman administration.
Agriculture and the life of the great estates and the countryside
also flourished where Roman peace was established. The local
people had to learn their place, but once they had done so their
way of life, their gods and their customs, were respected. In the
service of Rome, Syrian and African, Spaniard, Gaul and Briton
mingled. There was law and general peace, good communications
by sea, and a network of roads throughout the Empire which facili-
tated traffic and trade.

Despite the basic tension between Rome and Christianity that
resulted from the absolutism of the Roman State clashing with the
Christian insistence that their first loyalty must be to God, the
Roman order in many ways helped the spread of the Gospel. The
Jewish diaspora provided it with a base in most major centres, and
the peace and the comparative ease of travel throughout the
Roman world gave the Gospel access to every corner of it. Roman
civilization formed a bridge with Christianity; it had absorbed the
best in Greek philosophy, and many who began their quest for
wisdom in the schools, as did Justin Martyr and Augustine, ended
it in the Church. She provided a spiritual depth that the old
Roman religion lacked. The spiritual and theological awareness
aroused by the Oriental mystery religions would also find its fulfilment for many in Christianity; Roman religion faltered and faded
because it met none of the profounder needs of spirituality, theological enquiry a more rational morality or spiritual life, despite
having in its earlier days nurtured sound values.

The moral and spiritual collapse of Rome was progressive. The
wealth of the Empire, and the forms it took, were morally corrupting. The quantity of bullion of all kinds brought back from the East
in the wake of conquest was enormous, and the annual tributes
continued to pour in thereafter.[9] This new wealth financed luxuri-

ous living by the rich, and supplied funds for support of more clients; for the urban proletariat it provided bread and circuses. A stronger economic basis of the imperial order would have enabled better use to be made of the wealth, but the Roman imperial economy was, in modern parlance, underdeveloped and incapable of self-development.[10]

It was mainly agricultural, and the agriculture was technologically primitive and of low productivity. The Roman social order did not encourage the dynamism necessary if the Empire was to expand economically. There was little application of the technical skills which Romans showed in other areas. Most of the labour used was that of slaves or servile peasants whose incentives to work hard or well were minimal; making them work efficiently required close and harsh supervision. The Romans never valued trade, commerce or industrial development highly, though their legal system eased the way for private enterprise, which flourished within the limits imposed by cultural restraints. The needs and benefits of Empire made Rome into a centre of finance capitalism, collecting and disposing of the plunder of Empire and farming out the taxes, while Alexandria was the major centre of manufacturing and long-distance, mainly luxury trade. There was importation of grain from Sicily, North Africa and Egypt to feed the Roman plebs; to prevent the riots that accompanied any non-arrival of the shipments, agents were granted special privileges and the State itself assumed the task of provider. Throughout the Empire generally industrial production was for the local market and stuck in a pattern of low productivity; there was not sufficient money in the hands of the people at large to stimulate production, and organization and techniques remained unchanged from simpler times; inland transport was at all times expensive. Nor were there the credit institutions to encourage a funnelling of funds into profitable investment. The safest, and often the only, investment was land.

The urban civilization throughout the Empire, sophisticated and advanced though it was in many ways, was artificial and fragile, imposed from above, not a natural growth out of a local economy or people; it was also parasitic, draining, not creating wealth. It was the civilization of a leisured class, and as such it lived on the Empire's resources; expenditure on it was unproductive, and as the number of cities grew in the age of expansion, so the burden increased also. While it was peaceful and expanding the cracks could be papered over, since economic activity in absolute terms increased, but by the third century the expansion had stopped and neither the rural nor urban economies could adapt to counter the consequent decline.

The State's other expenditures meanwhile multiplied as the needs of defence grew, and the taxes and other burdens of the cities were raised accordingly. The plundered or exhausted resources of the countryside, ravaged by war and revolt for almost a century, made it impossible to meet the increased demands, and the wealthier individual members of the municipal authorities were made responsible for making up the shortfall. The towns were increasingly deserted by those who once had enjoyed their flourishing; nor was it possible to enforce effectively the laws seeking to control urban and rural labour, and it too abandoned its post.

The decline in moral standards accompanied the collapse of the political and economic structures of the Empire. The mother of the Gracchi bore 12 children; by the end of the first century AD, a woman who bore three was praised as an exception.[11] The availability of slaves as concubines, the unwillingness to accept the responsibilities of marriage, the frequency of abortion and infanticide were all part of the pattern. Roman citizens were reluctant to serve in the legions; the barbarian tribes took over responsibility for the Empire's defence. The frontiers were increasingly defended by mercenaries. There were fundamental social weaknesses too which sapped the Empire's will to survive.

Above all it offered the ordinary people no means of participation in its affairs, no way of identifying with it as their own. The senators and the knights, and below them the aristocracies of wealth and of those who occupied all the important positions in the Empire, the army, the professions, and commerce, flourished under it.[12] Though it boasted of its universalism, which it regarded as its distinctive feature, that universalism simply served the privileged. The barriers between freeman and slave, the rich and the poor, the civilized few and the barbarian many, and the ever-present danger that the free would for some reason sink into slavery, and so lose human status, made it a mockery.[13] Little survived of the once proud Roman plebs under threat from the slave labour which was so abundant.[14] The uprooted peasants, unemployed workers, the immigrants from all corners of the Empire, were kept alive on doles and entertained by the games, subject to every kind of degradation and debasement. It was an Empire thus weakened by its internal problems which gradually succumbed to the barbarians.

The attempt to restore order in the third century seemed at first to succeed, but the means used in fact destroyed what was left of the old order and all it stood for. The Senate, the citizenry, the city-

states throughout the provinces on which the Empire had been
built, all crumbled. The army and the imperial government alone
remained effective. Constantine's division of the Empire into East
and West, moving his capital to Constantinople in the East in 330,
did not stem the decline. In the West it was hastened. By the fifth
century, the Empire was little more than an empty shell. The
barbarians had long been settling within the imperial boundaries as
auxiliaries of the Roman army, and they increasingly proved
stronger than it. The Visigoths defeated the Emperor Valens in 378
and Theodosius I succeeded him. The nominal Emperors in the
West, recognized by the East and ruling from Ravenna from AD 404,
were insignificant and became increasingly so. With the deposition
of the last of them in AD 476, the Western Empire was no more.

4 The organization and growth of the Church

Cruelly but only sporadically persecuted from 64, the Church had
also been tolerated for long periods before her final acceptance in
313, and the persecutions had only served to strengthen her. The
resistance of the martyrs amounted to a peaceful campaign of civil
disobedience for which they paid with their lives, and it was
because Christ in his Church could command such love and loyalty
that her organization was, from the beginning, strongly compact.
Socially she was comparatively homogeneous. Christians were from
the first disproportionately from the lower ranks of society who
worked for a living.[15] The punishment meted out to the Roman
martyrs by Nero in the first century indicates that in Rome they
were overwhelmingly of the *humiliores*, the lowest class,[16] and their
enemies made this lowly status a taunt against them. Celsus (*c.*
178), the first pagan writer who took the Christians seriously
enough to undertake a lengthy refutation of their beliefs and practices in his *True Discourses*, dismissed them as being recruited from
among the slaves, the manual workers, the immature, children and
women,[17] but his sneers were not justified. Humble they were but
they were also capable of managing their lives effectively. They
were a cross-section of a hardworking urban society, not only slaves
and ex-slaves and unskilled workers, but freemen, skilled manual
workers, shopkeepers and owners of small businesses. Their capacity for solid self-organization in the Church reveals that they were
a capable people with reasonable resources of their own.[18] And
their social homogeneity was not deliberate. They excluded no one
who accepted Christ and his law of love.

The life of the Christian community was centred around the Eucharist and the bishop. St Ignatius of Antioch stressed that only the Eucharist celebrated by the bishop, or one approved by him, is lawful; where the bishop is there also is the Christian community.[19] His role was primarily to make sure the community was united in faith and practice, and bishops were particularly praised for their charity, their hospitality and their care of the poor; both the involuntary poor, those in need, and the voluntary poor, the widows and virgins consecrating their lives to prayer, were their charge.

From the second half of the second century the growing number of those of higher social rank and class becoming converts was notable – senators and their families, the members of the equestrian order, advocates, physicians, military officers, civil servants, judges, governors with their wives, sisters and daughters accompanying – or more frequently preceding – them into the Church. The growing problems of the Empire, and the unease that they induced, undermined confidence in the old values and encouraged men and women to look for others more durable. Justin speaks of the attraction that Christianity presented in the way it combined concern for philosophical and theological truth with the inspiration for moral reform.[20] The pagan religions had shown too little concern for the individual person; whereas such concern was central to Christian belief and practice.[21]

By the third century there were strong Christian communities in all the main centres of population in the Empire. The robust organization and social authority which stemmed from their hierarchical nature enabled the Church to survive threats from heresy and schism. She was a universal society able to withstand the threats from the pagan powers. She was not a state within a state, but an autonomous society, with her own organization and government, law, rules of initiation and membership. Her appeal was to all those who found no satisfaction in the existing order of things, the marginalized, the poor and the oppressed, the weak and those who were of no account in that order. Above all she offered to those who reacted against its corruption, its emptiness and materialism, a nobler way. By the fourth century only the vast military structures of the State could rival the compactness and discipline of the Church. Constantine had watched the failure of the last and longest attempt to crush Christianity; he had made it plain that he had no sympathy with repression, and it cannot have been difficult for him to accept the triumph of this new religion; through it new resources of spiritual and social vitality were made available to the exhausted Empire in return for its freedom.[22]

5 *Reasons for the success of the Church*

The reasons for the Church's survival and flourishing, despite the persecutions and the forces ranged against her, are to be found in the power of God. Historians can only suggest those characteristics which in human terms made her attractive to the people of her time. For Chadwick the practical application of charity was probably the most important single cause of that success.[23] These works of charity were not isolated instances and restricted to individuals; no Christian was excused from the obligation of contributing to the needs of the poor and the suffering, and the efficiency of the Church's organization was there to give them help where and when it was needed; dioceses were in contact with one another throughout the Empire.[24] Widows and orphans, the sick, infirm and disabled, prisoners and those working in the mines, the care of the poor needing burial, the care of slaves, those affected by natural calamities, and those seeking work; all were the Church's concern.[25]

Lecky notes the vast system of public relief that existed for the Roman plebs, but it was a charity given for reasons and in a manner which reflected little credit either on those who created it or those who received it. From time to time individual Emperors would make provision for strengthening marriage or for the relief of the poor. Nor were there lacking in classical Rome individuals who had a humane care for the unfortunate, but such efforts were piecemeal, relying on individuals and isolated initiatives or membership of some religious or cultural group. Christianity, which became coterminous with society, excluded no one and eventually united all social classes and cultural groups. 'There can be no question that neither in practice nor theory, neither in the institutions that were founded nor the place that was assigned to it in the scale of duties, did charity in antiquity occupy a position at all comparable to that which it has obtained by Christianity.'[26] It established charity as a rudimentary virtue, giving it a central place in moral thinking in both its teaching and practice. In making the love of Christ its motive, it revolutionized theory and practice in this matter and it produced a vast organization of charity, presided over by the bishop and directed by the deacons; the bond of charity became the bond of unity. The poor and humble were given a place in things. Care for the poor and the sick was provided free of charge and the Church 'reaped untold advantage from instilling the idea that helping the sick was a bounden duty from which neither the individual nor the community was exempt'.[27]

The Church began to take the place of the municipality as the focus of local loyalty. The city-state was collapsing as its supports one by one were taken away. Its institutions were increasingly empty shells, and political rights were exchanged for fiscal obligations. Membership of the Church became more meaningful than citizenship. In her was to be found economic assistance and spiritual freedom and the spontaneous social activity and freedom of which the Romans had been deprived by the state despotism of the third and fourth centuries. In consequence the most able and energetic minds and talents were attracted to her.

The example of the Christian life and the steadfastness of the martyrs attracted converts.[28] In moral matters, the contrast with the ethos of the pagan world was total. Christianity was a complete way of life and every aspect of life was its concern. Given the almost total breakdown of moral values in this area of personal life, its conflict was against sexual sins – fornication, adultery, homosexual practices. Faithful and permanent monogamous marriage was the only permissible union of the sexes. Life was also sacred from its beginning; abortion and the exposure of infants was forbidden. It also opposed all forms of social injustice and selfishness – covetousness, greed, dishonesty in business, worship of wealth or power, double dealing and falsehood.[29]

6 The Church and the Christian Roman Empire

(i) Introduction

On 15 June 313, Constantine and his ally Licinius issued the decree which gave Christians full freedom of worship and restored their confiscated goods. Christian images appeared on the coinage in 315, and by 323 had totally replaced the pagan. The churches were given a privileged legal status, being able to inherit property and so increase their endowments, and Christians could achieve the highest posts in government and public service. After his death in 337, Constantine's three sons who ruled after him were exercised by the need to preserve the Empire against the inroads by Germanic tribes from the North and the East. It was a losing battle; slowly the barbarians succeeded to the Empire by force and stealth.

The new faith was now important to the rulers politically as their Empire crumbled, and they increasingly interfered in its affairs. They sought to destroy paganism by legislation but they did not succeed because some attitudes and practices were too deep-rooted. The old ways still appealed to too many, the games and spectacles especially. Julian 'the Apostate', Constantine's nephew and Emperor (361–63) made attempts to restore paganism by law which were no more successful than his predecessors' attempts to eliminate it by the same means.

The Eastern Emperor Valens was defeated and killed in battle with the Visigoths at Adrianople in 378 and Theodosius (379–95) adopted the Christianity of the Nicene creed as the religion of the State to the exclusion of all others. Efforts to hold the Empire together and intact failed. In the fifth century the Western part of the Empire gradually disintegrated and was taken over by the invaders. In 401 the Visigoths had invaded Italy once more and in 410 Alaric sacked Rome. When the Huns came in 452 it was the Pope, Leo the Great, who saved the city. Ricimer and then Odoavacer, with their Germanic mercenaries, ruled Italy, with the latter finally replacing the last of the residual Western Emperors, Romulus Augustulus, in 476.

The Ostrogoths conquered Italy 487 to 493. Their leader Theodoric (493–526) proved to be a powerful and caring king, but as a Gothic Western ruler and an Arian, he was in conflict with his Catholic subjects and the Eastern Emperor Justin (518–27). His son Justinian (527–65) invaded Italy in 535 in an effort to recover it for the East, but despite the successes of his generals Belisarius and Narses, the effort was beyond the Eastern Empire's long-term strength. In 568 another wave of invaders, the Lombards, entered Italy and the imperial forces could not defeat them. Like their predecessors the Lombards then had a struggle to establish their hegemony in Italy.

The result was constant warfare, and as always the main victims of it were the ordinary, innocent people. During his Papacy, Gregory the Great (590–604) used his good offices to try to bring some order and justice to Rome and central Italy. Building on the tradition of service to the community which the Papacy both by choice and necessity had developed as the Roman power waned, he established it as a powerful force in European affairs.

(ii) The growth of the Church's social involvement

In considering the reasons for the success of the Church in the first three centuries, we have already noted the impact made by her social witness. The wide range of her social charity provisions was made possible by the systematic way in which the collection and distribution of funds was organized from the beginning, and by the provision of personnel to see that this was done. Tertullian describes how the voluntary contributions made by all were used to feed the poor, and to enable the old to be looked after, orphans and homeless assisted, and those in prison or condemned to the mines for the faith, supported. The funds were distributed by the deacons according to arrangement with the president. The local or regional churches helped not only their own people but others far distant when the need required. Because of its numbers, its comparative wealth and its outstanding Christian witness, Rome was notable for its generosity. It would seem that any church in need could call on it for help and receive it. Other major churches, for example Carthage, were also notably generous.[30]

In the time of Constantine and his immediate successors the Church's organization and personnel were used for many aspects of social organization. The State was generous in the property rights given to her, and the accession of wealth and influence that came with membership of, and office in her, inevitably brought with it problems of corruption and worldliness but there was no way in which the friendship now offered her by the State could be refused. The Church had always insisted that she was not an enemy of the secular order as such, and that her members were good citizens. Now that she was accepted, it was not possible for her to refuse the alliance offered her. It was a self-interested offer, it is true. The economic resources and the social and other privileges which came her way were offered so that her organizational strength and her moral leadership might be put at the service of society. The State hoped that the Christian virtues of honesty, integrity, acceptance of responsibility and generous service of others would help society to survive and thrive.

Generally the State and society did gain greatly from this link with the Church. In particular her services in the relief of social distress from various causes were particularly effective and much appreciated.[31] So too was the reliance now put on Church courts. They gave a swifter, fairer judgement than the civil courts and were overwhelmed by the demands made on them. The Church could defend those who claimed sanctuary and seek mitigation of their sentences and treatment, so helping to humanize the operation of the law. Under her influence, also in Constantine's time, legislation was passed on the treatment of slaves which was more favourable than any that had gone before. Wholesale emancipation was not favoured, however, nor did the Emperor have much understanding of the slaves' deeper human needs, but he did seek to lessen their hardships. He forbade the breakup of slave families, stopped the enslavement of foundlings and declared emancipation to be desirable, with the slaves being freed in Church.[32] Those in danger of being sold for immoral purposes, the condemned criminals and prisoners generally, were protected by the Church and she was given responsibility for the jails and their occupants.

The scope of care for the needy was extended. The Christian virtue of hospitality was initially very broadly interpreted, embracing not only the traveller but all who were in want, the poor, the sick, the aged, the foundlings, the orphans. Initially, from the second century, this was organized by the deacons, co-operating with the priests and bishops. As such they attended to all the groups listed, but only gradually were the different types of needy given separate care, with separate provision, however primitive, being provided for travellers, for the sick, the widows, the aged and the orphans. The freedom now given the Church enabled her to extend her work in this area[33] and to provide special buildings for the purpose. The Council of Nicea in 325 approved of the provision of facilities for the pilgrims, the sick and the poor in every city.

At Antioch in the time of John Chrysostom there were some 3000 widows and virgins supported by the Church, along with the sick, the travellers, the old, the orphans and the poor generally. It was part of a fourth-century movement which gradually established a comprehensive pattern of hospices and hospitals.[34] The houses of strangers, *xenodochia*, at first catered for all, but in time their prime function was more and more limited to providing for travellers, with other houses being set up for the sick, foundlings, orphans and the aged. We hear of a house for the poor at Sebaste in 356; and Basil of Caesarea's hospice, constructed in 372, was a complex of buildings, including workshops and a monastery, around which a hospital for the poor and a hospice for pilgrims were erected; for the sick there were as many wards as diseases, and lepers who had previously been kept in isolation were looked after there;[35] doctors and nurses were in attendance.

There are records of *xenodochia* in Pontus, Antioch and Constantinople; that at Alexandria was on a grand scale, its five hundred male nurses being given to rowdiness, providing the authorities with cause for some concern. In the light of the many calls on it, Pope Simplicius in 465 ordered that ecclesiastical income should be divided into four parts, one for the bishop, the second for the building of churches, the third for the maintenance of the clergy and the fourth for the strangers and the poor.[36] *Xenodochia* were established in Rome by Fabiola and Pammachius in the fourth century, and others were provided with the encouragement of St Gregory the Great and other popes. Episcopal hospitals appeared in Gaul in the sixth and seventh centuries.

This work of the Church far surpassed anything the State could do in this field, and all – the scattered hospitals in troubled Italy, the numerous ones of Syria, the tiny establishment at Clermont and the huge ones at Alexandria, Constantinople and Jerusalem – existed and worked in the same religious framework, which was one of love, care and compassion for the sick.[37]

7 Some social attitudes

(i) The right to life

The Church 'dogmatically asserted the sinfulness of all destruction of human life as a matter of amusement, or of simple convenience, and thereby formed a new standard higher than any which existed in the world'. Abortion was denounced as murder, in the same category as infanticide.[38] The latter was accepted in different degrees in both Greece and Rome, and the Church tried to make the moral enormity of the practice apparent.

Christians rejected also the bloodlust of the circus, to which by the fourth century 175 days were devoted annually – and these were only the ordinary festivals. For seven generations the Romans had been steeped in this cruelty, and their greatest writers and thinkers rationalized the bloodshed as a means of giving the citizens an example of brute courage in the face of death.[39] In the games, paganism had its strongest and most enduring hold on the people. Despite the attempted banning of gladiatorial combats as early as 325, not until the period 434–38 were these efforts effective.

(ii) Prohibited occupations

Christians had from the first been forbidden to take any active part in the games, and a number of other occupations were closed to them for fear of compromising their beliefs. Positions of leadership in the military, which involved a suspicion of idolatry or immorality, were denied them.[40]

The position changed somewhat as Christianity became more accepted towards the end of the second century. Christian apologists sought to calm the fears of their fellow citizens by stressing how like them Christians were. Tertullian affirmed that 'we frequent your forum, your market, your baths, your inns and your fairs. With you we take ship and serve as soldiers'; but in all this he stresses that they reject only what touches on immorality or idolatry.[41] Participation in commerce and trade, even if innocent of idolatrous purpose, was treated with reserve because of the fear of dishonesty and sharp practice that all business activity aroused. But 'the recognition of the ordinary forms of honest trade and industry as not only a legitimate but an obligatory means of support'[42] is found in Irenaeus and Clement of Alexandria; Tertullian also refers to the Christian frequentation of the markets as one of the signs of their involvement in ordinary life. Since there were restrictions on the occupation of Christians in some professions, trades or employments, it was accepted from the first that this obligation should be, and was, balanced by the readiness of the community to try to support those so displaced, at least temporarily, and to find them alternative work if necessary. Harnack goes so far as to say the churches had the functions of labour unions.[43]

(iii) War and military service

The strong but not absolute basis of Christian pacifism we have examined. The legions were originally recruited from Roman citizens only, and comparatively few Christians came into that category; military service was not compulsory until the fourth century[44] and those who wished to avoid it for reasons of conscience would have found little difficulty in doing so. The objection of some moralists to the military life was not only that the readiness to shed blood was part of it, but that its other obligations were not compatible with Christian belief. The passing of death sentences by officers of centurion rank and above and the carrying out of them by the soldiers, the infliction of scourging, torture and crucifixion, the unconditional military oath, the glorification of the military life, the religious sacrifices in which all had to participate in some way, the behaviour of the soldiers in peacetime, and the general immorality of the camps, all told against it.[45] Tertullian opposed military service but, in defending the Church from the charge that its members are not fully involved with the life of the Empire, he asserted that the fortresses and camps are filled with Christians.[46] He is however unimpressed by John Baptist's example of not requiring of soldiers the abandonment of their profession before being baptized, and does not accept it as compelling. As to the actual practice of Christians, there is one very well-attested case of their service in the legions in 171 to 173. The Twelfth Legion, the *Legio Fulminata* contained many, and their prayers on one occasion were called on, very successfully to aid its cause, as is recorded on a column erected by the Emperor Marcus Aurelius in Rome[47] after the conclusion of the campaign against the Quadi.

In the third century the problems of life in an Empire increasingly under siege complicated the task of the theologians on the general question of military service. St Cyprian of Carthage (d. 258) urged the incompatibility of the Christian faith with any act of violence; 'after the reception of the Eucharist, the hand is not to be stained with the sword and bloodshed', but he accepts that wars are inevitable: he sees the decline in the military power of the Empire as a sign of God's disfavour[48] and expresses the hope that the Empire's enemies would be kept at bay. The life of Lactantius (*c.* 240–320) spanned the period from the last of the persecutions to the acceptance of the Church by Rome and his work reflects the development of his original pacifism to meet the new situation.

This development had already been anticipated by Cyprian and Clement, and would accommodate the needs of life in a civil society which accepted the Church and expected its members to play a part in its legitimate undertakings. Initially, in his *Divine Institutes* written *c.* 304 to 311, Lactantius is opposed to all bloodshed. Constantine's victory over Maxentius in the battle of the Milvian bridge in 312 brought forth a different response. Later he sees the Emperor as God's vice-gerent punishing those who do evil and restoring justice.[49] The large number of soldiers who are found among the martyrs from the third century would seem to show a considerable Christian presence in the military; probably no other socially identifiable group was so well represented among them. They gave their lives for the faith in every Province of the Empire, Italy, Numidia, Mauretania, Spain, Asia, Egypt, Assyria and on the Danube.[50] St Alban, the first British martyr recorded was a Roman soldier.

(iv) Slavery

Following the New Testament example, there was no question of challenging the existence of the system of slavery. A Letter of Ignatius of Antioch to Polycarp, dating from about AD 105 advises that it is not right to treat slaves, male or female, condescendingly; nor is it right that the slaves give themselves airs or pine for release at the expense of the community[51] since it was clearly impractical for those communities to emancipate them all. Overall, as in the biblical times, the 'slave question' as Western society came to know it, did not occur to the early Church; it was no more a friend or an enemy of the institution than it was of the State; it was a fact of life with which it had to come to terms and no one of the time could imagine life without it.

The Christian community therefore concentrated on the practical task of relieving the sufferings of the slaves as far as possible by ensuring their more humane treatment. Converted slaves were regarded as brothers and sisters, they shared the rights of a member of the Church to the full. The sex of the female slave was respected. Masters and mistresses were charged to treat them as personal equals in the Christian community. Not all of them did this by any means, but it was recognized as wrong if they did not do so. Slaves for their part were expected to accept their master's authority over them in daily life. Emancipation was from the first regarded as praiseworthy but the slave was not to regard it as a right. Masters were to exercise authority over slaves in a Christian manner.[52]

Lecky sums up the effects of Christianity on slavery as encouraging a classless attitude and encouraging emancipation.[53] At the Eucharist and in the prayers they were side by side. At a time when the slave had no standing in civil law, being simply the master's property, the penitential system of the Church and its legislation treated wrongs done to a freeman and a slave equally. A master who killed a slave was excommunicated. But in her teaching there was no suggestion that the system itself should be challenged. Among the Fathers St Gregory of Nyssa expresses himself most strongly on the enormity of buying and selling human beings,[54] but we have no evidence that he believed slavery could be abolished. It did not occur to anyone that it was a practical possibility.

Some modern writers show surprise that the system was not rejected outright.[55] That they do reveals an innocence of the conditions of the time and ignores the fact that had it done this, the Church would have been in direct political, social, and eventually violent conflict with a society which regarded slavery as part of the basis of the civilized order of things. But as a community Christians had not used violence when they suffered gross injustices in times of persecution, though by the third century they had enough of the civil leaders and soldiers and ex-slaves in their ranks to have done so.[56] The Church was to conquer by goodness and love in the service of their master Christ, not by violence.

Finally we note that individual Christians often fell short of their duty to treat slaves properly. There were Christian households where treadmill, prison and scourges were used in the punishment of slaves and where, if they desired freedom, they were regarded as evil and deserving of punishment. That Christians could still be guilty of beating slaves to death in a fit of rage the Council of Elvira attests.[57] The corrupting influences of the institution continued to take their toll, therefore, and it is sad but not surprising that not all who professed belief in Christ were able to escape it.

(v) The dignity of labour

Uhlhorn outlines the effects of slavery on the classical world.[58] The Athenian citizen – and the Roman – was a member of a ruling caste: as such he was entitled to his share in the public property; his time was spent in the assembly or the court; he could not carry on a trade or business and he was maintained by the State and at its service. He grew unaccustomed to work; the slaves could do the work, and the free workers were degraded by doing work that slaves could do.

The industrial worker was undermined as the slave owners, rural or urban, produced goods by slave labour at prices with which the freeman could not fairly compete. Terms and conditions of labour were always at risk because of the possibility of replacing free workers by unfree labour if it became profitable to do so. The threat was not only to their economic well-being: it was to their dignity as human beings. Manual work and all who did it were esteemed no more highly than were slaves. Classical writers and society generally held manual work, and its workers, in contempt; it coarsened body, soul and manners. The labour of the free peasant was noble, but the peasants were a dying race.

The rebuilding of respect for honest work as a means of support for self and family, with all that this meant in a rebirth of moral responsibility and sound citizenship, was essential for a healthy society, and here the influence of Christianity was crucial. It was in the monasteries that the idea of free labour was born.[59] At the time when the problems of the Empire in the third century increasingly led to workers being tied to the work, the monk was free, and in the community work was done freely to obtain the means to live, to combat the enemies of the soul and to earn money to provide for the needs of the poor: it was not in response to State edict.

Both St Basil and St Benedict stressed the importance of work.[60] The monastery therefore became a community based on free labour. Work is done for love of God and neighbour; each has a calling to work and to pray. These communities therefore demonstrated by their existence that a livelihood should be gained through useful work for oneself and the community, and that through what is honestly earned by labour, a man should have the means to help others. In so doing they offered to the new civilization which would in time emerge a powerful pattern of cultural values affecting the world of work.

(vi) The role of women

Women were attracted to the Church from the beginning. She appealed to their deep religious sense, particularly in the personal attachment to her Founder which was central to her beliefs, and to the charitable work which grew out of those beliefs. They also saw the Church's teaching on sex and marriage as safeguarding the dignity of women. From the first also they were active in the Church's mission.[61] The order of widows gave themselves to prayer and the visiting of the sick. The order of deaconesses dates from apostolic times and by the third century had replaced the order of widows: besides attending the sick, they ministered to women, looking after the catechumens, instructing and encouraging them and attending at their baptism.

The order of virgins also existed from apostolic times; the example of Christ and his mother, and the strong commendation of the virtue in New Testament, made it very much a Gospel value. The significance of this way of life increased throughout the history of the early Church, and by the time of St Justin, in the mid-second century, it had become recognized even by non-Christians that for men and for women it was 'a form of physical heroism equivalent to the observed capacity of Christians to face down the fear of death'.[62] Through their witness to this virtue Christians demonstrated that their religion was truly universal, available to all in its simplicity. Virginity and celibacy were signs of a new order, a new creation.

It was then a sign given by both men and women, but in changing the status of women and giving them a wider influence in the Church as equals of Christian men, it had for them a greater significance. Through it they had freedom to develop their spiritual and intellectual talents, as individuals or in communities; their profession of this virtue gave them a wider influence within the Church because of the respect for it as a Gospel value. St Macrina, the sister of St Basil the Great and St Gregory of Nyssa, in sanctity and her way of life remained a model for her brothers. Heiresses such as Melania and Olympias who dedicated themselves to the Church were powerful witnesses to Christ. St Jerome encouraged Paula and others as Scripture scholars.[63]

Through martyrdom, Christian women demonstrated in the

most striking way that they were the full equals of men in their
dedication to Christ. The example of Saints Perpetua and Felicitas,
martyred in 203, was especially venerated in the early Church. The
former was a happily married young patrican woman and mother
of a small child, the latter a poor slave girl who was eight months
pregnant and was delivered of her daughter in prison just before
her death. So impressive was their bearing, their calm and joy in
face of the terrible death that faced them, that at one point the
crowds demanded they be spared, though in the issue they died in
a most cruel manner with their equally heroic companions.[64]

It is against this background that we must set those passages in
the Fathers which suggest that women were inferior and indeed a
snare. They centre around the interpretation of texts such as that
in Genesis concerning the punishment for the sin of Adam and
Eve in the Garden of Eden (Gen. 3:16).[65] Since these passages do
occur in Scripture the Fathers had to comment on them but in fact
any fairly representative selection from the writings of the Fathers
on the role of women contains far more passages which are compli-
mentary to women than are derogatory.[66] They held up the
example of women as models of asceticism and heroism, outstanding in their devotion, their faith and their generous service of their
master. They saw them also as outstanding also in their intellectual
powers and their simple human dignity, and Clark herself
concludes that in the light of this witness, the Fathers put aside
whatever cultural prejudices they had had against women and fully
accepted their sisters in Christ as worthy bearers of the new religion's ideals.[67]

(vii) Marriage and the family

Gnostic sects were from the second century claiming that celibacy
was the only option for the Christian – as Clement of Alexandria
tells us.[68] He takes up the challenge and answers it. The Christian
vocations to celibacy and to marriage are personal matters and
each must make a choice according to Christ's calling. Holiness is
the end of both and through either, properly lived, it can be
attained.[69]

Christian witness had increasingly and influentially been given
also from the beginning by the Christian family, especially in the
strength of the wife's faith and its impact on her menfolk and
society: so St Monica's prayers for the conversion of her son
Augustine. The ideal of marriage which the Church had inherited
from the Old Testament, and which in the New Christ had further

expounded and filled out, was a crucial one. It was central to the whole of human society: the family is the basis of Church and State.[70] In the family, the father was the head, but the head of a partnership of two personal equals; both partners were set a very high personal ideal, that of monogamy, total fidelity in marriage and an ethical and religious obligation to care for their children. Abortion, and also the exposure of children were therefore unthinkable, as were sterilization and contraception. Once the Church had been recognized, this ideal should have become the norm, but given the confused understanding of the family that existed in pagan society because of its corrupted understanding of human sexuality, any such attempt was beset with difficulties.[71] The consequent legislation on marriage in the Justinian code represented something of a compromise. For example, concubinage was allowed; divorce was also, although it was made more difficult: but slave marriages were protected and slave children who were emancipated were to receive the inheritance rights of the free born. The consent of the parties was considered the essence of marriage, as it was in Roman law, and several of the practices accompanying the pagan rite were kept – the veil, the joining of hands. All that was excluded was idolatry and, for example, the reading of horoscopes.[72]

The indissolubility of marriage, especially in the light of the teaching of St Paul in Ephesians 5, was stressed by most writers from the second century. Within Christian marriage the wife had equal rights with her partner. Man and wife were as Christ is to his Church and were to respect each other as equals in consequence. Second marriages were allowed but not encouraged because of the great reverence for the institution and the ascetical tendencies of the time. Adulterers were subject to ecclesiastical discipline; abortion was regarded as murder and the exposure of infants was strictly forbidden.

(viii) Individual freedom

The early Church left an indelible mark on the Western political tradition as a result of her conflict with the pagan Roman Empire. She did not seek that conflict; she wanted only the right to carry on her mission in peace, but there was an inevitability about her clash with the Roman order because she and the Empire had radically different views on rights of conscience in religious matters. In antiquity, and in Rome in particular, religion was national; a people revered its own gods and no others.[73] With the growth of

the Empire this changed: the Greek gods, and gradually the oriental, were admitted to the Roman pantheon: but the Jews and
Christians who worshipped the one true God could not accept
these conventions because they involved idolatry. The Romans saw
no distinction between their beliefs. The consequence was that
they were not only outside the national religion: they were seen as
atheists.

After the destruction of Jerusalem, however, the reality of
Judaism was accepted by the State; the Jews professed an approved
religion. Disturbances in Roman order as a result of disagreements
between Jews and Christians alerted the authorities to the differences between them. Trajan's reply to Pliny in 112 showed that
individuals could bring about the condemnation of Christians by
denouncing them to the authorities, but from the early third
century emperors themselves initiated persecutions. The martyrs
were prepared to obey the State when it acted within its competence, but they would not worship the imperial idea of the State,
for that was idolatry. There were limits to the State's authority. This
was the ultimate point of conflict with the Roman order, and this
introduced a new perspective on the relations of the citizen with
the State. It

> 'produced a unique problem which in the end contributed
> more than any other to the specific qualities of European
> political thought ... the belief in spiritual autonomy and the
> right of spiritual freedom left a residuum without which the
> modern ideas of individual privacy and liberty would scarcely be
> intelligible.'[74]

4

The social teaching of the Fathers of the Church

1 Introduction

In the last chapter we have already considered some aspects of the social teaching of the Fathers of the Church, but now we take a more systematic look at it overall.[1] The early or Apostolic Fathers, those who are linked with the first two generations of Christians, are the first group. They include the unknown writer of the *Didache* or 'The Teaching of the Twelve Apostles': its date is uncertain but it was used in the second century as a basis for Christian teaching.[2] The document known as the *Shepherd of Hermas* is also of uncertain date, perhaps as early as 70 or 90[3], and in one of the visions of the Shepherd which it recounts, the importance of solidarity between rich and poor is examined in the light of the parable of the vine and the branches.

The next group of Fathers, the Apologists, appear in the second century, from about 120, and they were, as their title suggests, mainly concerned with explaining and defending the faith against attack. Prominent among them was Justin Martyr who was put to death in Rome in 165. In his *Apologies* and the *Dialogue with Trypho* he comments on the relation of the Christians with the State and society, the sharing of property in the early Christian communities and the social implications of the Christian law of love.[4]

The third-century Fathers wrote more extensively. St Clement of Alexandria (*c.* 155–220) and Origen (*c.* 185–254) were prominent in the Catechetical or Theological school of Alexandria, and Tertullian (*c.* 160–215), St Cyprian of Carthage (*c.* 200–258) and Lactantius (*c.* 240–320) were from the province of North Africa. St Clement's homily on Mark 10:17–31 'Who is the rich man who will be saved?' (*Quis dives salvetur?*) deals at length with the attitude to

* The notes and references for Chapter 4 are to be found on p. 382

riches in the early Church[5] and reveals a very comprehensive approach to its subject.

The fourth century, the golden age of the Greek and Latin Fathers, so called because they wrote in those languages, included among the former Eusebius of Caesarea (*c.* 265–339), a church historian who was the first to consider in depth the relations between Church and State.[6] St Basil the Great (*c.* 329–379), St Gregory of Nazianzus (330–90) and St Gregory of Nyssa (335–94) are collectively referred to as 'the Cappadocians'.[7] Basil's Homily *In Illud Lucae* (on Luke 12:16–21),[8] is another important source for understanding the patristic attitude to private property. St John Chrysostom (*c.* 344–407), Patriarch of Constantinople in 398, was very much concerned with practical ethics and social ethics in his ministry, and dealt extensively with the ethics of property and wealth.[9]

Of the Latin Fathers, St Ambrose (*c.* 339–397) dealt with Church–State relations and, in his homily *On Naboth*, with economic ethics;[10] St Jerome (*c.* 345–419) stressed the legitimacy of private property, advocating sharing of it; St Augustine (354–430) was influential through his writings on the social order, on peace and war, and on property. Of the later Fathers, St Gregory the Great (540–604), wrote on wealth and property, and also on the origin and nature of political power.[11]

2 Natural law and patristic social teaching

The theology of the Fathers developed to meet the challenges to which the Gospel was increasingly being exposed as it was preached more widely. In this the formulation of the faith was the main concern, not social issues. Only one of the Fathers, John Chrysostom, can be said to have concentrated on the latter to any degree. At the same time, the relationship between Church and State, the problems of riches and poverty, of the need to see that property fulfilled its social obligations, were pressing on the Christian conscience. They were not ignored therefore, but in their treatment of them the Fathers were not concerned with social, political or economic analysis or policy in themselves, only with their moral implications. We do not then expect to find in them any lengthy treatment of theoretical or practical issues in these secular fields; they had neither the mandate nor the competence for it. They were, however, aware that some of the classical pagan writers dealt with some of the central problems of social

ethics, and they were ready to use such of their insights as were
compatible with the Scriptures and the tradition in dealing with
them. Jurisprudence, the philosophy of law,[12] especially the
natural law theory of the Roman jurists, was their starting point.

Natural law is a concept which has been used in different ways by
different thinkers and writers over the centuries. It had its philosophical roots in ancient Greece[13] but it was because it proved so
valuable in the elucidation of law and the strengthening of the
philosophy of law in the hands of the Roman jurists, whose skill in
this area of intellectual and practical achievement has never been
excelled, that it made its most lasting mark on the Western tradition. The concept itself received its classic definition from the
Roman Stoic and philosopher Cicero.

> There is in fact a true law – namely right reason which is in
> accordance with nature and eternal ... to invalidate this law by
> human legislation is never morally right ... it will not lay down
> one rule at Rome and another at Athens, nor will it be one rule
> today and another tomorrow ... but there will be ... one law
> eternal and unchangeable ... there will be one common master
> and ruler of men, namely God the author of this law and its
> sponsor.[14]

Natural law then is a thing of reason, and it lies behind all positive,
man-made law, including the *ius gentium,* the law of the peoples,
the nations, and knowledge of it enables man to correct the weakness of all positive law. In the *Institutes* of Justinian the natural law
is understood as, in effect, the God-given permanent law which is
superior to man-made law, an understanding which is fundamentally that of Cicero.[15]

The reason why the Fathers found this natural law theory attractive is clear. It was philosophical/juristic reason converging with
the Christian understanding that there was an absolute morality
based on belief in God. Men could attain to it independently of
revelation. The doctrine of the Fall of man as the Church understood it implied such a belief: man was not totally corrupted by sin,
and therefore it was possible for him to arrive at belief in a morality given him by God through his reason. The surest way to God is
of course through Christ and through the revealed moral law.[16]
But where, through no fault of their own, men do not know Christ
or the revealed moral law, they can still attain to knowledge of the
moral truth through the use of right reason. This capacity is
referred to in the Epistle to the Romans: 'Pagans who have never
heard of the law, but are led by reason to do what the law

commands' (Rom. 2:14–15). Origen speaks of the law of nature as king, and generally the early Christian writers accepted the natural law, identifying it with the law of God, as did Cicero.[17] Isidore of Seville restated it in the seventh century.[18] It passed from there to Gratian in the twelfth century, and from him via canon law to medieval theology. It was to be clarified by the scholastics and received its classic statement in the *Summa* of St Thomas Aquinas in the thirteenth century.

3 The equality of all men and the fact of slavery

The idea of natural law therefore was useful to the Fathers in confronting the key issues in social ethics which the Church faced, and one of these was the fact of slavery. The Aristotelian theory of the natural inequality of men, with some being only capable of slave work and destined to spend their lives in that capacity,[19] had been increasingly rejected as the Greek and Roman world became aware of the customs and character of other peoples throughout the Middle East and the Mediterranean: all human beings were capable of reasoning and living virtuously, and there were no inferior classes or races. Cicero so believed: it is evil habits and false conceptions which have made some groups of men appear to be of less worth than others. But since nature has given all men right reason, and a true law stemming from that right reason, the incidental differences do not argue against the general equality of men. Cicero taught that slaves should be treated like hired workers, and though he can be quoted to support the view that some men are incapable of governing themselves and so can justly be made slaves, he is on the whole not convinced this is the way it should be, or once was.[20]

Seneca was fuller and more complete on this matter. Slaves had the same nature as their masters; all men can be virtuous, the free, the freedman and the king. In the golden age when there was peace and justice slavery was not in the original scheme of things. This reference to a golden age resonated with the Christian view of a state of innocence before the Fall of which slavery was a result. But neither Stoic nor Christian considered it possible to challenge slavery as an institution.[21] Neither did the Roman jurists who taught that by natural law all men are equal, and by it all men are born free: slavery was of the *ius gentium* not the *ius naturalis.*

Some of the Fathers used this Stoic and Jurist tradition in their elucidation of the Christian understanding of slavery. St Augustine

taught that God did not create man to have control over his
fellows, and that by nature man is not a slave of man or of sin; in
the primitive state all were free and equal. St Gregory emphasized
that all are by nature equal and that it is only by God's dispensation
that some are set over others. The inequalities of life affect only the
body, St Ambrose stressed; mind and soul are unaffected by them.
The slave may be his master's superior in qualities of mind and
soul. These ideas are essentially the same as Seneca's, but they are
given greater force by the truth that in Christ all are one.

The Fathers therefore see slavery as lawful, and the slave is
exhorted to obedience. A man should patiently accept his lot, was
Ambrose's advice. Christ will make good slaves of bad ones, was
Augustine's view.[22] The idea of the liberation of slaves in the
seventh year, which was the law among the Hebrews, was rejected
by him. But equally the Fathers urged masters to treat slaves as
fellow men and not as things; Augustine tells them to bring up
their households in the service of God, their slaves as well as their
children, and Gregory warns that those who own slaves will have to
give an account to God for them.[23]

To the modern mind, the idea that freedom was according to
nature and slavery the result of original sin seems to have curiously
unjust consequences; since all men sinned in Adam, it would therefore seem to be required that, if slavery is part of the punishment
for that sin, or simply the result of it, all men should at some time
in their lives have to endure a period of slavery. That the wretched
large minority who found themselves slaves should continue to
suffer its evils life-long, while the majority at best sympathized with
them in the hardness of their lot, does not seem good enough.
This only reminds us once more of the gap that lies between those
who were conditioned to see slavery as a fact of life, and accepted
by all men at all times of which they had record, and we who have
seen a world largely rid of it. Slavery was hard to endure, imposed
on those who for one reason or another society accepted should be
reduced to it. Any such solution as here suggested, that it would
have been fairer that all should at some time experience it, would
have been condemned as wrong in principle and impossible in
practice.

But there were those more conscious of the evil. St Gregory of
Nyssa, commenting on the phrase 'I have bought male and female
slaves', which must have been common currency in a society dominated by the institution, asks, 'Tell me, how much is your life
worth? What have you found among creatures which is as valuable
as your human nature? How many cents did you pay for reason?

How many pence did you think God's image is worth? How many coins were charged for the creature that God has made?'[24] The intrinsic injustice of slavery was never better put, and was based on Christian theology, but there is no record that Gregory contemplated a world without slavery.

4 Society and political authority

Cicero was aware of two theories concerning the origin and nature of society and of the State; the first, that of the Epicureans, was that men were naturally solitary and possessed no tendency to join with others in society; it is only the dangers of the solitary life which move them to co-operate with others in this. The other, that of Aristotle and the Stoics, was that men are indeed by nature drawn to others, and form political societies because they are made this way, and it is the latter which is Cicero's view also.[25] Man is made for society, which grows out of that original society, the family. Society is of its nature organic, not mechanistic, and Cicero adopts Cato's view that the strength of the Roman constitution lay in its slow evolution over many generations.

The State must be founded on just law, and have as its purpose the promotion of the good of its citizens. The commonwealth must concern all the people, and they must all participate in it; it is a gathering of the multitude associated under a common law, in order to enjoy well-being. Forms of state may vary but they all must be based on justice and exist for the common good. Government there must be in order that the State may continue to exist, but it must serve the purposes for which it exists. It may be a government of one, of several or of the whole people, its legitimacy stemming from its serving the purposes stated. An unjust State is no State at all; there can be no *respublica*, no commonwealth, where there is oppression, disregard for law, absence of true union.[26]

So far Cicero follows Aristotle, but he lays more emphasis on the importance of the right form of government. While he thinks that the worst government is that in which all power is in the hands of the people, neither monarchy nor aristocracy please him either. The only government which can be trusted is one in which all share in some way; it must be founded in the consent of the whole people. The various capacities and abilities of all the citizens must be exercised in it and all should be duly recognized.[27] The theory of the Roman jurists of the second century AD, that the Emperor is the source of law, seems to be in conflict with Cicero's idea that government must rest on the consent of the governed and that all must share in the commonwealth, but the jurists conceded that people were the ultimate sources of the Emperor's power. This of course was the theory only. 'No Emperor gained power by popular appointment.'[28]

The Apostolic Fathers and Apologists pay some attention to the origin and nature of political authority, but they are mainly concerned to stress the need for obedience to it. So St Irenaeus sees authority over men as given to government so that the evil tendencies in them might be controlled and that righteousness and justice might prevail. St Justin stresses the need to render to Caesar his due.[29] St Augustine develops the idea of the innate sociability of man. Every man is part of the human race. Man has the capacity for friendship. God created man, and mankind is held together in society not only by the similarity of race, but also by the bond of blood relationship.[30]

The social order exists first in the family, then in the political society, State or city, and finally in the universal society of all mankind; each of these forms has its own structure, of which the essential elements are authority and law, which in their turn are ordered by the eternal law. However, at the heart of all there is charity, because there is no one of the human race who does not deserve our love. Justice also is needed; it is the condition and the foundation of peace which is in its turn 'the tranquillity of order'.[31] Society may be natural to man, who is of his being sociable, but coercive government of man by man is not natural; it is a result of the desire to dominate which is in all of us. With Seneca, Augustine believed that in the natural state all would obey those who were wise, so the question of coercion did not arise. Nor was it denied that, in the real world, government and the coercive powers it needed were essential. Like slavery, it was a result of man's sin.[32]

The general view of the Fathers therefore was that the coercive State as we know it was not natural to man, not part of the primitive state of the golden age of Seneca, or before the Fall according to the Scriptures. It was made necessary by the corruption of human nature. Government none the less is of divine institution. But does the divine institution of the State imply that he who exercises it gets authority directly from God, or is the citizen body involved in some way in determining who should rule; is the people sovereign? Some thought so, most notably Gregory the Great. The good ruler is God's gift to his people, an evil ruler a punishment, but both are to be obeyed. He takes David's attitude to Saul as his model: as a good subject David could not even criticize his king violently because to resist the powers was to resist God himself. Gregory was quoted by advocates divine right throughout the Middle Ages. Living in the wreck of the Roman Empire, and seeing on all sides the anarchy that followed in the sixth century, these views are understandable. But it was a fore-shortened view of the matter, and the tradition as it developed abandoned it.

The State therefore must be founded on law, which embodies justice, and has as its purpose the promotion of the good of its citizens. St Paul's words to the Romans on the necessity of obeying the State stress that if citizens live honestly they have nothing to fear; it is because it punishes evil and rewards good that authority is to be obeyed, and the necessity for rulers to do this was then implicit in the possession of that authority. Justice builds up the State: it is its purpose, said St Ambrose.[33]

It is possible that the tendency in Augustine, as in Gregory, to confuse the divine institution of State and government with the divine authority of the individual who governs, buttresses the conviction that the State can lack the qualities of law and justice. If the ruler is directly appointed by God, then he must be obeyed whether he is morally right or not, he argues.[34] Augustine's definition of the State does not embrace the idea of justice. Deane's account of his political philosophy as it can be gleaned from the *City of God* is that the State is only an external, coercive agent for the maintenance of social peace. It does not seek to make men virtuous; it is a punishment for sin and a remedy for it; it is needed to curb the anarchy that would exist without it. The thesis is perhaps sustained a little relentlessly, but there is no doubt that Augustine can be interpreted in this way.[35] But we keep in mind that it was in defence of Christianity that he wrote the *City of God*; he was not setting out a comprehensive political philosophy. It is possible to think that had he been taking a more positive look at the political order beyond the needs of the polemic of the moment, he would have looked to the healthier elements in political theory as it had been evolved by pagan writers. Be that as it may, his views did not affect the mainstream view. Isidore sums that up: the *civitas*, the body politic, is a multitude bound together in society by agreement of law and harmonious fellowship; if the king does what is right he will keep his name, if not he will lose it; justice and equity is the duty of the ruler.[36]

5 The State and the Church

According to the reported speech of the Emperor Constantine to the Council of Nicea, the Roman State initially disclaimed any right of jurisdiction in spiritual matters; that belonged to the bishops. However, practical problems soon tended to blur the line. St Optatus, Bishop of Milevis, was prepared to admit the right of the State to intervene on the Church's behalf in the Donatist controversy, but the situation was a complex one which raised unique issues; responses to it must be assessed accordingly. Bishop Donatus became the leader in 313 of a group of Christians who had a strict attitude to those who had weakened under persecution.[37] They said that bishops who had been *traditores*, who had handed over the sacred books and vessels in the face of persecution, could no longer perform valid ordinations, and they refused to accept the unfavourable decision on their views given by the episcopal commission which the Emperor, with the knowledge of the Bishop of Rome, had set up. The Council of Arles was also ignored when it decided against them in 314. When they then resorted to force against their theological opponents, Constantine retaliated in kind in 317, but the martyrs made subsequently only hardened opposition and the policy was abandoned. The schism continued to grow, the Catholics becoming a minority. The dispute went on for the rest of the century. Conflicts within the sect and participation in a revolt in Mauretania in 372, followed by Donatist participation in an attempted coup, led to imperial intervention which curbed them for a while, but from 377 they were in the ascendant once more. They felt strong enough in 397 to help Gildo in his revolt against Rome, the imperial army under Stilicho finally defeating them in 398.

Appeal to State power in a religious dispute had therefore first been made by the Donatists, who then consistently used violence and stirred up social unrest and rebellion in their cause when they had the opportunity. St Optatus was therefore not facing a purely theological dispute; he had to contend with a sect which turned to public disorder when thwarted in gaining its ends. In those circumstances the State had the right and the duty to protect the public peace which had been broken on such a scale. St Augustine's involvement with Donatists must be understood against this background. He first sought to reconcile them, but when the increased pastoral activity of the Catholics had led to violent attacks on their clergy, especially on those who had been Donatists but who had been reconciled, he and his fellow bishops sought State protection.

It does not seem that Augustine intended to establish the general principle of persecution for theological error. What he said on the matter was said in the light of the activities of a specific religious-revolutionary group which had consistently, and of direct intent, threatened and carried out violence against State and Church and its personnel for nearly a century. In this situation the secular authority had a right and a duty to restore peace and order.[38] The reasoning he used, however, could be used by those less threatened by violence to justify repressive policies where the dangers were not so extreme, persistent and beyond doubt proven.

St Ambrose, Archbishop of Milan (373–97) had been governor of the province in which Milan was situated before being chosen bishop of that city by acclamation. Milan had eclipsed Rome in the West in the late fourth century because of its strategic importance, and it was to it that the Western Emperor Gratian (375–83) moved his capital after he succeeded to the imperial crown. Ambrose accepted the State and civil government as ordained of God, and that the Christian had a duty in conscience to obey the law: at the same time the rulers were subject to the Church in spiritual and moral matters.[39] But he clashed on several occasions with the Emperor Theodosius over the demarcation line between Church and State authority. Specifically the massacre of some 7000 citizens after riots in Thessalonica in 390 outraged the Archbishop; the Emperor was excommunicated, and only after had he done public penance was the excommunication lifted. Ambrose also judged that the Emperor went beyond his powers in imposing penances on some Christians for their excessive zeal against Jews and Valentinians, and compelled him to desist. Nor would he accept that there were any circumstances in which the Emperor could seize Church property, though he could impose tribute on it.[40]

The classic theoretical statement of Church–State relationships was set out by Pope Gelasius I (492–96). According to it, Christ had separated the offices of king and priest, knowing the weaknesses of human nature and wanting to secure the well-being of his people. Hence there are two powers in the world, that of Church and State; the first is concerned with the attainment of eternal life, the second with temporal things. These two powers rule the world, but the burden on the former is greater because the ecclesiastics will have to account to God's judgement for kings as well as for their subjects. The Emperor therefore looks to the Church for the means to his salvation and accordingly submits to her in matters which concern her. The authority of the ruler is likewise derived from God and the ecclesiastical powers must obey his laws; he in his turn should be all the more ready to obey theirs. If the bishop fails to speak when he should on religious matters, he will be in great spiritual danger, as also will those who hold his authority in contempt.[41] The problem with the theory is that the question of when the Church should claim precedence is left unclear, and the human judgement of the Church's ministers and the secular authorities in such matters would not necessarily coincide; it remains the best theory not least because it implies Christ's own teaching – that tension will always remain between Church and State, but, like that teaching, it implies that working together is possible.

6   The teaching of the Fathers on private property

(i)   The social economic background

The economic system of the Roman Empire was dominated by agriculture. Crafts and industries, mining and quarrying existed on a large scale also, but it was the land and its produce which was the heart of the economy; taxes on it provided the vast majority of the State revenues. Land, farm stock and people were assessed, and by contrast with these revenues those levied on trade and industry were minimal. Likewise most of the revenues of the corporations, the cities and the rentier class, the senators and curialists, the professions and the Church, derived from agriculture; properties in the towns yielded only ten per cent of taxes, the land the rest.[42]

The tradition of the small peasant soldier/farmer as the typical Roman citizen had died with the Republic, indeed had been dying long before its end. Under the Empire the concentration of land in the hands of fewer and fewer accelerated, and as increasing numbers of the displaced peasants and their families left for the cities, the supply of wage workers to till the estates decreased and the owners then turned to slave labour, the conquests of an expanding Empire guaranteeing them their supply.[43]

Capture in war as the Empire expanded had been a major source of the supply of slaves, and as that expansion slowed in the first century AD, the supply dwindled. In order to keep their lands in cultivation, the large estate owners broke them up in whole or in part, and former free peasants were glad to settle on them as *coloni*, alongside others who were manumitted slaves, and alongside a residual slave labour force also. Initially it was a free agreement, but the *colonus* found himself increasingly tied to his master and to the land. The position varied in the different parts of the Empire but generally the free peasantry was becoming enserfed.[44] The breakdown of order within the Empire in the third and fourth centuries led to desperate efforts being made to ensure that where land remained under cultivation it should continue to produce revenues, and so repression of those who worked the land increased.[45] The currency was meanwhile debased as imperial income declined and inflation ran on unchecked; war and invasion destroyed capital; the economy stagnated, and taxes were gouged out of town and countryside to pay armies and administration.

Diocletian (284–303) and Constantine (306–37) restored order, but at the cost of military absolutism. The army doubled in size. Tax gathering achieved a new level of efficiency and cruelty.[46] The peasants were particularly hard hit and many more gave up their freedom. A higher proportion of the land was now controlled by the State and by a small group of the wealthy owners who were beyond its control. Urban workers were no better off; those employed in State factories and in the crafts were bound to their posts for life: semi-slavery, declining into slavery for many, had replaced freedom.[47] There were occasional peasant rebellions, for example among the Bacudae in Gaul and Spain in the fourth and fifth centuries.[48] They were the result of despair and fatalism and were doomed to failure. Although Jones notes that the picture of the peasant's lot was not one of unrelieved gloom, he judges that 'taken as a whole the peasantry were an oppressed and hapless class'.[49]

They were exploited by the tax collector if they were freeholders, by the landlord's agents if they were tenants. On the failure of the harvest they were still expected to pay their rent in kind; the tax collector and the agents compelled them to surrender their dues, even if this left them with nothing to feed their families.[50] They suffered first and hardest from all natural disasters, begging for food in times of bad harvest, being expelled from the cities for doing so, and denied the right to draw on the food stocks that existed in government or private hands. Saving the dramatic interventions which the public-spirited often made, they starved.

The Roman property law centred on the concept of absolute ownership, and the action by which that absolutism was asserted; there was an 'unrestricted right of control over a physical thing and whosoever has this right could claim the thing he owns wherever it is and no matter who possesses it'.[51] There were few restrictions on it in public law and for the rest *dominium* or *proprietas* was for practical purposes unrestrained;[52] it included not only the right of using, but also of abusing.[53] He who was in possession had unlimited power over him who was not, and gradually distinctions between types of property and their different natures were elided. What remained was the concept of absolute ownership.

Against this tyranny of abuse by holders of private property, the Fathers were to set the concept of the socially responsible ownership of that property. Since the gift of the world was made to all men in general by its creator, all men had a right to earn a living from it. Man has a right to private property, but that property has of its nature a social mortgage on it. It has to be socially responsible. Implicit in Aristotle's idea that the State had the right to control the ownership and use of property for the common good, it was here made explicit, an absolute moral principle, obligatory, the condition for the moral existence and use of private property established by God's law.

(ii) Clement of Alexandria

Earlier writers such as St Justin had stressed the need for a total renunciation of property and wealth as a powerful witness to the working of the Spirit in the Church, but since the Gospel did not demand this, other approaches were possible and Clement of Alexandria developed one. He was a disciple, and later head, of the Catechetical School in Alexandria, which was a great commercial centre. It handled the exports of Egypt and the trade with Arabia, East Africa and India and it was also a major industrial region.[54] At the turn of the third century the troubles of the Empire had little affected it; it remained a prosperous and thriving city.[55] In addressing the problems of the ownership and use of wealth Clement stresses the Christian duty of being ready to share. He condemns the man who says 'I have more than enough, why should I not enjoy it'. The attitude should be, 'I have something, why should I not share it with those in need?' God has given us the power to use our possessions[56] but there is an element of common ownership in all property. It cannot be used selfishly but must help others too. This approach rejected the Roman idea of the absolute ownership of property as it has been set out above, and it was the heart of the Christian ethic of property ownership.

The Lord does not forbid us to be rich but only to 'be rich insatiably and unjustly'.[57] It is not necessary to abandon riches, but it is wrong to be over-attached to them. Being without money is not necessarily in itself a good; it is being without it for the sake of heaven which is good. It is also good 'to possess enough without having to worry about possessions oneself and to be able to help others also'.[58] Matthew and Zaccheus were rich and were followers of Christ. A man is poor in spirit if he sees his possessions as gifts of God, serves him by using them for the welfare of mankind and shows he is not a slave of his possessions, if necessary being able to accept their loss as cheerfully as their abundance. By contrast the man who has riches, gold, money and land in his soul instead of the Spirit of God is trapped in the snares of the world and cannot have in him desire for heaven.[59]

(iii) Basil of Caesarea

St Basil the Great (329–79) was born and lived in Caesarea in Cappadocia, centre of an agricultural region and directly involved with it because the city owned great tracts of the surrounding land. Asia Minor was still a wealthy province in his time, but the problems of poverty and injustice in it were very evident. Some of the city lands were worked by slaves or tenants employed by wealthy citizens; others were worked by natives who were not full citizens, were too poor to employ tenants or slaves and lived in villages outside the city. Beyond the city territories were the large estates of the wealthy families, which were tilled by the tenants, the *coloni*, dependent on their masters in the manner already described; for all practical purposes they were tied to the land, and they were frequently in debt.[60]

Basil, a wealthy landowner, decided on the religious life, sold his property, gave the proceeds to the poor and entered a monastery. His hopes of obscurity, however, were disappointed: he was elected Bishop of Caesarea in 370, and was soon noted for his concern for the poor, in 372 setting up on the outskirts of the city his famous *xenodochion*, and exhorting his flock on their duty regarding their riches and their proper use. His Homily *In illud Lucae* (on Luke 12:18 'I will pull down my barns') is a powerful statement of the Christian insights on this matter and is a classic.

The rich man in question had received God's bounty. It was God's land, sun and showers, seed and oxen, which had made it possible for 'covetous hands that tilled it' to prosper. 'And what is the reaction of the beneficiary?' he asks. Selfishness: he had no thought of distributing his surplus to those in need, only in storing this wealth. He was not cheered to have full granaries he feared that it might in some way come to be used to help to relieve the destitute.[61] As we have seen, the picture painted here is drawn from life. Men and women were deprived of the means of life at a time when barns were overflowing, while those who owned them were only concerned to keep them so. This is not rhetoric, therefore, but a commentary on the facts. Those who are rich are to remember that they are the stewards of God's goods. Their wealth belongs to others in their need, and the rich will be asked to give a strict account of it. They are, however, like the rich man of St Luke's gospel who could have opened his barns and invited the poor to enjoy the bounty, but did not do so. Basil also ponders the anguish of the poor man compelled by necessity to sell his sons, the battle between starvation and fatherhood, and the hardened manner in which the merchant, buying them, haggles over the price.

Facing the fact that the greedy rich do cheat the poor out of their land, Basil does not spare them. The rich seize what belongs to all and claim the right of possession to monopolize it, whereas if everyone took for himself for his own wants and gave the rest to those who needed it, there would be no rich and poor.[62] The rich are so in order that they may win the reward of their charity and faithful stewardship. When they deny to the poor the things needed for existence, they are in fact thieves. We note here that Basil is talking about what is just, not about what is due out of charity. There would be no rich or poor if the wealth were distributed justly. He is also eloquent on the evils of usury, a reminder to us that the moralist's objection to this practice lies in that the usurer lends money at interest to those who require it for the necessities of life. He considers the usurer, whose duty it was to relieve the destitution of the poor man, but who instead increased his need. It is as if some physician, visiting the sick, instead of restoring bodily health to them, deliberately took away their little remnant of bodily strength.[63]

Basil and the Fathers had no knowledge of the science of economics as we understand it; it did not exist in their time, so Basil did not look to increasing the wealth of the time in order that there might be more for the needy, but he saw the actual link between injustice in the uses of property and the poverty of the many and was angered by it. He knew from experience and observation there was wealth enough for all, provided only that those who had surpluses used them correctly.

(iv) John Chrysostom

John Chrysostom was born about 344 at Antioch. He was ordained to the priesthood in his early twenties and his bishop appointed him preacher at Antioch's main church, his twelve years in this capacity winning for him the title of 'chrysostom', golden mouthed. In 398 he was chosen as Bishop of Constantinople, but his outspokenness offended the Empress Eudoxia, and this, and other problems, complicated his life there; he was banished in 404 and died in exile in 407.[64]

Chrysostom 'stands alone among the great ecclesiastics of the later Empire in that his supreme interest lay not in controversial theology but in practical ethics'.[65] He was particularly critical of the social inequalities of the time, and his phraseology on occasion seemed to suggest that he was stirring up the people against the rich; the poor certainly looked upon him as their champion. Preaching on Luke 16:19ff., the parable of Dives and Lazarus, he said that Dives had not robbed Lazarus by depriving him of what was his, but, by refusing him some of his own possession when he was in need, Dives was guilty of a species of robbery.[66]

There were, he claimed, 10 per cent of the population of Antioch who were rich, the same proportion who were poor, and the rest were at least moderately prosperous. It was therefore unjust that the 90 per cent who were able to succour the poor did not do so. The example of what the Church did was relevant. Compared with the wealthy, her total revenues were not great, but she assisted three thousand widows and virgins every day, apart from those in prison, in hospitals or convalescence, the travellers, the maimed, those who daily came seeking food and clothing. Yet her substance did not diminish. He therefore concluded that if ten men only were willing to spend the same proportion of their wealth as the Church did on charity, there would be no more poor. He asked them to give away not their capital, but their revenues, so making the poor sharers with them.[67]

Here, as with Basil, we may consider his arguments for overcoming the problems of poverty as naive, concentrating on distribution instead of wealth creation. The same answer holds. Neither he nor his times had any scientific knowledge of economics. He was concerned with the ethics of the situation as he saw it; private ownership of productive goods in an agricultural economy should fulfil its social obligations. At the time it could only do this by fairer distribution of the wealth that existed and if the figures he quoted were accurate, this could have been done, had the will been there.

He is not however impressed with the attitude of his wealthy auditors in general. He argues in one place that it is possible to get rich without injustice. He asks, When we see possessors of good things guilty of fraud and robbery, shall we call them good? Clearly

not, for if so, the greedier a man is, the better must he be. But is
this not plainly a contradiction? But suppose the wealth is not
gained wrongfully. But how is this possible? So destructive a
passion is greed, that to grow rich without injustice is impossible,
and he calls Christ's saying about the mammon of iniquity (Luke
16:9) to witness to this. And it is no excuse to claim that wealth is
received by inheritance, for this is simply to receive the fruits of
earlier injustice.[68]

Elsewhere, however, he allows that goods can be gained justly, as
the patriarch Jacob gained them. Nor is a wealthy man responsible
for the covetous acts of his father. But the earth is the Lord's and
the fullness thereof, and so one's possessions belong to one
common Lord; they belong also to others. The possessions of the
Lord are common. It is about personal possessions, houses, money,
property that disputes arise.[69] Yet he does not deny the rich the
right to riches in themselves if they use them well. The purpose of
money is that we may use it – not that it may use us. We are to
possess our possessions, not to be possessed by them.[70]

(iv) Ambrose

We have already considered St Ambrose's antecedents and considered his episcopate in terms of the evolution of Church–State
relations. The first thing he did when he was appointed bishop was
to distribute his wealth to the poor, directly and indirectly, the
latter through the management of his investments on behalf of the
community. Italy in Ambrose's day had long lost its standing as one
of the wealthiest agricultural regions of the Empire. The large
landowners continued to prosper at the expense of the peasants
and also of the smaller landowners. Most of the land of the aristocracy had passed to the Emperor, and those who administered it
plundered it for their own benefit. Landlords rarely lived on their
estates. They preferred the cities and left their lands to be tilled by
tenants supervised by agents. It was against this background that
Ambrose faced the problems of justice and charity in economic
matters as a bishop.

His *de Nabuthae* (On Naboth) is a commentary on the first
chapter of the First Book of Kings, in which the story of Naboth's
vineyard and King Ahab is recounted. The lesson is that this
ancient problem is also a very modern one. Daily the rich and prosperous covet other people's goods; they steal from the humble,
robbing the poor of their possessions. Discontented with what they
have, their craving for goods is stimulated by the property of their

neighbours. Earth at its beginning, however, 'was for all in common, it was meant for rich and poor alike; what right have you to monopolize the soil? Nature knows nothing of the rich; all are poor when she brings them forth.' And he reminds them that at the end 'a little turf suffices for the poor and the rich'.

Ahab's dealings with Naboth precisely outline the problem. The rich are not so much anxious to own for use, as to deprive others of ownership, whereas they should see that sharing their riches is their duty; it is a matter of justice. When giving to the poor they are giving them what is already theirs. What is common to all has been given to all to make use of, not to be usurped by the few.

Ambrose does not deny that there are rich men who are not slaves of their riches. 'There is a blessing for the rich man "who has been found without blemish and who has not gone after gold or put his trust in money",' but it seems he is hard to find. His actions are to be praised as rare rather than accepted as customary. But the man who remains commendable amid riches is a man truly perfect and one to be glorified – he who might have transgressed and did not transgress, and might have done evil and did not (Sir. 31:7–10). It is possible to amass riches and do good. 'Wealth is a redemption if one uses it well; it is a snare if one does not know how to use it.'[71]

Elsewhere he considers social justice. Justice concerns society and community because what holds society together is justice and goodwill. The latter is called liberality or kindness. Justice is the loftier, liberality the more pleasing of the two; one gives judgement, the other shows goodness. Nature, in the sense of God's plan, indicates to us the lines of this justice. It has given all things for common use. God has ordered all things to be produced so there should be food in common for all, and earth should be a common possession for all. It is greed that has made it a right for a few.

Even the sacred vessels should be used for charitable purposes when necessary. He was once criticized for doing this, he notes, but he replied that the Church possesses gold, not to store it up, but to distribute it and to use it to help those in want, especially when there is a risk anyway that the precious vessels will be plundered and defiled by sacrilegious enemies.[72] Ambrose stresses social solidarity and the universal purpose of created things; that is, the solidarity which makes the wealthy consider it their duty to act justly with their wealth, accepting the universal purpose of created goods which God gave to humanity in common in the first instance; all, the poor included, have to have access to what they need for a decent human life from the rich world he has given to us all. He does not deny the rich the right to their riches if honestly gained and properly used. He lays emphasis on how hard it is to meet these criteria, but they can be met for all that.

7 Property in common or private property a natural right?

Some of the early Fathers urged that property in common was more fitting for the Christian. The *Didache* urges 'sharing all things with thy brother'; the *Epistle of Barnabas* reflects the same teaching, both echoing the Acts of the Apostles: 'they all lived together and owned everything in common' (Acts 2:46). St Justin tells us that Christians put what they possessed into the common pool and shared with all in need. St Cyprian a century later, commenting on the same passage in Acts, believed that this is the way that the true sons of God behave.[73]

Clement of Alexandria, seeing the realities of economic life in a wealthy commercial city, was clearly not convinced that property could or should be denounced by all; the important thing was to see it was used properly. Poverty in itself is not to be recommended, unless it is for some good motive; the better thing generally is to be able to support oneself reasonably and have a surplus with which to help others. Wealth, riches, property can be used for good to oneself and others. Among the followers and close friends of Christ there were wealthy or moderately wealthy persons too. Provided they had gained it justly, or made restitution if they had not, they were welcome to become his followers. Lactantius, commenting on Plato's recommendation of common ownership, rejects it as unworkable and unjust; he accepts that there was a golden age, the natural state of things, but not that there was a complete community of goods at that time; no one was in want during it because there was generosity and kindness which prevented the sort of injustices that occur after the Fall.

What was common to the Fathers in their treatment of economic issues was their concern that economic life should reflect solidarity, brotherhood, so that everyone could claim the means, or access to the means, to support life properly.[74] Although the Scriptures did not condemn the institution of private property as in itself wrong, in the early days the strong warnings against the dangers of wealth in the New Testament, the example of the Church at Jerusalem and the difficulties of the Christian life under threat of sporadic persecution, emphasized the ephemeral nature of much that the world held dear, and so encouraged the belief in property in common;

but, as the Christian mission took root and the Church's theology developed, the Fathers, following Clement of Alexandria, recognized the right to private property as a good in itself.

Augustine, writing against the Manichees who were maintaining the contrary, sets out the case. It is not wrong to have possessions; it is only wrong to love them inordinately so that we put them before the love of God and neighbour. But both he and St Jerome, commenting on the words of Christ to the rich young man, suggest that property was originally held in common before the Fall.[75] St Ambrose held that opinion most emphatically. 'Nature produced a common right for all, but greed has made it a right for a few';[76] since avarice and greed have produced private property, it is only right that those who own property should accept the responsibility for supporting the poor, because property was given in the first to all in common so that all might have enough to live on. This argument is very much like that used by Seneca.[77]

The majority of the Fathers therefore see that common possession had been the original state and that, in imitation of that original state, it was preferable. Private property was, as for Seneca, not primitive and natural, but conventional, introduced by human reason and in the light of experience. That does not mean that they did not think it was morally defensible or legitimate, but it does make more emphatic the teaching that the social obligations of property are crucial for the Christian. The Stoic tradition concerning private property was, however, balanced in the ancient world by the views of some of the Roman jurists who saw private property as natural: Gaius for example, Florentinus, and possibly Ulpian.[78]

Some would question whether the Church's access to wealth and property, once she was accepted by the Roman Empire, changed her attitude. Did she originally possess an 'essentially socialist' faith vision which faded away with the accumulation of properties and power?[79] First, of course, the vision of the Fathers was not socialist, it was solidarist. Seeing all men as one in Christ, accepting that God gave the earth to all men in common initially that all might enjoy a good life therefrom, they asked that the mechanics of society allow this to come to be through justice and charity. Generally they regarded property not as natural but as conventional, but none of them denied the right to property in the present dispensation, a denial presumably being the 'essentially socialist' criterion referred to.

As to the accumulation of properties and power, to see the Church's possession of lands in a cynical light is to forget two things. The first is that she in the first instance built up her considerable strength as a social organization without the patronage of the State or its gifts, indeed while being persecuted by it. She would have survived and flourished without that patronage. It was precisely because the Church had attained such a level of influence as would make her a powerful ally, and had done so by being true to her spiritual ideal, that her favour was worth courting: she not only gave to deteriorating Roman society the spiritual and moral strength it no longer possessed of itself, but also put the same resources at the disposition of the barbarian peoples in developing a new civilization. The Papacy, the monastic orders and ecclesiastical organization generally were essential to this task.

The second thing to remember is that in an agricultural economy land was the basic source and form of wealth. Only by owning it could the social organization which was the Church live. To speak as if the refusal to own, or to run, estates was an option for her in late Roman or early medieval times is to ignore the facts and realities of life as it was then lived. The Church became responsible for all education, spiritual, moral and intellectual, and for providing social welfare, and since her personnel were almost the only educated men of the time, they were essential for the administration of the State. To fulfil her primary role as spiritual and moral leader of her people, as well as all these other functions she was called on to discharge, she needed economic resources, and the only ones available were the possession and use of land.

8 Industry, trade and commerce

The teaching of the Fathers on private property and its use is therefore overwhelmingly concerned with the moral obligation to ensure that distribution of wealth was just, and that those who were wealthy accepted and fulfilled their social obligations. They did not concern themselves much with the ethical problems of production in industry or through trade and commerce, which is not surprising since the vast majority of people were engaged in agricultural pursuits. Where they did pay such attention, it was usually to warn of the moral dangers that such occupations presented for those engaged in them. Tertullian can be quoted as equiparating trade and avarice, and John Chrysostom as judging that the merchant wanted to be rich irrespective of the means used to that end. Jerome expressed the opinion that trade and fraud were one, while Augustine saw it as diverting man's mind from true rest. Pope

Leo I concluded that it was difficult for buyers and sellers not to fall into sin.[80]

Yet as already noted,[81] Tertullian drew attention to Christians' participation in normal economic life and even praised it. They reject no fruit of God's works though they renounce excess. Christians are to be found in the forum, shops, workrooms, markets and other places of business, they till the soil and trade, exercise their crafts and put what they make at the service of the public:[82] Irenaeus and Clement of Alexandria accepted the participation of Christians in the ordinary economic life of the time as a fact which did not require unfavourable comment.[83] Augustine, as St Thomas was later to note, summed the matter up: some men of business are greedy and perjurers, but these are the vices of the man, not of the craft, which can be exercised without these vices.[84] To quote Cadoux again, Christians saw 'the ordinary forms of honest trade and industry ... [as] ... not only legitimate but necessary'.[85]

9 Usury

The taking of interest on a money loan was condemned by the Fathers on the grounds of injustice where the borrower was a poor man seeking for the means to live and the lender was a rich man who had the necessary resources to help if he would. They were in fact loans for subsistence, not for business purposes; it was money to use as a means of exchange, not as capital, that was sought. Lactantius envisages such a situation. 'If someone lends money, he should not exact interest, so that he may not lose the merit of assisting a person in need ... he should be content with receiving back what is his and should be willing to lose some of it in order to do good.' St Basil contrasts the borrower and the lender. 'It is extremely inhuman that one has to beg for the most basic necessities to support his life while another is not satisfied with the capital he has, but excogitates ways of increasing his opulence at the expense of the poor in distress.' Ambrose condemns the usurer: 'You subject the poor to usury; you know how to oblige them to pay you interest even when they have nothing to eat. Can one imagine anything more perverse?' 'Lend your money' says Augustine, '... give to a man and do not turn away from him ... and if what you gave and what he received is due and he perhaps does not have it to hand ... do not make new troubles for him.'[86] St Jerome was convinced that the urban unrest of the time was caused by the extortionate rates charged by moneylenders. 'But it does not appear that objection was seriously taken to loan capital for commerce and there is considerable evidence of the clergy providing a banking service for their congregations.'[87]

10 *War and military service: the just war*

The teaching of the Fathers on war and military service until the time of the Christian Roman Empire has already been briefly outlined. With the advent of that Empire a new situation had arisen. Christians were now accepted and the Church was part of the normal life of society; different questions would press on the Christian conscience in this matter. They had to look to their responsibilities as citizens and consider what the State could reasonably ask of the Christian community in preserving public order against internal enemies, and defending the commonwealth against external foes. It was in the Western Church that the issue was most live. In the East the Emperor still ruled effectively; the *pax Romana* and its traditional defences and defenders still held sway. It was not so taxed by questions of *ius belli* (the right to make war in a just cause), or the *ius in bello* (the question of what was just in the waging of war).

St Basil of Caesarea (*c.* 329–79) made the important distinction between him who sheds innocent blood, the murderer, and him who sheds it fighting on the side of moderation and piety, while at the same time counselling that those who shed it in this cause should abstain from communion for a period. His views were further modified by his becoming acquainted with a serving soldier whose character and demeanour convinced him that perfect love of God and the military profession were compatible; it was the disposition of the soul, not the profession of a man which mattered.[88]

St Ambrose of Milan was the first Western bishop to face the question of reconciling the Christian preference for non-violence with the broader problem of order in society, in a world where there were threats to both from many sides. The responsibilities of Christians who had the duty of handling affairs of State had to be determined. Ambrose had held high office in the Roman Empire before he was chosen Bishop of Milan, and accordingly he brought with him experience of the need for justice, courage and loyalty, and a sense of responsibility towards society for those in such office. Any use of violence for one's own advantage was to be condemned, but defence of the Empire, and the protection of the weak against the strong and of property against plunder, 'is wholly just'.[89] On the morality of war, civil wars were condemned but in principle those against barbarians and non-Christians could be defended.

The State had the right to wage war in order to right a wrong or repel an aggressor,[90] but in waging war there were certain conventions to be observed; agreements with an enemy should be kept, and there should be mercy for the enemy in defeat.[91] Military success too often breeds pride and arrogance, the desire to fight for the sake of it, whereas establishing peace should be the purpose of war. Far from it being always better to avoid violence, anyone who does not use it when it is necessary to prevent injury to others is as much at fault as he who does the injury.[92] The importance of this principle for the development of just war theory was fundamental. It is of course implicitly present in the Scriptures.[93] Ambrose uses the example of Moses killing the Egyptian as a case in point. The spirit of vengeance can be overcome by keeping in mind that it is the evil that is to be hated, not the evildoer.[94]

St Augustine is the most significant contributor to the development of just war theory, which is too readily understood as elaborating on the conditions which would make war just, in the sense of being a positive good. But for Augustine the main concern was the justice that brings peace. In writing to the Roman General Boniface in 418 he says 'peace should be your aim; war should be a matter of necessity so that ... God might preserve you in peace'. And to Darius, an ambassador sent to North Africa in 428 to try to negotiate peace, he wrote that

> 'preventing war through persuasion, and seeking or attaining peace through peaceful means rather than through war, are more glorious things than slaying men with the sword'.[95]

The theory of the just war then is an attempt to determine in what circumstances war might reluctantly be pronounced morally acceptable, an option which might be taken by good Christians, rather than a set of principles in favour of war as if it were in itself a positively good thing. The wise man will wage war when necessary, but he will decry the fact that he is forced to.[96] Like Ambrose, he did not see that military duty and love of enemies to be incompatible.[97] He instances Christ rebuking the man who struck him to illustrate that the correction of the wrongdoer was not forbidden by the beatitudes.[98]

A just war can only be waged by the decision of the properly-constituted public authority, the 'chief of state'. Its purpose must be to punish a wrongdoing which cannot be rectified by peaceful means, and can be either defensive or offensive to this end.[99] Wars of aggrandizement therefore are never justified. War can only be justified an external enemy when all else has failed to put right a wrong so serious that this is the only way to right it, and when it can be reasonably claimed that the suffering caused by the war will be less than that inflicted by tolerating the wrong it is intended to right±[100]. Civil war, revolutionary war is never just and even when the State commands something against the law of God, passive resistance alone is permissible.[101]

Agreements with the enemy must be kept and mercy must be shown to captives in defeat. Augustine's reaction to indiscriminate killing suggests that he accepted the principle of noncombatant immunity also.[102] Those engaged in such wars have a right to refuse any order from a superior which is against the law of God, but they must do this by passive resistance only.[103] In cases of doubt about the justness of the war, the assumption must be in favour of the legitimate authority. Where there is certainty about the injustice of an order, however, it can be refused. On spiritual matters, for example the offering of sacrifice to a false God, there was a clear right and duty of refusal.[104]

Because of his involvement in the Donatist controversy it has been said that Augustine was in favour of using force in purely ecclesiastical disputes and matters of conscience, but from what is said above it can be seen that this was not so.[105] The Donatists were serious disturbers of the social order because of the conclusions they drew from their religious beliefs. They were not persecuted for religion's sake; they were rebels who had to be curbed to defend the common good.

Part 2

Western Christendom
c. 604–1500:
The social role of the Church

5

The Church, society and politics in the early Middle Ages

1 The idea of Christendom[1]

With the gradual collapse of the centralized power of Rome in the West from the fifth century, the self-governing municipalities throughout the Empire, on which its structure depended, lost their last support also. An old order was ending, and a new one was about to be formed. The Church, founded by Christ and bringing with her a unique and powerful understanding of man, his potentialities and his destiny, had been born into a civilization in whose making she had played no part, and to whose self-understanding she had made no contribution; but now that only the Church remained of the old civilized order, she was able, by her presence and the organizational strength that a vital faith supported, to provide the spiritual, moral and intellectual leadership which in time helped bring to birth a new and brilliant civilization. That organization was manifested first in the college of bishops, united with one another and with Rome throughout the West. In this unity she provided a disintegrating society with a reminder of what had been and could be again; her administration embodied the traditions of civilized order and as an educator she preserved a tradition older than herself, that of Rome and ultimately Greece, as well as of her own Old Testament origins.

The old culture and its learning lasted down to the beginning of the seventh century but from that time the Christian ecclesiastical tradition took over from it, preserving much of the old learning in

* The notes and references for Chapter 5 are to be found on p. 387

so doing. However, the real achievement lay not in these things, any more than it lay in the complex developments of Europe under the Papacy from the eleventh century. It lay in this: Christianity was not merely accepted as a philosophy or theology, though its intellectual contribution to the new civilization through its learning was crucial, but it was above all accepted as a living faith in its Divine master and his Gospel teaching. 'Catholic ideals did not by any means always conquer in the world the Church created, but they never ceased to fight, and therein lies the glory of these centuries.'[2]

The Church had originally been urban based and it was the presence of the bishops in the towns, which continued to function as the centres of ecclesiastical administration for their regions, which mainly sustained their existence. In the countryside the monasteries were the focus of ordered life and education, and it was mainly the monks who brought Christianity to the peasants. Church and society were then inextricably linked at the foundation of Western Christendom; the result was that the history of the Church in medieval times

> is the history of the most elaborate and thoroughly integrated system of religious thought and practice the world has ever known. It is also the history of European society through eight hundred years ... when the outlines of our institutions and habits of thought were drawn.[3]

Medieval societies were, as a result of their permeation by the Church at all levels,

> the first in history to have a basic religious uniformity for a very large population as a whole ... this fact, combined with its organizational features and relatively this-worldly orientation, enabled the Church to exert an unprecedented influence on the process of social development.[4]

She had grown strong in the first three centuries by deliberately refusing to get involved in secular matters, and that strength eventually resisted the Roman Empire's attempt to crush her. Under the Christian Roman Empire the Church received favours from the State and did it many in return, but she was not dependent on it; she survived its collapse because of her strong social organization, centred round the Eucharist, and under the leadership of her bishops. She did not seek or choose the secular roles that were now expected of her by the barbarians, and accepting them was to cause her many problems. But the people of Western Europe elected to let the Church lead Latin society[5] and she could not, in justice or in charity, refuse help to a world which was in such desperate need of a more stable social order. It was because she was so involved with society from the first that she was able to influence and form it at all levels.

The Christendom which this alliance between Church and society formed was distinguished from idolatrous evil societies outside it. The distinction was sharply focused in the crusading twelfth century, but it was at least implicit from the fifth. The Franks were the most able and warlike of the barbarian invaders of the Western Empire and they formed the most effective State; the conversion of their king Clovis to Roman Catholicism in 496[6] had a crucial effect on European history. The reality that the word 'Christendom' refers to, dates from the crowning of Charlemagne, King of the Franks, as Roman Emperor in 800, when for the first time it appeared that a Christian kingdom might become a reality. In that context, Christendom is seen as defined by its conflict with the Muslims, whose advance into Europe had been halted by the leader of the Franks, Charles Martel, at Poitiers in 732, a victory which established them as the most powerful military as well as political force in the then forming Europe.

In time the Papacy would approve of the accession to the Frankish throne of Charles Martel's son, Pepin III, in the place of the enfeebled Merovingians, and it was Pepin's son Charlemagne who was to establish the new Empire, however fragile, and with the aid of the Church to reintroduce into Europe the idea of a civilized State. 'The Frankish empire, papal supremacy, monastic foundations and ecclesiastical organization were the principal springs of medieval civilization.'[7]

The bishops of Rome had played an increasingly important part in the services the Church gave to society from the time of St Leo the Great (440–61), who provided central Italy with political leadership when there was no other to give it. He was prevailed upon, for example, to intervene with Attila the Hun in 452 and the Vandal leader Gaiseric in 455 when they were threatening the city. St Gregory the Great, (590–604) a patrician of patricians, who had been Prefect of Rome before retiring from public life to become a monk, even more emphatically combined his roles of spiritual and secular leadership. The breakdown of order in central Italy placed upon him, as Pope, a heavy burden from the first. The feeding of a starving population was his responsibility. In warding off threats to Rome, he became effectively the secular ruler in central Italy. It was his pastoral and practical instinct which led him to send Augustine and his monks to convert the barbarian Anglo-Saxons in 597,[8] an event which in time, through the agency of St Boniface, gave

English Catholicism a key role in the formation of the new Europe.

Charlemagne's Empire was always an uncertain construction, despite its achievements, and did not long outlive his death. Yet in securing basic learning, mainly by recruiting the Church's educationalists, the Benedictines especially, in the cause, and through the labours of the monks in the copying and disseminating essential texts, it saved the classical tradition for the West and made possible the revival of the twelfth and thirteenth centuries, and all that stemmed from it in the service of the modern world.

2 The Middle Ages and the early Middle Ages[9]

One hundred years ago 'everyone deplored the Middle Ages'.[10] It was seen as a Rip van Winkle period from which Europe was awakened by the Renaissance and the Reformation. The phrase itself was coined in the time of the Renaissance and the prejudices it enshrined were increased by the contempt of the Enlightenment. Voltaire regarded the Middle Ages as superstitious and irrational; the labelling of Gothic architecture by that title was intended to dismiss it as barbarian. The truth is that this was an intensively creative time: the long formative period of a new civilisation in the development of which the spiritual, moral and intellectual resources of Christianity were the most important influence. In these years the ideas of Western civilisation on economics, society, politics and philosophy were being formed and many of the institutions of modern times had their beginnings.[11] They include representative government, constitutional monarchy, trial by jury and the universities in which

> were laid the foundations of the scientific culture of the modern world, in them grew up the disciplined thinking, followed by systematic investigation, which made possible the rise of the natural sciences and of the technical civilisation necessary to large industrial societies[12]. By the close of the middle ages – about 1500, Europe's technology and political and economic organization had given her a decisive lead over all other civilisations on earth[13]

The period embraces at least three different sub-periods, if we may call them so, which represent the very different experiences of their times. The first is the early period from AD 604, the death of Gregory the Great, to 1050. The second is the central or high Middle Ages from 1050 to about 1300. The third is the late Middle Ages, from about 1300 to 1500.

The first of these, the early Middle Ages, with which we are here concerned, was marked by the gradual ending of the Germanic invasions and a period of settlement which produced in the eighth century the remarkable intellectual interlude of Christian Northumbria and the genius of Bede (d. 735). The Muslims invaded Spain and France as far as Poitiers until defeated by Charles Martel in 732, and the kingdom of Charlemagne, his grandson, emerged (768–800) blending into the Empire (800–814). Though the latter declined rapidly after Charlemagne's death, there was now no chance that Europe would fall back into the chaos and ignorance of the sixth and seventh centuries.[14] The end of Charlemagne's empire in the ninth century overlapped with and was partly caused by the last invasions of Europe – that of the Vikings from Scandinavia, the Magyars from Hungary in the east, and the Saracens from the south, in the ninth and tenth centuries.

3 The mainsprings of medieval civilization

(i) The Frankish Empire and the Papacy

The waves of infiltrations and invasions[15] by the Barbarians beyond her frontiers, which the Roman Empire found it impossible to stem, repeopled Europe and the pattern of their settlement determined the political map of the future. The Germanic tribes had been pressing on the Empire's borders for centuries. By the time the Empire finally collapsed it had been comprehensively infiltrated: first as war captives, then as workers on the deserted lands of the Empire, and finally as mercenaries, barbarians had been introduced to Roman ways and settled within its borders.

The Visigoths were allowed by the Eastern Emperor Valens to settle within its territory in 376; they rebelled and defeated Valens in battle at Adrianople in 378 and sacked Rome in 410, before moving into Gaul and establishing a kingdom there. The Vandals occupied Spain, passing the Straits of Gibraltar and into North Africa in 429; as a sea power they raided Italy, plundering Rome for example in 455. The Ostrogoths invaded Italy in 493. The Alemanni and the Franks crossed the Rhine frontier in 420; the former founded a kingdom in central, the latter in northern Gaul. Those who settled on the Channel coast down to the Loire on the Bay of Biscay, had Merovech, the founder of the Merovingian dynasty, for their king: his grandson Clovis (481–511) was to make the dynasty influential in European history.[16]

The Gothic invaders had been introduced to Arian Christianity early in the fourth century.[17] The Franks were pagans until their leader, Clovis, was baptized with his warriors at Rheims in 496. Clovis combined the military and political skills necessary for effective leadership, and his marriage in 493 to Clotilda, a Burgundian Catholic princess, helped him to consolidate his hold on his conquest. By 508 his rule extended far into what is modern northern Germany, and down to the Mediterranean and the Pyrenees in the south, his chief residence being Paris. The manner in which he had achieved that union had been violent and treacherous after the fashion of his house, and the Merovingians continued in this tradition of fraticidal bloodshed over crowns and territories.[18] The dissolute ways of the Merovingians were their undoing. They gradually sank to insignificance, 'dying young, weakened by debauchery in their secluded villas',[19] and their kingdom disintegrated. Power passed to the hereditary Mayors of the Palace, an office which made them responsible for the administration of the royal estates, the chief source of revenues and the power of the crown.

Charles Martel, Mayor of the Palace (717–41), decided to have his sons Carloman and Pepin educated by the monks of St Denis near Paris in order to prepare them for the kingship. They succeeded their father as rulers of the Franks in 741 but Carloman finally chose the monastic life in 747; he had encouraged the reform movement in the Frankish Church and Pepin continued this when he was sole ruler.[20] In this they co-operated with the English Benedictine St Boniface (c. 672–754) who in 714 had received a commission from Pope Gregory to convert the barbarians and was working under Frankish protection.

Pepin needed sound moral grounds for claiming the throne and he found it when Pope Zacharias declared in 750 that kings should be seen to rule.[21] Boniface's, and later Pope Stephen's, consecration of him as king confirmed him in the eyes of his people as the Lord's anointed. The Papacy now had the political and military protector it needed, threatened as it was by the Lombard King Liutprand (712–44) who seemed intent on absorbing the papal territories and reducing the popes to dependence on him. Even if the Byzantines had been in a position to help, theological difficulties with them would have prevented an alliance since the Emperor Leo the Isaurian (717–40) had broken with Rome over iconoclasm. Pepin, aware of his debt to the Papacy, invaded Italy in 754 and 756, compelling Liutprand's successor Aistulf (749–57) to give up the lands in question. In substance the Papal States date from this time.[22]

(ii) The monastic orders, ecclesiastical organization and the Carolingian theocratic State

The Irish monks and monasteries evangelized in the Frankish kingdom in the sixth century, and the followers of Benedict of Nursia (*c.* 480–547), the Benedictines, consolidated their pioneering work.[23] The monk's aim was to lead a good Christian life and so save his soul, and to achieve this end in the circumstances of the time the community had to be a self-contained social and economic unit. The abbot was elected and he had sole authority under the rule once elected, though he had to consult with his community on the affairs of the monastery.[24] The monastic day was based on prayer, liturgical and personal, on study and on work. Idleness was seen as the enemy of the soul, so there were specified periods for manual labour as well as for prayerful reading.[25] The rule allowed for the reception of child oblates, offered to the monastery by their parents, 'nobles or the poor',[26] and a school had to be provided for their basic education.

Though in all this the prime concern was to provide an atmosphere of peace and calm so that the monk could serve God through a life of prayer, it was inevitable that since the world around them lacked those marks of ordered, peaceful and purposeful social life and discipline which the monastery evidenced, it had immense social influence. It loomed large in the local communities, spiritually, educationally and economically. The monks had most influence in the conversion of the peasants, which not only made Christians of them but incorporated them into Western society. Among them St Martin of Tours (*c.* 316–97) at Marmoutier, St Honoratus (*c.* 350–429) at Lerins and St Columba (521–97) at Iona in Scotland stand out. The monastery at Luxeuil, founded about 590, flourished under Columban, and his disciple Gallus established what became St Gall on Lake Constance. Bobbio was also a Celtic foundation. The monks, most of them countrymen themselves, found their way to the hearts of the peasants not least because they, like them, were compelled to till the earth for their living; they cleared the forests and reclaimed the land for their monastic settlements.[27]

The conversion of the people in the rural areas and their baptism made them participators in the life of Christ in his Church, and also bound them with their fellow Christians into the larger society of Christendom. Through its sacraments and liturgy, its preaching, the cult of the saints and pilgrimages, the work of evangelization and civilization 'must have proved powerful in holding before the consciences of the newly converted and their immediate descendants, ideals of forgiveness, kindness to the underprivileged and self-control'.[28]

Education generally was in the Church's hands. The collapse of urban society from the sixth century meant that the municipal schools languished, while the efficacy of episcopal schools depended on the interest of the bishop, which was often lacking. The monastery filled the gap by default. The large Benedictine abbey in the ninth century was also a centre of culture and economic development with upwards of one hundred monks; around it sprang up a township whose citizens provided the workers needed for its maintenance, its lands were worked by serfs of the monastery, and the abbot was their feudal lord. The whole was an image of a State which sought to bring law, culture and civilized peace. Abbots were men of importance, and as such the emperor or king was interested in who held the office, with the result that too often they appointed, or strongly influenced, the election of abbots. It was a practice that was to have disastrous consequences in due time.[29]

The clergy generally were the only class which desired to possess even the rudiments of knowledge,[30] and improvement of education was part of the programme of every ecclesiastical reformer from the days of Gregory the Great. The provision of schools for their own pupils and outsiders, noble and poor alike, was there in Benedict's rule but Rashdall asserts that it was only from the ninth century that they opened them to outsiders. As agriculturalists in an agricultural economy the monasteries also made a major contribution in these centuries. They encouraged the best scientific methods of the time. They were savers, investors: the cattle not slaughtered, the corn not consumed, were a guarantee of increased herds and better crops tomorrow. They also educated by the example of their disciplined order of work.

The large monastery was a civilizing agent and its vast land-holdings gave it a major role in developing a region. Monasteries were also leaders in what manufactures there were at the time. The records of St Germain near Paris in the period 875 to 925 show the scale of their operations; in many cases monasteries were the basis of a later urban industrial and commercial centre. St Gall, of which we have a ninth-century plan, has the appearance of a small town, including within its walls not only churches and schools but workshops and granaries, baths and hospital, farm buildings and mills.[31] The growing population and its needs led to the establishment of markets, and as centres of pilgrimage and piety they also encouraged traffic and trade.[32]

The Church and her organization was essential to Charlemagne's plans for a civilized and theocratic state. Charlemagne[33] had become King of the Franks in 768 and the first thirty years of his reign was dedicated to strengthening his kingdom against dissent at home and threats abroad. Political insight and ambition moved him but so also did the sincere zeal to guard and extend Christendom and civilization.[34] His person and reign reveal the growing benefits of a new intelligent leadership born of the union between the classical, Christian and Germanic elements in Europe, which gave a sense of direction and purpose.

Civilization presumes a military capacity able to ensure order. Charlemagne was ruthless and his actions at times indefensible as he fought primarily for the survival of the forming Christendom in his 53 campaigns against the Danes, Slavs, Saxons, Avars, Dalmatians and Spaniards. He did not seek to Latinize them; his was a fight for survival, protecting the Latin Christians of the West against the encircling forces of the anti-Christian world.[35] The effects of Charles Martel's committing his sons to the monks of St Denis for their education had indeed been epoch-making. They were imbued with a conviction of a ruler's duties to his people which was new in Francia. The most durable effects of Charlemagne's rule were spiritual and intellectual; only the Church in his domains, revived during his reign, survived with any vitality. Her ideal of kingship lived on, as did her revival of learning and culture which henceforth did not fail.

The intellectual inheritance from the immediate Christian past had been limited but not negligible. Much of the patrimony of Christian learning saved by Boethius (480–541) and Cassiodorus (485–577), passed through Benedict Biscop to England, and centres of learning had survived in papal Rome, in Celtic Ireland, in Lombard Italy, and Visigothic Spain: from them all Charlemagne drew as he revived basic learning in his domains.[36]

Alcuin (d. 804), first a pupil and then headmaster at the Benedictine cathedral school at York, was called on to direct the campaign. The initial requirements were very basic; to save Latin as the language of the Church, of learning and communication, and to establish a clear and easily mastered script for the written word. This was done. What has come to be called the Carolingian minuscule replaced the previous practice of using capitals only, so facilitating the production of texts. Latin was saved as the language of communication and scholarship; classical grammar was retained, but the vocabulary was more flexible; using it, scholars, travellers and administrators could be understood throughout Europe. Saving the Latin heritage also enabled scholars of later generations to return to the classical heritage; meanwhile it formed the basis of the vernacular languages of Europe, their vocabularies being mainly based on the scholars' Latin. Key texts were saved and multiplied – the Vulgate Bible and the original Benedictine rule, for example, among them. We owe most of the Latin classics which have survived to the labour of these years.

Alcuin also rationalized the school curriculum based on the seven liberal arts of grammar, rhetoric, logic (the *trivium*), and arithmetic, astronomy, geometry and music (the *quadrivium*). Charlemagne established a palace school and encouraged cathedral and monastic, even parish schools.[37] The copyists in the monasteries in central Europe were to work on throughout the troubled years of the late ninth and early tenth centuries, long after Charlemagne's empire had collapsed. There was little higher learning, though canon law was studied and so was dogmatic theology: John the Scot (d. 877) made original contributions in the field of philosophy.

Politically, Charlemagne had a very exalted notion of his role as ruler of Christ's people, derived from the Bible and St Augustine rather than the Roman tradition. He was seen as the new David, and he wielded the two swords. The lofty claims of Charlemagne were accepted by the Frankish clergy; he was a great king and he worked with the Church, whose educational and missionary work he supported to the full. As the Lord's anointed he seemed to loom much larger, and more importantly, in both Church and State than the Pope. Charlemagne answered Hadrian I's (772–95) appeal for help against the Lombards and destroyed their kingdom, but added 'King of the Lombards' to his other titles and sidestepped when Hadrian requested that the promises made in 754 be honoured. He made it plain that his title as 'patrician of the Romans' made him Roman overlord and that he could intervene in their affairs when he thought fit.

He was later to claim that Leo III's (795–815) coronation of him in St Peter's on 25 December 800 was a surprise to him. In fact he wished to become Roman Emperor in the West in a way which the Byzantines would accept: for that he was ready to do as the Pope wanted, but he still sought as much independence of the papacy as he could. He remained first and foremost a Frankish king, but he used his powers positively; his government amounted to a sustained and intelligent attempt to devise means of ruling more effectively and justly. In this too the resources of the Church were crucial.

Since the clergy were fast becoming the only literate class, the Carolingians had used the clerks of the royal writing-office since the time of Pepin to conduct the clerical, notarial and other official business of the realm, and these clerks were awarded benefices accordingly, the higher officials frequently being bishops.[38] A major problem Charlemagne faced was that of ensuring effective government at all levels where communications were very primitive and vast regions had to be covered. Experience showed that the local count who represented the king in legal and financial affairs, and the local duke who did the same in military affairs, too readily favoured local loyalties over central, and the cessation of royal perambulations increased the problem. The Emperor therefore introduced a regular pattern of legates, *missi dominici*, who toured the provinces annually with full powers to inspect, redress and reform. Many of them were bishops.

Customary law was put in writing, and written law was edited authoritatively. No code emerged, but there was a greater systematization than before: the result was that the law was better understood and administered. A new and reliable coinage was established, one pound of silver providing 240 denarii, the origin of the English pound and of the penny which lasted until the 1970s. Weights and measures, bridges and roads, tolls and customs were regulated. Trade in the hours of darkness was forbidden, as well as the export of corn in dearth; price tariffs were issued and speculation in corn and wine forbidden. The poor were to be supported by a levy, a poor rate, to which the great ones, clerical and lay, contributed according to their means.[39]

Under Christian influence the laws of the barbarian states were becoming more socially conscious. Before this time, the new Western kingdoms had kept the old tribal codes and any Christian modification was extraneous to them. Now Christendom enacted its own laws, which covered the whole field of social activity in Church and State and referred all things to the single standard of the Christian ethos.[40] Kings were interpreters of the law of God for God's people. The people were bound in justice to obey the king: he was bound by his coronation oath, as God's minister, to give them justice and peace. Priest and king alike were servants of the same Christian society and, most important for the development of a constitutional State, the right of the ruler was countered by the conditional, revocable character of kingship.

4 After Charlemagne

(i) New invasions

Charlemagne's son, Louis the Pious (814–40), could not secure the succession of his sons, and by 834 internal disorder had become endemic. The powerful landowners within the Empire infringed on the King's rights, while the coasts, main river valleys and central Europe were being ravaged by the Viking, Magyar and Saracen invasions.[41] The Vikings and the Danes colonized as they went, and the settlement led to their conversion and absorption into the countries they had invaded; Europe, as after the first invasions, was being welded into one by the action of the Church through baptism. The Saracens raided central and northern Italy, and the south coast of France and into the interior. The Magyars, horsemen from the region of modern Hungary, also raided in central Europe and Italy; they were finally defeated by Otto I at Lechfeld in 955, converted and absorbed.

The Empire was divided but the ideal of unity remained, mainly among the churchmen who were champions of peace and of Carolingian kingship as the best hope of order and good government,[42] but there was little of either. Lay encroachment on Church lands was constant, and she was helpless against it. The bishops looked to the Papacy to solve their own problems and counterbalance the secular forces, and for a while Pope St Nicholas I 'the Great' (858–67) could act as supreme arbiter, but the violent insubordination of the Roman nobles who wished to use the Papacy for their own secular ends was causing increasing problems.

Charles the Fat, Emperor and King of France, was deposed in 887 and died in the same year, and the last pretence of the imperial power died with him. From now on the kingdoms chose their own monarchs and the torrent of civil wars, invasions and feuds, marked the decline into chaos. Only Alfred the Great (871–99) in England maintained something of the Carolingian ideal. He was a profoundly Christian king. His law code, probably issued about 890, declared that it was based on the Ten Commandments. With this as his guide, he had selected the best of the laws promulgated by previous English kings, the whole approved by Councillors. Under his leadership, England became a nation. In France in 911, Charles the Simple and the Viking King Rollo reached a settlement by which the invaders were ceded the Duchy of Normandy. Elsewhere the turmoil created by the onslaught, and the strife among the native rulers continued for most of the century; not until 987 did the Capetian dynasty establish itself. The Saracens who ravaged the coasts of Europe from 827 were eventually defeated in 1016 when the Pope rallied the Genoans and Pisans to evict them from Sardinia.

(ii) The development of feudalism

The system we know as feudalism was born of the conditions of the eighth and ninth centuries in Europe, though the word was coined by French and English lawyers in the eighteenth century, popularized by Montesquieu and used pejoratively to characterize the old regime rejected at the French revolution.[43] Marc Bloch summed up the essential characteristics of the system: it embraced

> a subject peasantry; widespread use of the service tenement (i.e. the fief) instead of a salary, which was out of the question; the supremacy of a class of specialized warriors, ties of obedience and protection which bind man to man and, within the warrior class, assume the distinctive form called vassalage; fragmentation of authority leading to disorder; and in the midst of all this, the survival of other forms of association, family and State.[44]

The pattern of development of the system was patchy. It was strongest in France; elsewhere it varied, and there were always landowners who owed no feudal obligations; not all peasant settlements were subject to them either, but it was the dominant, social, political and economic system of the day.

The feudalism of the historian or the lawyer was a rationalization of the realities of the time, when the only hope of order was a local order under a military leader. The virtue of the system was that it did provide some government when none else was available; it enabled society to survive and nurture more positive political structures, since it possessed within itself the means to do so. The feudal states were more compact than the unwieldy Empire, and their consolidation in time encouraged civilization. Normandy for example was large and strong enough to be a true, small kingdom which one man could control, and as such kingdoms flourished so did not only trade and towns, but religious, intellectual and artistic life. William the Great of Poitou (993–1030), was a man of culture, the friend of Fulbert of Chartres. In their role of supporters of church reform such men also had great influence. It was William of Auvergne, Duke of Aquitaine who founded Cluny in 910.

The system had come to be, therefore, in order to meet the needs of society engulfed in chaos; it was not of Christian origin; the Church regretted the destruction of the incipient Christian Empire, the collapse of which led to that chaos, but she soon realized that feudalism was here to stay. As a major landowner, her lands were taken up into the system anyway. She sought to modify the violence of the system by providing a liturgical setting for the act of homage and by encouraging the concept of Christian knight-hood and chivalry. She also did her best to protect the merchant, the pilgrim and traveller, as well as the peasants and the churches, from brigandage; in this she had the co-operation of some of the major feudatories who were coming to realize that casual violence was a social disease. From 989, starting with Aquitaine and Burgundy, which were the most ravaged provinces, synods strongly condemned the evil. Sworn promises were obtained from those concerned to avoid violence towards noncombatants, and to abstain from all aggression in certain religious seasons. Often broken, it was sufficiently observed in a lawless time to reckon as a triumph of reason over brute strength. In the 1040s the Truce of God was introduced to supplement the Peace, forbidding fighting from Thursday afternoon to Monday morning the year round. In Germany the 'indulgence' was introduced under Henry III to prevent private feuds.[45]

5 The end of the invasions and the outlines of a new Europe

The signs of a new beginning appeared first in Germany where Otto (936–73), the victor at Lechfeld in 955, consciously sought to revive the Carolingian ideal and that of the Holy Roman Empire, being crowned in Charlemagne's capital Aachen by the Archbishop of Mainz. In facing the tribal duchies which chal-lenged his rights, he used the resources and personnel of the Church to provide a sound institutional basis for royal power. They gave him the wealth, the military means and the skilled adminis-trators he needed for his task, while the German clergy for their part were glad of his protection against the nobility; they also appreciated his endowments of churches, and the opportunity to serve him as administrators and executives.

By insisting on his right to invest bishops and abbots with the symbols of their office, a right he claimed as the Lord's anointed, he ensured that all the senior clergy were his men. Through the control exercised over proprietary churches he reinforced his rights regarding ecclesiastical offices, he shared their revenues and could better control the people. Finally, every large ecclesiastical estate required a secular manager to undertake tasks in regard to their administration and defence that the ecclesiastics themselves were forbidden by their calling to do. Since the majority of these 'advocates' were Ottonians, further control was exercised through them.

His successors followed the same policies. By 981 almost half the army was of men provided for by the monastic estates, and senior clergy were not only chancery officials but were given specific political tasks.[46] On the strength of the political, economic and military support of the Church, the king was well able to control the duchies. The stability and coherence of the Ottonian State gave its kings considerable influence in Rome over the next one hundred years. Much of it was used for good, in helping to release the Papacy from those malign local influences which had corrupted it, but the long-term problems of excessive lay control of the Church were embodied in her structures and not until a reformed Papacy had broken free of this could true reform of the Church make headway.

Hugh (987–96), head of the House of Capet, emerged as the most powerful and capable claimant to the throne as France recovered from the confusions of the tenth century. Though there was a Carolingian candidate – Charles of Lotharingia – the bishops of Francia, who were the most stable element among the king's vassals and the strongest supporters of the throne, chose the Capetian as the more throne-worthy. Hugh Capet possessed the territory which gave him the necessary power base in facing his task, and the proved ability to rule with a firm hand, yet he and his successors still faced problems from the turbulent aristocracy. Their main problem was with the strong Duchy of Normandy where the descendants of Rollo had shown remarkable shrewdness in building up the strength of their kingdom. Norman adventurers also sought their fortunes abroad; they fought in south Italy and in Spain, for example, from 1016, and in 1066 Duke William invaded and conquered England. Not until the twelfth century were the Capetians able to master their over-mighty vassals and begin to form a coherent and powerful State.

In England the Danes resumed their intrusions during the reign of Ethelred the Unready (978–1016), and they came to stay. The defence against them was marked by ineptitude, treason and panic, and Ethelred was defeated by Canute, the second son of Sweyn, King of Denmark. Canute (1016–42), who was conqueror of Norway as well as of England and who ruled a formidable North Sea empire, was no pagan or bloodthirsty Viking, but a good Christian, a lawgiver and a ruler capable of maintaining the peace, respecting the traditions established by Alfred, and ruling better through them than Ethelred had done. His empire did not survive him none the less, and in 1042 the English throne passed peacefully into the hands of Edward the Confessor. Edward, who had married late and had no heir, promised his cousin, William of

Normandy, that he would succeed him. The claim was disputed
and the country taken by force; it was a goodly prize, strong and
well organized internally, used to respecting its king and possessed
of a sound political and legal tradition.

6 The Papacy and the beginnings of Church reform[47]

The anarchy that followed the disintegration of Charlemagne's
empire, in the ninth century and after, affected every aspect of
the life of the Church and involved her in the corruption of the
time. Many of the bishops became almost indistinguishable from
the violent and devious feudal lords whose background they
shared, and from whose families they were largely drawn, and they
could not resist the pressure to alienate church lands by enfeoff-
ment. When a see became vacant its lands were seized, along with
the former occupant's personal property, and the new bishop on
appointment paid feudal homage to his lord, just as did the
secular magnates. He was then invested with the insignia of his
spiritual office, namely his staff and ring, the metropolitan bishop
consecrating him and receiving his profession of obedience when
this had been done.[48] The new bishop was therefore, according
to the understanding of the time, primarily a feudal vassal holding
his lands under feudal obligations; his ecclesiastical status was
secondary. Like an heir entering into his inheritance he had to
pay the stipulated sum for the privilege, and he then recouped
the cost from the fees he took for ordinations and other spiritual
administrations. He was selling his spiritual functions; he was a
simonist.

Ownership of a church and its income belonged to the founder,
bishop, king or more usually the local landowner, and the priest
was the lord's vassal serving on his terms. Often a married man, he
used the church's property for his own and his family's benefit; the
clergy too often became almost indistinguishable in every aspect
from their lay contemporaries in a degenerate society. Great
nobles were customarily abbots of the wealthiest monasteries and
such monks as remained were rarely models of their profession.

It was a situation which compelled those who had not been
corrupted by it to take stock. The prelates of the Province of
Rheims meeting at Troslé in 909 were aware that 'God's flock
perishes through our charge. It has come about by our negligence.'[49] A reform movement emerged, Cluny being central to it.
In 910 William I of Aquitaine had founded this Burgundian

monastery which lay beyond the reach of the invaders plaguing the country at the time. There were also other reformers and reform movements.[50] But Cluny was the most significant.

Its first abbot, Berno, and its founder Duke William, ensured that its constitution gave the monks the right to choose their own abbot after Berno's death, vesting the proprietorship of the foundation in the Holy See. Despite the Papacy being bogged down and intermittently corrupted by the struggles with the Roman nobility, the remarkable series of abbots the monastery possessed was able to work with the many good popes of this unhappy time in strengthening the spiritual life of the Church and encouraging reform. It was under its second abbot, Odo (927–42), that Cluny achieved its first prominence[51] and his successors were men of equal distinction who brought their holiness and their other talents to the task. The monasteries of France, Italy and Spain, which had already accepted the Cluny reform, were joined by others given to it by their patrons; this spreading empire was consolidated by increasing co-operation with the Papacy. The Cluniac reform in this way became the first of the centralized religious orders because its houses were independent of any local ecclesiastical control, being directly under the authority of the Abbot of Cluny who was directly answerable to the Pope.

Old and new foundations throughout the West were affiliated and became priories subject to the mother house. The priors met together in annual chapter at Cluny and their houses, 200 hundred eventually, formed ten provinces for regular visitation. Hugh respected theocratic kingship and its implications for the relationship between Church and State, and worked in co-operation with it. In these, the last stages of at least the formal Christianization of Europe, this was plausible enough; the rulers knew that they depended on the Church's existence and co-operation for the secular well-being of their realms, and where they were sincere in their Christian profession, the belief in peaceful co-operation and avoidance of confrontation was reasonable. Where they became less dependent on that co-operation, or where their sincerity was questionable, the Church reformer had some hard questions to ask and answers to face. As the eleventh century went on, increasing numbers were prepared to ask those questions and face the implications of the answers.

The need in society as a whole was to reintroduce respect for law, and this gradually happened. Bishop Fulbert of Chartres in 1020 could set out for Duke William of Aquitaine what the vassal's duties were. The Peace of God and the Truce of God were efforts to civilize the profession of arms. Where there had been a tradition of written law it was gradually revived. The Benedictine reform itself was based on a return to the original rule, the law of the founder, and canon law, the study of the Church's law generally, was the guide to those who would reform the Church. One problem was that the older collections were difficult to consult, and to make that law more accessible Burchard, the Bishop of Worms, produced a *Decretum* in 1021.

The reform of the Church at large, however, could only be undertaken when the Papacy itself was freed from its subjection to the Roman nobility, for in the breakdown of order that followed on the collapse of Charlemagne's Empire, the process of choosing and electing popes suffered as all else. The papal office represented a great prize in terms of temporal wealth and power for those who were prepared to ignore, or marginalize, its spiritual nature and obligations, and a corrupt local aristocracy was prepared to do this; the tradition of lay interference with papal elections had been building up since Carolingian times and there was now no power in Church or State to prevent them using it for their purpose. Not all were equally irresponsible in exercising their power; many of the popes they effectively elected or appointed were good men and reformers, but too many were not.

The scandals were intermittent over a period of some one hundred and fifty years from about 900 to 1050. The family of Theophylact was the first to exercise consistent control over the Papacy. From being a simple papal official, Theophylact progressed to treasurer and commander of its militia and in 915 'Senator of the Romans'. His influence and control was excessive, but not as evil as its political enemies portrayed it.[52] The charges that his wife Theodora had been the mistress of Pope John X (914–28) and his daughter mistress of Pope Sergius III (904–11), for example, once widely accepted, now appear to have been unfounded, but the overall result of Theophylact power was malign. Marozia was the dominant influence towards the end of John X's reign, but he broke with, and found himself at war with her, being imprisoned after riots in Rome; there he died, smothered it is said on her orders. She nominated the next three popes, the last of whom, John XI (931–5), was her son. Another son, Alberic, rebelled against her and she was herself imprisoned. The next four popes, from 936 to 955, were his nominees and they were men of good life, reformers guided by Odo of Cluny. When Alberic however died in 954 the full evil of lay control of the Papacy was demonstrated once more, because his sixteen-year-old son not only succeeded him as civil ruler, but also, in accordance with his father's wishes, was elected pope as John XII (955–64). His pleasures were boorish and his lifestyle debauched; it is said he died in the arms of a woman. Strangely however this totally unworthy occupant of the office accepted his official responsibilities in its administration in a way which the Church found acceptable.

The Crescenti family succeeded the Theophylacts as the dominant Roman family, and the catalogue of politically appointed popes went on. From Benedict VII (974–83) to Benedict VIII (1012–24) in particular, the appointees were all virtuous men, but with John XIX (1024–32) corruption and immorality returned and were continued under Benedict IX (1032–44). The Emperor Henry III now took a hand in bringing the scandals to an end and at the Council of Sutri in 1046 the contested papacy of Gregory VI was ended with his abdication: eventually in 1048 Leo IX was nominated by the Emperor and lasting reform was under way.

Reform of the Church required that bishops and abbots had to be chosen solely for their virtue and abilities by the proper ecclesiastical authorities according to canon law; as it was, they were under the control of secular authority which was concerned primarily with the election of men who would serve the local interests of the State well. The Church, her personnel and resources, had become so much part of the order of things that even the reforming emperors themselves were determined that they should continue so to serve the State, although they normally took care to see that good men were appointed to prelacies. If there came an emperor who was less concerned with the good of the Church, and less concerned about ends and means, there would be a clash between him and the reformers in which one interest or the other would prevail. There could be no half measures.

As noted above, Otto I had literally relied on the Church to rule Germany. Despite his large family and estates his resources were insufficient, even with all the other sources of royal income, to support his power. Hereditary feudalism had already sapped the kingdom's strength; the counts and magnates were intent on family aggrandizement, while their private wars were a main cause of the country's disorders. Reformed bishops and monks, however, he knew would not cheat him. The heavy military dues their estates bore would be met, as would all the other royal demands for hospitality for the king and his companions as he travelled the realm. Bishops were also literate, even learned, and staffed his chancery. If then he was generous to them in gifts of land and the rest, he was underpinning his throne in the most practical manner. But such a system made the Church subservient to the State. By insisting on the right to invest members of the hierarchy with their insignia of spiritual office, Otto made his bishops feudal lords and civil servants first, and put the Church, her resources and personnel at the State's service as he intended they should be.

His successors, including the reforming and holy men among them, insisted on their right to appoint bishops and enfeoffed knights on church lands. Henry III (1039–56), for example, was strongly religious; he was also a political realist and knew that the bishops in a disintegrating province were the best hope of holding it together.[53] He was not about to do anything which would relax his grip on the Church. A keen reformer, it was he who intervened at Sutri in 1046 and as we have seen he appointed Pope Leo IX in 1048; ironically it was Leo's reforms which would challenge the basis of the German kingdom that Otto had established and his successors had continued, and which led eventually to the conflict in which that hold was broken.

Leo, son of Count Hugh of Egisheim in Alsace, had been the reforming Bishop of Toul since 1027. When nominated pope by Henry III he accepted on condition that the choice was ratified by the Roman Church and people, acclaimed by them on his arrival on 12 February 1049 he took the name of Leo in order to demonstrate his will to reform. At his first synod in April he denounced simony and clerical concubinage and marriage, deposing several simoniacal bishops and reimposing Clement II's penance on clergy knowingly ordained by simonists. He travelled widely, addressing reforming synods in the main centres from Mainz and Rheims (1049) to Bari (1053). The failure of his mission to the Eastern Churches and of his attempt to control the Normans in south Italy overshadowed his last years, but he had given essential reform at the centre a momentum it would not lose.

6

The Church, society and economics in the early Middle Ages

1 Barbarian settlement, agricultural economy and the Church

The general pattern of social conditions in the rural areas during late Roman times we have already examined. It was one dominated by large estates or *villae*, State or privately owned, the peasants gradually becoming increasingly at the mercy of their masters. Slavery had been in decline since the second century, but the independent peasant and the *colonus* were increasingly subject to conditions which reduced their freedom; the burden of their obligations to their masters and to the State resulted in many fleeing the land despite the efforts to tie them to it.

The barbarian invaders were agriculturalists; they came with the intention of gaining more land for themselves and adapted their own traditions to this pattern as they settled.[1] Within two hundred years every corner of Europe experienced a change of land ownership but it was one which, on the whole, blended the old and new orders. The number of the invaders overall cannot have been great; it is calculated, for example, that the Vandals and Alans together probably numbered only 80,000. The barbarian chiefs took over the large *villae*; the degree of dispossession varied but generally the two orders fused, the land being plentiful. In Italy the Goths were content to be co-owners with the Romans; the Lombards who dispossessed the Goths were less accommodating; the previous incumbents seem at best to have been made *tributarii* while many were enslaved or evicted. The Franks had acquired

* The notes and references for Chapter 6 are to be found on p. 389

land by steady colonization and settlement so that they possessed much of the domain of northern France before the collapse of the Empire. They were then able to blend in with the Gallo-Romans. Gregory of Tours tells us that under the Merovingians there was only one aristocracy, which was both Gallo-Roman and Frankish; since the need was for more manpower to maintain the existing *villae*, dispossession was rarely required. In England on the other hand it would seem that the Romans fled before the invaders and those who remained were either displaced or enslaved.[2]

Many types and sizes of *villae* or manors existed: there was no such thing as a typical one since geography and conditions differed so widely, but they were all so organized 'that the greater part of the profits derived from working it accrued to one man, the lord who held it',[3] and all had certain general features with additions and modification according to local or regional variations. There was arable, pasture, meadow, woodland, forest and waste land, divided between the lord's domain, the holdings of the peasants and the common land; the domain could account for up to 30 per cent of the total and was worked by the peasants, according to their status and dues. It embraced the manor house, occupied by the steward if the lord held several manors, and barns, stables, workshops and gardens, and possibly a vineyard or orchard.

The land of the peasants was in the open fields, divided into strips of which each family had up to 20 or more, distributed throughout the whole so that all shared the good and bad areas. There were grazing rights on the commons and access to firewood, and perhaps for building, from the forests. The village, or villages, in which they lived were on the manor, often clustered around the manor house. Cottages were very simple, usually two rooms, possibly with a loft for sleeping, and in winter the livestock were frequently housed under the same roof. Life was, by modern standards, incredibly simple and harsh.

The dues which the peasant owed his lord varied, generally consisted of week work, boon work and deliveries in kind. The serf might have to work on the domain for several days, three out of six being common. Boon work was due at harvest time in addition, tasks rather than time being the norm. The produce to which the lord was entitled consisted of specified foodstuffs, and there were extra payments for special occasions, as when a daughter was given in marriage; the use of the grinding mill or bakery had also to be paid for. The only difference between serfs and freemen was that the latter were not subject to servile restrictions, in particular they could leave the land if they wished; but they had similar obligations to the lord of the manor in terms of work and produce.[4]

The whole of life revolved around the manor and the village and the seasonal needs of both, and because of her status as a landowner, the Church necessarily had an important role to play in that economy. Land and its produce were the only economic resources she, as others, possessed and she had to see it efficiently worked in order that the means to meet her obligations were available. Many members of the Roman aristocracy had become bishops, adding their own estates to those of the Church, and they also brought with them their knowledge of the arts of Roman estate management. The Church's estates had to support not only her ministers, buildings and liturgical needs, but the poor: one fourth of her income was to be expended on their care; they were registered as *matricularii* in the church records and *xenodochia* were provided for the sick.[5]

The monastic presence overcame the Germanic superstition that the forests were sacred; the woodlands were cleared and settled, and the peasants followed and further developed the region. Monastic endeavours of this kind completely changed the environment. There were extra burdens on the Church's land managers: they had to support the Church's work of evangelization, to make good losses of land to the plundering nobility, and to offer hospitality to the king and his entourage on their journeys. The parish system had constantly to be enlarged and the only way this could be done was by bringing larger areas under cultivation. The clearing of forests and reclamation of waste land, and the settlement of peasants on it was a distinctive mark of monastic settlements in remote areas. Hence 'the needs of the Church harmonized admirably with the craving of small freemen and peasants for fresh property'.[6] In France, in the growing anarchy of the ninth and tenth centuries, monasteries were particularly anxious to get land cleared and cultivated. The families of their own dependants needed it as did landless peasants, from devastated places or in flight from tyrannous lords, who sought assistance from the Church.[7] The monks suffered also from that same tyranny. The fugitives needed not only land but security against the violence, in the form of denser settlements which would provide stronger village units of settlers for self-protection. The monks negotiated for neglected land, being given it, and the right to receive dues from it, in return for certain dues; they thus secured the right to forest clearances which would provide both land and the timber needed for building material for the settlers.

The monasteries admitted the peasants as *hospites*, they received a piece of land, a *hospitium*, enough for a house and a small plot, probably one quarter acre in all, paying a yearly rent of a few pence and gifts of foodstuffs. In return they agreed to help with clearances and were given the right to lease the land they cleared in return for a fixed share of the yield. The settlers were then congregated in strong village colonies of 30 to 80 independent farmers and their households. Members of these villages had no easy task before them, but their legal position was sound enough. They were free; if a previous lord still had claim on them, this expired after a year and a day, and they were protected from him and his officials. The useful capacity for self-defence of the enlarged villages was all the protection they needed from the casual violence of the time, and once their utility was recognized the establishment of these colonies was imitated by kings and by the nobility.[8]

The Carolingian agricultural economy was vastly underdeveloped. It is calculated that some seven million hectares were under cultivation, as against the estimated total land area of some one and half million square kilometres potentially available.[9] The rest was forest, waste and untilled lands. The villa was factory and farm in one. It was on the products of his estates that the king relied for the equipment, as well as for the sustenance of his armies, when major campaigns were waged each year.

We are fortunate in possessing the records of the operations of a major estate, those of the Abbey of St Germain near Paris, the *Polypticon* of Abbot Irminion, covering the period 875 to 925, because it gives us detailed information on the working of such an estate.[10] Such monasteries were the industrial as well as the agricultural leaders of their day; they knew how to make the best use of the techniques of production then available in organizing their resources and their application scientifically.[11]

2 Urban life, economy and the Church

The cities which had been the administrative and cultural centres of the Roman Empire, and which also possessed an active population of merchants and craftsmen, were the preferred place of residence for the owners of the great estates when those cities were flourishing. With the withering away of the Empire, the life of such cities flagged; the declining purchasing power of a shrinking economy hastened their decline, and the wealthy landowners abandoned the city for their country residences. In Italy, the urban tradition was more deeply rooted and the contacts with the Byzantines and then the Muslims enabled them to maintain what long-distance trade there was between Europe and the east, a trade almost entirely in luxury goods. City life there did not experience the same eclipse as in the rest of Roman Europe. Venice, Amalfi, Naples and Gaeta held on to their official affiliation to the Eastern Empire, to Constantinople, and were the main intermediaries through which Syrian and Jewish traders kept trade to the north alive. Venice owes its origins to those inhabitants of the plain at the northern end of the Adriatic who fled the lagoons to escape the Lombard invaders in the sixth century. Cut off from their agricultural hinterland they developed a port, receiving and redispatching the goods traded between east and west. Pisa and Genoa developed as sea powers and had to protect themselves from the Muslim raiders: by degrees they came to control the western Mediterranean.

In the north 'it was the Church which, more than any other institution, gave continuity to the life of the town'.[13] The building of the cathedral, the pilgrimages to the shrines of saints, the clerical communities there and the centre of administration for the diocese provided them with an active if small community and economy. Men like Germanus of Auxerre, Avitus of Vienna and Anianus of Orleans were *defensores civitatis*, maintaining town ramparts and aqueducts, distributing public aid to the poor and providing hospitality for travellers and the sick in the *xenodochia*.[14] The cathedral was still the only religious building of importance in a diocese apart from the monasteries, and when churches were built in the villages and on estates, this increased the significance of the main church in the city where the most important ceremonies took place. The shrines of saints also helped cities to survive or develop; that of St Martin of Tours, who died in 397, ensured the city's flourishing. Pilgrimages were a favourite form of piety. When travel was hard and dangerous these were something more than an early form of tourism. Culturally, pilgrimages were one way in which society was prevented from being more turned in on itself. As the establishment of a see and the building of its cathedral or the presence of a saint's shrine helped secure a town's future, so too did the location of churches. They had initially been built near the Christian cemeteries that were situated outside the city walls, and although monasteries were mainly established in rural areas, some were founded in the vicinity of these older churches. The manual workers, domestics, farmhands and craftsmen who were essential for the running of a large abbey lived nearby and their settlements in time developed into suburbs of those towns. Hence the frequency with which, for example in

France, the streets bear the names of saints borne by monasteries which disappeared a long time ago. So the Abbey of St Rémy became the site of an important burgh. The development of such monasteries was one of the reasons that there was a moderate but steady expansion of some towns before the economic revival.

But overall the European urban economy underwent a long slow decline in the wake of the Germanic invasions, given the disruption of long-distance trade. It did not die altogether, and there was still a small market for luxury goods from the east, for royalty, aristocracy and the Church, regalia for the bishops and archbishops and for the adornment of churches, but its vitality flagged as life became simpler; the spices, silks and precious stones and metals which were its staples were less in demand. The Gallo-Romans had not been engaged in such trade, still less had the Merovingians. It was mainly conducted by Jews and Syrians, though abbeys would also sometimes appoint agents to secure more basic supplies from distant cities in Gaul. Such trading as there was, within or without the kingdom, was a dangerous undertaking in unsettled times and those who participated formed associations for protection; the merchants of Verdun in the sixth century for example formed one, as Gregory of Tours records.

Much of the trade that existed was in slaves. The Slavs, east of the Elbe, were a major source as Europe expanded eastwards: the word 'slave', originally indicating a Slav national, replaced the Latin *mancipia* or *servus* to denote one of unfree status. Although in 743 Pope Zacharias condemned the selling of Christians into slavery the practice went on; many however saw the evil of trading in those who shared the same faith. So Eloi, Dagobert's Minister, thought it his Christian duty to rescue these souls who were being treated as cattle, and he used his considerable wealth to buy them in batches from the traders to free them.[15] Where slavery existed, Christian influences worked to mitigate it: they gained certain rights by custom.[16] Bishop Wulfstan of Worcester shamed the merchants of Bristol into reducing their activities in this field of commerce.[17] Manumission of the slaves of bishops was made mandatory on the death of their owner and many lay landowners made provision for the manumission of their slaves in their wills, while the practice of redeeming slaves from captivity was commended.

The declining importance of urban life meant that towns and cities, currency, public works, roads, communications, shipping, were neglected. The failure to recognize the importance of maintaining a sound currency was particularly damaging, so crucial was it to trading confidence. Charlemagne's economic measures have already been mentioned: the livre with its twenty solidi each of 12 deniers, the standardization of weights and measures, and conditions for fair trading. In matters concerning economic and political morality, as in all those which the kings and their advisers sought to introduce more civilized ways, the Carolingians were guided by the Church's teaching.[18] Lending money at interest was a real problem because the debtor was usually borrowing for consumption needs.[19]

There is evidence that other kinds of loans at interest were morally acceptable, for example, the Bishop of Verdun obtained one from the King of Austrasia on behalf of the citizens of the city; the bishop agreed to legitimate interest being paid[20] on what was a commercial loan. Efforts were made to ensure that the consumer was not exploited in the local markets; the markets themselves were numerous enough, held in towns but also in the villages and on the estates, meeting the need for food and clothing and essential items not necessarily available locally. The prices prevailing in these markets provided a guide to what was fair.

Levies and tolls were also regularized, a great need at a time when abuses in this matter were so frequent. There was also effort made to ensure that only honest trading took place, the sale of particularly valuable goods, gold and silver, horses and other animals, was restricted to daylight hours and public transactions in order to limit the possibility of dishonest dealing. Efforts were made to limit the slave trade and ensure the personal status and faith of the slaves where it still existed. Christians continued to be sold to non-Christians, this abuse leading the Council of Meaux in 845 to urge princes to stop the practice; it continued none the less.[21] Towns which dealt with more than local trading continued to exist in Italy throughout the early medieval period and there were such centres established in parts of the north, Dinant on the Meuse, Cambrai on the Scheldt for example, Dorstad on the Rhine and Quentovic on the Canche being the most prominent.[22] Some were destroyed by the Norse invasions and the protection of trading centres was the first requirement of any revival of that trade.

3 The last invasions, recovery and growth

(i) Agricultural revival

In the wide areas affected by the invasions, agriculture as everything else was severely disrupted, but once they tailed off from the late tenth century a new growth was discernible; population, trade, the reclamation of the land and its productivity were all growing. Documentary evidence that we have from the tenth century contrasts notably in quantity with that which remains from the ninth; recovery meant trying to sort out property rights – for example, what was left of the land and properties of plundered abbeys had to be recorded as their communities returned, and the sorting out of rights involved an increase in litigation and the paperwork it produced. Slaves were disappearing, and as the movement to clear the land gathered pace the position of the peasant improved. Tenants paid only money rent and certain agreed dues in kind; most of the domain was divided among them, only enough for the needs of their own families was kept by the landowners. In this way the number of small farms and farmers, the free peasants, the freemen, increased.

The reclamation of wastes and the clearing of the forest went on throughout Europe during these years.[23] That done by the Counts of Flanders in the late tenth century was one of the most remarkable examples of the reclamation of marshland which was dyked and drained, and what was a wilderness at the beginning of the century was brought under cultivation by settlers; this work was parallelled in other parts of the Low Countries and the Atlantic seaboard. The resulting holdings were surrounded by ditches, banks and hedges – declarations that the strenuous toil of the settlers was responsible for whatever fruits were produced. By the second half of the eleventh century these settlements were developing into rural burghs, country equivalents of the social organization of the towns. Everywhere in these regions the peasants' impulse to establish farms for themselves and their families was evident.[24]

(ii) The growth of towns and trade[25]

In northern Europe it had been mainly the various activities of the Church within them which kept the towns alive. They had almost no free population living by trade or industry; their weekly markets were purely local affairs, their storehouses were for the crops of the local landowner, bishop or layman. However, the walls of the older towns were often not strong enough to protect them against the raiders, and new fortifications were built by the local magnates; they were called *castra*, but were usually earthworks with palisades and moat. They were centres for the temporary protection of the local people; later they sheltered merchants and craftsmen, and many developed into towns. Fortified abbeys gave rise to communities and some became the nucleus of medieval towns also, overshadowing the older episcopal cities whose walls had not provided sufficient protection. The lay burghs, like the episcopal cities, lived initially on the land; they had no economic life of their own; they were an extension of the agricultural economy. With the revival of commerce between 950 and 1000, a new type of town began to emerge.

These were the commercial centres which developed wherever there were active groups of merchants and traders; they were also centres of industry and manufacture, however basic, and they were profitable and expanding. They were economically active, giving back to the region more than they took from it; they were centres of economic growth, of development. The merchants had sought the safety of the walls of castles, or older towns, at a time when security required travel in large groups and the assurance of protection overnight when travelling and when trading. As trade grew, the merchant settlements became permanent.

Where and how these enterprising groups of merchants formed we cannot be sure.[26] If they were landowners or officials of abbeys and manors they would have had some, perhaps considerable, capital to launch them. Pirenne, however, considers that they came predominantly from among the landless at a time when it was land which defined a man and gave him a right to a livelihood, or from those uprooted by war or other disaster, wandering from monastery to monastery, living on alms or finding casual work in season. Pirenne's classical example of one type was Godric, a merchant from Lincolnshire. He had been born of poor parents and helped them to survive by beachcombing. He then became a peddler and then merchant, so prospering that he eventually progressed to shipowner and international trader. Ironically we have this knowledge of him, not because of his business ability, but because he abandoned trade in search of sanctity and found it; his fame as a living saint led to his biography being written by one of his admirers, and it is from this we glean knowledge of his trading activities as a young man.

It was the merchants who sparked the economic expansion, and liberty was the essential mark of their status. The merchant was assumed to be a freeman because it was impossible to prove he was not, and if he retained his freedom for one year he was free legally; that 'town air makes a man free' was the proverb. In some places, where towns grew up under the shelter of the Church, many of their inhabitants declared themselves 'serfs' of its patron saint.

This had involved paying a few pence yearly, in return for which they were in practice free; for example, such serfs at one time formed a very large part of the populations of Amiens and Mons.[27]

To the towns which dealt with the long-distance trade came the merchants who plied the roads and rivers between northern Europe and Lombardy in north Italy, bringing the mainly luxury goods from the south and returning with more basic necessities from the north. Around them gathered an artisan population working to meet local needs and making the export items which the traders then purchased for sale elsewhere. It is increased traffic in ordinary goods, however, not the limited luxury trade, which marks the difference between the developed and the underdeveloped economy. Neglect of roads between towns, the almost total absence of inns along them, the lack of shops in the towns, and the suspicion that strangers offering items for sale were probably thieves, did not help the growth but it happened none the less. Free or inexpensive hospitality was available for pilgrims, and wayfarers generally, in hospices and *xenodochia* supported by the Church or lay confraternities, and merchants could put up there. Pious organizations and confraternities also did something to keep roads and bridges under repair, and water transport was highly developed for internal and coastal handling of salt, grain, wine, oil and other staples to be sold in the local markets by full-time or part-time merchants.[28]

The towns as they grew also developed politically. They needed to ensure peace within their walls, protection from outside, and a tax system which could meet the costs of defence and administration. They could secure these by obtaining charters from the local lord by bargaining; in other cases they acted together independently of the feudal pattern; they were 'sworn' or revolutionary communes. There were bitter contests with local bishops in some places over such breaches of the feudal code. In either case, whether chartered or not, the townsman had to be politically as well as economically active from the start.[29]

(iii) Technological developments[30]

Population growth and technological advance was a mark of the period; it was the result mainly of factors whose collective impact, accumulating since the sixth century, made themselves increasingly apparent from the ninth. The first was the adoption by the Slavs in the sixth century of a plough which was better adapted to the heavy wet soils of Northern Europe than was the scratch plough, adequate for the drier regions of the Mediterranean. Its value was not only that it enabled heavier soils to be effectively cultivated; it also was labour-saving, turning the furrow, so that cross ploughing was not necessary. Its drawback initially was that it required a team of eight oxen to pull it,[31] but the problem was overcome by the medieval capacity for social co-operation, groups of peasants joining together and pooling their oxen. The adoption of the improved plough also required the holdings of the peasants to be in long strips so that the ploughing was not wastefully done, and this involved a complete change in the previous working pattern. The village's holdings were divided into two large fields, one for planting yearly, the other left fallow. The members of the village community had to work together, so that sowing and reaping could be co-ordinated, and this they did through the village council – an exercise in solidarity which helped impress that virtue on those involved.

The fenced two-field system also provided grazing in the fallow years for the herds whose grazing increased the fertility of the soil. The scythe, the typical haymaking tool, became a common sight among the Frankish farmers whereas it had been a rarity among the Romans, and hay cropping allowed stall feeding for the animals and their more efficient and economical management. By the eighth century the northern peasants were producing more meat, dairy products, hides and wool than ever before, and they had also improved the grain harvests.[32] In the late eighth century the three-field system was introduced wherever the land was fertile enough to support it. It involved leaving one field fallow, sowing a second for an autumn crop of wheat, rye or barley and a third for a spring crop of oats and beans and other vegetables, the crops rotating to leave one field fallow each year. This provided an insurance against crop failure; work was more equally spread, and the diet improved as more protein-rich vegetables became available and the productivity of the land increased by 50 per cent.[33]

The horse was a more efficient farm animal than the ox, and its diet of oats was now more widely available; it was more expensive to maintain, however, and it was economic to employ it only where there was a sufficient work-load to keep it busy. It also required a suitable system of harnessing the animal to the plough without restricting the horse's breathing or movement, as the Roman method did. The horse collar, long known in China, was the answer; it was in use in Europe by 800 and it meant horses could pull four or five times more weight than before. The invention of the spiked harrow improved agricultural productivity further still, as did the use of the iron horseshoe, common from the ninth century. A more efficient means of yoking horses to carts by using shafts meant they could manoeuvre more readily and safely, and increased the load that could be carried.[34]

The gradual application of machine power to agricultural and manufacturing needs was also made during these years. The water-mill, known in China before the time of Christ, became more common in Northern Europe than were the ubiquitous churches. Most of the 3000 settlements recorded in England's Domesday Book in the late eleventh century had two such mills in operation, and there is no reason for assuming that England was ahead of other European countries in this. The use of the cam, also a Chinese invention, and the crankshaft, enabled water mills to perform other functions apart from grinding – powering trip hammers and bellows for example. From the eleventh century the former revolutionized the fulling of cloth and were used in the iron manufacturing process.[35] Wind power was harnessed in the twelfth century with the development of the windmill, whose efficiency could be increased if it was mounted on a stout oaken post where it could be turned into the wind as it changed direction..

Iron ore was to be found in most parts of Europe, in Gaul, the Rhineland, Saxony, Bohemia and Tuscany, for example. The developed technologies of mining and metallurgy of Greece and Rome had been almost entirely lost by the Merovingian period, though small quantities of ore were produced and there was some development in metallurgy. After the eighth century, the advent of the mounted and armoured warrior and the use of the iron stirrup increased the demand for the metal throughout Europe. Iron was an item of export also, being extracted from the eastern Alps and shipped to the east through Venice. There is evidence that by the tenth century production of iron had considerably increased.[36] Medieval peasants made a greater use of iron than before, there being a smithy in every village; they wanted the best, and the best had iron cutting edges and fittings. Iron was also needed for horse-shoes and nails and the iron fittings on harnesses, carts and ploughs.[37]

7

The Church and society in the central Middle Ages

1 Characteristics of the period

Europe possessed a new creative energy in these years. It was one of those epochs in which man 'made a leap forward that would have been unthinkable under normal evolutionary conditions',[1] comparable with the period about 3000 BC when civilization appeared in Egypt, Mesopotamia and the Indus valley, or with the late sixth century BC when, in Ionia and Greece, philosophy, the sciences and the arts achieved astonishing heights at the same time as, in India, did spiritual enlightenment. The whole world felt it, but nowhere more than did Europe, which most needed it. In spirit, in action, in philosophy, social organization and technology, a new power exerted itself; life became larger than life.

The gradual ending of the last wave of invasions and the settlement of the invaders had left Europe poised for economic development, and the growth of population, the clearing of the waste lands, and the revival of trade, commerce, industry and urban life, charted its course. The reform of the Papacy and the Church brought a new spiritual and moral growth; the development of universities responded to the thirst for learning that gripped the young men of Europe. The whole resulted in

> 'a flowering of new ways of life ... which grew up around the cathedrals and universities, the royal courts and the commercial cities between 900 and 1500 ... The forms of thought and action which we take for granted ... were implanted in the mentalities of our ancestors in the struggles of the medieval centuries.'[2]

---

* The notes and references for Chapter 7 are to be found on p. 391

The Church was at the heart of all the activities of this vigorous new society. Not for nothing has it been characterized as 'the papal monarchy'. The title is, of course, a misnomer.[3] The Papacy had no mandate for temporal rule in itself, and the Papal States always lacked the coherence, economically and militarily, which would make them a credible secular power in their own right even in central Italy; they were of their nature, ecclesiastical, clerical. Yet, as we have seen, the pressure of events from the fifth century compelled the Church and the Papacy into a role of political leadership that extended far beyond the Papal States, and became determinative of the political future of the whole of Europe. In so doing popes and Church became so entangled in Europe's political structures, increasingly disjointed and corrupted in the collapse of Charlemagne's empire and during the last wave of invasions, that when the Church tried to reform herself in the eleventh century she came into violent conflict with the power of the feudalized Empire. It was a conflict which in its implications was to shake Europe to its roots.

The first pope who was able to make reform effective was Leo IX (1049–54). Deciding to break free of the corrupting influences of the Roman nobility he went on a whirlwind tour of northern Italy, Germany and France, exerting Papal authority on faith, morals and discipline as it had never been exerted before, deposing simoniacal bishops on the spot and defying the French king. A new force was at work in Europe which all aspects of the Church's life combined to support and manifest. The monastic reformers remained its cutting edge. The revivified cathedral and monastic schools from the eleventh and the universities from the twelfth centuries provided the educated Bishops, priests and monks reform needed. The heroic years of Cathedral construction in the new Gothic style 1130 to 1280 were eloquent testimony to a new age of faith, with Suger's Abbey Church of St. Denis finished in 1144, Notre Dame in 1250.[4] The great expansion of charitable works in the towns – hospitals, schools and almshouses – and the confraternities and religious who staffed them, were another affirmation of that same faith.

The leadership that Europe demanded of the Papacy was most dramatically demonstrated in the Crusades, which inspired and dominated the new culture for over two hundred years, and were still influential down to the sixteenth century. The abuses of the crusading ideal, like the Inquisition, the ill-treatment of the Jews, the very speed with which the apparently bright prospects of the thirteenth century gave way to the horrors of the fourteenth, remind us of how frail Christian civilization was; but it achieved much of lasting value and leaves us in its debt.

2 The investiture controversy: Gregory VII and Henry IV

Gregory VII, Hildebrand, a Roman who had been an active reformer before Leo became Pope, had realized the importance of canon law in effective reform and had organized scholars to rationalize existing collections. The *Dictatus Papae*[5] brought together previous teaching on papal authority to demonstrate that the Pope had power over the whole Church and all its members. None of it was novel, but since they were unused to an assertive Papacy, those who had gained from the appropriation of powers that rightly belonged to the Church reacted strongly, the Emperor Henry IV (1050–1106) in particular.

Gregory was determined to do what was necessary to end that lay domination of the Church which he and other reformers considered had made her corruption endemic; that domination was apparent in the practice of the king 'investing' the bishop, that is, handing him the symbols of his spiritual power, his staff and ring. Gregory saw himself as having the right to correct the Christian king if necessary, as he could any Christian, and having the right also as pope to decide ultimately who is of God and who is of the devil, so reaching the revolutionary conclusion that he could depose an unworthy ruler and free his subjects from their allegiance.[6]

Henry showed, by investing his own man as Archbishop of Milan and appointing bishops to Spoleto and Fermo, that he had no intention of respecting papal authority, for these were Roman metropolitan sees.[7] Challenged by Gregory with the threat of excommunication, the Emperor informed the Pope that he had forfeited his office and must renounce it. Thereupon at the Lenten Synod 1076 Gregory did suspend Henry, oaths sworn to him were annulled and he was excommunicated. Henry at this time had just finally survived a ten-year struggle for the control of Germany, in which most of the bishops had supported him; he now faced another rebellion from a much weaker position; two thirds of his army consisted of knights from ecclesiastical lands. The princes warned Henry that unless the excommunication of 22 February was lifted within the year, they would elect a new king. They would meet again at Augsburg on 2 February 1077 to consider the situation once more. Gregory, who was staying at Canossa on his way to Augsburg, was confronted dramatically by the Emperor who for three days, dressed as a penitent, petitioned Gregory the priest for forgiveness. Much against his instinct's promptings that the Emperor was feigning, the Pope did forgive and absolve him.[8]

Henry now, through a penitence which turned out to be feigned, regained his throne.

His political adversaries had elected a new king, Rudolf of Swabia in March 1077. Gregory had not supported him; instead he stood by ready to act as arbiter; he saw his role not in political but spiritual terms; he would decide for the one who had justice on his side. It was an attitude which only alienated both parties since both feared their interests were going to suffer. As the proposed arbitration was postponed again and again, time worked in Henry's favour. Finally his threat to have an antipope elected unless Rudolf was excommunicated forced Gregory's hand and he excommunicated Henry instead; thereupon an antipope was elected in June 1080. Henry promised to renounce him if Gregory would crown him Emperor; but the Pope had learned to distrust his promises; he saw him now as an enemy of the divine order who had to do penance and make reparation for his broken oaths. Whereupon 13 Cardinals deserted Gregory for Henry; in 1084 Henry besieged Rome and ultimately the city gates were opened to him; his antipope was crowned as Clement III and Gregory retired into the Castle of St Angelo. Gregory's Norman allies sacked the city after rescuing him, which so angered the citizens that he had to flee their wrath: he died at Salerno in May 1085.

His earnestness in reform had been unusual even in a reforming age. At the end he seemed a failure but

> he conquered in his successors, fashioning the face of Europe for more than two centuries and determining the figuration of the Church into our own day.[9]

Concerning the dispute with Henry IV, two things seem certain; first, the sort of hold that the German kings had on the appointment of prelates was not such as the Church could tolerate if she was to be 'Free, Chaste and Catholic' to proclaim her message and carry on her mission. Second, nothing in the character of German kingship, even in its best examples such as Henry II and III, showed that they were freely prepared to abandon the power that control over the Church gave them, and Henry IV was not among its best examples. If there was to be any effective reform of the Church, there was going to be an outright clash with him, whoever was pope.

3 The Gregorian Reform and society

The insistence on priestly celibacy had important secular implications. Latin Christianity required that those who wished to be priests should first have the vocation to celibacy, freely making the commitment for the sake of the kingdom (Matt. 19:29) and the reformers' emphasis on this helped spiritualize European society. It was one of the many ways in which the reform challenged feudal earthiness and brutality, its contempt for the bonds of morality – and it was profoundly popular with the masses for this.[10] The movement also affected the new culture's attitude to reforming society. Led by Gregory its supporters were seeking to correct abuses by moral force alone in their effort to make Church and society truer to their Christian ideals. It demonstrated that good men could face the arrogance of worldly corruption by spiritual and moral force alone and prevail. This faith in the ability of man to change society for the good by concerted action despite the bitter opposition of worldly powers impressed itself on the culture of the time, and Western man has not since abandoned it.[11]

Gregory's aim of righteousness had embraced more than an insistence on obedience to Church authority. It opposed pagan lawlessness, ferocity and oppression. It helped undermine the barbaric violence of the times. Knighthood was Christianized. Courage and loyalty could serve the cross, courtesy to women and the protection of the weak against the injustices of the strong. The attempt to make canon law effective against the might of the State was an assertion of the superiority of law over lawlessness not lost on the finer minds of the time. The asceticism of the reform, its spirit of renunciation and austerity, induced a feeling of reverence. The reformed monks gave the Papacy 'its most disciplined adherents and its most potent means of swaying opinion'[12] and the bishops and diocesan clergy revitalized by it were at the heart of the initiatives of the Church directed to improving society. They gave energetic assistance to the efforts of princes to suppress private war. They were prominent in the rebuilding of the Church's educational system. They were also leaders in the extension of the social welfare work of the Church in a society whose rapid economic growth was leaving the weak more open to unjust treatment.

Urban II (1088–99) in calling the First Crusade at Clermont in 1095 revealed the Papacy's latent capacity to lead a whole culture,[13] at last responding to the appeals that had been made by the Christian East for help against the Seljuk Turks who had won a great victory at Manzikert in 1071. The crusading movement is hard for the modern world to understand; it was abused for political and economic purposes, and the behaviour of the crusaders often belied their professed aim, but that was because of human weakness and cupidity which has shown a capacity to corrupt all good things.

The good, however, remains and we see it at its best in the ideal put before Europe by Urban. It was an appeal to the pilgrim spirit to rescue the lands that Christ had sanctified by his presence on earth;[14] and to the half-Christianized Westerners to stop fighting one another and unite instead against Europe's ancient enemy. It appealed then to a twin patriotism, and for more than two centuries provided Europe with a purpose and ideal which seemed to the majority to be based on a true reading of the signs of the times.

The investiture problem remained to be solved, and by degrees, and after a fashion, it was. Exiled during the reign of William II,[15] St Anselm of Canterbury (1093–1109) had become convinced of the evils of lay investiture and William's successor Henry I was prepared to accept the compromise proposed by Bishop Ivo of Chartres in 1106. In 1107 he renounced his right to investiture with the ring and crozier, but kept the right to receive homage from the bishops for their temporalities before they were conse-crated: he also continued to have influence on the election of bishops by being present in person during the process. The same policy was accepted by the Concordat of Worms in 1122.

The conflict between the Empire and the Papacy ended then in a compromise. An important victory for Church reform was won; imperial theocracy was no more, the king could not do directly as he liked with the Church and her ministers, though he still exer-cised considerable indirect influence through his presence at elections to hierarchical office. Events were to show that it was not quite as simple as that; the ways in which the secular authority could get its way with the spiritual were still manifold. However, the reform achieved much. The clearer delineation of the clerical order from the laity emphasized the awareness of the call to holi-ness for the latter also. The reformed clergy and the new religious orders became a powerful force for good; priests were more united with their bishops, as were the bishops with the Papacy, and the links between diocese, province and Rome were aided by the growing practice of appeal to Rome. The spirit of reform was reflected in the number of councils held in the next one hundred and forty years. There were seven such ecumenical councils between 1123 and 1311 – the four Lateran called in 1123, 1139, 1179 and 1215, the two at Lyons in 1245 and 1274, and that at Vienne in 1311.[16] The great constructive period was that between Third Lateran and the Second at Lyons, between 1179 and 1274.

The business of the papal court multiplied as the hope of an ordered Christian society manifested itself in clergy and laity seeking in Roman courts the justice they could not get elsewhere, but the scale on which it developed swamped the system by 1150. From the time of Calixtus II (1119–24) there had been a growing awareness of the dangers of this but the beneficiaries of the system drowned out the protests. St Bernard was eloquent on those dangers;[17] the Pope acting the role of Moses 'to teach ordinances and laws and the way wherein they must walk', was one thing. But Rome's judging in every small matter he opposed. The problem was that papal justice was stronger and better than any other. It gave solid and lasting benefits and its litigants were willing to pay the price. For the laity it made the main obligations of Christian life, baptism, the sacraments generally, marriage and alms giving, clear: it also provided essential legal documents, wills and testaments. Order was being established: the problems presented by a rapidly developing society could be dealt with rationally. Such a service justified the claim of Rome to be the mother Church and she had no need to urge its services; those seeking justice sought her out.

Meanwhile, the State was little inconvenienced by the Church. Should it be necessary to appeal to the papal court over a disputed bishopric, for example, the revenues of the vacant see went to the State in the meantime, so a swift settlement was not in the royal interests. By the time the matter was decided, all concerned had gained in one way or another, but it also looked as if king, nobility and senior clerics were conspiring to plunder the Church for their own benefit, and the authority of Rome was being used to maintain the system. Rulers could not appoint bishops at will, and through them use ecclesiastical property directly, or interfere with ecclesiastical law as they pleased. But they could employ clerics as agents of government. Church offices therefore were the main source of income from which rulers paid their ministers. The number of royal officials multiplied, and papal dispensations enabled them to be paid out of Church funds; there were rules to be kept, of course, and there was nothing overtly corrupt about most of the transactions involved; but the conspiracy of exploitation of ecclesiastical resources was a fact.[18]

The papal legal traditions of law and government were unique in Europe, and they were valuable to society at large because they alone provided a living model for the new Europe, still learning the arts of civilized living, which is above all living with law. The older traditions in these matters had left little or no trace in the European mind or its institutions but the Papacy's legal system was intact; it gave them something on which the developing secular order of the times could build. The great lawyer popes from the time of Alexander III (1159–81) knew this and put the Church's expertise and knowledge at the service of society. They were clearheaded, men of principle and of great practical wisdom, and their leadership gave outstanding service to Europe. All this was much to their credit and much to the advantage of civil society, but it was involving the Church and the Papacy more and more in secular business and ways of thinking. From the thirteenth century the underfinanced Papacy[19] would be involved even more deeply in politics, and meeting its political obligations would lead it and its advisers into financial practices which did not sit well with the ideals which the Church existed to serve. Political involvements had equally undesirable spin-offs as they became engaged increasingly in the task of maintaining the Papal States. Here the Pope appeared to be just another ruler of a petty Italian principality seeking to sustain its power with the help of his own relatives, his nephews, cousins and kinsfolk generally, supporting the family interest which happened to be the Papacy.[20] It was a pattern of its nature inimical to the Papacy's true role in Europe's affairs which was that of spiritual leader and moral guide.

4 The growth of urbanization and piety: the Augustinians

From the tenth century the number and size of towns and cities grew and the service of the urban dwellers offered the Church new challenges and opportunities to which she responded spontaneously in a typical medieval fashion, through the initiative of some of her ministers at local level. The first group, the Augustinian Canons, emerged some time during the middle of the eleventh century. Their origins were as diverse as their initial organization was casual but as they grew in number the need for a rule became plain, and they adopted the simple one which St Augustine had provided for such simple communities.[21]

They were predominantly active and apostolic in their orientation but also included contemplatives – responding as they were to felt and immediate needs, their work was as varied as those needs. They restored churches and religious communities, ran schools, hospitals for the sick, for pregnant women, for the blind and lepers, and places of retirement for the aged, applying formerly misappropriated ecclesiastical tithes, which the Gregorian reforms were reclaiming, for these purposes. They were everywhere identified with the reforms and were a spearhead of them. Unlike the great monastic centres, their needs were simple, and large endowments for them were not required; those endowments they attracted as they established themselves were typically from townsmen who wanted to support a small Augustinian community in or near their town so that their families could benefit from its ministrations. They were the most prolific of all medieval religious orders; their foundations certainly must be numbered in many thousands in the thirteenth century and their ramifications were great.[22]

5 Learning and the universities

Though Greece and Rome, Byzantium, Islam and China had their systems of higher education, the university

> as a community of teachers and taught, accorded certain rights, such as administrative autonomy and the determination and realization of curricula [courses of study] and of the objectives of research and publicly recognized degrees, is a creation of medieval Europe which was the Europe of Papal Christianity[23]

Monasteries had been the most important centres of higher education in the early Middle Ages; what educational institutions there were in the cities declined with them, and the cathedral schools had wilted in the disorders of the time. The urban revival from about 1050, however, along with the Gregorian reformers' insistence on an educated clergy, and contact with Muslim culture, revived the schools; those in Paris, Rheims, Chartres, Laon, Tournai and Liège for example flourished, and it was in them that the northern university was incubated – most notably that of Paris where William of Campeaux (c. 1070–1121) and the brilliant but erratic Peter Abelard (1079–1142) taught.

The crucial development, which responded to the need to introduce some order in these schools, was the introduction of the *licentia docendi*, the licence to teach, which ensured the competence and responsibility of the masters and was made mandatory in the cathedral schools in the twelfth century; it was in fact the first university degree. Its introduction led to a proper system of training for those who wished to secure it, the formation of syllabuses, organized courses of study and graded examinations. The spontaneous organizational instinct of the times meanwhile led the increasing number of masters and students in the schools to form guilds, *universitates*, to protect their interests. These immediately attracted the interest of the Church because it was through them that academic and disciplinary standards could be established and maintained; they were also of interest to the secular authorities, initially because of problems of local order, but increasingly because they were a new, positive and vital element in urban life.

Hence the *universitas* of Paris obtained a royal charter in 1200 and a papal bull *Parens Scientiarum* in 1230. These confirmed its autonomy and ensured its academic standards; it had legal status. The *universitas*, a private organization, had become a university, public and legalized, autonomous under the law and capable of organizing its own affairs. There were two centres of higher education in Italy which predated Paris, namely Bologna and Salerno, specializing in law and in medicine respectively; in them the *universitas* initially had been of students, not masters, and other southern universities followed this pattern. But it was the northern universities, which outnumbered them seven to one, which were more significant in terms of Europe's intellectual revival and growth overall. There had been no Bolognas or Salernos in the north.

The long-term cultural influence of the universities, north and south, has been beneficial beyond measure to society in Europe, and they became the model for advanced education throughout the world. Some 72 of them existed by the fifteenth century, spread throughout Europe from north to south and from east to west, staffed by men professionally dedicated to a life of study and the search for knowledge, training generations of graduates who permeated society and served it in every profession and position of responsibility. If the universities were not ecclesiastical organizations they were always very close to the Church.[24] The university developed primarily out of the need of the reformed Church. The vast majority of the masters who taught in them were clerics; the most active agents in their spread were the reform popes who wished to see a rationally intelligible theology elaborated in response to controversies within the Church, and also required trained canon lawyers and administrators; they also sought to provide a counterweight to the political powers and regional feudal interests.[25] Several twelfth-century popes were university men and from the thirteenth most of them were. Papal involvement with the university movement seemed to make the world of study and of the Church one.[26] In particular it was the initiatives of the Papacy in providing for the sustenance of masters and pupils out of Church funds which made the universities viable.

Alexander III (1159–81), former Professor of Law at Bologna, decreed that proper examinations to judge the competence of teachers should be provided, and at the Third Lateran Council in 1179 it was confirmed that both the licence to teach, and the teaching itself, should be free; the masters were to be supported not by student's fees but by benefices, as also were approved clerics and priests studying there. It was this financial support which made it possible for the university system to develop and flourish. Princes and municipalities co-operated with the Church, or obtained the co-operation of the Church, in establishing them, but the entire material existence of academic institutions depended on her financial support. The Church was also the largest subsequent employer and wage-payer of university graduates after they had left the university, because they worked either for the Church or in the royal service paid by the Church through the benefice system.[27]

The studies and examinations, and degrees awarded were designed only to form academics. The bachelor's and master's and doctor's degrees and the *licentia docendi* equipped a man for this task, but in fact a university education became increasingly a characteristic of the elites not only in the Church, but in law, medicine and government administration, as well as in education. But while such vocational training became increasingly important, it took place in institutions whose fundamental aim and purpose – the search for and the honest love of knowledge – remained unchanged.[28] The academic ethic of the time was based on belief in a world made by God in which man made in God's image had to be free to seek the truth. Honest scholarship and teaching, respect for evidence, and openness to honest criticism and free debate were the way to it. Scholars were to be equal and in solidarity with each other, respectful of those who differed from them and ready always to rethink in the light of new knowledge.[29]

Finally, the assumption in the early days of university development was that all students were clerics, in at least minor orders. It was not an assumption that meant much, and it grew to mean less. Universities bred careerism and worldliness as well as love of truth, and the bawdiness and the disorder of so much of medieval university life was proverbial: but at their best they were true to their origins. For example, the scholars of such Oxford colleges as New College, Magdalen, Brasenose, Corpus Christi, Christ Church, Trinity and St John's were to proceed to priestly ordination after degrees or regency in order to promote the faith and welfare of the Church.[30]

The universities ensured that direction of private and public affairs was in the hands of men who had devoted a considerable part of their lives to severe and exacting mental labour. They offered a poor man of ability the opportunity to advance himself, and there was probably a larger proportion of the population receiving a university education at the close of the Middle Ages than was the case in the first part of this century. We think of medieval man as little concerned with intellectual matters, that it was the care of the soul, not the mind, that he concentrated on.

The existence of the universities should correct that view. The period was one of intense intellectual enthusiasm.[31]

It was in the universities that the science of theology was developed. St Anselm (1033–1109), pioneering theologian and teacher of the subject in the monastic school of Bec and later Archbishop of Canterbury, can be accounted the founder of this scholastic theology, as it came to be called; but it was Peter Abelard (1079–1142), of Chartres and Paris, who set the schools alight with the dialectic adapted from the lawyers and set out in *Sic et non* ('Yes and no'). This method, while having the good effect of opening up all questions to examination, required more positive and systematic development if it was to serve theology adequately, and that Abelard could not provide. The schools needed an influx of new ideas in order to enable them to do this, and the revival of Roman Law and the rediscovery of Greek learning mediated by scholars in Sicily and Arabic Spain provided the impetus required.[32]

Parts of Aristotle's works were coming to be known through translation in the West in the period between 1130 and 1180 but much of what was taken as by Aristotle was in fact the thought of his Muslim translators and commentators.[33] It was the problems raised by these commentators which were the main reason for the condemnations of Aristotelianism by the University of Paris and Gregory IX after 1210. The new and more accurate translations of his works made by William of Moerbeck (1215–86), a Flemish Dominican, made it possible to separate the Philosopher from his commentators and to cope with his insights.[34]

The key problem was the relationship between the truths of reason and the truths of faith. Aquinas[35] was the first to define the distinction with the requisite lucidity and precision. Faith and reason, according to Thomas, are different and mutually exclusive ways of apprehending truth. Faith is about things unseen, of which we have an imperfect understanding. Reason proceeds by way of demonstration and is able fully to comprehend what it studies. Some of the truths of faith may be demonstrable by reason; others may not, being beyond reason but not contrary to it.[36]

It is not our purpose to follow through the theological and philosophical questions which arise in this context, but the question of human rationality itself, and its relation to faith, is central to our basic enquiry because it affects the heart of man's self-understanding and the nature of those natural powers which are behind all human development, especially those which affect his life in society and its needs. It was the refusal to confuse what faith and reason can tell us which helped lay the foundations of those modern physical sciences which have come to man's aid in solving many of the problems of developing the world's wealth in the service of mankind.

For those sciences to be pursued, the first requirement was belief in the rational intelligibility of the world, and the second was belief that that world was created by God. The Greeks had the first but they lacked the second. The medieval scholar had both. Knowing that the world was rational, because it was created by God, he also knew it was inscrutable because God transcended human understanding. It cannot therefore be explored by human reason alone, but since it is material it can be investigated, researched into by empirical processes, and in this way man can learn something about God who made it[37]. In an age of faith this was a powerful motive for empirical research and Western man has continued this tradition long after faith has for many, faded.

6 St Bernard and the Cistercians

The foundation of the Canons Regular of St Augustine predates the foundation of the reformed Benedictine Order of the Cistercians by a few decades – an order which presages the second wave of revivals of religious life in this period. In 1122 the latter, at the time very small in numbers, attracted to its service the young Burgundian nobleman who came to be known as St Bernard of Clairvaux (1090–1153).[38] Within two years, and with the order in the first fierce vigour of reform, he was made abbot of a new foundation at Clairvaux. The Cistercians stressed once again the importance of simplicity and asceticism, making hard manual work a part of the life of the monk. Seven houses were founded in the first twenty years between 1098 and 1118: when Bernard died in 1153, there were 328, by 1200 the number was 525 and in 1500, 742.

The principles of the Order's organization equipped it well to work with the spirit of the time. Most importantly it was federal; the General Chapter of Abbots which met annually at Cîteaux in September legislated for the whole order of affiliated houses, and regular visitations ensured uniformity of practice, though with considerable local autonomy. It was a self-governing international organization and initially suffered little from internal disputes. It abandoned elaborate religious observances and liturgies, as well as the feudal obligations that monasteries had undertaken. Food, clothing and buildings were of the simplest. It wanted as little to do with the outside world as was possible.

Refusing to accept the usual means of support for monks, that is by income from property or feudal rights, the Cistercians had perforce to work the land effectively. This is where the first conflict with realities came. The spiritual obligations and the administrative work of running the monastery, combined with hard manual work in the fields, could not be reconciled for the choir monks; they continued to do manual work, but they could not sustain all the abbey's needs by it. To meet the situation, the order developed in a unique way the role of the non-choir monks, the lay brothers, those who were not destined for the priesthood; they undertook the heavy agricultural tasks for the whole community. For the first 100 years lay brothers, or *conversi*, far outnumbered the choir monks; at the time of St Aelred's death in 1167 there were 500 lay brothers to 140 choir monks at Rievaulx.[39] During the time of the order's greatest expansion down to 1190 there was no evidence that the position of the *conversi* caused any discontent, but thereafter there clearly was and the system gradually fell into disuse.[40]

The characteristics of Cistercian monasticism had made it one of the great agents of the land reclamation movement and of technical innovation in their time. The strictness of the rule which prevented them indulging in needless expense of any kind meant that they were accumulators of surpluses from their efficiently-run farms; since they could not accumulate gold, treasure or precious stones for the service of their churches they invested what they earned in extending their estates and increasing their efficiency in running them.[41] They also built new abbeys which were very advanced in their construction and facilities for their time. All were built to the same plan, and they used the best techniques in the daily operations of the monastery. Water power was adopted very effectively in them. At Clairvaux it performed four industrial functions, crushing wheat, sieving flour, fulling cloth and tanning. Monasteries in other regions adapted it to their needs; where olives were grown they were crushed by specially-made grindstones, where there was iron to be found, hammer forges were developed to exploit it. Running water was piped to the kitchens and to the gardens for irrigation; it was also used to cleanse the drains.

Three hundred and thirty-five Cistercian monasteries were set up in the thirty-five years between 1118 and 1153 and this helped the clearing of forest and marsh throughout the Western world, especially on its frontiers. In Aragon, Hungary, Poland, Sweden, Austria, northern England, Wales and the Scottish Borders, wherever the land was wildest and most neglected, they were pioneers. In time criticism was levelled at them for some of their methods and attitudes. Charges of being avaricious and acquisitive were brought against them.[42] Renouncing riches, they became rich and powerful because they invested wisely. This won them the resentment of those who sought riches but invested badly or not at all.[43]

The organization of the Order is interesting in terms of the political developments of the time. The annual general chapters, presided over by the Abbot of Cîteaux and at which all the abbots were expected to be present, were international assemblies which required considerable planning and organization, and in this they bear comparison with the general councils of the Church. They also bear comparison with the councils in their representative nature and in one respect went beyond them in this. Since the journey to the chapter could take as long as three or four months for the abbots from the more remote monasteries, and such long absences were not in the best interests of the religious life of the houses concerned, they were allowed to send representatives in place of the abbot in three years out of four. Overall the achievements of the Cistercian general chapters so impressed the Church by their effectiveness that the Fourth Lateran Council in 1215 recommended them to all other religious orders.[44]

7 The Church and the urban economy

The slowly reviving commerce of the West from the tenth century resulted in an expansion of urbanization and trade, industry, and commerce which continued through the next two hundred years. The pattern of trade initially centred round the Flanders–north Italian axis. The Italian cities of Venice, Amalfi, Naples and Gaeta had kept their contact with Byzantium and Islam in the early period, and acted as intermediaries with the poorer north, helping to keep alive what international trade there was. Pisa and Genoa, dependent on the sea trade, developed rapidly after they had gained control of the western Mediterranean. The northern Hansa (the word means 'group of merchants') developed a little later; the founding the town of Lübeck in 1158 marked its emergence, and the axis of its activities was London, Bruges, and Riga – the latter being the gateway to trade with Novgorod, Vitebsk and Smolensk in Russia.[45] The wood, wax, fur, rye and wheat of the north-east were traded with the wool, wine and salt of the west.

Venice, the city of sixty or so islands or inlets, had to obtain everything from trade except salt, but since she was not condemned to fight for her existence, as were Pisa and Genoa, she was able to concentrate her energies on developing the advantages she possessed in being in direct contact with the vast market of Byzantium. In the ninth century we hear of Venetians who brought the riches of the east, ribbons, ermine, balsam, spices, medicaments to Charlemagne, for which he traded horses, mules and Frisian woollen cloth.[46] Pisa and Genoa flourished along with Venice and their prosperity stimulated the economy of the inland towns on the fertile plains of Lombardy and Tuscany, Milan in the former, Florence in the latter especially; the consequent demand for food and other agricultural products also raised prices and increased the income of the farmers of the region. Population in the country areas rose and more workers were available for employment in the expanding ports and cities.

In northern Europe it was the clothmaking industry of Flanders which was the engine of development in the twelfth century. It was one of the wonder stories of medieval economic history, indeed the earliest case-book example of economic development as now discussed in relation to the underdeveloped countries.[47] It was made possible by the peaceful and orderly government the Counts of Flanders had established, the reclaiming of land from the sea, and the concurrent increase in population and agricultural production; population pressures encouraged emigration to the towns where the traditional clothmaking industry was ready for development; the skill of the craftsmen, the larger workforce, the availability of wood supplies from England, together with the vast market eager to absorb the high-quality cloths produced there, were the recipe for success. Bruges, the main port for handling the cloth in Flanders, came to be known as the Venice of the north, because of the prosperity the trade brought the town and the countryside around. The link with the Italians and the southern market established by contact with the Fleming merchants in Cologne, Paris and the 'fair' towns of Champagne, was the core of the commercial axis between north-west and southern Europe from the eleventh to the thirteenth century. The Florentines in particular appreciated the quality of the Flemish product, finishing it themselves to the requirements of their export market in the east.[48]

Until the twelfth century, the merchants tended to be itinerants. On land, they travelled in caravan, armed against possible banditry. At sea they went armed also for fear of pirates, and there was the added hazard of possible shipwreck. They originally traded each on his own account, their capital tied up in the stocks they took with them, but soon partnerships were formed between merchants, and risks and profits could be shared. The Italians were

leaders in this; from their offices in Florence or Milan they operated branches in whatever city they had business. Banking and
credit arrangements were the next development, and here the
Italians again were the leaders; the numerous Lombard Streets
which were found in cities throughout Europe were so called
because there the Italian bankers were to be found.[49]

A framework of industrial, commercial and financial practices of
which ours are the descendants was being established; a town-
centred commercial and industrial market economy was
flourishing and a productive agricultural sector was linked to it. The
long-distance trade was important but it was secondary to the mass
of transactions carried out locally. After 1150 Europe moved
beyond self-sufficiency in food and could support industrial expansion as the towns attracted the skilled crafts and monopolized
industrial production.

> Over a very wide area the crucial move was made from a domes-
> tic to a market economy ... the towns were beginning to tower
> over their rural surroundings, and to look beyond their imme-
> diate horizons. This was the great leap forward, the first in the
> series that created European society and launched it on its
> successful career. It marked Europe's true renaissance ... two or
> three hundred years before the traditional renaissance of the
> fifteenth century.[50]

Commerce from now on dominated the European economy, not
agriculture. Economic depression, periods of starvation and
plague, destructive wars it would suffer in the coming centuries,
but the European economy would never turn back on the progress
made in these years.

The cities were makers of their own destiny from the beginning.
The distinctive element in them was the merchant class which
made its appearance in the late tenth and the early eleventh
centuries.[51] The main influences on its development, and that of
its guilds, were the principles of voluntary association under religious protection which enabled their members to establish their
place in a feudal society. They were fellowships of the highway;
travelling together was essential for their protection, and at the
same time they were voluntary religious organizations, confraternities or guilds which were organized for social purpose under the
protection of a patron saint.

The first associations emerged in Flanders in the tenth century
under the protection of a fortified or an ecclesiastical town. They
gradually began to take responsibility for the needs of the growing

communities in those towns, and as they did so they produced the
structures of a new form of city government, unknown to the classical or the feudal tradition. It was the organization of a single
unprivileged class, a self-constituted group of merchants who
elected their own officials, looked to the good of their members
and raised funds for their common needs.

The general merchant Guilds were given valuable privileges by
those who granted them charters; so for example the Count of
Flanders in 1127 gave to that of St. Omers[52], freedom from tolls
among other concessions. They were also charged with supervision of
the crafts, and as their trade and the towns expanded, those which
dealt in one commodity formed their own specialized guilds. The
manner in which they began to deal in an unofficial way with all the
needs of the new urban communities distinguished them from the
cities of classical antiquity as well as the feudal society around them[53].
Eventually they developed as a power in their own right, taking over
the political, juridical, and military functions of the Bishops and the
feudal authorities and out of them rose the urban communes, associations of all the citizens, bound by oath to keep the peace, defend
common liberties and obey common officers. Often anti episcopal,
they were not anticlerical; many worked with the reform movement.

Craft guilds we hear of from early in the twelfth century.[54] They
too originated in confraternities or guilds with their charitable
educational and religious purposes serving many needs, one of
them being that of economic and trade organization. Men who
followed the same calling, living in the same area, worshipping in
the same church, buying and selling in the same markets, inevitably
combined for mutual protection and help.[55] This origin is reflected
in their history, in their building or maintaining their own church
or chapel and contributing to the upkeep of hospitals or charities.

Troeltsch speaks of 'the ethical significance of the medieval town'.
Feudalism never fully met the needs of the Christian life because of
its social distinctions and its violence. The city by contrast, was a
community of equals, free workers who needed peace so that they
could go about their business, earn their living and become men of
property. Politically and economically the towns laid the foundations of modern urbanized life, and the Church was an integral part
of them; its religious guilds and confraternities nurtured the guilds
and its commitment to the spiritual and material well being of the
citizens, its parish schools and its charitable work meant that the
churches framed the whole undertaking. The towns and the Church
also fostered an intense intellectual life[56] evidenced in the growth
and development of the Universities. The medieval cities were

crabbed and confined; there was always factionalism and conflict within them, and as conditions worsened in the later Middle Ages these became more marked; but its essential organization secured important civic values and functions on which later generations built. Above all it was based on free labour, and citizenship was open to all who would obey its laws. It was then much more real in terms of community than the privileged cities of the classical world. The common faith of the citizens, and the presence in their midst of a vital Church providing for their spiritual needs and in particular forming consciences with Christian ideals, aided the natural instinct of men to combine for common purposes.

8 The friars, lay piety, and heresy

The Augustinian Friars continued their fruitful apostolate in the towns. But the wealth and importance of the urban areas was growing, and with it the need for new initiatives by the Church to meet their needs – especially in the universities which were multiplying in them. It was met by the providential emergence of a new kind of religious order – the Franciscans and the Dominicans. St Francis was born in about 1180 in Assisi, an Italian town in Umbria some twenty kilometres north of Perugia, the son of a wealthy cloth merchant who traded in the fairs of the Champagne country, the cross-roads of the overland trade of an economically booming Europe. He was not happy however in following in his father's profession, and being an attractive and generous character he became the leader of the youth of the time. For a while he toyed with the idea of becoming a soldier, and indeed was captured during a minor skirmish between the citizens of Assisi and Perugia. In prison he underwent a conversion experience and became convinced on his release that he had to restore churches.

He took it upon himself to sell some of his father's goods for the purpose: this marked the final break with his father and the beginnings of Francis' lifetime's work. He went around proclaiming the kingdom as the Gospel inspired him to do, going barefoot and preaching repentance. His fellow citizens at first regarded him as demented, but his sheer goodness conquered; as the number of his disciples grew he drew up a simple rule of life based on the Gospel teaching on poverty, and he set off in the summer of 1210 to get for it the approval of Pope Innocent III. He got it; his Friars Minor were commissioned to preach repentance. St Clare, a young heiress of Assisi, who had followed his way, also received approval for her work.

Rapid growth meant that strict, literal, evangelical poverty was impossible. A regular and more detailed constitution was required if the Order was to serve the Church more effectively and carry on after Francis' death; a more stable and reliable source of funds was likewise needed if the young men who were preaching the Gospel were to be adequately educated for the task. The pattern of informal nomadic preachers of the good news, most of them laymen, supported mainly by manual work and, where that could not be had, by begging, was no longer the best way of fulfilling its mission.[57] By the time of Francis' death in 1226, changes were already in train. Over the next few years the new pattern of owning churches and permanent houses and of funding their maintenance was established. With these came a regular income, and in particular the means to train their men in the universities, but the controversies over Franciscan poverty were to continue for many years.

The growing strength of the Order of Preachers, the Dominicans, helped to shape Franciscan development. Though both were friars and involved in the urban apostolate the Dominicans were from the first a priestly order oriented to meeting the needs of the universities. Their founder Dominic Guzman, born in Castille in 1170 of wealthy parents, was a canon of the cathedral at Osma who in 1203 came in contact with the Cistercian mission which was countering the Albigensian heretics in the region of Montpellier; Dominic joined them, spending ten years on this task, and as he did so gathering around him a growing number of companions who became the nucleus of the Dominican Order. In 1215 Dominic attended the Fourth Lateran Council, where his work was approved by Innocent III.

It was in effect a new religious order with a constitution based on that of the Augustinians. Unlike older orders, the Dominican and Franciscan friars were not attached to one house; they took no vow of stability. They went where their work took them. From the first it took the Dominicans to the university towns. Seven of the first Dominicans were in Paris in 1217, others were in Bologna in 1218 and others in Oxford in 1221. The Franciscans were later drawn into university life by their need to train their future priests adequately, and were soon as deeply engaged in the intellectual apostolate as the Dominicans.

The popes were quick to appreciate how providential the appearance of these orders was. Honorius III (1216–26) saw that in them the Church possessed the means of carrying out the programme of conciliar legislation and providing the professors of theology the Church so needed. The discovery of the corpus of Aristotelian writings, interpreted initially by Arabic commentators, required able

Christian thinkers to meet the challenge. The friars proved apt for the task, and by the middle of the thirteenth century all but a handful of the leading theologians and philosophers in the universities were Dominicans or Franciscans.

One result of the new currents of thought was the reappearance of heresy, a problem which had hardly occurred in the previous period.[58] The first serious challenge came from the Cathars or Albigensians; it was against them that Dominic and his companions had originally contended. The creed was a strange mixture, there being much in it that attacked not only orthodoxy but civilized society; the idea of equal and opposite principles of good and evil was a denial both of the God of revelation and the possibility of social unity; the equation of marriage and prostitution[59] undermined the basic social institution, marriage and family life. The Waldensians, or Poor men of Lyons, were another dissident group who appeared about 1174 in Lyons, taking their name from Valdes, a rich merchant who had undergone a spiritual conversion, embraced poverty, went about preaching the Gospel and gathered disciples around him. At first approved, they were condemned by the Council of Verona in 1184; the sect thereafter scattered and spread its teaching widely in southern France.

Gradually it was recognized that something had to be done to try to counter the disturbances they caused and in 1153, at the Council of Tours, Alexander III instructed that the heretics were to be excommunicated and separated from the community: it was the beginning of a pattern of attempted repression which continued to develop. The heretic was bracketed with the infidel.[60]

The problem was that in medieval times Christianity was the basis of the whole social order and to preach heresy was to seek to destroy that basis; inevitably society tried to defend itself. In our day the racialists and the political terrorists seek to undermine our social order and we do what we can to thwart them. It was the public profession of heresy therefore, with its socially dissolvent effects, which was the problem, not dissent in itself. St Thomas More's attitude at a later time is here relevant. As responsible for public order he proceeded against those who were not content to keep their dissenting consciences privately instead agitating publicly, so threatening that order. When he, in his turn had a dissenting conscience against his king he specifically refused to encourage others to do the same, he kept his private conscience to the end, and died for the privilege. Had religious dissenters so behaved when he was magistrate there would have been no reason to proceed against them. His attitude was fair and just in both cases.

In tackling the problem of the Albigensians, Innocent III first
sought to persuade them, but when his legate, Peter Castelnau, was
assassinated on a mission to them in 1208, it was decided that
stronger measures were needed. So was launched the crusade which
was disgraced by the massacre after the taking of Beziers in 1209,
when some 7000 old men, women and children in the church of La
Madeleine were put to death. Innocent's purpose had been to bring
the wanderers back to the way of truth, not to exterminate them, but
such excesses were inevitable, given the nature of the times, once
military action had been decided on. Not until 1229, when King
Louis IX of France made peace with Count Raymond, did the
Albigensian wars end. In 1231 Gregory IX completed the basic legislation for what became the Inquisition, having power to punish the
unrepentant with spiritual penances or with flogging, the loss of civil
and political rights, banishment, deprivation of property and, in the
last resort, the death penalty.[61] The sentenced were to be turned over
to the civil power for the execution of physical penalties. The passing
of the death sentence was mercifully infrequent: Bernard of Gui for
example sentenced 613 persons before his court over a period of
seventeen years; of those 307 were imprisoned and 45 executed.[62]

The Inquisition was confined in the main to central and western
Europe; in the British Isles and Scandinavia it never operated. It
was active at times in Germany and Italy but not to the extent it was
in France, where it helped to bring the country under the control
of the French kings and therefore was supported by them. It was at
first only sporadically and never energetically active in medieval
Spain; the country was notably tolerant and treated the recon-
quered Muslims on the whole with fairness. It was the hold of
Ferdinand and Isabella over it in the late fifteenth century, and its
use for predominantly political purposes, which rightly gave it
notoriety.[63] It was at the service of Spain also when it was translated
to South America, where the Church's writ ran only under the total
control of the crown.

The lesson of the Inquisition is plain; active leadership and direct
involvement in secular affairs, no matter how socially valuable, in the
end puts the Church in a position where she takes on tasks which are
not hers to perform. The heretic in these years was one who threatened the basis of the social order and civilized life as well as the unity
and peace of the Church, and it seemed reasonable for the Church
to seek to defend herself and society against him, if necessary using
at one remove physical force and execution. It is precisely because
her mission is incompatible with such a course of action that we can
see that she must never find herself in such a situation again.

9 The Papacy loses control of reform

Until the 1240s, it looked as though the Papacy, with the friars as
its close collaborators and agents, would be able to consolidate
some of the wider aims of the reform. The great age of scholasti-
cism was yet to come, crowned by the achievements of St Thomas,
while the Franciscans, John of Plan Carpino and William of
Rubrouck, in 1246 to 1247 and 1253 to 1254 respectively, carried
embassies to the Great Khan in Inner Mongolia to try to mitigate
the latter's harsh policies in eastern Europe and open up the possibilities of new missionary endeavour.[64] But Gregory IX and his
successors Innocent IV and Martin IV were not in a position to
emulate Innocent III.

It was that continuing conflict between the Papacy and the
Empire which was the problem. In 1152 the prince electors had
chosen the Hohenstaufen Frederick Barbarossa as Emperor, and
his attempts to establish a strong basis in Lombardy brought him
into conflict with the Papacy, which feared his power would be
detrimental to its mission; it also brought him into conflict with the
Lombard cities who had no desire to lose their autonomy, and
their army defeated the Emperor's forces at Legnano in 1178.
Frederick's death on crusade in 1190 was followed by that of his
son Henry VI in 1197 and his widow Constance in 1198. On
Constance's death Innocent III claimed regency and the care of
the young Frederick II, on grounds of his sovereign rights, the
terms of Constance's will and his duty to protect orphans. In the
disputes over the imperial throne that now occurred Innocent
backed the claims of the young Frederick II who had undertaken
to abdicate as King of Sicily and separate it from the Empire, so
relieving the Papacy of the danger of the encirclement it feared. In
1216, however, Frederick reneged and further sought to bring all
Italy under his control, so bringing himself into open conflict with
the Papacy. His plan never had a chance of success. He lacked the
skills, the patience or self-control to follow it. He conceded too
much to the German princes in his effort to keep the peace there,
and he overtaxed Sicily to finance his interminable wars. He died
in 1250, excommunicated by the Council of Lyons, deposed and
facing rebellion throughout his kingdom.

The Papacy in one sense therefore emerged victoriously from its
struggle with the Hohenstaufen, but the cost at which it had done
so was a serious loss of moral prestige, given the political manoeu-
vring that was involved. Any attempt to grapple with the Empire
and the two Fredericks meant trying to outface them in a struggle

where power and its requirements was paramount, and it tainted all involved.[65] During the medieval period the Papacy never regained the control of the movement for reform which it lost in these years. Reformers were now predominantly anti-papal in spirit as were, for example, the spiritual Franciscans, Wycliffe, and the supporters of secular power, William of Ockham and Marsilius of Padua.

In the thirteenth century therefore the Papacy's international religious mission became obscured by its local political problems. It was apparently successful in the political battle, but the political means it had to use, and much more the spiritual weapons it overused, such as excommunication and crusade, were slowly eroding its moral standing. There was also the increasing problem of financing all this secular activity, the cost of which in one way or another had to be borne by the Church; the situation was worsened by the insecure basis of papal finances at the best of times, given the inadequacy of the revenues from the Papal States and the increasing cost of protecting and defending them.[66] Now her tax system had to be made as efficient as possible and the step from efficiency to the dangers of doubtful uses of that efficiency was a short one.

The political pattern of Europe now began to change also as the national monarchies of France and England in particular grew stronger. As they did so, they found it increasingly difficult to live with aspects of Roman Catholicism as an international Church, with its head on earth, the Pope, ruling it from Rome. It was around the reforming efforts of the Papacy that all had revolved in the last two hundred years, and it no longer had that role. As the Kings of England and France found themselves more and more aware of their power, they began to resent any form of submission to the Papacy in matters they considered were theirs alone to decide.

For fifty years following the death of Innocent III in 1215, however, a new period of stability and coherence in the culture of Christendom seemed established. By 1260 popular heresy had subsided, as the Dominicans and Franciscans met the needs of the urban Christians. France and England were ruled by saintly kings, St Louis IX (1214–70) and Henry III (1207–72), who respected Church and Papacy. The system of St Thomas Aquinas seemed to have reconciled faith and reason, while the building of the magnificent cathedrals and other churches gave an architectural and artistic witness to the same harmony of things.

St Thomas's synthesis also developed the Catholic tradition

towards a more positive acceptance of the political order at a time when there were true Christian kings in France and England; representative government was developing also, suggesting that its ideals were not impracticable. Meanwhile the defeat of the Hohenstaufen in seeking to defy papal monarchy appeared to confirm that those who did not accept this particular vision of the social order could be thwarted. Religious, cultural, political and economic developments in Europe seemed to be favouring the idea of Christendom.

Yet already the signs that challenged such an assumption were becoming clear. The death within the space of five years (1270–74) of St Louis, Henry III and St Thomas Aquinas, who represented so much of what was best in the lay life and the clerical life of the Church, and its harmonious coexistence in the creation of the new culture, turned out to be symbolic. The condemnation by the Bishop of Paris in 1277 of some of the errors of Averroism, which was taken as a condemnation also of Thomism, combined with the accession to the throne of Philip the Fair in 1285, with his new ruthlessness in the royal style of government, were portents of confusion and violence to come; the fall of Acre in 1291 also marked the end of the hopes raised by the Crusades, though they lingered on yet a while. The long period of economic expansion, population growth and inflation that had begun in the eleventh century, and which formed the right sort of economic background to the other achievements of the period, was coming to an end. Christendom was not to be triumphant; the next century reintroduced sufferings, savageries and violence that it had thought were behind it, and the ideal itself was to fade, in the fifteenth century, into insignificance in the affairs of Europe.

8

The Church and society in the late Middle Ages

1 Characteristics of the period

It is a truism that all historical periods are ages of transition: history is a record of change and development. But some periods are more markedly so than others and such was the late Middle Ages.[1] It was a time of political violence and confusion, of scepticism and negativism in theology and philosophy, corruption and schism in the Church. The economic expansionism which had marked the central Middle Ages now gave way to a period of decline and recession. It was a different prospect from that which the period of the papal monarchy at its best had offered: a vision of one Christian kingdom, a fellowship of nations under the spiritual and moral leadership of a reformed Church – free, chaste and Catholic – enjoying the fruits of a thriving economy under monarchies which were being modified by the parliamentary systems evolving in the thirteenth century.

Man needs a true vision to guide the social order if it is to serve his needs properly, and it can be argued that that of Christendom was as good as any offered to him before or since. But there is one serious reservation one must make. In the light of the Church's true mission it had a fatal weakness: it had required of the Church and the Papacy the role of secular leadership and involvement which they had had thrust upon them by events and which in the end undermined both. In the previous period good men with high ideals occupied the See of Peter and they were actively engaged in trying to improve the world of their time; in so doing "they tragically, perhaps inevitably, soiled their hands".[2] For all the idealism

* The notes and references for Chapter 8 are to be found on p. 394

of the endeavour, the price for the Church was some surrender of the spiritual and moral standards her founder gave her. All modern pleas for the Church to perform tasks which belong to the secular order should be measured by the experience of the medieval Church. The corruption brought on her by secular over-involvement severely undermined her true mission.

2 Avignon Papacy, Conciliarism and Renaissance

With the success of the reform movement, the Papacy was in a position to claim the right to judge the political order if it was found wanting. The implication of this was that as soon as the State or states recovered some coherence and credibility once more, they might well challenge this scheme of things. With the clash between Philip IV of France (1285–1314) and Pope Boniface VIII (1294–1303)[3] such a challenge came, and it did so at a time when the Papacy no longer held the moral high ground as it had during the eleventh century.

The new concept of royal sovereignty was abroad, and those who held to it resented the presence in their realms of a Church which claimed independence or semi-independence of them. The beginning of the conflict between England and France in 1294 led to increased expenses for their respective monarchs, and they made new financial claims on the Church within their boundaries. Philip IV and Boniface VIII clashed over the matter, with the former claiming the right to tax the clergy. Boniface, quoting canon law, denied that the king had power to do this and he published a bull *Clericis Laicos* (1296) which forbade all clerical taxation that did not have his approval. Philip brought the full force of his might to bear on the Church in France while stressing the State's right to tax the clergy in defence of the realm: Boniface was forced to concede in 1297.

In 1302 he returned to the attack with the bull *Unam Sanctam* which stated the extreme case of the supremacy of the spiritual over the temporal power and the necessity for salvation of submission to the Papacy. Philip, counselled by a new type of adviser, de Nogaret,[4] approved the seizure of the Pope by a band of mercenaries while he was staying at the papal palace at Agnani in 1303; he was rescued by the citizens, but the shock proved too great for him and he died a few months later. The incident was, as has often been noted, the antithesis of Canossa, where a Pope gave absolution to one who appeared before him as a penitent. Boniface had misjudged the situation, but he believed in law and the rule of law, in government of Church and State. Philip was shortly to show himself to be less confined by legality and truth in the suppression of the Templars.[5] The amoral advisers he had taken into his service had convinced him that the law was what he wanted it to be.

The period of dominance by the Papacy was now at an end, and it was increasingly under French influence. A French Pope, Clement V (1305–14), was elected and established his court at Avignon because of the political instability of Italy and Rome and also because Philip asked him to do so; though not strictly French territory, it was under the rule of the King of Naples, who was Philip's vassal, and in all other respects it was a French city.[6] In 1348, however, Benedict XIII bought it and it became formally a part of the Papal States. The cost of supporting the papal court at Avignon led to practices in church finances which brought forth further criticism of it and the Papacy alike, but contemporary charges of excessive luxury in a 'second Babylon' are not justified. The six French popes of the period were admirable men, competent, beyond moral reproach, and sincerely concerned for the Church's well-being, and the period in Avignon offered them the opportunity to sort out the Papacy's affairs. This was done, though the manner of its doing, especially regarding its financial affairs and the control of preferment for ecclesiastical offices in particular, was open to criticism. There was intense competition for these offices, and at every stage money came into the papal coffers on appeals and litigation. There were also annual levies on the clergy, and the sale of indulgences,[7] and to make sure they were all paid there was a papal collector in each metropolitan province of the Church; he deposited the sums collected with bankers who saw it was transferred to the Holy See, but more was spent on trying to recover control of the patrimony of St Peter in Italy than on the luxury and living costs at Avignon.

As a result of the Avignon reforms, disputes over episcopal elections were fewer, and better men were appointed to benefices which previously had too often been reserved for appointees of local nobility. Yet there were drawbacks also. The system offended vested interests and so provoked animosity. Pluralism and absenteeism remained rife, and to nationalists the whole system could be seen as a means of giving foreigners undue influence and taking large sums of money out of the country; yet it is likely, Keen suggests, that the system, with all its faults, was less easy to abuse than would have been any other system possible at the time.[8]

There was increasing pressure on the popes to return to Rome, and in 1376 Gregory XI did so. Tragically, he died within the year. Urban VI (1378–89) who succeeded him had been known for his austere mode of life and his efficiency. As Pope he sought to reform the cardinalate and make the Church more independent, but his manner was both truculent and violent, and support for him dwindled among the French Cardinals, who eventually withdrew it altogether, electing Clement VIII (1379–94) as antipope. The break was complete[9] and the states of Europe had to choose which pope to support; inevitably politics rather than the good of the Church determined choices.

Yet a third 'pope', Alexander V, was elected as a result of a Council at Pisa which had been called to end the schism. The position was worsened when Alexander died a year later, because Anti Pope who succeeded him as John XXIII was a thoroughly disreputable libertine. Finally the Emperor Sigismund forced the calling of a Council at Constance in 1414. John XXIII and Benedict XIII were deposed by it, and the Roman claimant Gregory XII agreed to go on condition that the abdication was received by a new Council called by his proxies; this was done on 4 July 1415. The circumstances since 1376 had encouraged discussion of church reform, as well as the means of ending the schism, and as a result there had emerged a conservative consensus, which said that radical reform was needed, either by making general councils superior to the Pope or by making him more accountable to them. Councils were being seen as superior to the Pope; they were the Church's sovereign body.[10]

Pope Martin V was elected by the Council of Constance in November 1417: the arrangement for the control of the Papacy by the Council was laid down in the decree *Frequens* which required councils to be called at stated intervals; proposals were also made for reform. In fact the Council was incapable of bringing it about. The five nations within it reflected nationalist and secular interests and the princes and kings wanted above all to control the Church in their own countries; reform was not their concern. They were opposed to papal taxation of those churches and this the Council limited; but the question of how the Papacy was to be financed, the problems of which had led to the practices they disliked, they ignored.[11]

As Constance had determined, another Council was called in 1423; it was transferred to Siena where it petered out for lack of interest. The next one was to be at Basle in 1431, Martin V dying before it met. Eugenius IV (1431–47) succeeded him and the Council duly assembled. Though bitterly divided at the outset, the majority of the Council accepted the Pope's invitation to reassemble at Ferrara, which it did in 1438: a rump remained in Basle and the two halves were in open opposition. The Council moved again to Florence in July 1439, and Basle became irrelevant; by 1447 the Emperor and most of the other crowned heads of Europe had abandoned it, so that the new Pope Nicholas V (1447–55) was able to effect the reconciliation of the last remnants of the schism by 1449.

The Popes who succeeded him over the next seventy years were caught up in the beguiling atmosphere of the Renaissance. Mainly Italians, they struggled to hold on to the Papal States, since Avignon had taught them that he who was not clearly a sovereign was soon someone's subject. Most of them were men of good life: one of them manifestly was not; but their fixation with the Italian problems of the Papacy which beset them, and with the need to stem the threat from the Turks, obscured the more fundamental task of church reform. Meanwhile, the power conceded to the northern churches in the Avignon period consolidated into a national church mentality. Corruption in the Church ran on and produced the conditions in which a demand for root and branch reform was conceded by default; when it came it was led by Martin Luther, and the Church itself was under threat.

The Renaissance context[12] also obscured the need for reform. The movement itself was not anti-Christian or anti-Church in itself: quite the contrary. It was born of Christian Europe and was part of a natural cultural development: the rediscovery of classical literature and the ancient languages of that literature could only enrich it. At the same time, the emphasis placed by it on the powers and the freedom of the individual, and the delights of civilized life in all its aspects, meant that it was in tension with the traditional emphasis; the latter had stressed that this life is a pilgrimage to the richer life of the next, gained by faithful service to God and the love of our neighbours. It did not exclude the enjoyment of its honest pleasures, but like its Master it stressed the dangers of the dishonest.

Nicholas V[13] was the first Renaissance Pope. A man of good life who avoided nepotism, he sought to put the Papacy back at the centre of things through its cultural leadership, but he initiated no reform. The three occupants of the Holy See between 1455 and 1471 were none of them unworthy of their office. Two were humanists and friends of the Renaissance but they did not allow it to cloud their vision; all three were concerned with the need for a crusade against the Turks and for church reform, but on both they were unable to make progress.

It was with the pontificate of Sixtus IV (1471–84) that the disastrous implications of the Papacy as a Renaissance princedom first became apparent.

Cardinal della Rovere was a theologian and a man of austere life. His administration was none the less scandalously corrupt and financially profligate. His nepotism was notorious, while his extensive building projects and his ill-advised political-military involvements put an immense burden on papal finances, so encouraging the raising of money by questionable means. To his credit was his support of humanism and scholarship, and his work in beautifying the city of Rome. Innocent VII (1484–92) was probably simoniacally elected and proved weak and indecisive at a time when effective government was needed. The financial difficulties of the Papacy resulted in further corrupt practices being encouraged during his pontificate: he was also a nepotist who used his office to advance the prospects of the natural children of his early unreformed life. But on his death there was worse to come, because the conclave was bribed to elect as Alexander VI (1492–1503) Rodrigo Borgia, an able man but one whose life after 40 years as a Cardinal was notoriously unworthy of that honour.

As Pope he continued in much the same way. He gave office to his illegitimate children and continued his immoral relations with women. Politically he faced a French invasion of Italy and the Franco–Spanish war to which it led, his policies always being conditioned by his family interests. He was a supporter of the arts, and it was he who commissioned Michelangelo to draw plans for the rebuilding of St Peter's. After the short pontificate of Pius III (1503), Julius II (1503–13), a nephew of Sixtus IV, was elected. He had fled Rome for fear of Alexander VII and served the King of France until he was able to fulfil his ambition of becoming Pope by plentiful promises and ample bribes. For the Papacy as a Renaissance princedom he was a good choice. He quickly crushed the Roman barons and organized the Papal States under his effective rule. As a nepotist he elevated only those who would serve the Church well, and when a Council was called in May 1511 to challenge him, he called his own, the Fifth Lateran, in 1512. A great patron of the arts, he began the building of the new St Peter's and laid the foundation stone in 1508; the sale of indulgences to meet the cost of the building was the immediate cause of Luther's revolt. Though he forbade simony in papal elections, he introduced no reforms. No pope until Paul III (1534–48) was sufficiently convinced of the need for reform to do anything effective about it, and so laid the Church hostage to a reform which split her.

3 Cross currents. Theology, devotion and sanctity

For all its problems, this period showed a vigorous manifestation of piety and a thirst for spiritual things, particularly among the laity.[14] It had been there in the early thirteenth century when the friars founded their third orders; it was from the preaching of the Dominicans Eckhart, Suso and Tauler in the late thirteenth and early fourteenth century that a corporate mysticism developed in the Rhineland and northern France and it was in this context that the Brethren of the Common Life, associated with Ruysbroeck (1293–1381) and founded by Gerard Groote (1340–84) flourished. There were other like movements, such as the Friends of God, groups of dedicated men and women in the cities of the Rhineland who sought a deeper spirituality in their ordinary lives under Dominican direction.

Margery Kempe, an illiterate Englishwoman who died in about 1440, attained high sanctity; her fame spread and accounts of her spiritual experiences were recorded and published. Julian of Norwich (d. circa 1413) was a mystic whose *Revelations of Divine Love* have been recognized as a classic, and St Bridget of Sweden (1303–73), an aristocrat who became a nun after her husband's death, went to France and then to Italy in 1394, possessed of the desire to help reform the Church; her revelations were published after her death, and the convent she founded at Vadstena became the centre of the Order of Brigettine nuns. St Catherine of Siena (1347–80) was the daughter of a guildsman; she achieved great holiness and worked for the reform of the Church, being influential in persuading Gregory XI to return to Rome. Her writings on spiritual matters have resulted in her being declared a Doctor of the Church.

There were also great saints among the clergy. In the first half of the fifteenth century St Vincent Ferrer, who was born in Valencia in 1350 and died in Brittany in 1419, preached throughout both Spain and France. St Antoninus of Florence (1389–1459), a Dominican friar, Archbishop of Florence, was famed as a confessor and director of souls, champion of the poor, confidant and adviser of Popes Eugenius IV and Nicholas V. He is one of the outstanding moralists of the Church, ranking with St Thomas Aquinas and St Alphonsus Liguori in his contributions in this field. St Bernardino of Siena (1390–1444), a Franciscan, evangelized tirelessly throughout Italy; he was an outstanding moral theologian, and the greatest preacher of his time, attracting thousands to his open-air sermons. Another Franciscan, St John Capistrano, who died of the plague in Hungary in 1456, had preached in Austria, Germany and Poland.

Yet piety and the search for holiness was no longer parallelled by comparable theological developments in the Church.[15] The Thomistic synthesis seemed adequate to meet the needs of a more demanding time and to provide the required healthy development in the life of thought and spirit, but that St Thomas himself had been sufficiently under suspicion as an Averroist to incur condemnation by the Archbishop of Paris in 1277 indicated that it was by no means as simple as that. Meanwhile Duns Scotus (1266–1308), a Franciscan who taught at Oxford, was one among many who challenged St Thomas's Aristotelianism; he did not intend to undermine the tradition of positive philosophy and theology within which St Thomas stood, 'but after the supreme medieval synthesis of Thomism ... the moderate criticism by Scotus prepared the way, as a matter of fact, for the radical and destructive criticism which is characteristic of Ockhamism'.[16]

The Franciscans numbered among them the Spirituals who considered it against the spirit of their founder that the Order should own property.[17] They rejected the Pope's insistence that property was in accordance with the Gospel and St Francis' teaching, and demanded apostolic poverty for the whole Church. William of Ockham (d. 1350), an Oxford Franciscan, developed Scotus's theories to arrive at a radical nominalism; we could in no way demonstrate God's existence by rational argument – faith and revelation alone had to be our guide. He was a supporter of the Spiritual Franciscans in their dispute with John XXII (1316–34) on the question of property and papal temporal power and took refuge at the court of King Louis of Bavaria where he found Marsilius of Padua (d. 1343), likewise in conflict with the Papacy over his views. They posited a totally lay State, with the Church and religion having no active part in guiding it – and both would be entirely under the control of the ruler.[18]

4 Political and social violence

From the eleventh century a consistent effort was made to reduce the level of violence in Europe, and it was not entirely unsuccessful; in the fourteenth and fifteenth centuries this trend was reversed. Warfare was more widespread and prolonged during this period than before.[19] The conflict between England and France which dragged on intermittently between 1337 and 1453, and has come to be known as the Hundred Years' War, was the most destructive.

The kings of England, as successors of a Norman baron, still had extensive lands in France and were therefore vassals of French kings who were determined to retrieve these lands. Philip Augustus (1180–1223) was able to deprive John (1199–1216) of Anjou and Normandy and all but a portion of Acquitaine. The kings of England were equally determined to regain them and Edward III (1330–77) decided to force the issue so that by 1337 the two nations were at war. The French armies proved to be less well trained and led and were outdated in arms and tactics; and the victories by the Black Prince at Crecy in 1346 and Poitiers in 1356 shattered French military power. Two decades of exposure to roving armies and armed bands who plundered and massacred, enraged the French peasants, and in 1358 the Jacquerie from Picardy to the Seine rose in revolt, and was duly crushed.[21]

Social unrest intensified. Revolts against taxation took place in Paris in 1382. Flanders had long been agitated. There were five years of civil war in defence of the liberties and privileges of the people from 1323 to 1328, and divisions between towns and crafts later caused more civil conflict. A time of comparative quiet after 1361 was followed by another series of upheavals from 1379, in which the weavers, aligned against the nobles, merchants and craftsmen, after some initial success, went down to defeat in 1382.[22]

The Peasants' Revolt in England was partly sparked by the war in France which, by the 1380s, was going badly for her. The revolt affected all areas from the Scottish borders to the south coast and it forced the young king Richard II to make concessions. His people trusted him, but once revolt had subsided, the promises were forgotten and repression was the order of the day.[23] Florence had experienced disturbances since 1340 because of discontent over taxes, the food supply, and wages. Not only were the poorer workers badly paid, but inflation was eating away the value of money, and they were allowed no right of association in their own defence. The protest was initially that of the more affluent workers who were being denied advancement, but the lesser arts or guilds gradually took the lead, with the *Ciompi*, the lowliest of the woollen workers among them, being the most vociferous. For a moment it seemed the rebellion would succeed, but a counter-revolution violently restored the position of the greater arts or guilds, and the *Ciompi* and their friends returned to their obscurity.[24]

The disturbances in Europe caused by the Hundred Years' War overlapped therefore with social and economic conflict resulting from economic decline, and the effects of the Black Death (1347–50) on society. In France, the victories of Henry V (1413–22) and subsequent events led to his being recognized as heir to the French throne in 1420, but he died of camp fever in 1422 before he could claim it. Not till the Siege of Orleans in 1428, and the intervention of Joan of Arc, did the tide begin to turn for the French.[25] Joan was a peasant's daughter who claimed she had a mission to rescue Orleans. This she did and she won another great victory at Patay in 1429 before she fell prisoner to the Burgundians, was handed over to the English and burned at the stake in 1430. In 1456, just three years after the invaders departed from France with Calais alone left to them, a new court vindicated Joan.

5 Economic and social decline and revival[26]

The period of growth that had begun in the eleventh century ended in the late thirteenth. The problems became apparent in the years 1290–1320; famines recurred and the price of cereals rose sharply. There was a series of bank failures as the inability of monarchs to pay their debts ruined their Tuscan financiers, and these badly affected trade, finance and industry. Population was no longer increasing, the mining of silver and gold slowed down, and the textile industries of Flanders and Italy, engines of the expansion of industry, trade, commerce and finance in the previous two centuries, saw demand for their products dwindle.

The problems were compounded by specific and catastrophic events which were unique and extraordinary. The early fourteenth century, for example, experienced unusually cold weather, which marked the beginning of a new minor ice age, lasting until the 1700s. In the years 1303 to 1308 the Baltic froze over, and cold, storms and rain of unusual and unseasonable intensity were experienced. The colder weather affected the delicate balance between population and an agricultural technique not developing rapidly enough to meet its needs properly.[27] In 1315 heavy rains destroyed crops throughout Europe and widespread famine was the result. The effect of the Black Death, bubonic plague, on a society which had already been weakened in so many ways was therefore multiplied when it struck. It ravaged Europe between 1347 and 1350 and killed at least one third, 20 million, of its people, at a conservative estimate.[28] The death of so many was, apart from all else, an economic disaster whose effects were felt down to the next century; it was growing population which accompanied the previous prosperity; its decline was hastened by the sudden reduction. Meanwhile brigandage and wars continued to take their toll, as did the sporadic recurrences of the plague which afflicted particular areas over the next fifty years.

When things settled down, it became clear that the devastation of the plague had left the peasants in a strong position. Rents were reduced, even waived, so desperate were owners to get their land in production again. Where they could not, many villages in areas where the land was poor were turned over to sheep pasturing. Prices rose, and the inflation reduced the value of the rents received by landowners, leading to governments attempting to maintain old wage rates by law, as with the Statute of Artificers in England in 1351. In France legislation more reasonably allowed some readjustment upwards, but the repeated attempts to apply both measures indicates their widespread inefficacy. The underlying discontents of the people as a result of these efforts, added to those which affected workers in the textile-producing regions as markets collapsed,[29] and the terrible sufferings that the war between France and England imposed on them, contributed to the social upheavals of the period – the Flemish revolt of 1323 to 1328, the French Jacquerie of 1358 and the English Peasants' Revolt of 1381.

The first decades of the fifteenth century did not augur any improvement, but mysteriously by the 1450s it was clear the tide had turned. Population was increasing and with it came the increase in prices of agricultural products, and in wages for the initially still scarce labour; more land was also brought under cultivation to meet the demand as prosperity returned. For the rise in population no clear cause seems to present itself, but of the fact there is no doubt. For the next two hundred years from 1450, Europe's second period of economic expansionism, its second logistic as Cameron calls it, saw a steady such increase; by 1650 Europe's population had increased by two thirds. None the less, the accumulated effect of natural disasters and war did not dispose the economy to steady development. Violence and uncertainty had created local scarcities, destroyed accumulated social capital, and driven from their homes those who had been reduced to destitution by this combination of disasters, leaving them to wander from place to place. Violence notoriously breeds violence: banditry was rampant, the social structure challenged.[30]

There were however more positive aspects to the times. The achievements of the previous period could not be entirely destroyed. Agriculture, commerce, industry and business organization had been revolutionized during it and this provided strong foundations for future development down to the nineteenth century.[31] However, many were not greatly helped by the social

and economic changes. Death and inheritance led to a concentration of wealth, and a minority possessed increased purchasing
power as their conspicuous consumption made plain. By contrast,
those at the bottom of the social scale, the lowest third or quarter
of the people, were worse off in the fourteenth and fifteenth
centuries; certainly the number of paupers grew.[32]

9

The Church and politics in the central and late Middle Ages

1 The Church and social solidarity

As we have seen, 'it is not possible in studying the medieval world to distinguish between the history of the Church and that of secular society.'[1] F.W. Maitland insisted that there is no acceptable definition of the State which would not include the Church. She was a sovereign power, she made law and applied it through her own courts and had judges and lawyers to do so. She possessed an elaborate system of appeal, an imposing bureaucracy, with a centralized administration with its own permanent officials, visited and supervised by its own legates.[2] She raised her own revenues and dispensed them, in so doing profoundly influencing many aspects of economic life. The circumstances of society and civilization of the time gave her a role in political and military leadership in matters which concerned Christendom.

The social ideal held out was unity based on the oneness of all men in Christ – solidarity – and it was by baptism that one entered European society. In that society marriage, the basis of the family and society, was blessed by the sacramental seal of the Church.[3] As result of her influence there was, despite the brutality of the times, an emphasis on brotherhood, the equality of men and the value of the individual. The parish guilds and confraternities fostered the human instinct of social co-operation.

Solidarity was imperfectly achieved. The distinction between clergy and laity frequently seemed to imply second-class Christian status for the latter. The conflict of Church and State had a disturbing effect on cultural unity on many matters and occasions. Social

* The notes and reference for Chapter 9 are to be found on p. 396

conflicts and violence were endemic because of the nature of feudalism and the tendency to exclusiveness of the privileged classes in the towns. Heresy, which was of its nature socially divisive, was in part a reaction against the corrupt aspects of clericalism. The Inquisition and persecution of dissenters was the result of the over-involvement of the Church in secular affairs. The maltreatment of the Jewish people was a denial of solidarity.[4]

The limitations on solidarity were therefore real, but its achievements were real also. Medieval society was clearheaded about social problems and finding solutions to them. The Church, present throughout society at all levels, sought to make sure that Christian principles were applied in a broad range of human affairs. The merchant, the manual worker and the farmer were well-pleasing to God if they faithfully fulfilled their duties in life and work; every order and profession had, in the Catholic faith and doctrine, a rule suited to its quality which could assure a man's salvation, as St Bernard taught. The medieval Church has been much criticized for giving no place to the lay professions, but this criticism is not well-founded.[5]

The society in which the Church existed was feudal society. It was not favoured by the Church initially; she preferred a strong civilized monarchy which would give justice under the law and protect the weak. But society had evolved an alternative form in the light of its needs, and its legitimate autonomy demanded that the Church accept it. The mass of the ordinary people were peasants, and in the eleventh century most of them were serfs, tied to the land but with accepted rights. Gradually over the next three centuries they gained their freedom.

2 *The main principles of political theory in the Middle Ages*

The political ideas of the early Middle Ages were derived from the classical writers, the Scriptures, the Fathers and the Germanic tradition. In the ninth century there were three such,[6] centering around the concepts of (i) freedom, (ii) the foundation of the political order in God and (iii) the need for law to check the possibilities of injustice. The first was implicit in the Scriptures, asserted by Cicero and taken up by the Fathers; basically, human nature was one, and all men were in that sense equal and free.[7] Man's weakness and faults produced the social conventions which limit that freedom. The second conviction was also Scripture-based: that the political order was God-ordained. Divine right theory, however, was being

eased out by the idea that the king could be removed if he did not
rule in accordance with justice.[8] The third principle, found in the
classical and Roman tradition, was that it is law, not the ruler, which
is supreme. Law requires the assent of wise men representing their
community; the lawmaker gets his authority not directly from God
but indirectly. He gets it directly or immediately from the people.[9]

The typical political ideas of the central Middle Ages concerned
(i) justice and the political order (ii) law and justice and (iii) the
relationship of ruler and ruled. The first was that the purpose and
function of political authority and organization is ethical – to give
justice. The second specifies the first: justice is established by the
supremacy of law which embodies it. The third concerns the relationship between ruler and ruled; this is founded, and depends on,
the mutual obligation and agreement to maintain justice under
the law; agreement on this establishes political society.[10]

The first of these was a principle of both Roman and canon law
and was equivalently contained in the barbarian tradition. It was
embodied in the feudal law and its courts were concerned with
applying it. The king's authority, Bracton said, is one which has as
its purpose the doing of right, not wrong, judging with equity and
mercy.[11] That St Augustine had seemed to deny that the State can
provide justice did not affect the general opinion. The second
principle was the supremacy of law as the embodiment of justice.
The king is then elected to do justice to all men; God is giving
justice through him because law requires someone to enforce it. In
this capacity therefore the king is God's vicar on earth, to judge
right from wrong, just from unjust, so that none harms another
and all may live at peace. The king

> has his title from the fact that he governs well, and not from the
> fact that he reigns, for he is a king when he governs well, but a
> tyrant when he oppresses the people entrusted to him.[12]

Though subject to no man, the king is under the law by which he
became king; he is also under it because he is God's vicar, subject
to the law lest his rule be unrestrained.

The third principle was that the relation between king and
people was founded and depended on the mutual obligation of
maintaining justice and law. Belief in the supremacy of law and king
was one thing, but the procedures which would enable that justice
to be given effectively and constantly were less easy to provide. The
most fundamental requirement was a method of ensuring that the
right sort of ruler would emerge and that he would, once in office,
provide the justice which was the purpose of his rule. While gener-

ally respecting the hereditary right of the eldest son to succeed to
the throne, it was required that the succession should have the
consent of bishops and chief men of the realm, representing the
whole community, and that during his reign the king should
continue to administer the State with their advice and judgement.[13]
These provisions were intended to guarantee that the king's rule
was not arbitrary, that he did preserve the justice that was present in
the law. That the king could not be expected to handle the affairs of
the kingdom and give justice without the advice of the representatives of the community, is the key to later constitutional
developments. Implicit in it was the social contract, and the possibility of challenge to the king if he did not rule justly.

Manegold of Lautenbach elaborated such a theory in the
context of the conflict between Henry IV and the Papacy. No man,
according to Manegold, can make himself king or emperor; the
people elect someone to that position in order that he may protect
the good and punish the wicked, administering justice to everyman. If he violates this agreement and disturbs what was entrusted
to him to order justly, he has broken the faith that bound him to
his people and they are consequently free from their obedience to
him. This was not an eccentric view but probably represented that
of the majority of canonists at the time. In the case of the king
becoming a tyrant he has violated that agreement (*pactum*) that
validated his right to rule[14] and his people are released from obligations which depended on his keeping faith. Manegold is giving
the first formal expression to what we know as the theory of the
social contract. But as Manegold lays it out it is not constructed

> on some quasi-historical conception of the beginnings of politi-
> cal society but rather represents the constitutional principle of
> the medieval states as embodied in the traditional method of
> election or recognition and its reciprocal oaths of the corona-
> tion ceremonies.[15]

The king was not absolute; his succession depended on the
consent of the people through the council of the great men, and if
the monarch broke the terms of the agreement which led to his
being accepted, then the people could be absolved from their
oaths of allegiance.

The emergence of the Papacy as apparent victor from the conflict
over investitures seemed to change the balance that the Gelasian
theory assumed, making it appear that the Pope was superior to the
Emperor in political matters. Yet that theory was still the general
understanding of the relationship between the two powers. Where

they differed was on what constituted the divine law under which both State and Church operated. Some papalists seemed inclined to claim that civil law should always cede to canon law when they clashed; others pointed out that fallible human judgement was all too evident in the latter; it was Innocent III himself who cautioned that the judgement of God is always true but that the judgement of the ministers of the Church in practical matters could be in error.[16]

Gregory VII in practice only claimed that authority over the Emperor Henry IV which he had over any other Christian, including the right to excommunicate them in certain circumstances. His conclusion that he had a right to depose rulers seems to have arisen from his belief that excommunication of the king in a Christian society would have made his position untenable and therefore would imply loss of authority as king.[17] That he did not think that he had himself assumed supreme power in the State by deposing Henry is shown by his actions in 1076. The resolution of matters between the Emperor and his challenger Rudolph was for the German people to determine; if he was to be present at their deliberations it was only by invitation, and the role he sought in them was that of mediator. In the thirteenth century the popes who followed Innocent III (1098–1215) seemed to their opponents to have extended the Church's claims to authority over the State beyond all reason. To those who defended the Church's position it appeared that, on the contrary, she was only engaged in necessary self-defence; we will look at these matters a little more closely below.

3 Political organization and the development of representative government[18]

The principle of representation 'means that one or more persons stand or act on behalf of others and that, at least for the purposes at hand, an identity of interests between them is assumed'.[19] Representatives are more than mere delegates of constituents; they owe those they represent not obedience but judgement, knowing they are responsible to those whom they represent. Representative government evolved when medieval civilization was in full flower and was 'the natural and logical outcome of its political conditions and ideas.'[20] This judgement regarding 'the ubiquity of these [representative] assemblies in Latin Christendom from the thirteenth century' has been corroborated by the researches of the last thirty years.[21]

It is in Spain, at Laon in 1188, that we first have record of representation of all three classes, or estates, of society in a national assembly, and by the end of the next century such representative assemblies were to be found in all the kingdoms of Spain, and widely throughout Europe generally.[22] They were, then, a Christian European phenomenon; no one country can claim the distinction of developing them out of its own genius. Accidental factors, however, resulted in representative institutions taking root in England so firmly that they survived essentially down to our own times, and the manner of their doing so has a special significance.

The foundations of the English system were laid in the Anglo-Saxon period. The beginnings of Parliament itself have their origins in the meeting of the folkmoots; these were restricted assemblies of local lords, lay and ecclesiastical, together with royal officials, and were held usually at the time of great feasts such as Easter or Whitsun. These the Normans incorporated into the state structure[23] and by the time of Henry I (1100–1135) they had become a fixed tradition, described as *curiae* or *consilia* and eventually, Parliaments.

King John's arbitrary rule at home and his disastrous adventures in France finally exasperated the northern barons in particular and they persuaded the rest to refuse to pay the taxes being levied on them; instead, at a conference in London in January 1215, they demanded once more their ancient and accustomed liberties.[24] John sought compromise, accepting the main complaints and making concessions. Under the guidance of the Archbishop of Canterbury, Stephen Langton, a group of counsellors acted as mediators and on 19 June the charter was signed. The Church's rights were guaranteed, as were the liberties and customs of all cities, boroughs, towns and ports. Traders were given freedom to come and go as they wished except in time of war, and standard weights and measures were guaranteed to consumers. Local abusers of power, and the oppressive activities of forest officers in particular, were also restrained, and among the judicial provisions was included the assertion that no freeman would be proceeded against except by due process of law. Penalties were to be proportionate to the offence and no freeman, merchant or villein was to be penalized to the point where he was deprived of his livelihood.

The Great Charter was not a revolutionary measure; it simply bound the king and his servants to observance of established custom. But he could no longer disregard the law; if he did he could be restrained by the national community which was given the legal right of resistance to him. The victorious barons, however, showed that they had no intention of abiding by that law once they were in the ascendant. John appealed to the Pope, who condemned the whole proceedings and their outcome, the king dying during his attempts to quell the baronial rebellion.[25] The value of the Charter is that it stands as the first firm step towards formal representative goverment and then its democratic form. William the Conqueror had left to his heirs the strongest and best founded state in Christendom, and Stephen Langton, in acting as mediator, was carrying on the tradition of the English Church in resisting excessive royal power – St Anselm had stood out against William Rufus, St Thomas of Canterbury against Henry II. As in the time of Anselm and Thomas Becket,

> had the power of the clergy not checked the monarch's power the course of English history might have been very different. For the monarchy fastened on England by the Norman conqueror was a tyranny in the making.[26]

The next major stage in the development of representative government[27] after the Great Charter came in 1264. The king, Henry III (1234–72) had increasingly angered the nobility with what they saw as his unpredictability, incompetence and extravagance,[28] and Simon de Montfort, Earl of Leicester, rebelled and defeated the royal forces at Lewes in May 1264. To muster fullest support he called a Parliament in January 1265 and to it not only the greater nobles and the royal officials, but two knights from every shire, and two burgesses from each town. This pattern of Parliament became established by 1295 as the model, though it had yet to establish itself as normative. Only a few of the next twenty Parliaments were fully representative; some of them had no representative of the towns at all.

Within the Parliament, the knights, realizing they were closer to the prosperous burghers than to the great barons with whom they had traditionally been allied, began to identify with the Commons in petitions for legislation. The burghers generally, however, were not initially enthusiastic participators in the affairs of State and did not always respond to the summons to attend; the expenses to the borough were quite considerable and the inconvenience to those chosen was often resented as it was seen as a duty, not a privilege. Sometime about 1450 this changed; being a member of Parliament was appreciated, probably as a result of a growing sense of national unity and spirit. Henry VIII's need for the support of the Commons in the 1530s established its power firmly, though from then on it was controlled by the aristocracy.[29] Its numbers increased as a result of the Crown's interest in packing it with its friends; eldest sons of peers sought membership, the merely wealthy bought boroughs to provide themselves or their friends with seats. Not until the reform of the franchise in the second half of the nineteenth century did the pattern change and the Commons begin to represent the commons with any fidelity.

4 The Church and politics

(i) The papacy, the Church and temporal authority

The key figure in the later developments in the relationship between Church and State was Innocent III, who stressed that as the Vicar of Christ the Pope has authority not only over all the faithful and the Church universal but over the world (*saeculum*) also.[30] However, he did not bring out the full practical conclusions of such a theory as it affected the relationship between the Papacy and the Emperor; his successors and their advisers were to do that.[31] His claims however were far-reaching.

In the crisis following the death of Henry VI in 1197, two lines of thought concerning that relationship were developed. The first was that set out by Hugh of St Victor: that in the Old Testament the priesthood had provided the leadership for the chosen people, and that in the New Testament, Christ's Vicar has the same role in his Church. The dual functions of the king and the Church existed within this framework; the Church was one body under the control of its head on earth, the Pope. Innocent III then applied this idea to his relationship with the imperial power in the new situation. Since it was the Pope who had translated the empire to the Germans in Charlemagne's time, the Pope had the right to verify any election of an emperor, scrutinizing the choice and vetoing it if the man chosen was judged unworthy. If he was confirmed, he was anointed and crowned by the Pope, receiving his sword from him.

From this the decretalists concluded that, in the language of the time, the Pope possessed the two swords.[32] This phrase is taken from Luke 22:38 where, before his Passion, the uncomprehending disciples offer Christ two swords, as if he wished to see them used in his defence. By allegory, commentators saw this event as relevant to Church–State relationships; one sword was Paul's 'sword of the Spirit' (Eph. 6:17) wielded by the priests; the other was the sword used by power of the civil authority in punishment of evildoers. Both were needed in the Christian warfare against evil. The king fights with the material, the priest with the spiritual sword.

The imperialist case was that the two swords implied the autonomy of the State, which possessed the temporal sword, and the Pope had no authority over it. The papalists claimed that, on the contrary, the Pope held both, and could use them both. It was not a claim that had arisen during the investiture controversy but from remarks of St Bernard of Clairvaux in 1150 in which he suggested that the Church could direct the king to act on her behalf in temporal matters, and from this it was concluded by some that this was a general power of the Church. It was also assumed by some that, if he did not do so, the King would be failing in his duty, and could be deposed.

The matter was of practical relevance in the deposition of Frederick II by Innocent IV in 1245. The decree of deposition stated that it was Frederick's lack of penitence for his evil deeds which made him unfit to be the Holy Roman Emperor and king of Sicily. It was God who cast him out; the Pope simply declared the judgement. The consequence was that all Frederick's subjects were released from their obedience to him; they were excommunicated if they maintained that obedience, and the imperial electors were ordered to find a successor to the deposed monarch.

The predicament of the Church and Papacy in face of Frederick II had been a real one, and one which showed the impossibility of popes ever being able to act as a moral arbiter of princes in any way which left them with their spiritual and moral integrity intact. Frederick had determined to restore his divided and disorganized realm. But to do this he would have had to live in Germany and work patiently at the task, avoiding conflict with the Papacy and the communes, and resisting the lure of imperial ambition. He was incapable of doing either. His heart was in the warm south, and he wanted to bring both Italy and Sicily under his autocratic rule and unite them with Germany in one great Empire.

> The scheme was a chimera, opposed equally to the interests of the Papacy and to the passion of the Northern communes for republican autonomy, and it led to the fall of his house and of the Empire itself.[33]

Faced with so unscrupulous a ruler, the Papacy was in a no-win situation. The idea of the two powers in Christendom those powers balanced but co-operating for the common good, always assumed they were bound by the same moral law and were in some way equal in authority and power. But experiences with Frederick II and Philip IV showed that the same morality did not apply. Where the Church was at her strongest and the ruler weak, she could hold her own, but where both were at their strength, the latter would always win because the secular authority was backed by armed force of its own which the Papacy could not match; it also had many other ways of bringing pressure to bear on the Pope and the Church at all levels, irrespective of moral considerations.[34] The Papacy could only use its power where the mood of the time allowed. It could not match any strong State in the worldly means of enforcing policy when it did not; in so far as the popes did use such means there were always limits to their ability to do this, limits imposed by the fact that it was the Papacy and the Church that was involved; some moral restraints therefore always existed. At the same time they could no longer claim that they occupied the moral high ground once they became involved with political and military means to their ends.

Marsilius of Padua and William of Ockham were to make the arrogance of papal claims, as they saw them, a particular object of their attack on the Church as the obstacle to imperial and Italian unity. In truth, Europe's problem was one of the historical weakness of the civil authority, and the Papacy's concern had always been to secure sound government to protect the weak, and to defend the Church's right to carry on its mission. The failure to bring order out of the chaos of European politics was due to the secular rulers, emperors, kings and princes, choosing to follow their own sectional interests and disregarding the common good.

The Church had direct political power because of her services to society in the first instance, services she undertook because they were essential for the social order, not because she wanted to control society or State, and she served a weak and insecure society well by her actions. It was the Church's services to Europe in secular terms which gave it its political coherence, replacing that given it initially by Imperial Rome, just as she had played the major role in forming a culture which was becoming sufficiently politically conscious to claim the right to control its own destiny. The result was that she was embedded in the political structures of the time in a way which did not sit well with her primarily spiritual role, and as the states of Europe grew stronger they resented the Church's power; they did not reflect that it was because the Church had been there to take the lead when they were not able to do, that they now had a chance to develop their own polity. They saw the Church as the power-hungry intruder. Some popes were extremely political, and many thought it was the only way they could sustain the independence of their spiritual role. But initially she was no intruder, but, as Mundy put it, she was elected to lead Europe because at the time no other could.

Did the Church try to establish the idea that it was superior to the secular authorities? It is R.W. and A.J. Carlyle's claim that ultimately the dualism inherent in the Gelasian theory was always dominant in principle. Watt on the other hand argues that increasingly the unitary view dominated.[35] Whatever the theories behind the actions, the State was always in charge when it chose to be so; the problem was not that of unitary Church authority, which would always lack teeth, but the threat of a unitary secular authority which had very sharp teeth indeed, backed up as it was by force, and sometimes brute force. It was against the unitary power of Imperial Rome that the Church had struggled in the early days and, in surviving it, had given to the Western world the idea of individual freedom against the almighty State. In insisting on the independence of the moral and spiritual power in the Middle Ages, even if she did so somewhat over-zealously, she was, as the Carlyles point out, still defending the freedom of the individual conscience against the State.[36]

(ii) The Church and representative government

In that the Benedictine rule provided a constitution for a self-governing community, electing its abbot to rule in consultation with the brethren, the early Middle Ages had, in the life which was accepted as a Christian ideal, an example of government under the law in a constitutional form. But each monastery was independent of the others; there was no structure of a religious order in the modern sense. The needs of the Cluniac reform in the tenth century led to developments which pointed in that direction. Cluniac houses secured themselves exemption from supervision by local bishops, being immediately responsible to Rome; the individual houses remained closely linked to Cluny which appointed their superiors.[37] The overall plan beyond this was not clearly conceived, however, and soon it was beyond any one man to supervise the Order effectively.

The Cistercian reform of the twelfth century was better organized. Initially it was strictly monarchic, the Abbot of Cîteaux having absolute powers regarding the daughter houses, but it gradually moved towards a representative model.[38] A strong federal framework was combined with a system of mutual supervision through the annual general chapter of the order, which all abbots attended, and a system of filiation, where each founder house was responsible for the well-being of its daughter houses through regular visitations. We have seen that the obligation of attending the annual general chapter led to the sending of representatives in the other years. Year by year from the early twelfth century, this order at its most influential and flourishing demonstrated the value of such meetings, partly representative, deliberating on matters which concerned all.

With the orders of friars in the next century, a more fundamentally representative system was developed. Friars were religious, bound by the vows of poverty, chastity and obedience, but they were not monks; monasteries had been mainly, but not exclusively, rural-based. Founded for service in the growing towns and cities, the friars organized themselves with it in mind. They were mobile, moving from town to town as their work demanded, whereas the monks were stable, vowed to the one monastery for life. Members of organizations which from the outset were international, the Friars, by contrast, were sent to different countries by their superiors, and they lived in different houses as required by their states of training and apostolates.

The Order of Preachers (the Dominicans) in particular, while it retained the monastic spirit in matters such as office in choir, had a system of government which was unique for a religious order in its day.

> It gave effect to principles of representation and responsibility to an extent then unknown in either the ecclesiastical or the secular world.[39]

At all levels, superiors were elected by and were answerable to those who elected them. The priory, the basic unit of the order, elected its prior in chapter. The prior provincial of each province of the order was elected by the chapter of priors of its individual houses, plus two representatives of each house, and he was responsible to that chapter. The general chapter of the order met annually under the presiding master general and one representative elected by each of the provinces; one year in three it was the provincial priors who attended instead of representatives, and any new statute had to have the approval of three consecutive meetings, so ensuring a veto for the provincials if they wished.

The master general himself was elected by a specially enlarged general chapter. Elected for life, he could, however, resign, and the rule made him answerable to the chapter which could correct him, and if necessary remove him from office. This complete system of representative government, with elected officials answerable to their constituents at every level, existed from 1220. It was a form of government which was basically in harmony with that which political society was evolving, and both sprang from the conviction that the ordinary members of a community or society should have a share in its government; in its turn this conviction was entirely in harmony with the Christian understanding of the dignity of man, indeed might be seen as demanded by it.

Several other aspects of church organization were relevant to political development. One was the general organization of the

Church since the fall of the Roman Empire; it did much to keep alive the idea of ordered and constitutional government in Europe.[42] The example of the provincial councils of the Empire influenced those of the Church, while the Roman diocese or groups of provinces were parallelled by metropolitan dioceses of the Church under their archbishops. The councils had consisted of appointed or representative members of the cities, and the bishops represented the Christian communities in their areas in virtue of their office when deliberating on Church affairs. The first Church assembly or council was that at Jerusalem as recorded in Acts (15:1–29), and before Constantine regional or local gatherings of bishops met regularly to treat of matters in common. Once the Church was recognized it was easier for general councils to assemble. 'The Council of Nicea [for example] was a representative assembly which exercised both judicial and legislative functions; the powers were maintained in succeeding assemblies.'[41]

Provincial councils and synods continued to meet until the unsettled conditions of the ninth century caused by the renewal of invasions disrupted the pattern in many areas, but they were resumed as the disturbances decreased in the tenth and eleventh centuries. Pope Leo IX (1049–54) held councils in Rome and crossed the Alps to hold others in northern Europe, and with the reform movement, general councils began to assemble again, there having been none since the eighth, that of Constantinople in 869. The First Lateran in 1123 was the ninth and, as we have seen, five others followed in quick succession, the Second, Third and Fourth Lateran called in 1139, 1179 and 1215, and two more at Lyons in 1245 and 1275. The great period of the revival of the councils therefore coincided with the growth of representative national assemblies.

The Fourth Lateran council (1215) was particularly significant in representing the whole Church at a time when the reforming movement of the previous two centuries was having its full effect. It was a reforming council, called two and a half years before it met; attendance at it for all those called, the Pope warned, was a solemn obligation. Along with the hierarchies, and the monastic representatives, all the monarchs of Europe were also invited. It was the greatest such deliberative gathering since Roman times; over twelve hundred bishops, abbots and priors, apart from numerous proctors representing cathedral chapters, were there. The latter attended at Innocent III's insistence, since he intended to tax all chapters to offer one prebend for the support of a schoolmaster: and according to the principle already established by him in his canons – *quod omnes tangit, ab omnibus approbetur*, i.e. 'what concerns all should be approved by all' – he wished to have the approval of this measure from those concerned.[42] The importance of this gathering made the deliberations of representative assemblies and their value known throughout Europe. It prescribed provincial councils for all metropolitans and their suffragans for the purpose of reform, appointing individuals to report on the situation existing with suggestions for improving it where necessary, and these reports were submitted to the bishops; the resulting decrees were then to be published. Provincial and diocesan synods were to meet annually; these were also enjoined for religious orders which had not previously had them.

In the Church the custom of representation of the clergy so that response could be made to requests for financial aid, for purposes of Church or State, was well developed by the mid-thirteenth century. In 1254 the English bishops had refused to agree to impose such an aid on their clergy without their assent and, having met to discuss it, the latter acceded to the request, but with so many conditions attached that the King refused it. Clarke suggests that the decision of the King in the same year to appeal over the heads of the tenants-in-chief by inviting two knights from the shires to come before the Great Council at Westminster may have been influenced by the bishops' appeal to their clergy. Certainly they were not called for the purpose of bearing the record of their counties, but to gain the consent, on behalf of those they represented, to the King's request for aid.[43]

(iii) St Thomas and political theory[44]

Though St Thomas wrote no comprehensive treatise on political theory, his concern with Christian ethics led him to deal with most of the important ethical issues which were considered by political theorists. He adopted Aristotle's theory of the natural origin of political society and the State, so moving away from the position of St Augustine who saw it as conventional, the result of the Fall.[45] He agreed with St Augustine that in the natural state before the Fall there would have been no absolute dominion of man by man, such as a slave-master had over his slave, but argued that since man is a social animal, he would have needed someone to direct the State anyway, and those with special gifts for this task would have done this for the common good.[46] Even before the Fall, therefore, the need and special aptitude for politics would have asserted itself.

The State is natural to man because there is in him a social tendency. It is not the result of sin, nor is it merely the result of a selfish desire for security, although egoism does play a part in convincing man of the necessity of the State; were it egoism alone, however, force would be required to keep it united, and such a State could not endure; a State based on man's natural social tendency, on the other hand, can survive. Since it is founded in human nature the State is God-ordained and as such is a perfect society, that is, it has within itself all the means needful for the attainment of its ends.[47] This is relevant to its relationship with the Church. As a perfect society, it cannot be just an appendage, directly subject to the latter. The end of the Church, which is a supernatural one, is higher than that of the State, it is true, and in matters which affect salvation the latter must subordinate itself to the Church; but in its own sphere, the political and economic ordering of the State for the common good, it is autonomous and in that sphere Church authority over it must be indirect.

The end of society being the good, the virtuous life on earth,[48] there is a possible tension here between it and the Christian citizen, because his end is not only to live virtuously in the natural sense, but to attain to the enjoyment of God, which exceeds the purely natural good. It is then the task of the monarch to direct earthly affairs in such a way that his subjects can do this, but it is not for the Church to exercise any direct power over the secular authority in what concerns the common good for which the State exists. That good requires peace within the State, protection from external enemies, directing the citizen body in well-doing and countering crime; the State must therefore have armed force at its disposal and an effective judicial system.[49]

The relationship between the individual and the State is left somewhat ambiguous in the *Summa*. It notes that the part is ordered to the whole, as imperfect is to the perfect, which seems to suggest that the individual is subject to the whole; the State for example can impose the death penalty for the graver crimes.[50] These passages have, however, to be balanced against Christian theology, and natural theology, which framed all St Thomas's thought according to it man has a final end outside and independent of his role as a citizen, so any interpretation in a totalitarian sense of what he says cannot be sustained. There are some things which cannot be rendered to Caesar, and it is this right of conscience which has secured Western man in his instinct for freedom since the martyrs' conflict with the Roman Empire.

St Thomas's theory of law brings this into focus.[51] Law is first of all the law of God, and within this framework the lawfulness of Governments and their actions can be judged; it was his understanding of law which covers the question of sovereignty, the power of the ruler over law itself. Law according to Thomas is that rule and measure of acts by which a man is to act or be prevented from acting. And since the rule and measure of acts is reason, law too is of reason.[52] It is a command of the practical reason of one who governs a perfect community: and since the whole of the community of the universe is ruled by divine eternal reason, hence an eternal law.[53] All things therefore derive their respective inclinations to their proper acts and ends from this law. Now man, the only rational being, is subject to providence in a particularly significant way because, in that he is provident both for himself and for others, he has a share in the eternal reason, and this participation in the eternal law is called the natural law; it is by it that we discern good from evil and as such it is an imprint on us of the divine light.[54] Natural law tells us to do good and avoid evil, preserve and foster life and do all that is necessary to that end, and to seek to know the truth and to cultivate the social virtues.[55] Divine positive law is that moral law which God has revealed to us through the Scriptures. Among the reasons for its being given to us is that man's natural moral sense can go astray. Human positive law, both the *ius gentium* and the *ius civile*, must relate correctly to the divine eternal and divine positive law.[56]

St Thomas therefore saw law as a thing of reason, the eternal reason of God in the first instance, in which all things participate in so far as given their essential orientation by him: man, because he has reason and free will, participates in a unique manner; through natural law he knows and can move freely to obey the essential moral law. The human positive law, that determined by governments and judges, insofar as it embodies right reason, derives from this natural law. If it disagrees with that law, it is not true law but a perversion of it.[57]

Concerning the origin of political authority, St Thomas of course saw it as coming from God and it seems probable, though it is not certain, that he saw it coming to the ruler through the people. He certainly speaks of the ruler representing the people.[58] Perhaps his teaching on sedition may have relevance to this question. The purpose of the State was to give justice, he noted, but a tyrannical government, which is one that is not directed to the common good but to the private good of the ruler, is not just, as Aristotle states (*Ethics* viii 10 and *Politics* iii 5). To disturb such a government is not sedition therefore, unless it be disturbed to such an extent that the people suffer more from that disturbance than they do from the rule of the tyrant. Otherwise it is the tyrant who is being seditious in so acting against the public good that he gives rise to that sedition.[59]

It would seem that if the people have the right to rebel against an unjust ruler, which they have in principle no matter how hedged about is that right, then they are sovereign. If power came to the ruler directly from God, then those who were oppressed by him to the point of considering rebellion would have no appeal against him despite his injustices, as defenders of the divine right of kings have been ready to point out in defence of their beliefs. If they do have the moral right to dislodge the unjust ruler it can only be because his exercise of power is conditional upon their consent; ultimately political power has been given to them by God, and they can reclaim it from the unjust ruler.

On forms of government he follows Aristotle, that the right ordering of rulers in a State or nation requires that all should have a share in that government, because such a form will commend itself to all and there will be peace, as Aristotle's *Politics* (ii 6) states. There should also be one head of all, and a number of men set in authority, while all should be eligible to rule. Hence the best form of government should be 'partly kingdom, since there is one head of all; partly aristocracy insofar as a number of persons are set in authority: partly democracy, i.e. government by the people, insofar as rulers can be chosen from the people and the people have a right to choose their rulers (*in quantum ex popularibus possunt eligi principes, et ad populum pertinet electio principum*).[60]

The phrase 'the rulers can be chosen from the people', however, had no feudal precedent; feudalism was an order established by armed might and one's place in it was determined by custom. There was a new element in his reasoning. That rulers can be chosen from the people and the people can choose their rulers suggests the operation of the representative principle in town government, where the citizens did in fact choose rulers from among themselves. The political development of the towns has been a neglected aspect of political development in medieval times; with this phrase St Thomas put them in the centre of it.

5 Political theory and organization in the late Middle Ages

(i) Marsilius and Ockham

With Marsilius of Padua (1274–1342), the common ground which all previous medieval political thinkers had shared was abandoned, and it is notable that the years of Marsilius's maturity are those of the first period of the Avignon Papacy with its financial and administrative efficiency but when it was increasingly under criticism from within the Church. Pope John XXII (1316–34) had quarrelled with the Emperor Lewis the Bavarian (1314–47) who had been elected without papal ratification and on this count, and on the charge of aiding heretics, had been excommunicated in 1324. The consequence was that his court was a natural rallying-point for anyone who had in any way come in conflict with the Papacy.

Marsilius of Padua was among those who found themselves in this position. He had fled to Lewis's court in 1326 when his authorship of *Defensor Pacis*, which was dedicated to the Emperor, became imminent; the particular target of the work was papal imperialism, which he blamed for the problems of Italy and its city states.[61] He also went further than any other writer in seeking to put the Church under secular control. He argued that reason shows the need for civil government to procure peace and order, and religion has its place in civic life for teaching the scriptural truths of salvation, but there is no place for an independent Church. The truths she has to teach are beyond rational discussion, and faith is from a secular point of view irrelevant: in all things the Church and her officials are simply part of civil life, as for example are farmers, and like them she and her officials are subject to State control.

Divine law has no sanction in this life and therefore it too is irrelevant to the life of the State. Human law is not related to it because the latter imposes earthly penalties and human authority. The lawmaker is the people and the State is the body of men who make that law; this latter he calls 'the Legislator'. The *pars valentior* of the legislators, the group within it which carries the greatest weight, decides matters, not the simple numerical majority. In government, unity is to be assured by a supreme executive so that factions can be mastered and the law effectively applied. The whole concern is for a system which will protect the city-state from the strife which so often afflicted it. His reliance on a general council as the answer to the Church's problems at the time placed that council at the disposal of the secular authority; it was to be called by the State and its decisions were to rely on the State for their application.

For the individual, as for the Church, the implication of Marsilius's theories were not encouraging; they emphasized the strong State but did not show how the freedom and the rights of individuals and social organizations were to be preserved under it. Trying to avoid what he saw as papal absolutism, he substituted another absolutism, that of the secular State; against it the citizen had little assurance of freedom. Marsilius's analysis was defective in making the Papacy the scapegoat for Italy's ills. The roots of Italian disunity lay in a tortured history for which the Papacy was not responsible; indeed it had frequently supplied for the lack of any effective political society in central Italy in the early Middle Ages. Representing one of many interests in later years and looking to its own survival, it had formed and joined alliances which its enemies could claim maintained or exacerbated the disunity, but the disunity itself was not due to its machinations.

William of Ockham was called to Avignon in 1324 to answer questions about his teaching. Ockham did not reflect systematically on the nature of political society;[62] his theories on these matters were set out in the context of disputes with the Holy See over what he regarded as papal aggressiveness and absolutism. Insofar as he took issue on them he was not setting out to be revolutionary. He respected law and custom and feared the absolutism which is capricious and arbitrary. In rejecting the Papacy's attempt to intervene in the election of Lewis of Bavaria he stressed the independence of the secular power from the spiritual. The Papacy is not the source of that power, which comes to the secular ruler through the people, either immediately by direct choice, or mediately through their agreement, implicit or explicit. The people therefore have a right to choose their rulers, and if they wish to choose a hereditary monarchy they may do so, but any ruler can be deposed if he abuses his authority.

His insights into the sovereignty of the people and the independence of the secular order brought out clearly what had been accepted by the medieval tradition. It went beyond that tradition, and against it in the controversy with the Papacy over religious poverty, suggesting that the Church should renounce all worldly functions. He underestimated the dangers of absolutism, conceding to the State excessive powers. He denied to the Pope the right to defend the liberty of the Church, arguing that 'liberty and honour in the world are among the least important goods'. The freedom of the Church must give way before the expansionist ambitions of the king.[63]

(ii) Absolutism and the decline of representative government

The political theory of the fifteenth century continued to favour the view that political authority came ultimately from God, but immediately from the community. The monarch had considerable freedom in the exercise of his power but he usually consulted the leading men of the land, who in this role were seen as representatives of the whole community. The king's power was treated with respect but it was not regarded as absolute; he could be deprived of it if he did not rule by the law and protect his people's liberties.[64]

However, there was a contrary trend detectable among the civilian lawyers of the time. They accepted that it was from the community that all legislative authority was immediately derived, but since they were concerned with law of the Roman Empire, they saw this authority as having been conferred on the Emperor. As to whether the community had completely alienated legislative power from itself or could reclaim it, there had been controversy among the lawyers in the twelfth and thirteenth centuries; there were some who were sure that the people no longer had any formal legislative role: the Emperor's power over positive law was absolute and unconditional. He was, however, bound by any contract he had made with his subjects.[65]

Divine right theory, explicitly stated by St Gregory the Great, had been almost completely abandoned by the eleventh and twelfth centuries, only a small number of imperialist writers maintaining it. St Thomas Aquinas, as we have seen, ignored it and justified the right to rebellion against a tyrannical ruler if the circumstances warranted it. Wycliffe resurrected the theory, and we have examples of it in the fifteenth century also, from the Cortés of Olmedo in 1415 in particular, which instanced the disorder and disturbances of the State at the time. Divine law forbade men to touch the king who was the Lord's anointed; to resist the king was to resist God's ordinances.

The first meeting of the Estates General in France took place in 1302, the occasion being the need of the Crown to get support, and subventions, from the country at large for the King's policies in the conflict with the Papacy. By 1357 the Estates were attempting to use their position to gain more political control, but they lacked the unity to present a united front to the monarch, and in 1439 they voted to accept a perpetual tax which theoretically had to be periodically renewed. It was only imposed on the third estate, the clergy and nobility arguing that their prayers and their swords respectively were their means of serving it; nor was it periodically renewed, although the clergy made periodic grants to the Crown. At the meeting of the Estates in 1612 the nobility sundered themselves from the third estate, refusing to accept them as an equal partner in the proceedings,[66] and there was no further meeting of the Estates General until 1789.

In Aragon and Castile the monarchy was able to exploit the jealousies among the towns, and their willingness to accept privileges at each other's expense. The nobility obtained exemption from taxation on the grounds of their military contribution to the State, and so they had no incentive to join the bourgeois in limiting royal power here. As we have seen above, representative government in England did not atrophy. The lesser aristocracy, the knights of the shires, found it more to their advantage to identify with the burghers in the Commons, and the English king was not able to divide the opposition in the same way as in France and Spain, for example. Though in the fourteenth century most of the towns, and their representatives, found attendance in Parliament more of a burden than a privilege, this changed in the fifteenth, possibly because a sense of national identity was developing, and with it a desire to participate in the affairs of the realm. Then in the sixteenth century Henry VIII increasingly turned to the Commons in his difficulties with Rome and his people: as he did so it became more and more dominated by the gentry and the wealthy, with the true Commons having little or no voice, and so it continued until the nineteenth century with little change. However, the structures and privileges of a representative system remained and, with the gradual extension of the franchise, the mother of parliaments was gradually able to emerge as truly representative. By that time a more thoroughgoing form of democracy was gathering strength in the former North American colonies, the United States of America.

10

The Church and economics in the central and late Middle Ages

1 The wealth of the Church

The wealth of the Church lay first in land; in the early period it has been calculated that one-third of it was in her hands; by the thirteenth century it was one-seventh,[1] the fall in the proportion indicating not that her holdings had declined in absolute terms but that more land had been brought into use as a result of the reclamation over two centuries. It lay secondly in her money income which gave her control over a large part of the liquid wealth of the times. There was the tithe, mass offerings, Easter offerings, those which accompanied the ministration of baptism, marriage, the last sacraments and burials. The tithe, the tenth part of the increase yearly arising from the profits of land and industry of the parishioners, was payable for the maintenance of the parish clergy by all who had things titheable, unless they were for some reason exempted. They were at first paid spontaneously as offerings in kind – corn, wool or agricultural products in the main – and they gradually came to be seen as recognized payments. By the eleventh century the majority of parishes had become part of the system of proprietary churches owned by laymen or monasteries who thereby owned also what was paid in tithe; the administration of the parish in practice was carried out by a priest or priests appointed by them. Such tithes had in fact become a feudal due which could be bought and sold, divided or inherited. It was part of the reformers' task to recover these tithes and with them

* The notes and references for Chapter 10 are to be found on p. 399

provide benefices for a better-educated and a celibate clergy who
would be financially independent and free of simony. They had to
settle for the patron giving up one-quarter of the tithe to the parish
church; eventually the bishops recovered the churches owned or
served by the monasteries,[2] but many of those in the ownership of
lay patrons remained so.

The wealth of the Papacy came from the tenths, an income tax
on the clergy, dues paid by prelates when appointed to office,
annates from priests given benefices, the tribute paid by bishops
on their *ad limina* visits to Rome, chancery fees and taxes on religious orders, gifts and legacies, and the preaching of indulgences.
Temporal revenues came from the Papal States, the *census* paid by
papal monasteries and churches, and finally Peter's Pence. To
collect these funds agents were used, the Templars initially, but
then Sienese and Florentine bankers. The organization and direction of such operations made the Church overall the most efficient
economic organization and policy maker of the times.

The basis of the Papacy's finances were, however, always weak. It
became weaker during the Avignon period; income dropped, and
the expenses incurred in trying to protect and regain control of
the Italians lands increased. The efficiency of the administration
managed to compensate for this, until the return to Rome and the
resultant schism destroyed all their good work:[3] papal revenues
consequently fell by two-thirds between 1378 and 1429.[4] Reformers
within the Church were rightly scandalized by some of the methods
used to make up this deficit, of which the sale of indulgences was
just one, but if the Church had control over all her revenues there
would have been no need for resort to such measures. Far from the
Church regaining those revenues, Christian princes gradually
compelled her to make more of them available for secular
purposes; what they were capable of is demonstrated by Henry
VIII's demands once he got total control. Taxation of the English
church by Rome amounted to some £4,816 annually in the early
Tudor period; when the King had made himself head of it he took
£46,000 in 1536, rising to £53,000 in 1540 – and from a church
which had been considerably impoverished by seizure by the
Crown of a large part of its assets.[5]

The monastic orders also disposed of considerable wealth; some
of them, the Cistercians in particular, knew a great deal about
wealth creation in practice, and aspects of their activities brought
criticism; general chapters sought to restrict excesses but with only
limited results.[6] The concentration on the maximization of returns
by monasteries from the late thirteenth century was the result

partly of inflationary pressures and the changing nature of tenancy; many were certainly accused of striking hard bargains with tenants. Decline in fervour affected monasteries in the late Middle Ages, certainly, yet their contribution to the commonweal remained well appreciated by the people at large. Those who supported the 'Pilgrimage of Grace' rebellion against Henry VIII (1536), were divided on many things but they were as one in demanding that the suppression of the monasteries should cease.[7]

The problems of making ownership of property or wealth compatible with the Christian life as lived by clergy and monks had always troubled the Franciscans. It had started while St Francis was still alive and only eased off after the condemnation by John XXII in November 1323 of the proposition that 'Christ and his apostles had possessed [nothing] neither as individuals nor as a group'.[8] The theoretical question settled, the Church had to possess property in order to do her work; the main problem was making sure that it was not appropriated in any way by the clergy for other than these purposes.

The insistence on celibacy for her ministers was based on its being a Gospel value, but on a practical level one of its advantages was that it prevented alienation of Church property for personal or family reasons. Her revenues were 'for the Church's own use or to provide food for the needy and sustenance for pilgrims.[9] Traditionally they were intended to be divided into four portions, for the bishop's work, for the clergy, for the fabric of the churches and for the support of the poor and the needy. These Gratian embodied in his *Decretum.*[10]

The Church then had to possess property in order to do her work, and that property had to be administered by the clergy, but it proved difficult in a society which was expanding economically to prevent some of the clergy who were in a position to exploit their positions for gain from doing so. There were vast differences between the clergy in their birth, offices and income and it was difficult to impose any policy on them if they chose to oppose it. The question of apostolic poverty agitated the Franciscans, as we have seen, and their problems illustrate that any attempt at correction of abuses could rouse a fanaticism on both sides which was, to say the least, unseemly. For example, attempts to apply the law limiting pluralism which had been passed by the Fourth Lateran Council were so resented by London clergy that some of them threatened to have powerful friends use force to resist them.

The abuse of the benefice system was at the heart of the problem. A benefice was a method of providing for those who were serving

the Church as priests and bishops the means to live without having
to engage in other paid work of any kind; since apostolic times (Acts
6:2) such provision had been seen as seemly, and the benefice
system made it formal from the eleventh century. Unfortunately too
many priests and bishops, affected simultaneously by a feudal and a
capitalist mentality, saw benefices as a profitable right, while the
services which were attached could be turned over to a poorly-paid
vicar, they themselves enjoying the rest.[11] In this way several bishoprics or other pastoral offices could be occupied by one person –
there were cases in which this was as many as 10 bishoprics, 26
monasteries and 133 other benefices. In some cases bishoprics and
abbacies were controlled by the nobility, who used them to provide
for their younger children. However, the main responsibility for the
scandals and the damage to the Church's mission that resulted lies
with the clergy concerned. The effect of their weakness was cumulative over the centuries, and it was summed up with chilling clarity by
the Papal Commission on the Reform of the Church, *de Emendanda
Ecclesia*, set up in 1536, and reporting in February 1537. It identified
as the root of all the problems,

> the reckless exaggeration of Papal authority by unscrupulous
> canonists, asserting that the pope was not merely the legitimate
> dispenser of benefices but their absolute master, with the right
> of selling them without thereby incurring the guilt of simony ...
> according to his own pleasure.[12]

The result was the admission of ignorant and completely unworthy
men to holy orders, as the distribution of benefices was based on
considerations regarding the candidate, and not the welfare of the
souls for whom the benefices existed. It also encouraged simony,
dispensations given to the illegitimate sons of priests preferred to
worthy candidates, pluralism of incompatible benefices and of
bishoprics, pastors entrusting their flocks to poorly-paid vicars, and
general advoidance of the regulations concerning the holding of
multiple benefices. All this was added to the problems caused by
the pope as a temporal prince attracting support by distributing
favours and money, and by the weakness in the papal finances
which encouraged the cutting of corners and the use of dubious
means of raising funds.

We have seen that this always inadequate income was cut by
two-thirds between 1378 and 1429; the conciliar movement
increased the problems the Papacy faced, Constance for example
limiting its right to levy taxes. The preaching of indulgences,
exploitation of lawsuits and the sale of offices were some of the

means used to make up the shortfall; by 1486 the majority of offices in the Curia were manned by men who had bought them. As spiritual revenues declined and the Papacy had more and more to depend on the Papal States to meet its commitments, spiritual weapons were used in the struggle – for example, bankers charged with collecting them were protected by the threat of excommunication or interdict.[13]

2 The development of the Church's economic ethics

(i) Economics and ethics

Economic theory as we know it did not exist in the Middle Ages, though the beginning of one emerged in the fifteenth century. There were at all times, however, economic ideas, on economic organization, for example; they were embodied in the old feudal agricultural, and the new urban industrial and commercial systems. But economic life as a whole process, with a distinct and coherent role and a place of its own in civil society, and theories to match, was not known. The model of economic life was domestic; the word itself is taken from the Greek *oikonomia* which means the art of household management; it was the art practised by the prudent head of the household, managing the income and expenditure for the whole family and the work by which the family's needs are met. Above the family, the State and its policies had effects on aspects of economic life, but its role was perceived on the paternalistic model: as the father of the family having responsibility for its provision and its finances.

The canonist and theologians were concerned with economic morality only; the determination of the economic structures of society and their operation were for society to decide. At the same time, since these structures and the policies of the State had important effects on the daily life of the individual, and in particular raised many moral questions concerning means and ends, dealing with them was very much the Church's concern. From the Old Testament, confirmed by the New, a cautious attitude to wealth creation and abundance was inculcated, but honest trade and industry were not only a legitimate but also an obligatory means of support.[14]

When a self-sustaining economic growth began in the central Middle Ages it brought with it a range of new problems in moral terms, and canonists and moral theologians had to guide the

consciences of those facing them. Moral theology and canon law
are practical sciences and they respond to the questions asked of
them by Christians facing new real-life situations. The insight into
the consciences of their people in these matters taught the priests
concerned to see the good in the marketplace, as well as the bad,
and moral theology developed accordingly.

(ii) Markets and profits

The practice of exchange of goods, by barter or selling and registering a profit, has always been a part of the pattern of human life
and we have seen that this was accepted by moralists from the
beginning; it was possible to distinguish between the honest and
the dishonest trader and merchant: if the suspicion of sharp practice remained because it was so easy for the dishonest to flourish in
its ever-changing world, this was not allowed to obscure the basic
necessity and honesty of the craft as such.

The medieval economy was basically agricultural, and the sort of
business practices which gave the moralist pause for thought in
commerce and trading was less evident in a manorial economy.
There was a pattern of exchange in local markets for the disposal
of surpluses and the obtaining of household and other goods at all
times, but initially it did not challenge the basic subsistence
pattern of such an economy as a whole; production was in general
for consumption, not the market. The task of the Church in giving
guidance on economic matters in this context was not as complex
as that of the developing urban areas of the central Middle Ages
from the tenth to twelfth centuries, when the world of trade and
commerce was involving a larger and larger number of her people,
and a genuine, profit-driven market was appearing across a whole
culture.

The general outline of this development has already been
sketched in dealing with the Church and the urban economy. The
development of commerce and industry on the Flanders/north
Italian axis through the Champagne fairs in the first instance, and
the outreach through the Hansa and the trade with Russia, were the
crux – while the Italian trade with Byzantium and Islam in the early
Middle Ages linked that axis with the outer world to the great advantage of Europe and the East. In North Western Europe, the engine of
economic development was woollen manufacture and trade – first in
Flanders then in England. Northern Italy later developed a woollen
industry and trade which surpassed them and Italy also became the
commercial and banking centre of the west. The result of these

developments was that from about 1150 Europe moved from self-sufficiency in food to support industrial expansion as the towns attracted the skilled crafts and monopolized industrial production; the move from a domestic and manorial agricultural economy began, a market economy was emerging, and Europe took the first great economic leap forward, the basis of all that followed over the next centuries. 'It was the central middle ages, not the Renaissance period that was the age of the rebirth of the European economy.'[15]

There was capitalism, and industrial capitalism, in the Middle Ages, and at its worst it was liberal capitalism, the 'cult of money, the frenzied search for profit which considers nothing but cold reason'.[16] The zenith of northern European industrial capitalism was reached in the woollen industry in the thirteenth century.[17] Woollens were produced for a wide and expanding international market; the industry was dependent on imported materials, there was subdivision of labour, with organizing entrepreneurs co-ordinating production, purchasing raw materials directly from producers, putting it out to the crafts, owning the finished product and marketing it. Such were Jean Boine Broke of Douai in Flanders, and in England Henry Houhil of Leicester, and John Winchcombe – Jack o' Newbury – in the thirteenth and fourteenth centuries.

Financial and commercial organization was of its nature capitalistic. Their geographical position and experience of trading with, as well as fighting, the Arabs on a contested maritime frontier, gave the Italians the lead in international commerce. Self-defence and the hope of booty in conquest intermingled capitalist enterprise with the profession of arms. With the development of that trade came credit institutions, the use of the bill of exchange, and the growth of banking, the Venetians developing the latter out of their merchant activities. The growing complexity of economic life led to improved business organization and better accounting, with the Italians again being the pioneers.[18]

This then was the general background against which the canonists and moralists had to explain, and seek to see applied, the insights on commercial morality which were embodied in the tradition that guided them. Gratian had condemned trade and its profits outright with no distinction between unjust and unjust profits, or even between those earned by trading and those that came from money-lending. A more balanced consideration of the tradition did not justify this blanket dismissal. Rufinus, in his *Summa* written about 1157, allowed that profits were moral when they were based on expenses incurred or labour expended. These ideas were further developed so that eventually,

according to the best judgement of canonists and theologians of
the twelfth and thirteenth centuries, if the merchant was careful
and wise he could live with honour in medieval society.[19]

St Thomas was very cautious in handling the matter, but he was also
positive. Profit from trade was justifiable if it was for a good purpose.
Trading for profit[20] 'has about it a certain debasement' but a man
'may intend a moderate gain which he seeks to acquire by trading,
for advantage ... lest his country lack the necessaries of life' – a gain
which is a payment for his labour. Such adjustments came from
experience of the more complex economic life of the times; the
temptations and possibilities of dishonesty in commerce, trade,
industry and finance remained, as did the social problems it
brought with it, but it was impossible to maintain that these occupations could not be pursued honestly. Thomas, quoting Augustine,
had pointed out that the evil practices of some traders could not be
made the basis of a condemnation of their craft. Good men with the
right values could ply it honestly, and since there was a need for
their services, they, with the help of the authorities, could set the
tone. The Church was at home in the developing economy of the
time, which was in itself good because it was fulfilling God's instruction to use the world for man's purpose. But economic life, as
political, must be morally responsible.

(iii) The just price

A profit then, was, acceptable from trading if it was not sought for
its own sake, and any honest trader who met a legitimate need by
his foresight, sound judgement and the expense of time and
money, was entitled to the profit that it brought him. But how
much profit? What price could he charge for his goods? The
concept of the just price was one the medieval moralists and
canonists inherited from Roman law: parties to a contract of sale
had the right to bargain for the best price, getting the advantage of
one another if they could, and in this context the play of the
market in terms of supply and demand should determine what was
the just price; it could so be set by the State or the town. If it turned
out that the seller in a particular case had received less than half of
what was the just price, i.e. what the market would have determined, then he had suffered a considerable loss (i.e. *laesio enormis*)
and could sue for recovery. These ideas were adopted and
extended by canonists; the principle of the just price was made a
general one and it applied to buyers as well as sellers.

Baldwin thoroughly investigated the use of the term by the

canonists. He concluded that the canonical just price was simply the current price fixed by the market or by the public authority, plus the principle of *laesio enormis*.[21] The free market determined the price. The theologians saw the value of an object in terms of its social utility, its capacity to satisfy needs. The just price then could fluctuate. St Thomas considered the case of a merchant possessing a cargo of grain during a time of famine but also knowing that more grain was on the way. Should he tell his prospective customers that this was the case and so reduce the price he obtained for his own cargo? Thomas's answer was that a virtuous man would probably do this but there is no obligation on him to do so.[22] He also notes that the just price of things, 'cannot be fixed with mathematical precision, but only approximately estimated'.[23] As Augustine says, it is their usefulness to the buyer which determines the price of things sold.[24]

The nub of the matter then was the need for a free market which enabled buyer and seller to agree on a price that was not fixed by anyone operating it for his own purposes, and it is on this that the canonists and moralists concentrated, their enemy being monopoly or price discrimination of any kind. In particular they abhorred the activities of the middleman who contributed nothing and tried to rig the market in his favour; the practices of forestalling (buying goods before they came to market and so pushing up their price), regrating (cornering goods for resale at a higher price in the same market) and engrossing (hoarding in expectation of rising prices) were forbidden. Far from the medieval moralist being a protector of the inefficient producer or overpriced goods, 'the most consistent thread in scholastic economic thought is horror of monopoly'[25] for it is monopoly which is the great enemy of that free market which served the common good. The monopolies that the towns offered to those who would supply the right goods and the right quantity and quality, to be sold in an open market, were offered to those concerned in order that the town could be assured of supplies in a world where they were often uncertain; they were monopolies which all three parties, the public authority, the consumer and the producer agreed were fair to them. Outside suppliers could also participate and did, provided their goods were of the quality wanted. This sort of monopoly was a world away from one in which the supplier so dominated customer and producer that a free market was denied.[26]

(iv) Usury and interest

Making an honest profit, then, was morally acceptable and such a profit could be earned by providing needed goods in a free market. But could such a profit be earned by 'selling money', that is, lending it at interest, charging a price for it? This question of usury, taking interest on a money loan, was a central moral problem at the time and we must make some effort to see the problem in its context. The idea that a rich man had the obligation to lend without charge to the poor who were in desperate need was one that was inherited from the Old Testament; it was a basic obligation of human solidarity. The lender was entitled in justice to expect the return of the loan in due time, though it was better that he should forgo if he could reasonably afford to. The starting point of the moral thinking on the matter was then the law of God, and the context of its application was an undeveloped economy where investment opportunities were few. Those who had surplus wealth were rarely deprived of good investment opportunities if they made loans; it was otherwise simply hoarded. There was at all times, in the primitive society of the period, a danger of the peasant, and the poor generally, falling into the hands of the usurers, the men who took interest, at penal rates, on loans from those pressed by absolute necessity to borrow. Every village had its usurers.[27] The overwhelming need therefore was to prevent such abuses, and one of the great services that the teaching on usury performed for the poor in these times was to condemn outright such injustice.

The insistence that in return for what is borrowed for use or for consumption, whether it be goods or money, only the same value should be required, 'prevented the peasant of the middle ages from being as hopelessly in debt as was the peasant in the ancient and the Muslim worlds'.[28] The Church's usury laws were then of the greatest relevance to the peasants and the poor generally, the vast majority of the people at the time; they made good sense in terms of Christian social charity and justice. They were a way of trying to ensure that the goods given by God to all should serve the needs of all.

When the possibility of wealth creation through trade, commerce and industry became real, as it did in this period in a way which it had never done before in western Europe, so too did the demand for money, not only as a means of exchange to be spent immediately for consumption purposes, but as a store or measure of value. It could then be used to make more money by investment; it was capital. This was a natural and inevitable development as the increase in population required a more efficient exploitation of the resources of the world to meet human needs, the purpose of economic life. The possibility of making an honest profit by supplying those needs was in itself moral: the business-man was using his talents and his energies in meeting the needs of others. Those who had money could, by a simple *societas* contract, go into business on a speculative manufacturing or trading venture and make a profit on it. But was it right to lend money to a businessman at interest in order that he might use it on a business venture? To us it seems a matter of common sense, but the moralist of the time knew that to allow interest on money loans would put at risk the culturally, and morally, valuable prin-ciple that the poor should have access to money loans in their need. It entailed a static view of economic activity because the science of economics was not yet developed; it was the best they had and in its time was justified, but economic necessity and right reason required that economic theory and ethics had to develop to meet more complex human needs.

The question of capital loans between businessmen affected a far smaller proportion of the people, and they were those who were engaged in the markets. There, those who struck bargains were not doing so in the desperate circumstances of a peasant or craftsman faced with beggary or starvation if he did not get the consumption loan he needed; these were men of some substance dealing with others of the same kind for trading purposes. This was clearly a different case from that which led to the prohibition of usury, and canonists and theologians were capable of seeing that. What they had to do was to maintain the socially necessary protection of usury laws for the benefit of the poor, while providing means by which the need for commercial loans could be met. The theoretical problem according to the understanding of the times was illus-trated by Roman law; the *mutuum*, the personal loan between man and man,[29] could not bear interest.[30] Money was regarded as sterile in the sense that since it is only the human agent who puts it to use who makes it profitable, it is only that agent who should profit from such increase. A charge cannot be made by the lender, because he no longer owns the money; it is not his efforts that make it fruitful.

The question of business loans was not pressing in the early Middle Ages, and it is possible that the prohibition of usury applied only to clerics until 800; usury was defined as asking for more than is given and by 806 was understood to be a sin against justice.[31] The Second Lateran Council (1139) ruled that manifest usurers should not be admitted to communion and that, if they died in their sin, they were not to receive Christian burial. This it would hardly have done if the problem had not been a widespread and an obvious social evil; the poor were being exploited at a time when the economy was expanding and developing; many were the victims of rapid change and had to turn to moneylenders for help. Protecting them was the Church's concern.

Business loans required different treatment. They could be offset against profits, so that both loan and interest could be self-liquidating if the venture was a sound one and no untoward circumstances were to intervene. At the same time there was still a great need for close watch on whether interest was asked on a particular loan and whether, if it was asked on a commercial loan, it was a fair rate. In the absence of a true money market such as modern economies have, the Church's role as moral watchdog in this area was socially valuable.[32]

The practices of moneylending and borrowing at the time varied. There were pawnbrokers and moneylenders, giving loans secured by pledging lands or personal possessions. The going rate here was about 43 per cent per annum. Merchants borrowed, and lent, money for commercial purposes, while the Italian banks could also be approached for business loans; here the rate was something between 7 and 15 per cent. A business loan could be regarded as an investment, rewarded by a share in the profits if the risk was high. In rationalizing developments which were clearly socially beneficial, while seeking to make sure that the usury laws which protected the poor remained in force, the canonists made exceptions to the latter in the light of what experience was teaching.

The *mutuum* by definition excluded any possibility of a charge intrinsic to the loan itself, but in a market situation reasons extrinsic to the loan could justify it.

> 'The failure of modern historians to understand this leads them to make such bald and unqualified statements as that the taking of interest was forbidden in the middle ages or that the Church came to change its doctrine. Without asking what is meant by interest or was there ever such a thing as a doctrine on usury, which people today take as some infallibly defined teaching, then only confusion and misunderstandings result.[32]

Had economic theory developed enough to allow a tidier handling of the problem to emerge, it would have been better for all concerned, but it had not; the moralists could only reflect on the matter in the light of the accepted economic thought of the time. Several of them made their contributions to the development of that thought in their concern with the moral issues; but they were not economic theorists. That genre of academic and intellectual interest was still unknown, and until it, and economic organization, had developed more fully, the moralist had to use what evidence was available on which to form judgements.

There were four such extrinsic titles. The first was the paying of a penalty if money was not repaid in time; a *poena conventionalis*, the difference between what had been due and what was paid; the 'fine' was the 'interest' (from the Latin *interesse*, to 'be between'). The lender could suffer because of the borrower's not returning it in time, and so could claim a *damnum emergens*. He could claim for loss of a possible profit, *lucrum cessans*, if he passed up a chance of making a gain as a result of lending to others, or finally there could be the risk of losing his capital, *periculum sortis*. Once delay in payment was recognized as a just title, penalty clauses against such a delay could be put in agreements. Further, a merchant who passed up a chance of making a profit if he made a distress loan could charge a modest interest provided he only occasionally performed this service.[34]

The theologians followed the canonists; usury was sinful but interest in itself was not. They were more hampered by the teaching that money is sterile and could not bear fruit. It cannot be lent because it is used up in the use; the lender has handed it over to another, and any profit from its use should go to him who has been the agency by which the profit was made. The borrower owns it and the profit, if any, belongs to him. However, the logic of events was showing them that money was not only a means of exchange, the purpose of the *mutuum*. As St Bernardino of Siena put it,

> Money has not only the character of money, but it has beyond this a productive character which we commonly call capital[35]

and capital could bear interest. Ultimately, the Fifth Lateran Council defined usury as

> nothing else than gain or profit drawn from the use of a thing that is by its nature sterile, a profit acquired without labour, cost or risk.[36]

Where capital is concerned, the use of which involves labour, cost or risk, then profit could, in principle, be taken.

(v) The impact of the Church's teaching on economic society

Economic life is part of the secular order and, like political life, has its own autonomy, its own purposes and logic under natural law. Individuals and groups realize they have surpluses of some goods

which can be exchanged in markets through barter or cash transactions, so that they have the means to purchase goods of which
they are short; in time specialist traders and manufacturers appear,
and a complex pattern of such exchange, markets, commerce,
industry, financial and credit institutions establishes itself.
Revealed religion, concerned as it is with the sacral order, has no
direct role in the technicalities of economics, though the Church
as a social organization affects and is affected by economic considerations, and as a moral teacher she is concerned with moral issues
which arise in the economic process.

Her guidance here can have profound effects, it is true. For
example her canonists rejected the Roman law's principle that the
simple verbal understanding between the parties to a business
agreement, a *nudum pactum*, was not binding. They taught that a
Christian's word must be his bond. This idea, which found its way
into both ecclesiastical and commercial law,

> facilitated commercial operations under the ultimate protection
> of the confessor and ecclesiastical authority. The ethics of the
> Church, so strict on this point, ensured the development of a
> free economy.[37]

Ensured it but did not create it; the free economy was a natural
development as man applied his reason to meeting the physical
needs of his existence.

Christianity and the Church's role is then reactive, guiding
natural developments to operate morally for the common good, not
initiating them. As has been said the economy has its own legitimate
purpose and authority. A market economy developed in the Middle
Ages, as we have seen, and as it did so the need for industry and
commerce to operate on a larger scale to meet the needs of wider
markets led to larger investment of capital in their operation. The
market economy and capitalism continued to expand in the
sixteenth and seventeenth centuries, and from the eighteenth capitalists began so to dominate society that they set its tone in a way they
had not done in previous times. But this was a matter of degree, not
kind; what burst forth into full flower in that century had been long
in germinating. The volume of medieval trade was small compared
with that of modern times, but it was large in proportion to the population of the day and to the scale of economic activity of the time.[38]

The words 'capitalist' and 'capitalism' were made pejorative by
socialists, and especially by Marx, because of the excesses of liberal
capitalism which accepted no moral restraints on its activity; profit
and loss alone mattered. But of itself capitalism, in the sense of larger

investment in the productive process in order to meet wider demand, represents a natural development in man's economic life. In itself is an economic good if it operates in accordance with the moral law.

The question of the interrelationship between capitalism, Christianity and the Church was raised in the nineteenth and early twentieth centuries by the German economic sociologist Max Weber.[39] The context was the rising appeal of Marxism with its thesis that economic relationships explain everything, leaving no room for metaphysics or objective morality, and that capitalism embodies this ideology – which will destroy it. If this were true it was a devastating condemnation of the Western economic system, and Weber, searching for defence against such a thesis,[40] found it in one of the more basic anthropological concepts of the time, the ideal type, identifying the Calvinistic businessman and his Protestant work ethic as this economic type.[41] But the choice of this was ideo-logical and quite arbitrary. Capitalism had a long gestation, and to see the spirit of it embodied in one small group of men at one particular time has nothing to do with the actual history of capital-ism. It had everything to do with Weber's desire to combat Marxism.

Weber did not imply that capitalists had not existed before Calvinism;[42] it was capitalism that did not. The thesis had some credibility because at the time no one realized how great had been the extent of the development of trade, commerce and industry, of economic development in the period c.1050–1250, which modern economic historians now know was a period in which a genuine market economy, and capitalism, existed[43] and in which the reli-gion of everyman was overwhelmingly Catholic. Weber's assertion that capitalism and Catholicism were incompatible was based on erroneous data.[44] Capitalism exists where there are many capitalists – as there were in the middle ages, many of them being as dismissive of the moral law as the liberal capitalist. But liberal capitalist culture came to be, as we shall see, when entrepreneurs embraced the mechanistic view of natural law elucidated by some thinkers of the enlightenment; it justified the absolute freedom of economic man, irrespective of objective morality, and so justified by the dominant ideology of the time he was free to inflict the injustices on his fellow men which by reaction in time produced Marxism.

As Schumpeter points out, 'there was no such thing as a new spirit of capitalism in the sense that people would have to acquire a new way of thinking in order to be able to transform a feudal world into a wholly different capitalist one ... pure feudalism and pure capitalism are equally unrealistic creations of our own mind'. The ideal feudal man and the ideal capitalist man and their opposition, he adds, has no counterpart in the realm of historical fact. It is a misuse of the method of ideal types to which Weber lent his great authority; he found his ideal capitalist type engendered by the Reformation – but the historical objections to such a theory, he concludes, are truly too obvious to mention.

Feudal society incubated the society of the capitalist period. It did so by degrees, each step 'teaching its lesson and producing another increment of capitalist method and spirit'.[45] The fact is that the idealist, single-factor explanation

> seeing capitalism as the incarnation of a certain mentality was simply the way out adopted in desperation by Werner Sombart and Max Weber to escape the conclusions of Marx. We are in no sense obliged to follow them.[46]

Capitalism cannot be explained by one set of material or social factors or relationships; it cannot be explained or be seen to have emerged from a single source. Political, social, economic, cultural, intellectual, moral and spiritual influences played their part; above all historical experience and development, trial and error, learning by doing, played their part too. It was a long slow formative experience embracing many cultures and centuries and it does not accommodate a single-factor explanation such as Weber's thesis propounds.

3 St Thomas on private property[47]

The right to private property in productive goods was taken for granted by the canonists and theologians of the Middle Ages because of the teaching of the Scriptures and the tradition. However, the theological understanding of the concept still left much to be desired because its development had not been systematic. St Thomas's treatment of the subject, although he wrote no specific treatise on it, provides us with such a systematic approach. For him, as for the Fathers, the community of spirit which would have existed before the Fall would have enabled people to use the goods God had given them without conflict; even in our present state there are those who can enjoy goods in common without strife, and the principle that in necessity all things are common underlines this universal purpose of created things.[48] Community of goods is not, however, one that will satisfy all men; for man has a natural right to possess access to some external goods.

Man cannot have absolute dominion, that is total control over the goods God had given him, that belongs to God alone but he can have conditional dominion over them because they were made for his use.[49] Man can possess things. He has first the power to procure and dispense them, and there are three reasons for this. The first is that every man is more careful when he is working for what will be his own than if he is working for the collectivity, for what belongs to all. Where each is working for the community, he will be more inclined to shirk the labour and leave it to others. Look, St Thomas says, at situations in which there are many servants, where we will see this happening. The second reason is that human affairs, in this case economic affairs, are conducted in a more orderly manner if each man is charged with taking exclusive responsibility for some particular task. If everyone has to look after everything, confusion results. People must have particular responsibilities if economic society is to flourish, and private property establishes them. The third reason is that a more peaceful state is ensured if each one has and is contented with his own; quarrels arise more frequently where there is no private property.[50]

But man ought to possess external things as in some way common to all, so that he is ready to communicate them to others in their need, and Thomas quotes St Ambrose and St Basil on the point. He goes on to say that community of goods does not belong to the natural law in the sense that it dictates that all things should be possessed in common and that nothing should be possessed as one's own, nor does natural law specify who should have what: that is decided by positive law.[51] Hence ownership of possessions is not contrary to the natural law, but is in addition to it as a result of man's reasoning on how best to make use of God's gift. But the right to private property gives exclusive power only to the procuring and dispensing of goods, and the right to use them is not absolute: the common good has to be respected. At the same time, things possessed are truly subject to the owners; they can be bought, sold or given away.[52]

Thomas therefore here puts forward arguments drawn from observation and experience, but the more fundamental reason for private property is that it is a natural right for man to own goods as his own. When he says that this right is not of natural law, he does not mean it is contrary to it, but in addition to it. Such rights imply commensurability. This can be established by private agreement – as when two parties agree on a price for an object[53] – or by positive law. The commensurability can also exist in the nature of things, as when people marry, each has the right to the other's love and from it the bringing to be of new life.

A thing can also be commensurate with another according to something resulting from it. So in the absolute there is no reason why a piece of land should belong to one man rather than another, but if we consider the practicalities of cultivating it, and the need for this to be done without disputes over ownership, then it is more apt that it should be privately owned, as Aristotle has shown.[54] In other words we can all see that the world over, men have a right to a share in the earth's riches. But they cannot assert that right globally, but only in reference to their own, and their own people's, location on the earth's surface. To be a practical gift to all men therefore, each race or nation has to have the right to own part of those riches and each member of that nation must have the right to own part of the riches of his country if he is ready to work for them and use them for the common good.

Experience confirms this theory: socially responsible private ownership has proved the best way of ensuring that the world can provide a living for man so long as it works within a framework of just law. It is relevant to note here that when God was forming his own people in Old Testament times, the promise of a land of their own was made, and when the promise was fulfilled it was through the gift of private property in land; it was truly private property but its social obligations were inbuilt. It was for the support of the family, and therefore of the clan, the tribe and the nation in accordance with the principle of subsidiarity.

Private property then is natural, not directly from the natural law, but by natural reason expressed by human agreement and positive law.[55] It is then in harmony with natural law because right reason tells man that private property is better for the common weal.

But social responsibilities of ownership are intrinsic to private property because the original gift was to all men in common, and private ownership must operate in such a way that these responsibilities are respected. We can own goods but once our own needs are taken care of the needs of others must be met out of what we own.[56] It is this common purpose in use which justifies the right, in extreme necessity, of taking what one needs from the goods of others. Apart from the case of extraordinary necessity, this sharing is accomplished by the exercise of social virtues. Riches are granted to some so that they may obtain merit by using them well. So the virtue of liberality moves us to use well those things that we could use ill; liberality means not spending recklessly, but prudently for the common good. At the same time it prevents the wealthy having such an immoderate love of that wealth that they refuse to use it as they should, clinging to it for its own sake under the pretence of prudence. In a sense justice demands liberality. Being directed to others, and being concerned with material things[57], namely money, it is consonant with justice, annexed to it.

Munificence (or *magnificentia*) is called for when there is need for some great work to be done for the community, and its relationship to liberality is that it is in addition to it.[58] Avarice therefore endangers not only the individual soul but the community, because it concentrates wealth in the hands of those who refuse to use it for the good of all, just as prodigality recklessly throws it away when it is needed for charitable or productive enterprises.

The social responsibilities of ownership, however, are not left to the consciences of individuals alone. St Thomas is sure that social supervision is needed; it contributes to the well-being of the whole community. He appeals to Aristotle, who reasoned that the regulation of possessions helps to preserve states or nations[59] because, if a few gain control of property and income, the future of the commonwealth is undermined. There must be for the individual a sufficiency of material goods because this is necessary for a virtuous way of life, for human well-being.[60] Extreme disparity in the distribution of wealth is accordingly a fertile field for social discontent because it is an affront to the human sense of justice; the regulation of property is therefore the task of the State which has care of that common good which can be threatened if this task is neglected. It can make property laws, impose taxes and exercise jurisdiction over ownership. It is for the good legislator to decide how this is to be done. This is the role of general justice, which orders the individual towards the community; it is primarily the responsibility of the legislator, secondarily of the citizen.[61] The legislator therefore has the duty to see that an adequate amount of the necessities of life is available to all who are ready and able to work for them, since these are needed for the practice of virtue. In return the citizen is bound to make his contribution to the common good.

Particular justice is either distributive or commutative. Distributive justice is concerned with the distribution of common goods according to what the rank of each deserves.[62] The goods which are in the State's gift are given to a private individual in return for his services to the State in some way which may be greater or smaller.[63] Distributive justice also requires in those who benefit from it, satisfaction with their reward.[64] It is to be noted then that it is legal justice which requires adequate access to the necessities of life for all. The honours and riches of the State are for citizens in accordance to their service to it, not according to basic human need.

Commutative justice by contrast is concerned about the mutual dealings between persons.[65] Here one gives to another something by way of exchange for something received, such as is paid to an individual in commercial exchange. Here the question is one of equity, strict justice. What is exchanged in commutations must be equal in some way to what is received.[66] Equity also requires taxation because of the administrative expenses of government and the need to provide public services for the community. But it must be just and not confiscatory.[67]

The demands of justice must therefore be met if society is to be peaceful and well-ordered; peace is the work of justice. But on its own it is not enough. Justice removes obstacles to peace, but love positively fosters it. Justice alone will not produce the needed social cohesion, solidarity; that comes only from the *vis unitiva* of society, charity.[68] This virtue implants the desire to help one's neighbour, and without this desire society cannot cohere. Laws can do much, but there is a great deal more that they cannot achieve; the rest must be done by private individuals.[69] Self-seeking and greed will always accompany the institution of private property. Justice cannot always be done. The proper moral and spiritual values are the only answer to these evils. The Divine law orders men to the community under God.[70]

4 Commercial and industrial organization

To commerce and industry the guild organization was central. A form of guild organization existed in Roman times, but the guilds which developed in medieval Europe were a new growth, initially an integral part of the Church life of the time.[71] The medieval economic guilds were commercial or industrial, of the merchants or the crafts, and they both had links with the life of the Church; they had a religious and a social welfare function, although they were primarily a form of commercial or industrial organization evolved to meet the needs of their day. It was the parish church which provided medieval man with the chance to organize collectively for any legitimate purpose in civil society, and religious guilds of all kinds proliferated; those of the parish often formed the nucleus of professional and trade guilds. When they were established in their own right the religious and social welfare aspect of their work remained with them. In the case of the merchants, their guilds originally developed on the road, as mutual support and protection societies of those travelling a particular road or trading in a particular commodity, but as trade expanded their organization became more settled in towns and they developed a religious and social welfare function also. Their regulations were also influenced by their Christian origins and context; they 'derived in part from contemporary religious teaching on man and society, price and profit'.[72]

It is because from their beginning their activities were influenced in this way, that a consideration of their operations must have its place in any account of the Church's economic ethics. The merchants' guilds were the first to emerge, and as they grew and consolidated they became important in the political and economic organization of the towns, usually being responsible, among other things, for the craft guilds which appeared as the towns became centres of manufacture. Given the primitive state of society at the time when the towns began to develop from the eleventh century, it was necessary for the municipal authorities to ensure the food supply and other necessaries of life for its citizens, many of whom who were becoming involved entirely in commerce or manufactures; a wet summer or a severe winter could put such supplies, and with them the life and prosperity of the town, at risk.

The supply had to be organized, its quality established and its prices agreed. Any attempt to rig the market had to be checked and needless middlemen eliminated; the guildsman who provided the supplies had to deal directly with the buyer and the prices were to be agreed by fair trading in a free market; regrating, forestalling and engrossing were forbidden. Suppliers of goods who would meet these terms were then offered a monopoly of the town's supply; having agreed to meet terms which would ensure the consumers had a fair deal, they had a right to be protected from those who, not being bound to these conditions, could undercut them. Provision was made for the long-distance traders to sell in the same market through authorized outlets, and other traders from outside the town could sell on stated days, subject to town rules.[73] The town authorities had no interest in prices being kept artificially high; after all, they bought in the town markets, supplied by the approved guilds, they were consumers of their products, and they had a vested interest in not being charged overmuch and in maintaining the quality of what was offered.

Individual trades within the guilds in big cities soon developed into specialized groups forming their own 'craft' and separating from the main body. In London no general merchant guild had ever existed; there were twelve independent crafts, some of them mercantile, some of them industrial.[74] Craft guilds were primarily those which organized the local manufacturers, the skilled craftsmen, the cobblers, carpenters and the rest. They were in many cases the product of conflict with the merchants of the towns, but they won their place and were incorporated into its economic organization. In return for participating in the town market, the crafts had to accept the same conditions as the merchants. Goods had to be up to standard and sold in a free market. In return for the honest trading of sound goods at fair prices they had a monopoly to protect them from unfair competition. The distinction between merchant and craft is not to be overemphasized, however, since the craftsman marketed his own goods and so was also a trader.

Craft guilds grew naturally out of religious guilds. 'People did not see a clear distinction between their roles as masters of a craft guild and as brothers and sisters in a confraternity, although occasionally the statutes of these associations reveal at least the difference of emphasis between the two roles.'[75] Whenever people of the time gathered for any social purpose, their common faith consolidated the bonds between them so that they were in honour bound to respect an obligation undertaken. The unity, and the disunity which comes from the common concern for the endeavours of daily work, made it natural for the moral dimension to be encouraged. One modern economist, Robert Frank,[76] suggests that people who have a strong moral sense do better in a market economy than those lacking one, because those who lack such a sense eventually become ruthless and selfish and so destroy the trust on which sound business practice builds; a convinced and sincere Christian would be by definition a good guildsman.

Later we will trace the problems with which the guild system had to contend as the social and economic context of the guilds' work changed. Those difficulties do not invalidate the achievement of the craft guilds in the years between c.1100 and 1250 when the medieval European economy was most vital; they mark an important stage in the growth of good business practice and the efficiency it produces.[77] Guild members were forbidden to try to rig the market, and they were to supply a free market with quality goods. For example woollen cloth had to be all wool and a yard wide, and night work which could lead to inferior workmanship was forbidden in its production. The craftsman had to work in shops facing the street and keep his goods in view for scrutiny, and none could practise more than one trade. Sanctions were severe, and an offender could be fined, suspended and ultimately expelled from the craft.

The craftsman underwent an apprenticeship which lasted on average for seven years, during which, in return for his labour, the master was responsible for feeding, clothing and housing him, teaching him his craft and looking after his welfare generally. At the end of his apprenticeship he had to satisfy the guild as to his competence, then serve a further specified period as a journeyman in which he accumulated the experience needed for full membership of the guild; in theory, if he had the small capital necessary and a wife to keep his house, which was also his workshop, he could then set up as a master on his own. Such a training was designed to teach the would-be craftsman the virtues of hard work and good workmanship. Not every craftsman could expect to become a master, but many more could than after industrialization and there was nothing like the gulf between them. The background of master and man were roughly similar and the small scale operations meant that they worked side by side. In Paris in 1300 masters and men were about equal in number and scattered evidence from Germany 1300–1500 suggests that ratio was one to three or four.[78] Since this guild system existed generally down to the eighteenth and nineteenth century, the great class gulf between employer and employed which later developed was not there.

The crafts were efficient in ensuring honesty, quality and fair prices[79] and they did this by respecting the consumer and the public authorities while maintaining the dignity of their labour. They had a powerful influence on the organization of the manual workers. They taught them solidarity and discipline, which was maintained by freely chosen leaders, under the rule of statutes and regulations drawn up by themselves and supervised by the urban community. They gave them a powerful position in society, which was founded on a professional competence and assured them of the independence and dignity of labour.[80] The guild system was primarily and above all an efficient system of industrial organization. That it was so is shown by its longevity; guilds had to evolve and adapt to changing times, but that they survived down to the modern age attests to their value in their very long day.[81] In fostering commercial skills in difficult conditions, providing some insurance and social security for their members and establishing traditions of sound craft training and standards they provided an ethos which fostered commerce and industry. In them was incubated modern economic enterprise.[82]

5 Economic thought in the Middle Ages

It was noted above that there was no such thing as economic theory in the Middle Ages, in the sense of a unified account of the economic process as an independent sphere with its own laws. The basic economic model was that of the family unit, with the State having, in theory, a paternalistic responsibility for some form of economic policy. Aquinas, like Aristotle, could not have imagined economic behaviour other than in a framework of rights and duties regarding the common good.[83] Economic morality he dealt with in moral theology, but like the rest of the men of his time, he could not see economics as a system.

The theological landscape after Thomas was, as we have seen, not dotted with positive theologians like the great Dominican. The Church became less certain of herself in the fourteenth century and theology reflected this, but the fifteenth century finally produced theologians of genius who reflected deeply, and had a feeling not only for the problems of economic society in a market economy but went some way towards thinking systematically about them; they were the Franciscan St Bernardino of Siena (1380–1444), and the Dominican St Antoninus of Florence (1389–1459), archbishop of that see and now Doctor of the Church. Schumpeter gives to the latter the distinction of being perhaps the first person 'to whom it is possible to ascribe a comprehensive vision of the economic process in all its aspects'[84] while de Roover thought that the all-round achievement of St Bernardino was as great if not greater; de Roover also had great respect for another lesser known Franciscan, Pierre-Jean Olivi, to whom St Bernardino owed some of his insights.

However their individual contributions rate, between them they were responsible for a value theory based on scarcity and utility, both subjective and objective, and for grasping the importance of the market economy and tackling the practices which would warp it. They were strenuously opposed to all monopoly, oligopoly, and agreements between producers or distributors which penalized the consumer. Schumpeter, de Roover notes, was ridiculed by some experts when he claimed that the scholastics were advocates of the market mechanism and of free competition rather than of guild socialism; he adds that if anything Schumpeter did not go far enough in his emphasis on this.

They saw price determination as the result of a social process and rejected the labour theory of value. Value was determined by competition in a genuinely free market. Medieval moralists

> were much more favourable to the maintenance of competition than is commonly assumed. Unlike the mercantilists, they were implacably opposed to exclusive privileges and monopolies, which included any conspiracy to raise the price of goods or services above the competitive level to the detriment of the public and for the benefit of private interests.[85]

Finally, the question of usury. The problem here is that the modern world, starting with the Enlightenment, has seen the Church's teaching on this matter out of context, noted that it was rather complex, discharged itself of the labour of understanding it and preferred the unscientific alternative of dismissing it as at best irrelevant. There are however modern writers who have shown a more scholarly understanding of the problems the medieval moralists were facing and the wisdom of their answers. The context was one in which the major concern of the Church was to protect the peasant or the urban worker from the loan shark, the money-lender who took advantage of the desperate need of the poor for a loan for consumption purposes. The vast majority of loans were for consumption, needed by the desperate. Any moral judgement on moneylending had to make protecting them the first priority, and the Church's first concern was with moral issues.

But there were others needing loans, not for consumption but for business purposes, either to make an investment, or to finance their own business activities. The Church, in other words had also to protect the rights of businessmen. The ecclesiastical position was this: interest on a pure money loan, in any form, is forbidden, but profit on capital is permitted, whether it flows from commerce, business, or from an industrial undertaking, from insurance against transport risks, or from shareholding in an enterprise. The scholastic theologians and the canonists were not splitting hairs but seeking to encourage both economic efficiency and justice to others.

John Maynard Keynes was brought up to believe that the attitude of the medieval church was inherently absurd, and that subtle discussions of usury and exceptions to it were attempts to wriggle out from under a foolish theory. But they were in truth honest efforts to distinguish money loans from the return on active investment, to keep separate what the classical theory had inextricably confused, namely the rate of interest and the marginal efficiency of capital – to allow the schedule of the marginal efficiency of capital to be high, while using the rule of moral law to keep down the rate of interest.[86]

6 *Social welfare*

Strictly speaking, the responsibility for seeing to the needs of the poor was that of the bishops, but, in the turmoil of the ninth and tenth centuries and until the Gregorian reform, it was one which the monasteries were in fact called on to provide. So, for example, in 1050 Cluny possessed a hospice for the poor as well as an infirmary for the monks, a guest house for rich travellers and a small almonry for resident pensioners.[87] They also provided help for the destitute where none else existed close at hand.[88] The monasteries appointed a special official, the almoner, to supervise their work in this matter; he was to be a man of active charity and we have the description of such a man and an account of his work at Velay.[89] The availability of this care in times of famine and social disorder was one of the greatest services rendered by the monasteries of the times.

The growth of urbanization and the market economy in the central and late Middle Ages posed challenges to the traditional role of the Church in social welfare, and her canonists and theologians had to reckon with the new situation. Gratian summed up the tradition as it had become embodied in the law of the Church: 'the bishop ought to be solicitous and vigilant concerning the defence of the poor and the relief of the oppressed'[90] but how and when to be solicitous was no longer so clear as it had been.

Huggucio, who produced the best of the commentaries on the *Decretum,* distinguished between three categories of poverty. The first was that of those who were born poor and bore their poverty gladly for the sake of Christ. The second was of those who gave up their possessions for the sake of Christ, and the third was that of the involuntary poor who did not see their state as a blessing but were eager to end it. It was recognized that this involuntary poverty was an evil and there was no tendency to blame the poor for it. It was not a kind of crime to be poor.

There was a realism then about the way poverty should be tackled, and the difference between poverty and parasitism was well understood. No one was more in love with the idea of poverty than St Francis, yet his ideal was not begging but honest work in self-support. In his testament he asserted

I have worked with my hands and I choose to work and I firmly wish that all my brothers should work at some honourable trade. And if they do not know how, let them learn.[91]

The medieval canonist was well aware of the problem of giving carelessly and without proper regard for the true needs of the petitioner; he was aware of the cheat, but he did not presume that the majority of those in need were cheats. Nor did he allow his realism to obscure the obligations of charity; deterrent or punitive measures were neither desirable nor necessary. In case of doubt 'it is better to do too much rather than nothing at all'.[92]

The temporary problems of poverty could often be met without resort to outside help in the central period. Family ties were strong and the religious guilds of town and parish, together with the commercial and industrial guilds, commonly assisted their less fortunate members. All this was seen as an obligation of social solidarity, a man receiving help in the first instance from his own. The parish system also enabled the priest to know which cases were likely to be genuine and which not, and those seeking to avoid Paul's injunction, 'if a man will not work neither shall he eat', would quickly be known as shirkers. The peasant's failure to meet his labour dues would also be brought to the attention of the steward of the manor and steps be taken to correct it.

Failing such support by the family or social group, the poor had a right to turn to the Church for help, to the parish priest in the first instance, especially for the very basics, particularly for food. Here the evidence from England is that this hospitality was rarely lacking. In the diocese of Exeter in 1342 there was only one complaint from the ninety parishes during the annual visitation that alms were lacking to the poor, and complaints were usually accompanied by attestations that this was a lapse from the accepted high standards.[93] The parishes in England therefore had some of the functions of local government and they were officially recognized in this role.[94] In summing up his study, Tierney allows himself the observation, on the basis of the English experience in the thirteenth century,

I am inclined to think that ... the poor were better looked after in [that] ... century, than in any subsequent century until the present one ... [though] that perhaps that is not saying much.[95]

However it might equally be said that, given the disparity of wealth, technology and social organization of the two centuries it is saying something.

The role of the monasteries in the institutional care of the poor was fading by the twelfth and thirteenth centuries, not least because the problem was becoming increasingly an urban one and the monasteries were on the whole established in rural areas; those nearer the towns had usually also been responsible for such *xenodochia* as there were in this early period. There had been such institutions run by the Church since the fourth century, as we have noted, and they were in existence in Carolingian Europe also. How far they survived the collapse of that empire is not clear.

What is clear is that they were either founded or revived in considerable numbers from the late eleventh century, the majority of them in the period from about 1150 to 1250. By 1150 Narbonne, for example, had two hospitals and two leper houses. Paris's long-established Hôtel Dieu, which may have been operating in the ninth century, was either revived or considerably extended in the twelfth to become one of the biggest in Europe, and it existed there on the same site until the nineteenth century. In Genoa the Knights Hospitaller founded the San Giovanni hospice, and St Ugone, who died in 1233, was outstanding in his devotion to the poor and the sick who there attended. Most of the institutions as they grew up were run initially by religious communities or congregations.[96]

Some hospices seen to have survived in the cities, but since almoners were not appointed by cathedrals until late in the twelfth century, institutional care for the poor may have been limited. What gave the impetus for this to change was the Gregorian reform. For example, Bishop Peter of Agnani (1062–1105) had been appointed to his see by Gregory, and when he built his new cathedral complex, accommodation for the poor and the travellers was part of it. Innocent III was active in support of the hospital movement. This included the Fathers of the Holy Spirit who ran a long-established hospital at Montpellier and who founded another in Rome. Innocent determined that all cities should possess such institutions. Within twenty years there were few cities without them; London for example had St Bartholomew's, which until then had been a hospice for sick pilgrims only, St Thomas's, Bethlehem, Bridewell and Christ's Hospital. Such hospitals are the forerunners of the city hospitals of today, intended for those who have had accidents or are suffering from acute illnesses, as well as the sick who have no one to care for them.

The original idea of a hospice or hospital then had been to cater for the poor, the sick and the travellers; their ethos was not that of a modern hospital, dedicated to the care of the sick only. Even when they concentrated on the care of the sick, the initial emphasis was on the provision of 'shelter, food, spiritual comfort and disciplined environment. Some contemporaries would have considered that these are all that is needed for man's recuperation and regeneration.'[97] But by the twelfh century the study of medicine was being developed in the universites and the best knowledge and practice of the time was applied by the doctors who attended the sick in the hospitals but, given the ecclesiastical origin of most of these institutions, they paid at least as much attention, in some cases more, to their spiritual and moral needs.

The impact of Christianity on the specialized care of the sick has been revolutionary, and it was in the central Middle Ages that it was first felt. Like other religious and philosophical beliefs which encouraged hospitals, Christianity first of all taught the value of human life and the value of preserving it by using the best techniques available. It also from the first saw it as a service of Christ in the poor and the suffering, and the care and the treatment was free. It also provided the doctrinal and organizational basis for the adequate staffing of these institutions. The charitable care of the suffering was stressed as one of the surest ways to being saved. Instead of sheltering women and so discouraging them from nursing the sick, the Church encouraged unmarried women to undertake this and to live away from home to do so if needed.

The Church also organized brotherhoods of monks, and orders for women, whose main work was nursing in hospitals. She set up hospitals,

> It organized hospitals, financed them through its extensive fund raising machinery, and maintained them … Christianity's ecclesiatical structure produced a continuity in hospital affairs regardless of fluctuations in State policy … for many centuries European hospitals were run by the Church or by associations of laymen with the Church and they were staffed by nuns … hospital systems created and maintained by the Church became the workshops of doctors and centers of medical education … lay physicians were welcomed and soon commanded all their medical practices.[98]

So much has modern social welfare depended on the cultural conditions of Europe where it was developed by the Church, that where the Western hospital in its modern form has spread throughout the world in non-Christian societies, it has been found difficult to provide the qualified nurses needed; Christian values have been the inspiration for lay as for religious medical staff in the West.

The development of hospitals was part of the general pattern of

confidence and success in facing new problems in all spheres
which were the mark of the period. The fourteenth and fifteenth
centuries tell a different tale as the strife and confusion of the
times replaced the former cultural constructiveness.[99] There was a
failure to recognize that the nature of the social problem had
changed. The recession of the fourteenth century affected larger
numbers of people and brought with it problems of structural
change which had not existed before. It was a situation in which
organized systems of private charity such as the Church provided,
and which acted as a social security net, were no longer adequate
on their own. In particular the role of the monasteries in relief of
need was no longer as effective as it once was. Knowles in fact calculated that one-tenth of their income was given to this cause, but it
is possible that it was much less than that.[100] The State and civil
society alone had the authority and the resources to tackle it. So
although the canonists had much to say about migratory workers,
they could not deal with the problems of depopulation, the
soldiers returning from wars, vagrancy, plague and famine, nor the
problems of guild restrictiveness in a time of recession, the
growing use of unskilled labour, the putting-out system in industry,
or the problem of consumer credit.[101]

The rise of the national states, and the strong Italian city states,
from the fourteenth century created a political framework through
which society could tackle these problems and they were aware that
it, as well as the Church, had duties in the social and economic
field. Unfortunately these new states had political and military
ambitions also, and national rivalries fanned them; military expenditure increased and the people, and the Church, were expected
to provide the resources to meet it at a time when economic
decline and inflation were reducing the means by which they could
do so. The two centuries present a picture of an ever-widening gap
between the rich and the poor. The Church was no longer in the
position, and she no longer had the means, to deal with the social
problems of the day. Particular demands were made of the Church
and the clergy in terms of increased taxes by the State, and the
disillusion with both at the time made it more demanding than it
might otherwise have been. In turn, the inflation and the recession
which increased the problems of society affected the Church also,
and she was inclined to interpret her rights very strictly in resisting
what were considered excessive exactions. It was a measure of the
way that events were making it impossible for her to provide the
constructive leadership she had given to Christian society in the
central Middle Ages.

11

The medieval Church:
some social attitudes

1 The role of women

Eileen Power[1] in her classic treatment of the role of women in
medieval society states the familiar paradox of the conflicting attitudes to women that the Christian tradition presents to us. Woman
on the one hand is the inferior being, a temptress, the daughter of
Eve, and on the other, she is the model not only of women but of
humanity, Mary the mother of Christ. Apart from the more
extreme monastic and clerical writers, however, the idea of all
women as temptresses was not taken seriously. What was accepted
was that woman should be subject to man in marriage. Yet the
women as superior beings because of the virtue and graces of the
Virgin Mary was also part of the culture, helping to inculcate a
special reverence for those of her sex, and encouraging their
chivalrous treatment, so necessary in a violent time.

Courtly love and chivalry were connected; that love was lauded
as chaste, platonic; woman was next to God, worthy of the highest
and purest devotion, the inspiration of brave and noble ideals. The
practice of course often fell short of the theory. However, the ideal
itself remained and has helped in framing better attitudes down to
our own day. Further down the social scale there were fewer formal
social conventions which would buttress respect for women, but in
the thirteenth century they seem to have improved their condition
overall.[2]

Yet they still were at a disadvantage generally; conditions of the
times meant that women on the whole led restricted lives. Few
opportunities were open to them other than to be wives and

mothers, and most married young.[3] If she was single, among the peasants a girl could have her own holding and, on the estate, women dominated the crafts of brewing and spinning. For the upper-class girl who did not marry, there was the alternative of the convent, if she had a strong religious sense. It offered her opportunities, not only of spiritual progress but also of a better education, and a fuller exercise of responsibility, and of its nature it stressed her worth as a person, since her role in marriage was one secondary to that of her husband. There were sisterhoods in the towns which offered the same advantages for young women there.

Feudal marriage for the daughter of an upper-class family meant marrying the man chosen for her. It led to unhappiness for many, but the records show little evidence of the secondary role resulting in a state of subjection. The lady of the manor had to stand in for her husband on his frequent absences in service of his feudal superior. Nor did widowhood, too frequent in these violent times, deter her from her task, as the record of many a valiant woman shows. The country housewife had to be adaptable and self-reliant. Apart from the responsibilities of motherhood, she also had to supervise the making of cloth and linen, to be something of a doctor, and to assist her farmer husband when needed. The town wife helped in the workshop as well as being responsible for the household tasks. A marriage had to be a real partnership, the very opposite of the picture of a woman dominated by her husband. Further down the social scale the partnership was even more evident; the poor peasant's wife had a very hard life indeed, having to do her part of the heavy fieldwork as well as being wife and mother. It could not have worked without a rough and ready equality between husband and wife.

If medieval civilization is then to be judged by the actual records we have of the women of every class it would seem to come out of it reasonably well.[4] The theory was one of subjection, that she was not a free and lawful person, had no share in public life nor access to higher education. In practice the private rights and duties secured respect for her as a person. 'Taking the rough with the smooth, and balancing theory with practice, the medieval woman played an active and dignified part in the society of the middle ages.'[5]

Shahar's conclusion from her study recognizes the positive elements that Power considers sum up the real attitude of the times, but thinks that women suffered much more than her account allows, and she takes the idea of woman as the devil's ally as an example of this, as demonstrated in the treatment of witches.[6] Witchcraft survived in the Middle Ages but it did not flourish until after 1450 when the Church's influence was waning; the great witch-hunts were of the sixteenth and seventeenth centuries, not the fourteenth and fifteenth. The practice of witch-craft was a form of paganism and the Church sought to uproot it accordingly. She was more lenient than the secular authorities, because she was not convinced that there was a real witchcraft. Demons were scriptural and could be accepted, but that men and women could work magic with their help was nonsense.[7] Some of the clergy came to accept the reality of the phenomenon, but most of the learned among them rejected it. From the thirteenth century, however, the awareness of the reality of the devil led to a growing popular belief in witches, and by 1450 witchcraft was being identified by theologians as devil-worship. There was also an accompanying stress on woman as a temptress and source of evil. Belief in witchcraft resulted in and incited mob irrationality and violence, which was of its nature pathological. Though the worst of it did not occur during medieval times, Shahar sees it as a delayed result of them.

2 Slavery and labour

(i) Slavery[8]

The agricultural economy of the central Middle Ages was not based on slavery but on serfdom, which was slowly but surely giving way to free status. Slavery had persisted in Christian Europe in the early Middle Ages but it gradually disappeared in the period from AD 800 to 1100, reappearing in the Iberian peninsula where black African slaves were used in a domestic and urban role, with free labour predominating in all sections of the economy. The Portuguese had been connected with the existing networks of Muslim slave traders in Africa, but from 1500 bought slaves directly from the Africans just at the time when the need for them in the Indies was being felt. The transatlantic slave trade had started.[9]

Slavery in western Europe outside the Iberian peninsula, however, continued to fade away. According to Marc Bloch, this 'is incontestably one of the most notable facts in our Western history'[10] and he suggests that there were three causes for this. One of them was that the supply of slaves had to come from weaker soci-eties. From the second century AD the Romans found it difficult to maintain this supply and the slave population was reduced in consequence. Secondly the warlike Middle Ages did not revive the slave system though slaves continued to be taken beyond the frontier and traded within it; Christian belief precluded one Christian taking another into slavery; if a Christian captured another Christian he was obliged to respect his free status.[11] Evidence of a positive effort by individuals to get rid of the institution is also there St Wulfstan's (c. 1009–1095) success at Bristol, which was a centre of the traffic in slaves, was a most notable one and was the result of a long and cautious persuading of the men engaged in it.[12] Its persistence elsewhere was condemned once more at the synod called by St Anselm of Canterbury in 1102.[13]

The third factor in the decline and death of slave trading and slave owning, Bloch suggested, lay in the general social and economic conditions of the time. In the Merovingian and Carolingian kingdoms, for example, the landowners did not have the skills required to handle large slave workforces; it was more convenient for them to settle what slaves they had on the land, where they provided for their own needs on their plots and fulfilled their work obligations on the demesne – which were established by custom. The slave had become a serf.

Ross Samson questions Bloch's thesis[14] on several points but he concludes that the influence of the Church was central to the decline of the institution because of her insistence on rights for the Christian slaves. One of these was the right to Christian marriage. Roman slaves were not recognized as being capable of marriage but they were allowed an informal union, and the threat of breaking it, or separating them from their children, gave the owners a very useful way of keeping slaves under control. The Church, by contrast, insisted on sacramental marriage and it would seem that she was able to get this established and respected by the laws of the Franks and the Lombards, for example. She also insisted on the sabbath rest. Slaves had been allowed certain holidays by Roman custom and the threat of withdrawing these privileged occasions was another instrument of social control. But the Church forbade sabbath work for slaves also and that gave them a guaranteed 52 days of rest; again there is evidence that she had the support of the kings in making sure that they did get them.

The right of sanctuary also limited the freedom of owners. Once a fugitive from the law was on sacred property he was safe from molestation. Those with no other power to defend them found a defender in the Church and slaves on the run could and did avail themselves of its protection. It was not a privilege the State appreciated or liked to tolerate, and it had to be constantly defended, but it seems that it survived. Roman law had also provided for slaves to be able to appeal to the State for arbitration in disputes with their masters. This was a matter of self-interest. If slaves were left without any recourse against injustice then they would be more likely to nurse their grievances to the point of open rebellion, a constant fear of the Romans, surrounded as they were by slaves whom they felt, with good cause, they could not trust. The appeal was theoretically to the Emperor, and since in practice he did little to help the slaves the Church was able to offer her services as arbitrator, making sure that there would be no retaliation if the slave was returned to his or her master. These rights and privileges collectively amounted to a formidable limitation on the freedom of the owners and they had little to lose when, from the tenth century, slaves were anxious for manumission. There was the immediate financial gain, the long-term loss was not so great, and the threat of losing a valuable piece of property if the slave absconded was removed; when a slave requested manumission, 'it may sometimes have appeared as an offer they could not refuse'.[15]

It was a good time to be manumitted. Europe was on the move and a runaway or manumitted slave could join the freeborn in the task of clearing the waste lands within Europe's borders which developed from the tenth century; in so doing he could get land of his own. In 900, villages were widely scattered among these wastes, and as trade, commerce, urbanization and population increased, reclamation of them was a natural development. More land was needed and it was there to be had for the labour of clearing it. To attract the workers, landlords were ready to renounce their normal rights to labour services and to dues; the newly settled peasants paid only a money rent; they could become free and independent tenant farmers.

The whole of this development of Europe over two centuries (900–1100) and beyond went along with a great growth in population. Any accurate estimates of its size are not possible, but it is likely that in 1000 there were about 18 million in west, central and eastern Europe, with Scandinavia, and that by 1300 it had increased to some 60 to 70 million.[16] Slavery had been the answer to labour shortages in the past, but now with a growing population eager and ready to work, there was no such shortage. That if a man would eat he should be prepared to work was impressed on minds by the scriptures, more positively the dignity of labour had been recognized by the new culture from the beginning. All honest work however was respected because it was man made in God's image who did it. The need for workers to open up the new lands was met by freemen, or men fleeing from slavery or serfdom who responded to the challenge.

The Greeks had regarded basic manual tasks as unworthy of a citizen, and the Romans saw them as work that slaves did, if slaves were to be had, and so despised the free men who were engaged in them. Christianity, on the contrary, maintaining the attitude of Old Testament times, respected free men who supported themselves and their families by manual work, and the example of Christ the carpenter, and the emphasis on self-support through work that was inculcated in the early Church gave it a central place in her system of values. This was testified to by the importance placed upon it by the monks.

The early monasteries were the birthplace of free labour as Troeltsch, quoting Uhlhorn, pointed out.[17] Christian people saw monks doing manual work to support themselves and to have money to help the poor. This respect for work and those who did it was reflected in medieval European attitudes; guild membership and status, and the honest trade that was expected of those who enjoyed it, gave the manual workers in the towns a respect from fellow citizens.[18] There was an underclass of the unskilled or less skilled who had not attained the same dignity, but their readiness to revolt in order to try improve their lot shows they knew they deserved better.

The peasant was often regarded as a boor or a clod; but that most English of poems, *Piers Plowman*, does not see it that way; Piers is a mystic and a thinker. And Eileen Power reminded us that the peasants had achievements to their credit which rival those of any of their contemporaries in the arts and government. It was they who fed and colonized Europe, and with infinite patience gradually progressed from serfdom to freedom, securing for themselves by their hard work 'a good proportion of that land which they loved with such passionate and tenacious devotion'.[19]

(ii) Agricultural labour

The peasant did not achieve his aims without a great deal of conflict.[20] Nor was the move to a more market-oriented agriculture without its downside – the break-up of the large estates had its disadvantages. The small peasant farmer rarely had the incentive or the resources to be innovative and he also had to rely on middlemen more, but the advantages for the peasantry on the whole were real.

The decrease in population after the Black Death in the fourteenth century initially gave the serfs, labourers and peasants an advantage against the landlords, but the attempts of the feudatories to limit their gains, and the general disorder and suffering that resulted from the long-drawn-out war between England and France, led to a series of revolts in France, England, Germany, Spain and Sweden. The State itself was an object of attack, its more impersonal and restrictive use of the law particularly resented. Religion was at some times used for revolutionary ends; at others it was a bulwark of the old order. The monastic landlords were tenacious of their ancient rights, while the combination of their ecclesiastical and territorial claims was an extra cause of exasperation for those who were subject to them.

Flanders in 1322 to 1328 experienced real rebellion. The peasants, many of whom were very prosperous and feared the loss of that prosperity, rose up against the prince with his agents and his taxes, and against the landlords and the clergy. Five years of bitter unrest and much bloodshed led to a merciless and successful repression. The French Jacquerie of May and June 1358 reflected the peasant's resentment at their sufferings from war and its aftermath, and from poor prices for their corn. The exactions of the nobility and its incompetence added to their anger. The peasants went down to total defeat.[21] In England in 1381, the Peasants' Revolt, precipitated by a poll tax, was soon the vehicle of every grievance of town and country. The regulation of wages by Act of Parliament, the Statute of Labourers, which affected the urban as well as the rural workers, ensured their support. In Majorca, Scandinavia, Denmark and Germany there were revolts and uprisings at various times in the fourteenth and fifteenth centuries.[22] It was only in the more prosperous regions, those affected by market forces, that the practice of farming developed. Elsewhere the demesne was worked by peasants, and they were subject to labour dues also. Eastern Europe was generally more backward, and there the trend in later periods was to the great estate, a servile labour force and the exaction of labour dues, although these were less onerous. Though not as much affected by local market pressures, the demand for grain in the towns of north-western Europe increased as population rose from the mid-fifteenth century and they preferred to import from the east. The profitability of this trade made the eastern landowner more determined to hang on to his land and increase its output. In the west desmesne farming was less and less profitable for two reasons – grain prices were low and farm labour in short supply and expensive to employ; hence the effort to put the clock back which led to rebellion.

The prospect for the peasant in the fifteenth century seemed to be an improving one, and it has been regarded as a time of pros-

perity for them. Food prices and the cost of living were not excessive, and in real terms fixed money rents were depreciating, but
there is no way of knowing how many of the peasants were able to
benefit from this. The richer could take advantage of the situation
and hire labour whose cost was offset by lower rent payments, but
the poorer, with little land of their own, had to sell their services.
Even if they were able to do this, they were usually unemployed for
a large part of the year between ploughing and harvesting; subsistence, not prosperity, was their lot. It was a time for the clever and
the unscrupulous to make their fortunes. Population was fluctuat-
ing, labour was more mobile and the relations between lord and
peasant were changing. This created conditions which favoured
speculation in commodities and land as old estates were broken up
and new ones were formed. Prosperous peasants could become
merchants, acquire more land and join the gentry. The poorer or
less fortunate or avaricious sold or mortgaged their land and
became poorer still.[23]

(iii) Industrial labour[24]

The discussion of the place, role and attitude to industrial labour
in the medieval period must centre on the craft guilds which were
a unique product of the times and the basic form of industrial
organization. As such, the principles on which and for which they
were organized reveal the attitude of society to industrial life and
labour. We have given above a summary of the craft guild and its
operation in its heyday; although like the feudal 'system' the guild
system was very varied and no two trades were exactly the same,
there were several characteristics they had in common. They represented a stage in the evolution of modern industry, where initially
the master craftsman owned the raw material and the instruments
of production and himself marketed what he had made; he
enjoyed the full fruits of his labour. The system of apprenticeship
was designed to provide a thorough craft training and initiation
into the ways of work which inculcated the essential virtues of
steady application, good craftsmanship and respect for the craft
and its customers. Though in many crafts promotion to master's
status became restricted, the number of crafts and their small-scale
operation made it likely that this was not the normal case.

The particularism with which the more prosperous guildsmen
and guilds began to use their privileges as their wealth grew in the
thirteenth century aroused the anger and resentment of those
outside the charmed circle. The former became patriciates which

kept out the small traders and craftsmen; they could only be entered by right of birth or fortune, on condition of doing no manual work and paying high fees. The reaction of the excluded was to form their own fraternities or charities, crafts and corporations and to seek political power. In Beauvais in 1233 the mayor and the moneychangers were attacked and 1500 rioters were imprisoned. In Paris in 1295 and 1307 the fraternities were dissolved because of the threat to public order. In Flanders where the central power was weaker, the crafts rebelled in Liège (1253), Dinant (1255), and Huy (1299), and from 1275 the country was in open rebellion that simmered and flared until 1328. Northern Italy was similarly intermittently disturbed: Milan and Brescia (1260–86), Genoa (1257–70), Bologna (1257–71) and Florence (1250–93). The patriciates were beaten and the exercise of a craft was made the condition of admission to political rights; but there was no emancipation for the wage earners who were outside the civic body.[25]

In the great industries, and in particular the woollen cloth manufacture of Flanders, northern France and Tuscany, the crafts were absorbed and reduced in influence by the growth of capitalist production.[26] Here the entrepreneur distributed orders and materials and organized the productive process, either through the specialist crafts in which the masters were as much beholden to them as their workers, or in their own workshops and through piecework; they were also the sole buyers of manufactured goods and so could impose their own conditions and rules. They advanced money to those they employed on terms which kept them in debt, paying famine wages and operating truck systems. Here then was a proletariat, but it was not overall a large one. The mass of the workers were employed in the small crafts which had direct contact with their customers in a local market, not in the few great industries which catered for the long-distance trades where economies of scale were available. The local urban market absorbed the goods they made, mastership in the guild was more open, wage labour was a fact but the worker could find employment by the day, the week or longer; it was hard work, on average for 8 to 13 hours a day according to the season, once meal breaks had been deducted. But night work was usually forbidden and there were numerous feast days and holidays.[27] Wages did not fluctuate wildly; they followed the cost of living, and journeymen did not fare badly in comparison with their masters: for example in the fourteenth century a master tiler made at most five and a half pence a day, the journeyman three and a half. Living standards

were rising, if slowly, as were the moral and cultural.[28] The majority of those who worked at the ordinary tasks of supplying the
needs of their fellows and supporting the structures of ordinary life
had demonstrated the dignity of labour and had attained political
power in the towns.

Generally during the fourteenth century, with the worsening
economic fortunes of the times, the wars and social upheavals that
split Europe, and the experience and aftermath of the Great
Plague, communal patriotism waned. Whereas in more favourable
times the guilds had been the leaders in progress and freedom,
they now became particularistic, inward-looking, monopolistic and
tyrannous in their economic affairs. As a result of their superior
business ability and their ruthlessness in exploiting it, small
numbers of capitalists dominated the cities where the great industries were centred; they controlled most of the house property, and
they were active in banking, commerce and industry. It was they
who were in control of international trade, corn, wine, fish, cattle,
spices; they speculated in industrial raw materials and in manufactures, in wood, hides, skins, furs, cotton, silk, wool and woollen
goods. They exploited the mineral resources and the processing of
metals, and everywhere their capitalistic enterprises were flourishing. They looked beyond the city and were the agents of the kings
and princes who were establishing themselves more securely and
gradually taking control of national economies. They adopted an
aristocratic manner of life and became patrons of the arts.
Through their economic ventures they infected Europe. Reckless
speculation, monopolies, cartels and disdain for morality was on
the increase. They crushed where they could the old urban organization, and forced a large part of industry and commerce into a
pattern of their own choosing; wage labour became harsh and
oppressive and the urban proletariat's attitudes reflected this.

The only check on their interests was the still strong small and
middle class of bourgeois, urban proprietors, the officials and the
traders and masters of the crafts who formed the majority in most
towns; in Basle for example some 95 per cent of the population
belonged to it. It was fostered by the monarchies which involved its
members in urban administration, through which popular
elements could participate. Even in the centres of big industry, the
crafts still existed. In Ypres for example while such industry
employed over 51 per cent of the workforce, small crafts employed
most of the rest.[29]

The tendency to exclusiveness and selfish fostering of particular
interests challenged worker solidarity. The major crafts sought to

dominate the minor, the masters sought to limit access to mastership to their own sons or relatives only and to make it more
difficult for the ordinary journeyman to become a guildsman.
Everything combined to keep the ordinary worker in his place
while a small number of the privileged enjoyed the rewards of
labour. The journeymen became a distinct class separated from the
masters, and guild regulations were brought to bear to prevent
them making any advance. In self-defence they formed journeymen's associations under cover of piety or charity or technical
instruction, but as they became established they in their turn
became intolerant and exclusive.

Capitalism at the top and pauperism at the bottom were then
both growing, yet masters, journeymen and wage workers in the
small crafts could enjoy a reasonable standard of living when war or
other crises did not intervene. Indeed the rise of wages that
followed the Black Death increased prosperity for many. Thorold
Rogers showed that in real terms the English workers' wage was
worth twice in the fifteenth what it was in the twelfth century.[30] But
from the second half of the fourteenth century the anger of the
increasing proletariat was shown in violent rebellion.

In Florence the textile workers rose up in 1342, and in 1378 the
much more violent and desperate *Ciompi*, the poorest section of
the community, rebelled. Initially successful in getting a share in
government, and some protection from the worst excesses of the
industrialists, they were misguided enough to seek total control, so
provoking a reaction which lead to their defeat in July. There were
risings in Flanders in 1345 and 1359, and in the climax of 1378 the
leaders from Ghent sought to set up a workers' dictatorship,
destroy the bourgeois and despoil the masters. For four years they
had their way until their defeat at Roosebek in 1382.[31] In one form
or another, labour unrest and rebellion of some kind, usually less
spectacular, wracked Europe and, except where mixed governments emerged, caste selfishness prevailed. Few showed interest in
breaking out of urban exclusiveness; they only wished to preserve
old privileges and attitudes and it was this which opened the way
for the princes and kings to bring them under control once more,
though it was not long before the exactions of the royal officers
bred further rebellion.

Most industries at the end of the period were then small-scale
crafts, the average shop employing the master and his few assistant
apprentices or journeymen, and where external conditions
allowed, they returned to those who manned them a basic livelihood. The textile industry was highly capitalized and free of any

control apart from the will of the masters and the needs of the market. It was here that the proletariat and all the bitter problems of injustice in that market were found, and this was a particularly dangerous inheritance that the Middle Ages left to the modern world. But the guild ideal at its best was the most successful of attempts made by man to balance the rights of the consumer, the producer and the community in the industrial process, and its insistence on good workmanship and honesty in the formation of masters and men marked a notable step in education and business education for the industrial worker. Above all it demonstrated that morality and economic enterprise could go together. Erasmus, who saw at Strasbourg a full guild constitution still flourishing during the Renaissance, was aware of the achievement at its best: 'I saw monarchy without tyranny, aristocracy without factions, democracy without tumult, wealth without luxury ... would that it had been your lot, divine Plato, to come upon such a republic'.[32]

(iv) Freedom

The idea that freedom was 'not a value of any importance in the Middle Ages',[33] has been due to the identification of freedom with the personal and civic freedom of today, whereas in medieval times the starting point for establishing freedom was finding protection against the infringement of the existing liberties which were established by custom. Medieval lordship could mean tyranny, the absolute use of brutal power over others. The practice of obtaining charters in which the customs were laid down was the first stage towards limiting this tyranny; with these secured, the way was open to the development of personal and civic freedom. Charters were sometimes granted to individuals, but more commonly to communities, fraternities and guilds, and the strong sense of solidarity these organizations evidenced also embodied a conviction of personal and civic freedom. The collective consciousness and the social action that stemmed from it developed from the parish, overlapping with the village in the rural areas; the parish was concerned not only with the spiritual well-being of its people but also with community action for secular improvement; parishes for example undertook road building and the clearance of the waste land.[34] This solidarity and collective consciousness in the parish was the focus of life for the people in the countryside and it was from it that the struggle to secure the basic minimum customs and liberties, rents, dues, rights of inheritance, legal exemptions, the right to elect their own officials, for example, began. Recognition of customs meant freedom to the peasant because, collectively, it meant free status.

For the townsmen, the burgh was the guarantor of freedom and rights. Their charters of liberties secured their right to carry on their businesses and trade; they embodied their claim to personal liberty and dignity, to organize their own lives and to have their rights respected. The struggle of the craft and journeymen's guilds was a struggle for the right of association and recognition of the dignity of their labour against the patricians, the greater industries, or the exclusive guilds. More than a matter of status was involved. Underlying these conflicts was the question of the spiritual nature of man. Their connection with a radical interpretation of Christianity was notable. The English Peasants' Revolt of 1381, which was in fact a revolt of townsmen too, evidenced this. The king's power was not in itself threatened, but obedience to him as God's representative was limited to all things proper and Christian. It indicated an idea of human dignity which was based on Christian belief in man as made in God's image and likeness. On this basis, the idea of civic as well as personal freedom, and the accompanying rights, was well alive in medieval society.[35] It was evident in the great store which peasants and burghers placed in their right to elect their leaders; at the village, parish and town level, participation was highly valued. It was basic democracy, communal decision making at the level that most affected daily life.

It was the absolute monarchies with their claim to the divine right to rule who were later to limit the Western idea of freedom. This

> audacious attenuation of the Western ideal of freedom did not occur in the middle ages. It was an excessive conceit of late antiquity that was reborn in modern Europe.[36]

Christian theology, the queen of the sciences, was essentially a theology of freedom, given to man by God as being in his image and likeness, restored to him by Christ through his passion, death and resurrection. The Reformation and Renaissance tradition has stressed that it was these movements which secured for the West the idea of personal freedom that the modern world knows. The truth is that it was the whole of the Western tradition, which achieved maturity in the Christian Middle Ages, which spoke of freedom. That the Son of God became incarnate and died to save man from sin gave more powerful values to society than any other culture possessed.

> Individually liberating, socially energizing and culturally regenerative, freedom is the undeniable source of Western intellectual mastery. The engine of its extraordinary creativity

and the open secret of the triumph of Western culture ... the facts that today, almost all peoples of today embrace the ideal of personal freedom ... are telling testimony to its overpowering appeal and inherent goodness.[37]

This same sense of freedom encouraged intellectual enquiry and tremendous intellectual vitality. It also supported those cultural trends which issued in representative government which made possible the modern democratic state.

There were also negative aspects to the medieval and Christian record on freedom which we have also examined; the treatment of the Jews, and the excesses of the Inquisition and of the crusaders in particular. These have to be taken into consideration in the balance. That they were real and deplorable has, however, in its turn to be seen against the background of a civilization which for the first time built itself up to prosperity and high achievement in all the fields of human endeavour open to it at the time, and did so on the basis of semi-free labour moving to full freedom on the land, and in the cities, free labour from the beginning. In all this the Church was at home, in many aspects of it she was the guiding force. She was at home in the urban economy whose institutions and methods heralded their modern forms, she was at home with representative government which made the development of modern democratic forms possible. The building of her Churches and Cathedrals produced a cultural epoch, and an art, that has never been surpassed. She played the dominant role in the development of the Universities which have become a model for the modern world, and played a similarly dominant role in the organized care for the poor and sick, and in particular developed a system of hospitals to which the modern world owes much. She also tried to civilize and human-ize, in so far as she could, the profession of arms and the conduct of war, leaving us the ideal of Christian knighthood and chivalry, of the strong protecting the weak, which still has much to offer us.

3 War, crusades, chivalry, the just war

The medieval Church was a peace society, yet war as part of the pattern of human affairs was a fact that the Church had to face the more she became involved in the role of leadership of that society. Her desire was always for peace, even when she became entangled with war. The peaceful and prayerful pattern of life of the monaster-ies in particular, at a time when they were at their most influential, stood in sharp contrast to the ethos of the warrior society surrounding them. The peace movements of the time – the Peace of God and the Truce of God – mark the attempt of the Church to restrain violence, while the councils of the ninth century repeat the prohibition of the carrying of arms by the clergy. Warriors could be penalized by the Church for their involvement in war, as were the Normans who shed blood in the invasion of England.[38]

The Church continued to take pacifism seriously, as the peace movements testify.[39] At the same time both justice and charity demanded that the right to use force in defence of right and in protection of the weak be recognized. Bishops throughout a large part of Europe sometimes raised militias from their own resources to join with all interested in suppressing the evildoers who broke the peace. The church reformers of the eleventh century however saw another aspect of the problem; some of them had been actively involved in war as churchmen. The Pope's responsibilities for central Italy and the weakness of the civil authority in the region impelled them, for example, to use force to protect the territories of the Church and of their people.[40] The Crusades marked a new stage in this Christian response. The destruction of the Holy Sepulchre in 1009 and the attack of the Pisans and Genoans on the Saracens in Sardinia in 1015 marked a revival of the conflict, and the subsequent clashes between them and the Normans in Sicily were a continuance of this trend. In 1064 a large German pilgrimage to the Holy Land had been attacked and forced to defend itself. The defeat of the Eastern Empire by the Seljuk Turks at the battle of Manzikert in 1071 was the background to the Crusades proper. The East appealed for help at that time but it was not until the Council of Clermont (1095) that the West was able to respond with the Crusade called by Pope Urban II.

The older attitude, which saw the emergence of warrior elites as a usurpation of the authority of the king, a kind of publicly accepted gangsterism where the only hope of salvation for a knight was in abandoning his arms and retiring to a monastery, was receding under these influences. The realization that in certain circumstances the use of force was necessary led to greater respect for the profession of arms. With the Crusades, the warriors were idealized; their knighthood itself, the life of battle for Christ, the Church and justice and peace in society, was a positive good. With the use of the term *milites Christi* for the crusaders, and the foundation of the Knights Templar, the first of the knightly religious orders, this was underlined. In St Bernard's *In Praise of the New Militia*, knighthood was seen as a Christian avocation. Its standards were high. The knight swore to love God and be steadfast in the faith, to defend the Church, and to keep his sworn word. He promised to be ready to defend the rights of widows and maidens and give them material help should they need it. He was to denounce wrong judgements and he must try to bring all murderers and extortioners to justice. After an all-night vigil he made his confession, heard mass and was given the spurs and the sword which were the mark of his knighthood.[41]

The medieval canonists and theologians took up the question of the morality of war, that is, armed conflict between sovereign states, and they did so on the basis of the teaching of St Augustine on the just war. They, like Augustine, did not set out to justify armed conflict, which was always seen as at best a regrettable necessity, but to try to ensure that when it was necessary, in the absence of any other means in defence of the State or of restoring peace and justice, it was conducted with as much respect for life and civilized values as was possible. Gratian in 1140 defended the soldiers' avocation; they can please God in that role in wars waged 'in order that the wicked may be corrected and the good relieved', for that war is just which after formal declaration is waged to regain what has been stolen, or to repel attack.[42]

Like Augustine, the medieval theologians preferred negotiation to violence in the settlement of disputes between nations but knew that it was necessary to deal with the question of the use of force in keeping of the peace and the maintenance of justice. For all that, they remained doubtful over positive recommendation of war as a means of advancing the cause of religion in any way. They discussed many issues that were of comparatively less importance in medieval times than were Crusades, but

> scholastic reticence to accord full treatment to the crusading movement stemmed from a nagging suspicion that the crusade was an unsuitable means to ecclesiastical and religious ends.[43]

Theologians and canonists were reluctant to commit themselves to the support of Crusades. Many crusading bulls were not included in official decretal collections and generally war insofar as it was necessary was a task for the laity; not even St Bernard's recommendation of the crusader monks of the knightly religious orders established them as a positive good; both canonists and theologians said as little as they could about them. That did not stop the Church using them, and Pope's insisting on them; it simply serves to show that the clerical mind was not altogether happy with the idea.

St Thomas's teaching on the just war theory was based on that of Augustine. For a war to be just it must be declared by the proper authority, namely by him who has the task of directing the affairs of the State, and not by private individuals. Secondly, it must have a just cause; self-defence, or the restoration of what has been unjustly taken from the State. Thirdly, it must be waged with the right intention, that is to avoid evil or to do a good, not for vengeance, hatred and the desire to dominate. War must be fought for the sake of peace; conquest must be directed to leading the conquered to the ways of peace.[44] He also excludes the clergy from the ranks of those who have a right to bear arms, not because it is in itself wrong to do so but because it is unbecoming for them as clergy; they can therefore encourage others to fight in a just war and help them spiritually.[45] Prayers and other spiritual means are the main means the clergy should use to prevent war.

The complete medieval just war theory has been summarized as follows:[46]

1. There is greater merit in preventing war by peaceful means than in vindicating rights by bloodshed.
2. Peace through conciliation is better than peace attained through victory.
3. There is a natural community of mankind which gives rise to certain rights and duties relevant to the morality of war.
4. The absence of a superior tribunal before which a prince can seek redress can alone justify him in making war, except when resisting actual attack.
5. The following conditions must in addition be fulfilled before a war can be just.
    (i)   It must have a just cause, a grave injury (actual invasion, unlawful annexation of territory, grave harm to citizens and their property, denial of peaceful trade or travel, violation of religious rights). Great injustice against those the State is obligated to help also gives a just cause.
    (ii) It must be necessary, the only way of restoring justice or preventing its continued violation.
    (iii) A formal warning and declaration of it must be made to the offending state.
    (iv) It must be declared by the proper authority within a sovereign State; if the defence of religious rights is involved, the consent of the Church is required.
    (v)   The good to be attained by the war must be reasonably supposed to be greater than the certain evils, material and spiritual, that war entails.
    (vi) A right intention, the restoration or attainment of true

peace, must actuate it in declaration, conduct and conclusion.

(vii) Only so much violence as is necessary in defence or repelling attackers must be used.

6. The moral responsibility for war rests with the sovereign authority, not with the individual soldier or citizen whose duty it is to obey, except when he is certainly convinced it is wrong to do so.

7. Priests may not fight even in a just war.

8. The duty of repelling injury inflicted upon another is the common obligation of all rulers and peoples.

As so stated the theory assumes many things. It is in a juridical and legal form. It assumes that private war is of its nature outlawed and that only kings and princes have the right to wage war. So stated it abstracts from the realities of feudal warfare where war often enough was the private war of one lord or vassal against another. It assumes there exists an impartial higher authority to which the prince can appeal for redress other than by arms, before the final resort to force can be justified. This again is purely theoretical; only the Emperor or the Pope could be seen as capable of fulfilling this role; in practice there were insuperable obstacles preventing them from acting effectively in it.

To be effective, such a final court of appeal must be able to apply meaningful sanctions. Without them, it could just be ignored. The Papacy did not possess such sanctions; spiritual measures only worked insofar as they were accepted by all concerned. Political and military sanctions could never be applied on a sufficient scale and the Papacy should not be put in a position, or accept a position, which demanded them. The Emperor in theory did possess them, but at no time would the states of Europe as a whole accept his right to use them. And so one could go on. Medieval just war theory was never as precise as it could have been, and insofar as it went it could usually be challenged or circumvented by the determined. Its significance is not that it worked in any full sense, but that it represents a consistent effort to avoid war if possible and where it was not, to civilize and humanize its conduct. In the last analysis, perhaps it can be said that the conditions set out were 'the best compromise between aggression and Christian pacifism that the Church could devise'.[47] Aggression was a fact of life among a warlike people and aggression was sometimes necessary if the right had to be protected by force for lack of an alternative. Yet in accepting its necessity, a Christian civilization had to keep in mind

its potential for brutalizing and degrading humanity. The attempt
to formulate a just war theory was an attempt to do that.

The flaw in such theories is that they assumed that an authority
responsible to no superior is competent to declare war under the
right conditions; they accepted in other words that a superior
acceptable to all would not necessarily be found. In fact one State
judges another as an unjust aggressor and declares itself judge, jury
and executioner in its own case. By the same token the supposed
aggressor counter-claims that justice was on its side; then, there
being no one to judge the issue impartially, both could claim they
were fighting just wars, and the fighting went on just the same.

In practice, the complexity of the just war theories had to cede
before the primary obligations of the State to defend itself; these
were seen as absolutely binding. The scholastics refused to
consider any preventive war, but once in war aggression was necessary to pursue what was authorized by the competent authority and
had been declared just; however, there were limits on that aggression: combatants must treat their defeated enemies justly and they
must not pursue the war in a spirit of vengeance. With all their
defects, just war theories

> placed the burden of proof on the would-be just warriors or
> demonstrate or rationalize the grounds for their actions accord-
> ing to generally acceptable principles.[48]

At the same time, a theory which at once seeks to restrain and
justify violence acquires a subtlety which tends to defeat its
purpose. Those involved in the terrible business of killing or being
killed rarely have, or have had, the opportunity of proceeding
entirely according to whatever rules of war exist or existed. In
Russell's view it is also unclear whether just war theories have
limited more wars than they have encouraged. This may be so, but
they must surely be given the benefit of the doubt, and the effort
to bring humane considerations to bear before, during and after
hostilities, must be maintained. The agreement between at least
some nations to provide proper treatment of the wounded and of
prisoners of war, for example, have been the result of the continu-
ation of these efforts, and the value of them is dramatically clear
when conflicts take place between nations which have not accepted
their binding force.

Part 3

The marginalization of the Church in the modern world (*c.* 1500–1878): absolutism, imperialism and revolutions

12

The Church, absolutism and imperialism

1 *Introduction*[1]

The failure of the Papacy, episcopate, clergy and religious orders generally to tackle the problems of corruption which afflicted both in the late Middle Ages brought about the Protestant Reformation; a Catholic reformation eventually came, but Christendom was already sundered. The idea and reality had both been on the wane since the Avignon Papacy (1306–78) and the conciliar movement in the fourteenth and fifteenth centuries, but with the Protestant Reformation the divisions within Europe became set. The religious and political conflicts in the sixteenth century resulted in the Empire, France, Spain and England variously being at odds with one another, the divisions between the first three being highlighted most clearly in the Thirty Years' War in Germany (1618–48). It was not primarily a religious war, but one for and against the German Princes; it was

> not fought by the German people, still less for religious motives. The defenders of princely liberties, the majority of whom were Catholic, called themselves Protestant; the protagonists of Imperial authority called themselves Roman Catholic, although Wallenstein, the greatest of them was an unbeliever.[2]

Thirty years of ferocity, frequently stimulated by appeals to Christian fervour, was, however, increasingly effective in giving the leaders of Europe, wearied of the theological controversies of the time, and more and more impatient of any attempt at moral restraint on their ambitions, the opportunity to claim that religious

* The notes and references for Chapter 12 are to found on p. 407

and moral considerations had no part to play in politics: reasons of State alone should move the minds of statesmen; any attempt to limit national sovereignty within the framework of a supranational law, justified by appeal to religious or any other higher ideal, was gone.

2 Absolutism and the decline of representative government

The Peace of Westphalia[3] encapsulated this secularism in its religious provisions which gave the State the right and the power to control churches. The Papacy still disputed that right, but the Papacy was under pressure on this matter even in the Catholic countries, the Catholic monarchs being intent on depriving it of what was left of its influence. The secularist tendency of the seventeenth century in Western culture was also accompanied by a deep institutional change in politics, namely the movement towards absolute monarchy. The development of representative government, which was so characteristic of the thirteenth century, faltered in the fifteenth as we have seen, mainly because of the failure of the three estates, the clergy, the nobles and the commons, to work together: kings were able, by concessions, to prevent them forming alliances which could have checked the excessive regal powers.[4]

The failure of representative government to adapt to the changing needs of society, the conflicts of the fifteenth century and the religious upheavals of the sixteenth encouraged the growth of strong national monarchies, or petty princedoms, apt to become absolutist because they promised peace and order to a Europe craving both. In France the Huguenot wars (1559–98) were ended by the accession of Henry IV (1594–1610), and when the regency for the young king Louis XIII (1624–43) was over Cardinal Richelieu set about making him the master of France, and France the master of Europe. Louis XIV, actual monarch from 1661 to 1715, was absolutism personified. Germany, which had achieved domination in central Europe in the early fifteenth century seemed on the point of doing the same in Europe generally at the beginning of the sixteenth. Two things[5] prevented her from doing so. The first was the economic decline brought about by the opening of the Cape route to India which transformed her from the centre of world commerce to being an economic backwater; her markets were taken by others and the wealth of her burghers shrank. The second was Martin Luther's (1483–1546) revolt against Rome, the circumstances of which meant that he would be overly subjected to political pressures from those who supported him. The result was that the main thrust of Lutheran political theory in early modern Europe was to encourage and legitimize absolutist monarchies.[6] He began by stressing the equality of man and ended by making all men subject to the iron will of rulers.[7] The man who first expressed Germany's national spirit rejected medieval universalism, made it impossible to unify the country for centuries and left to Europe an inheritance of states perpetually in conflict.[8]

In Spain the Crown reduced the number of towns which sent representatives to the Cortés, and the opposition of those still privileged to do so to the attempt to increase them once more, secured the power of the monarchs. Ferdinand and Isabella (1479–1516) also brought the Church firmly under control and by the reign of Philip II (1556–98) absolutism was firmly established. The wealth of Spain's colonial empire, and the share of it which went to the king, freed the monarch from the pressing need for subventions.

In England, developments worked more effectively to sustain the growth of representative government. The same class differences and jealousies of other countries were there in the fifteenth century but there were other influences to counterbalance them. In particular the minor landed gentry allied themselves with the merchants and towns in the House of Commons rather than their more noble colleagues in the Lords, and the Commons were strengthened as a result. However, under Henry VII the House of Commons had little influence because of the King's shrewd financial policies and the short shrift he gave to his enemies. It was under Henry VIII that Parliament came into its own, and the Commons became a coherent and compact entity and a national institution. Henry was no friend of freedom, but he needed to get approval for his controversial policies in Church and State and he used the Commons to do this; the wealthy merchants, landowners and professional classes who gained in one way or another from the dissolution of the monasteries and the sale of church lands, or prospered through the other social and economic changes of the time, were its backbone.[9] But the structures of representative government remained and in the seventeenth century they enabled Parliament to defeat the attempt of the Stuarts to impose royal absolutism.

On the Continent, however, absolute monarchy had established itself as the preferred form of government in key states by the mid-seventeenth century. Theoretically absolutism asserted that embodied within the State was a sovereign power beyond which there was no appeal, and in practical terms it was a reaction to the political and religious strife of the previous period. It personalized the effective centralization of power in the monarch who was not hindered in making effective decisions and putting them into practice by the need to depend on the will of a representative assembly. In reality there was a limit on the extent to which he could control the vested interests which had been consolidating over the centuries at all levels of society.

Whether the monarchs appealed to their own right or to divine right they all wished to be sovereign, to tolerate no higher authority within the State than themselves. This meant the end of any claim by the Christian Church or churches to dissent in conscience on specifics, or to bear allegiance on spiritual and moral issues to a supranational religious authority such as the Papacy. The powerful absolute states which proclaimed themselves Catholic sought to retain all the external forms of that religion, but to deny the authority of the Church generally and Rome in particular except on such matters as they chose to concede to them.

3 France, absolutism and the Church[10]

The foundations of French absolutism were laid by Richelieu when acting as regent during the minority of Louis XIII 1610–24; the Cardinal was then until 1642 his Secretary of State for foreign affairs. He set out to secure the prestige and power of the King and the strength of his kingdom, and he succeeded in both tasks. Louis XIV (1643–1715), was five years old in 1643 and became king in fact in 1661. In him, the 'Sun King', absolutism reached its zenith, though his power was always curbed by the inertia of the system and the vested interests within it. There was indeed a greatness about Louis XIV and about all he did. He presided over an empire more compact, efficient and powerful than Spain's. France's culture and brilliance was the glory of Europe; her administration in the hands of men like Colbert (1669–83) was regarded as a model for the world. Bossuet explained that 'Royal power is sacred, God raises up kings as his ministers'.[11] Sworn to protect the Church, he also knew that the Church, supporting him in his role of Catholic King, was the strongest foundation of this throne.

This did not stop him denying the hierarchy and clergy any influence on policy, while at the same time interfering wholesale in the affairs of the Church,[12] effectively choosing and appointing bishops, practically excluding the Papacy from any part in her life and distributing bishoprics and abbacies to reward favourites. The whole episcopate became increasingly his men, more attached to the throne and its needs as he understood them than to the international Church and the Papacy. That most of them were good men meant that the more obvious kind of scandals were avoided, but the long-term effect on the French Church of what has come to be called Gallicanism was disastrous.

Louis's policy of personal and national aggrandizement was misguided at best, not least in that it imposed great suffering on the ordinary people of France. He became increasingly rash in his political judgements; the War of the League of Augsburg (1689–97) involved conflict with Protestant and Catholic kings alike. That of the Spanish Succession (1701–14) was fought over the dubious claim of a grandson to the Spanish throne; his enemies were too numerous for his forces. He lived to regret having done so little to relieve the distress of his people. This sustained contempt for the needs of common good which had first claim on his care mocked his title of Most Christian King. The splendour of Versailles, the dazzling brilliance of French culture, were achievements of which he and France could be proud. Against the wretchedness of constant war, which had little discernible moral justification, and which imposed upon his people immense suffering, and the excessive and unjust taxation which bore hardest on the poorest, the boast must be muted. There were not lacking those with courage to warn him of his failings in this; Bossuet and Fénelon, Boisguilbert and Vauban, did so but in vain. Bossuet's words at the end show his disillusionment with his master:

> It is not proper for a man to have no superior. The very idea is bewildering, for man's condition does not lend itself to such independence.'[13]

4 Absolutism, social problems and the Church

The problem of dealing effectively with the social problems created by the changing conditions of the fourteenth and fifteenth centuries had not been solved in their day. The task was beyond the resources and personnel of the Church which had been, until the central Middle Ages, responsible for dealing with them. At the same time the same changes were undermining what structures had existed in the earlier period for the purpose. The basic solidarity that existed in the medieval village and town, and which ensured that the problems were recognized and social efforts to combat them could be organized, had crumbled. St Vincent de Paul (1580–1660),[14] realized the scale of the need and sought to meet it.

Born near Dax in Gascony of a poor peasant family, Vincent's abilities gained him an education at the local Franciscan College and the University of Toulouse. In 1625 he founded the Lazarist Fathers whose work was to minister to the spiritual needs of the smaller towns and villages, and in 1633 he also founded the Sisters of Charity to work among the sick and the poor. He was loved and trusted by Louis XIII, and his widow Anne of Austria, when regent for the young Louis XIV, relied on Vincent and supported his efforts. The ravaging of Pontoise, Champagne, Burgundy, Picardy and Lorraine after Richelieu committed his country to open warfare against the Austrians and Spaniards had left the people in great need. Two or three hundred thousand men, with their camp followers, lived off the land they plundered for years. The fields were not ploughed, the peasants starved, epidemic followed on war and floods compounded the misery. When peace came in this conflict, there was the war against the Huguenots, the peasant risings in the Périgord and the rebellions of the Fronde against Mazarin. Bad harvests from 1647 to 1651 worsened the situation; nor did it substantially improve over the century as a whole.[15]

Vincent identified with the poor and spent himself for them; because Christ was in them especially, they were 'our lords, the poor' and he fought first to get true Christian charity, charity which was respectful of their dignity, for them. His initial experience of the need had been in his parish at Châtillon. Being told that one of its families was in danger of dying of neglect, he exhorted his people to do something about it, and they did; the entire market town responded by seeking out and helping all those who were destitute. By the time Richelieu's wars had led to the ravaging of France by her enemies, Vincent was in a position, as chaplain to the Gondi family and famous for his work as missioner and educator of priests, to create a vast network of relief, organized by and for the charity of Christ, to help the poor. During the regency of Anne of Austria he became an unofficial Minister of social welfare, for he recognized that problems could not be handled piecemeal but needed comprehensive treatment. The work of relief in the war-ravaged provinces was turned over to him; money was raised, and relief teams appointed for the different regions worked systematically and thoroughly. The magistrates of

Rethel wrote to him thanking him for the two years of effort his workers had put into the Champagne region; it was entirely on this help that it had lived. The Lieutenant General of St Quentin was speaking for all when he wrote to thank Vincent for his work, without which the people of the district would have perished of hunger, and he implored him to continue to be the 'father of your country'.[16]

St Vincent died before Louis XIV assumed his duties as King and no such schemes for the relief of need were put in hand in his reign though they were more sorely needed than ever. The traditional works went on, new hospitals were opened, and confraternities of charity were encouraged but they were not a matter of major interest to him. By the last years of his reign, as we have seen above, his advisers were begging him to cease his endless wars and look to the internal affairs of the realm, but he either would not or could not respond.

Throughout Europe the basic unit of the Church, the parish, remained also the basic unit of society and it was primarily through the parish that the social work of the Church was done. In secular terms it served as the means of government making known its wishes to the people and was the first link in the chain of authority from village to royal councils. Its life revolved around the liturgy and its festivals; it gave the peasant an identity against the world beyond it.[17] However, the clergy throughout Europe as a whole were underpaid, often badly educated and unevenly distributed, and such conditions hindered the Church's mission in all its aspects, including her charitable and social work.

In France the parish system generally worked well; in Spain by contrast thousands were without priests, while in Italy an outdated parish structure made it difficult to care for an expanding population. Poland's problem was the relative poverty of the Church and the large and inefficient parishes that resulted. In Hungary new parishes had been created in areas where Turkish rule had recently ended, and in Austria the Emperor Joseph had used the resources released by closing monasteries to found new parishes.

A main weakness generally was that the wealth, power and prestige of the Church was concentrated in the urban areas, and the countryside, where most of the people worked and lived, was comparatively neglected. Much of her wealth was spent on church and monastic building. In the cities which were ecclesiastical centres the Church and her ministers were major consumers of goods and services, while her charities, parishes, monasteries, hospital and charitable foundations were the major sources of social welfare, though of themselves they were inadequate to meet the social needs of the time.[18]

The numbers of the poor we do not know with any accuracy, but it is calculated that in France generally one-third of the people were on the fringes of destitution and something between 16 and 20 per cent were destitute. Generally the French bishops did not neglect their duty to them. Hospitals – part for the workless, part for the sick – were a main agency, and voluntary workers were organized to serve the poor. The sheer size of the social problems swamped voluntary efforts, and the enlightened mocked the Church's efforts as too indiscriminate and causing more problems than they solved. It was not an opinion shared by the poor. From them the only complaint about these efforts was that there were not enough of them.[19] The nuns continued to be outstanding, the Sisters of Charity and the other orders provided the majority of nurses, and the most able ones in Europe until modern times.

The wealth of the Spanish church enabled her to fulfil her traditional role of providing charitable assistance on a large scale; it was done unevenly and not always dependably, but since the State accepted only little responsibility for the poor the Church still provided the only real barrier against starvation for the needy of town and country when times were difficult, and her record in the eighteenth century was impressive. The poor turned to her as a matter of course in their need; the first large-scale anticlerical riots in modern Spanish history took place in 1834–35 when the state of Church finances prevented her giving the extensive assistance that was expected during a serious food shortage.[20]

5 The Papacy and the old regime

There was little or no role for the Papacy in the social affairs of Europe in this period, and this goes for the states which regarded themselves as Catholic as well as for those which did not. The failure to establish any principles and practices for the reform of the Catholic princes was the unfinished business of the Council of Trent. Given their influence in the age of absolutism, no reform was more important, but had the Council attempted it its efforts would have been rejected.[21] Yet it was on these unreformed institutions that the Papacy had to rely in its efforts for the Church international, and the price of their co-operation was concession. Turned in on itself, worldliness infected the Papacy once more, though not to the extent of the Renaissance period; gold and honours were lavished, for example, on the Borghesi and the Barberini in the period 1605–67.

The problems of dealing with Philip II of Spain (1556–98), who was a man of genuinely deep piety and strong religious sense but yet who kept the Church in his realms firmly under his control, underline the difficulties of the Papacy in dealing with the Catholic kings. Philip searched out the heretics and punished them, but more for political than religious motives. He saw that monasteries were reformed and the Decrees of Trent were enforced, but he also controlled the appointment of bishops and controlled them, a practice which was totally incompatible with the Church's real good. He claimed no competence on matters of faith, but apart from that the Church was a State Church. He sought to pressure the Papacy through forcing his nominees for the cardinalate on it; there were fourteen of them in office on the death of Pius IV and three of them were the King's close relations.

The powers who negotiated the Peace of Westphalia disposed of properties and civil jurisdictions which belonged to the ecclesiastical princes without any reference to Rome. They also rejected the more than one thousand years of experience and achievement of Christian Europe and denied to the Church any role as a moral guide. The Church and the Papacy became marginalized. To the Catholic kings the Church was an instrument to be used for their purposes; the intellectual movements of the times rejected it, and its influence on the minds and hearts of the Catholic people was on the wane in many parts of Europe.

In the late seventeenth century the French church was agitated by the problem of Gallicanism, three of whose 'four articles' (1682) were fundamentally in error, stating that General Councils are superior to the Pope, that the papal primacy is limited by the rights of local churches and finally that the Papacy is not of itself infallible: the whole Church has to assent to its decrees.[22] Though in 1693 the King withdrew his edict compelling seminaries to teach these ideas, they continued to frame the mentality of the French church. The Jansenist heresy surfaced again in these years before it finally faded; in the meantime the campaign to have the Society of Jesus suppressed was under way since it was seen by the Church's enemies as the strongest bulwark in defence of Catholic internationalism and the Papacy.

Of the eighteenth-century popes, Benedict XIV (1740–58) was the most outstanding. He was a deeply devout and prayerful man, noted for his care for the poor and the sick, and was little concerned with political intrigue but much concerned with

improving Catholic scholarship and the presentation and imple-
mentation of Catholic doctrine. His pontificate was the last of the
eighteenth century which allowed its holder anything like peace.
Clement XIII (1758–69) died exhausted by his struggle in opposing the efforts of France, Spain and Naples to have the Society of
Jesus suppressed, as a preliminary to a final attack on the power of
the Papacy itself.[23] His successor, the unfortunate Clement XIV
(1769–74) failed in this task. A man elected as the Pope least likely
to oppose the will of the Bourbons inevitably caved in under pressures so enormous that he was unnerved. Ground down by the
threat of greater evils that the monarchs could inflict upon the
Church if he did not concede, he issued in August 1733 the brief
Dominus ac Redemptor which dissolved the Society. In practice, in
Russia where the rulers refused to accept the document's authority, it lived on and in 1814 was fully restored.[24]

   Pius VI (1775–99) was faced by the challenge of Febronianism –
Febronius being the pseudonym of Bishop von Hontheim
(1701–90), Co-adjutor of Trier. He regarded the Pope as accountable to bishops, who were the delegates of the community of the
faithful to which the authority of the Church belonged.[25] He faced
also the Emperor Joseph (1741–90) of Austria, who sought to make
the Church a department of State in his Empire, the Pope to be left
with residual powers regarding dogma, but disciplinary matters to
be entirely for the State to decide.[26] In the midst of these troubles,
the French Revolution broke out; Pope Pius VI died while
Napoleon's prisoner in 1799, but ironically it was the Revolution,
deposing the Bourbons who had set out effectively to destroy papal
power in the Church, which left the Papacy free in the nineteenth
century to take the lead in revitalizing it for its task in the modern
world.

6 Absolute monarchy and the right to resist

Jean Bodin (1530–96),[27] who had experienced in the France of his
time the confusion and the suffering that result from lack of clear
and effective government, was the first to put forth a complete
doctrine of sovereignty. According to it the State, whose origin was
in force, not in divine institution or social contract, was to have
ultimate control over all persons and corporations within its territory, and within the State one person or group was to exercise that
control. Sovereignty then is absolute and indivisible. Bodin was a
Christian and accepted the authority of the law of God and the

natural law but he gradually drops the pretence and 'retreats ... into an uncompromising defence of royal absolutism'.[28]

Thomas Hobbes (1588–1679),[29] had similarly witnessed the tumult of the Civil War, (1642–46 and 1648–49) but in England, and was equally convinced of the need of a strong State to the exclusion of almost all other considerations. He argued that insecurity and conflict of the most violent kind drive man to establish the State for protection; he gives up all his rights to the State, the Leviathan, the mortal god, for his purpose. The form of government could be democracy, aristocracy or monarchy but his own clear preference is for monarchy. In any case the power of Leviathan is absolute and, subject to the right to his own self-preservation in certain circumstances, the subject must obey it. Hobbes' theory of morality, which is entirely self-interested, makes that right to self-preservation entirely individualistic and self-interested too. He speaks of natural law, but it is not a natural law which is designed to secure the rights of all in an objective scheme of things; it is a 'dictate of egoistic prudence'[30] concerning self-preservation to the exclusion of all else.

The case for the right of rebellion was put by the Calvinists, in particular by the author of the *Vindiciae Contra Tyrannos* (published anonymously in France in 1579) which argued that the people had the right to resist a ruler who would enforce a false religion or rule unjustly. It was put more emphatically by the scholastics, developing the teaching of St Thomas on tyranny.[31] Suarez demonstrated that when the life of the community is threatened by an unjust ruler, then the citizens have a right to resist.[32] He is very stringent on the conditions to be met in invoking it, but the right exists. The Calvinist writers in fact relied more and more on scholastic and Roman sources for their argument against tyranny.

> We may say with very little exaggeration that the foundations of the Calvinist theory of revolution were in fact constructed entirely by their Catholic adversaries.[33]

Suarez was concerned with determining the conditions for a just and practical political order, in consideration of which the options open to the citizen in the face of gross injustice had to be faced. Theoretically, absolute monarchy could be justified, if the monarch accepted the limits set by divine and natural law upon the authority he wielded. It was because in practice absolute monarchs showed that they were above those laws, even if in theory they accepted them, that the scholastic moralists' theory of justified resistance was so relevant. As we have seen, the Catholic tradition insisted that positive law must be in conformity with both the natural law, which man can know by right reason without the aid of revelation, and also with the divine positive or revealed law.

God gives man the power to form a commonwealth and set up a political community, and the consent of the people is needed to establish a State and form a government. Suarez in his *Law and the Law Giver* had examined this proposition with great care, showing that while many states are established by force, they have valid authority only when the people have accepted them. The king's power is not from God by hereditary succession. Rather, in Bellarmine's words, writing against James I of England's claim to be God's anointed, 'The king's power is from God, not immediately, but by consent of human wills.[34]

As noted, Suarez was very strict on the rules for the invocation of the right to resist; they amount in fact to what we would call an overthrow by constitutional means in a stable State;[35] this raises the question of what is to be done when, because of a tyrant's actions, constitutional means do not exist; but it cannot be implied that the right ceases when clear constitutional means do not exist, otherwise the worst tyrants could never be challenged and the right would be meaningless.

Suarez' theories also accommodated the existing realities of an absolute monarchy provided the people wish to be ruled this way; in giving their consent they genuinely transfer their power to the king. He then can rule, not being bound by his own law, but he remains bound by divine and natural law. It is to these the people could appeal under an unjust absolute ruler. Since the right to rule depends on the monarch seeking not his own good, or that of his favourites, but the good of each and the good of all, the common good, a ruler can in principle be challenged if his rule 'becomes manifestly pernicious to the entire commonwealth'. Since he was making this point against the would-be absolutist James I, it was extremely radical.[36]

7 The growth of empires[37]

The emergence of strong monarchies in northern Europe in the late fifteenth century coincided with an interest in the exploration of the oceans of the world in the national interest of the exploring nations; it was a time of the development of colonialism and imperialism. The seafaring and trading tradition of the Mediterranean and north west Europe and their developed naval technology gave them the means to these ends. Portugal's Prince Henry 'the Navigator' had captured the port of Cueta on the North African coast in 1415, and, with gold and spices as their quarry, the Portuguese explored the west coast of Africa southwards, discovering the Gold Coast, and setting up trading stations where they could. Others worked their way further south until in 1500 Vasco da Gama rounded the Cape of Good Hope. Later the Portuguese penetrated to India and then to the rich spice islands of the Far East.

Christopher Columbus, sailing under the Spanish flag, made landfall in the West Indies in 1492 and further successive expeditions by Spaniards on the mainland in Central and South America led to the discovery of vast deposits of precious stones and metals. Yet the bullion brought back to the homeland did not make it wealthier in the long run;[38] one reason was that the structure of Spanish society and its social values discouraged economic development. The aristocracy, some 2 per cent of the population, owned more than 90 per cent of the land. There was no middle class; the small commercial, merchant and professional sector amounted to only 3 per cent of the population. The aristocracy had no interest in improving agriculture, and commerce and industry were held in disdain. There was lacking therefore the commercial and industrial expertise which would have developed a modern economy.

Spain then had an undeveloped agriculture, partly due to poor soils and primitive agricultural methods, but partly due also to the landowners' contempt for commercial development. England, France and the Netherlands, by contrast, had realized that a healthy agriculture was the key to a sound economy. Neither did Spain's limited industrial and commercial base equip it to make full use of more capital, since there was lacking the will or the means to develop industrially; it was easier to buy from abroad.

Neglect of the New World's agricultural potential in the greed for gold meant that Amsterdam developed the entrepôt trade in Europe, not Spain, while bullion was drained from it to northern Europe to buy the goods Spanish industry could not supply; the same defect meant that there was no balanced trade between the mother country and its dependants. The monarchs relied too heavily on the bullion imports to finance their overseas adventures, and they grossly overestimated the income that would come to them from this source, recklessly borrowing on the strength of those overestimates. Private bullion shipped from America was used to import goods from the north, and the king's share was backing the loans being made to finance a misguided foreign policy. It was the northern economies which prospered on Spanish

bullion; Spanish armies fighting an unwinnable war in the
Netherlands were financed in so doing by colonial gold. Spain was
like a huge sieve leaking more bullion to the north while at the
same time it was forfeiting any hope of developing a balanced and
healthy economy.

This economic eclipse of Spain was part of a decline of the
Mediterranean countries that had begun in the late Middle Ages as
the trade of the Baltic/North Sea region supplied the growing
mass market of ordinary people who were experiencing a slow
increase in living standards generally, overshadowing the older
trading pattern. The Dutch challenged the Hanseatic northern
and the Portuguese East Indian trade and took them over. Dutch
settlements were also made in South Africa, but tiny Holland could
not maintain its outposts of Empire against the French and British
and in the end it was the latter who, by the Treaty of Paris in 1763,
emerged as inheritors of the French possessions in North America
and in India. Helped by the French, the former colonies in what
became the United States of America were, in turn, able to expel
the British in 1781. The Portuguese in the mid-sixteenth century
had consolidated their hold on Brazil against the challenges from
Spanish, Dutch and French interlopers.

8 The Church in the New World[39]

(i) Latin America and the Indians

The Portuguese and the Spaniards founded their empires in the
fifteenth and sixteenth centuries, and their attitude to them was
conditioned by the *reconquista* from the mid-eleventh to the late
fifteenth centuries as the Muslims were expelled from the Iberian
peninsula and the inhabitants of the lands taken had to provide for
their new masters. The peoples of the New World were seen in the
same light, as enemies of God and Christian Spain, and it was their
duty to provide for the lords who had conquered them. The victors
showed great ruthlessness in the establishment of their colonies in
Central and South America, and they decimated the indigenous
peoples with their bloodletting, oppression and diseases. They saw
no problem in serving God, gold and glory at one and the same
time, and happily made the ends justify the means; yet they were by
the standards of their day 'for the most part, devout men whose
devotions took forms at once orthodox and practical'.[40]

The Spanish State was in almost total control of the Church in its dominions in the sixteenth century. Under the royal patronage, the *patronato*, all clerical appointments were made by the throne, all movement of missioners and hierarchy within the empire was subject to the royal permission, no Roman document could enter, be promulgated or given effect without its consent either. Clerical policy, clerical finances, every aspect of Church life was under the ultimate control of the secular authority. This was not a situation that Rome freely accepted; it was this issue after all which lay behind the investiture controversy of the eleventh century and its aftermath. Given the problems of the See of Peter in the late fifteenth and early sixteenth century, however, its attempts – and several were made – to deprive the State of this control were weak and ineffective.

In the first decades of the Spanish Empire, the Crown's use of its prerogatives regarding the Church was responsible, and it was able to call on the spiritual and moral resources of a Spanish church which had been spared the corruption it had experienced in some other parts of Europe. The Dominican and the Franciscan friars who were the spearhead of evangelization in South America were, by their way of life, their learning, and their dedication to the mission, well suited to the task of bringing Christ and his Church to the peoples of the New World. The average settler, on the other hand, unfortunately was not. The native population was treated badly from the beginning. Disease, maltreatment and war drastically reduced the number of the Indians; estimates of how many inhabitants there were in Central and South America before the Europeans came vary from 7.5 million to 100 million and it would seem that the decline in numbers from the time of contact to the nadir was as much as 96 per cent overall.[41]

In 1512, Antonio Montesimos, a Dominican friar in Hispaniola, protested to his mainly Spanish congregation that their treatment of the Indians was unacceptable, but it was when two years later another Spanish priest, Bartolomé de las Casas, took up their cause, that the matter became a central issue for the settlers and the Crown. Las Casas was himself an *encomendero*, a landowner who had Indians 'commended' to him, so that they could be taught the faith and be protected by him and in return would work for him on his estates. The way the settlers administered this system of *encomienda*, which could probably have worked if there had been the will, was the heart of the problem since it had in the main become a form of serfdom or slavery. Las Casas, on seeing the light, freed all his Indians and began exhorting others to do so. Meeting setbacks and disappointments until he was almost in

despair, he was saved by the support he received from the
Dominican friars and in 1523 he joined the Order, returning to his
work for the Indians in 1527, seeking their emancipation and
better treatment.[42]

The question of what should be the attitude of the Spaniards to
the native populations was considered by the neo-scholastic theologians, in particular Francisco de Vitoria (1483–1546), Dominic de
Soto (1494–1560) and Francisco Suarez (1548–1617). The discovery of the New World, and the divisions in Christendom, were
challenging them to find a new basis for international relations,
and this they found in the law of nations which they regarded as a
specification of the natural law. They argued that the existence in
all men of a sense of mercy and mutual help indicates that each
community is dependent on others. However this natural moral
sense, natural law, is not enough for all circumstances. There is
need for special laws and a special category of law, international
law, in order to fill it out. This was the argument of Vitoria taken
up by Suarez fifty years later.[43]

In 1537 Pope Paul III became involved in the controversy, issuing
the bull *Sublimis Deus*. Stressing that 'all mankind is one' he rejected
the argument that only true believers had the right to own property,
govern themselves and enjoy liberty,[44] which is what the settlers
wished to believe so that they could confiscate that property and
enslave the non-believers. It was around this matter of the capability
of the Indians to possess to the full the rights of human beings that
the debate occasioned by men like Las Casas in their championship
of the indigenous peoples revolved. To try to solve the matter once
for all, Charles V called for a formal academic debate on it at
Valladolid in 1550,[45] between Las Casas and Juan de Sepulveda, a
famous humanist who based his case for enslaving the Indians on
Aristotle's arguments about natural slavery, to which he saw the
former were clearly destined. He further argued that since they
were pagan barbarians, they could be compelled by force to become
Christians, and if they refused to do so freely and were caught, this
would be capture in a 'just' war, which justified enslavement.

Las Casas on the contrary argued that the Indian was truly
human and capable of being a good subject of the king, and to save
them from the rapacity of the settlers they must have their own
villages, under their own chiefs, and be given the protection of the
royal officials under the necessary laws. Such laws were passed, and
they achieved their end in that what once looked like the possible
extermination of the original inhabitants was prevented.

Las Casas also sought to demonstrate that his way was the best in practical terms. In this he had sufficient success to convince anyone capable of being convinced. He settled them in villages under the protection of the law and the care of the missioners so that they were not brought into exploitive relationship with the settlers. He showed, through several experiments, that it could be done; under imperial protection the villagers lived peacefully. They lost their former freedom in many ways, but since it was a freedom which left them open to enslavement, the move to the villages had much to commend it.

In Portuguese Brazil the missioners also set up similar villages for their people, but unlike Spanish South America there was no government backing in fending off the settlers, and to survive at all they had to make concessions to them which undermined the principle of the protective mission settlement. One of the most outstanding missioners in his work for the Indians was Antony Vieira, a Jesuit academic, writer, pulpit orator and confidant of the king Dom João IV, who in 1652 exchanged his brilliant career in Lisbon to work in Northern Brazil. So successfully did he and his companions struggle against the exploiters of the natives that the settlers in the end saw that he was expelled. The missioners made mistakes, it is true, but with the passing of Vieira in particular

> the Indians lost their most powerful champion. No one of similar stature and energy concerned himself with Indian welfare during the three centuries of Portuguese colonial rule or the nineteenth-century Brazilian empire. The tragedy was that the situation was impossible, even for Vieira.[46]

The villages were regarded as dangerous to the State and the rights of the Indians, and Portugal's First Minister Pombal ensured the passing of a law in 1755 which gave Indians 'freedom' – which resulted in their further merciless exploitation at the hands of the settlers.[47]

The Jesuit reductions of Paraguay[48] were set up in more fortunate circumstances than faced Las Casas in Central America, or the missioners, including their Jesuit brethren, in Brazil. They were in a part of the Spanish Empire that was more isolated and had fewer settlers, and they had a comparatively large and coherent group of missioners, a small Jesuit province in fact, centred on the work. They also had the protection of the Crown from the start. It also helped that they were working initially with the Guarani Indians who were particularly adaptable to the life of the reductions, the mission villages. Finally, they had time to work out what was the best way of proceeding, learning from their mistakes and being able to rebuild positively without interference. There was a false start in 1587, but the development that led to what became the famous 100 missions of Paraguay began on a firmer basis from 1609; they were in fact not all in Paraguay; some were in Brazil and Argentina, at the point where the three countries meet.

A typical settlement was laid out on the plan of a Spanish town with a central square, on which stood the church, the Jesuit residence and the buildings used for administrative and storage purposes. The rest of the area was divided into rectangular blocks around the square and these were subdivided into family plots large enough for a house and a garden to grow crops for home or market. The settlement was surrounded by a stockade or wall for protection. The settlement also had its communal lands on which all took their part in tilling for communal use; animals were also grazed there. Surplus products from private and communal plots were sold to finance the purchase of the things the settlement could not produce for itself. Work was the duty of all but it was made as pleasant as possible; the skills of the people in making musical instruments and in building and decorating the churches was highly developed. There were two Jesuits only in each mission and ultimate authority lay with them, but there was also a complete system of town government on the Spanish model, administered by the people themselves.

The reductions lasted for some 150 years; a few missioners met their deaths at the hand of the Indians, the vast majority of whom were content to live under their paternalistic guidance. They knew the alternative – being often under attack by the slavers, and they were prepared to defend their settlements. Since Spanish troops were lacking in that remote area, the missioners – with Spanish permission – appointed one of their number who had been a professional soldier to train the occupants of the reductions to defend themselves and their homes, which they did successfully. They would hardly have done this had they resented the way they were treated by their mentors.

In 1750, the old rivals Spain and Portugal signed the Treaty of Madrid which realigned the border between their territories in the Paraguay region, it being decreed that since some of the missions were on Brazilian territory they would have to leave and resettle on that of Spain. The process of uprooting was cruelly unjust to the Indians, since they had to cede their land, homes and buildings, which were worth more than a million pesos, for a mere 4000. There was no way the Jesuits, aware though they were of the immense injustice being done, could effectively oppose the

change, because the governments of the two countries were determined on it and the Jesuits' own superiors had told them they must
obey; to have actively encouraged or supported military action
designed to help the Indians would only have led to greater suffering for them and their families. The majority of the Indians
affected, however, decided otherwise and determined to defend
their towns by force. The idea that they could hope to be successful in this was forlorn; the War of the Seven Reductions, militiamen
against regular troops backed by artillery and cavalry, and experienced in waging modern war, was a massacre; they died in their
hundreds, and failed.[49] Tragically, the treaty was never viable
anyway; in 1761 Charles III of Spain renounced it and sought to
revive the abandoned missions.[50] By then however it was too late.
In 1767 the Jesuits were expelled from the Spanish domains altogether: the reductions they manned remained in being, but
without the guidance of the 'black robes' they faltered. Despite
efforts being made to revive them as their value in retrospect
became more appreciated, they had little success.

(ii) The problem of slavery

The Brazilians developing the sugar industry were anxious to find
a servile labour force which was more numerous and durable than
the Indians; they found them in Black Africa and the transatlantic
slave trade was really under way. It is calculated that some 9.5
million were transported from the fifteenth to the nineteenth
centuries, 6 million of them in the eighteenth. Down to 1700, the
largest number went to Brazil; thereafter it was to the British,
French and Dutch West Indies.[51] The slavers sailed to Africa with
salt, cloth, firearms, hardware, trinkets and rum and traded these
for the Africans captured by other Africans in the interior. The
'middle passage', the transatlantic crossing, with the slaves packed
in rows between decks, was reasonably swift, given the trade winds,
but it still exacted an appalling price in suffering from its black
cargo. After their initial capture they had been driven mercilessly
from dawn to dusk on the way to the coast and had died in
numbers. On the middle passage between 10 and 50 per cent died
because of the overcrowding, the heat, the insanitary conditions,
inhuman treatment and poor food, but the trade was so profitable
that the loss could be absorbed. After delivering their cargo, the
slave ships then turned homewards with sugar, molasses, tobacco
or rice. Urgings of the priests working among the Africans led to
Paul II condemning the trade in 1462, Urban VIII in 1639 and

Benedict XIV in 1744, but they had no effect.[52] The trade was too lucrative to be hindered by moral considerations. The spirit of liberal capitalism unrestrained was well illustrated in the slave trade; British slavers controlled the trade in the eighteenth century and they exploited it to the limit. It was as well that, in the late eighteenth century, the country developed a bad conscience about slavery, since it had so extended it and profited from it.

The institution of slavery remained an accepted part of the colonial economy and the Church was part of it, having slaves on her properties. She had learned in her long history that while society demanded the service of slaves to do its heavy work, slaves would be found to do it. While the cultural conditions supported it, there was no possibility of challenging the institution. Cultural conditions had eventually led to the disappearance of slavery on the European mainland by the twelfth century, though it survived on the fringes. Colonialism had revived it and the Church's role was to reduce as far as possible the suffering of the slaves. Individual popes condemned the trade, as we have mentioned. Fr Alonso de Sandoval, who worked tirelessly to relieve the needs of the slaves in Cartagena, passed on his experience and knowledge to his fellow Jesuit Fr Peter Claver, who was later canonized for his heroism in the work. They organized relief for the slaves at Cartagena, the port of entry for slaves to Spanish South America and the largest centre of slave transhipment for the trade. Every slave ship was met and the physical needs of the sufferers tended. Claver spent forty years of his life in this work.[53] Sandoval also wrote about the slaves and the conditions they had to face, and always condemned the trade in principle.[54] There was plenty of anti-slave literature in circulation in South America in the eighteenth century and other missionaries were active in speaking against it, for example Giovanni Antonio Andreoni and Jorge Benci in Brazil, and in New Spain there were Francisco Javier Clavigero and Francisco Javier Alegre.[55]

The argument about whether, on balance, the miseries of slavery overall were in any way lessened by what help the Church could give is never ending, but the testimonies to its effectiveness by those who have had no particular reason to overestimate it, and yet have affirmed it, is remarkable. Frank Tannenbaum was one of the more influential of them and 'there is a certain validity to his assertions' despite the controversy that has surrounded them.[56] At the least, the evidence that good was done 'cannot be lightly dismissed'.[57] In the light of Samson's observations[58] on the effect of the Church's concern on the decline of the institution in Europe, this is fair comment.

(iii) Social welfare and education

In extension of the tradition developed in Europe in the Middle Ages, the inhabitants of the Portuguese and Spanish colonies relied on the Church's work in education and social welfare to provide these for the colonists and for the indigenous peoples. Initially the Spanish Franciscans were enthusiastic about the academic education of the Indians in Mexico[59] but as the stress on racial superiority grew among the settlers in general it affected the missionaries also, and they lost their fervour in the matter, although more basic education was provided as part of the missionary work generally. All other educational institutions, including universities, were run by the Church. She was also responsible for the hospital system, providing for travellers and the aged as well as the sick, as in Europe; parish confraternities also provided mutual support systems for their members.

There have been accusations that the Church in Latin America was too wealthy, and that its clergy were exploitive or callous – accusations which in specific instances were all too true. Overall however neither the Church nor the clergy neglected the service of the people. Mecham notes the evidence of greed, backsliding and corruption but also

> the devotion and abnegation of the vast majority of the priests and friars who laboured for the faith among the Spaniards of the cities, the castas of the rural districts and the neophytes of the far flung frontiers

Those who condemn the clergy as heartless exploiters of the Indians make 'no mention of the fact that the Church was the Indian's staunchest defender from first to last'.[60] There are criticisms of the wealth of the Church but 'no admission that all educational and charitable work was ... supported by that institution'.[61] Of the Church in Mexico in particular,

> it would be a distortion to ignore indications that the majority of priests observed their vows, lived modestly and performed good works for their people.[62]

When political liberation came and the Church was despoiled, it was the rich, or those determined to be rich, who took over church property for their private gain; the last thing that occurred to the new owners of church property was that they had any responsibility towards the poor and less fortunate. With all its defects, the Church had safeguarded the only patrimony the poor had; once it was out of the Church's guardianship that patrimony was no more.

9 Nineteenth-century imperialism, the missions and new churches

(i) The resurgence of imperialism[63]

The nineteenth century witnessed a reawakening of interest in empire by the European powers, and it was connected with the growth of liberal capitalism, the search for new markets, more profitable investments and raw material supplies, but it also had much to do with desire for national glory and a rebirth of the Christian missions in pagan lands, a rebirth which was encouraged by the revival of interest in Empire, though it predated it. The significance of these missions is that they laid the foundations of new churches through which Christianity transplanted itself to all the major regions of the world from the European base to which history had previously largely confined it. With the Latin American Empires of Spain and Portugal breaking free in the nineteenth century also, their churches were finding their feet within the international Catholic community as free peoples, rather than as adjuncts of those of Europe.

The largest colonial power in the nineteenth century was Britain; the British Empire was mainly the result of the initiative of private individuals in search of fortune whose efforts were supported by national policy if they could persuade the government to do so. But there were always doubts. The doctrines of *laissez faire* and free trade were about, and these clashed with a colonial system which worked on the principle that the home country should regulate trade and traffic, within and to and from colonies, for its own benefit. It was a policy which commended itself in the seventeenth century and did serve the national interest as it was then conceived. But when, after the secession of the United States of America, trade between Britain and the thirteen American colonies actually increased, the benefits of the colonial system and empire were seen to be illusory.

But by the 1870s the mood was changing again. The old empires remained and sought to extend their bounds, while those who did not have empires wanted them. There were many reasons for this new interest. Empire, it was felt, was necessary for national greatness. It gave scope for political and military ambitions. Altruism, a sense of civilizing mission, however intermingled with self-seeking, awareness of the imperative to Christianize pagan people – all made their contribution. So too did the feeling of European racial superiority and destiny. Economics played their part also with the need for raw materials and new markets, living space for surplus population and new outlets for capital.

J. H. Hobson's *Imperialism, a Study* (1902) and V. Lenin's *Imperialism, the Highest Stage of Capitalism* (1917) correctly stressed the connection between the two, but it was a limited connection. European capital found little outlet in the colonial areas of Africa or Asia. Britain was the major investor but in 1913 only 12.5 per cent of its investment was in its dependent colonies, including India. The other 87.5 per cent was in the older established or former colonies such as the United States, South America, Canada, Australia and South Africa.[64] The main targets of new imperialism on the other hand were firstly the East, China especially, but also South East Asia and Oceania. Second came Africa – the 'Dark Continent'.

China, disorganized and militarily weak under the Manchu dynasty, was defeated by Britain in the two opium wars, in 1842 and 1857, which led to concessions being forced by her and other European nations, as well as by the USA. Not unnaturally the Chinese deeply resented the imposition of these conditions. By the end of the century, a reaction was building up, manifesting itself, for example, in the Boxer rebellion of 1899 which particularly targeted the missionaries as the enemy.

As to Africa, at mid-century Europe was ignorant of the great mass of the central and southern regions.[65] The north coast was known, and the Portuguese had rounded the Cape in 1500, establishing trading posts and making contact with African kingdoms in coastal regions. Europeans had also settled in some numbers in the Cape, but the interior was a mystery. From the 1790s this mystery was lifting and when on his last journey (1867–73) David Livingstone was finally sought out by the American newspaperman H.M. Stanley, the resultant publicity fully engaged popular opinion in favour of the work of bringing civilization to the Dark Continent.

The explorers and missioners were supported because it was thought they would, by their activities, spark an African regeneration, and that the Christian Gospel, plus man's trading instinct, would do this without any overt political influence from outside, because for one reason or another Europe had little such influence. European settlement in Africa, apart from the Cape region had not seemed feasible; only French Senegal and the British Gold Coast had European administrations. Then the French intervened in Algeria and Tunisia and the building of the Suez Canal meant deeper British involvement in Egypt and the Sudan. But what really gave the new Imperialism a kick start was King Leopold of

Belgium's Empire in the Congo. Germany then annexed South
West Africa, the Cameroons, Togoland and East Africa in 1883–85.
The British invaded Egypt in 1882 and remained there, and so it
was to go on, the eventual division of Africa reflecting European
political rivalries. In 1884 an International Conference in Berlin
approved of Leopold's Congo Free State and the partitioning of
the continent, which now went ahead.

(ii) The missionary background.[66]

The Catholic missionary activity in South America and Africa in the
fifteenth and sixteenth centuries had been the responsibility of the
monarchs of Spain and Portugal because they were strong enough
to insist on their own terms and conditions for the Church's evangelization of the new worlds they discovered. The intrinsic
disadvantages, the total abnegation of Gospel freedom that this
system involved, made it inevitable that it would end as soon as the
Papacy felt free to get rid of it, and with the establishment in 1622
of the Sacred Congregation for the Propagation of the Faith steps
were taken to see that this was done.[67]

The first Cardinal Secretary of the Congregation, Francesco
Ingoli, was remarkably clear-sighted and laid down what a sound
missionary effort required: namely, adequate knowledge of the
missionary world, freedom from the stranglehold of Spain and
Portugal, many more bishops with better communications with
Rome, more diocesan clergy, and above all, more native clergy so
that, among other things, the Church could be freed from that
connection with colonialism which marked her out as foreign to
the new lands in which she was trying to take root. To this end, the
maximum respect for local customs and cultures must be shown;
only those things contrary to religion and sound morals were
rejected. The founding of the Paris Seminary for Missions to
Foreign Countries in the 1660s was another very significant step
because, as the supply of priests from Spain and Portugal declined,
France became an importance source.

After St Francis Xavier's heroic exertions had extended the
Christian mission there, India in the seventeenth century
possessed in missionaries like Robert de Nobili (1577–1656) and
John de Britto, martyred in 1693, men who sought to consolidate
the initial gains and respect, but their work was necessarily slow
and painstaking. They and their few fellow missionaries had huge
areas to cover and only catechists to help them, living conditions
were poor and the climate very difficult. Matteo Ricci left the Jesuit

Mission in China flourishing on his death in 1610; a period of
persecution in 1664 gave way to toleration once more and other
religious orders came in to help with the work. Rome appointed a
Chinese bishop in 1674, and a seminary was established to train
Chinese priests. Sadly, misunderstandings over the Chinese rites
resulted in their condemnation by Rome and the process of accommodation to local cultures was severely hampered thereafter.

The Portuguese in Africa had made one attempt at sustained
evangelization and that was in the Congo at the end of the
fifteenth century; there they formed an alliance with the African
chiefs, sending missionaries and baptizing the Manikongo and his
eldest son.[68] Neighbouring São Tomé's slave hunting and trading
in the Congo undermined African confidence in Portuguese
promises and the experiment faltered. It never recovered, though
the Church maintained a presence. Later efforts of Propaganda to
revitalize it also failed.

The second half of the eighteenth century was a difficult time for
the missions. The decline of the major missionary nations Spain
and Portugal, and persecution in China were the main problems;
the suppression of the Society of Jesus in 1773 then deprived them
of the best part of 3000 men, and all the existing problems were
compounded. However, the impact of the French Revolution purified the Church in Europe, in France above all, leading among
other things to a great revival of the foreign missions. The Papacy
itself emerged from its maltreatment by Napoleon with its moral
and spiritual authority and prestige enhanced, and the foreign
missions were high on its list of priorities; the Society of Jesus was
revived in 1814 and new religious congregations concerned with
the missions sprang up. From 1816 the laity, through the Society
for the Propagation of the Faith, were more actively involved in the
promotion of the missions and Pope Gregory XVI (1831–46)
prepared the ground for later expansion by creating bishoprics
and prefectures in missionary areas throughout the world.

In India the Portuguese *padroado* still caused difficulty. Rome
pressed for a native priesthood also, but the European mentality of
the Portuguese, combined with the poor reputation of the Goan
and the Thomas Christian priests, did not help. Rome persisted,
however, the number of the native clergy rose, and in 1896 Indian
bishops were appointed in Kerala. The quiet work of mission and
missioner was meanwhile building up coherent and cohesive
Christian communities; educational work, dispensaries and hospitals were part of that care for the whole person which the Gospel
teaching on the importance of children and childhood, and on the

corporal works of mercy inculcates. Fr Constant Lievens, appointed to Chota Nagpur in 1885, found his small community in distress because of the injustice of their local overlords. Lacking the means to challenge the heavy taxes, they had turned to money-lenders and ended up in greater trouble. He therefore saw that they were provided with lawyers to plead their cases and this action on their behalf had the desired effect.[69]

China's resentment at the behaviour of the European powers did not help the missions there: it was then doubly unfortunate that the main Catholic missionaries in China, the French, were 'protected' by Napoleon III who was at the height of his power and influence and wanted to make the most of it. Particularly did he want to use French missionaries to expand French national interests as he understood them. Because of this support the French missions grew rapidly, but this brought problems. In China practical Christian charity, the setting up of schools, hospitals and orphanages, mainly staffed by nuns, was central to its work.[70] Yet the active role given to European women in this way was offensive to the Chinese, and persistence with it caused friction. Hence Christian missions, and missionaries, were a main target of the violence of the Boxers in 1899 to 1901. The failure of their rebellion lead to a greater freedom for the Church and to another great growth in Chinese Christianity before 1914.

On the opening-up of Japan in 1859 it was discovered that Christianity had survived for centuries without missionaries or contact with the Christian West, but it did not thereafter expand on any scale, even when it ceased to be a proscribed religion in 1873. The Korean persecution of the Church had also eased off by 1866 and growth was again possible. Indo-China was an area of rapid expansion but here the French influence on the missioners produced resentment. In Africa, the Catholic missions were at a very low ebb at the beginning of the nineteenth century.[71] Little remained of the older ones, and missionary effort had practically ceased. The sending of the first Sisters of St Joseph of Cluny to the island of Réunion in the Indian Ocean in 1817, followed by another group to Senegal two years later, marked a small revival, and the several other major congregations founded from the 1840s made a major impact; they included for example the Fathers of the Holy Spirit who went there in 1848, the Lyons Society of the African Missions in 1856, and the White Fathers in 1868.

The founder of the White Fathers, who were dedicated to the conversion of Africa, was Cardinal Lavigerie, Bishop of Nancy in 1863, Archbishop of Algeria and head of the Catholic Church in

North Africa in 1867. He insisted on religious freedom in the face of the governor's and the French government's opposition, and he proclaimed his intention of Christianizing first Algeria and then the whole of Africa, telling the Moslem people he claimed the right to love them as his children though they did not accept him as their father. Individual missioners and mission groups made their own distinctive contributions.

Some missioners found it helped their work among the people if they established settlements where freed slaves and foundlings could be fostered and Christian communities built up, but the danger here was that the very success of such efforts could alienate those who were helped in this way. In the Congo, Father van Henckxthoven developed a system which secured the essentials of such settlements while avoiding excessive paternalism. A group under the guidance of a catechist would be detached from the main station to settle near a non-Christian settlement. Farming, handicraft skills and the care of abandoned children occupied the inhabitants and, if they wished, young men would return after marriage on a permanent basis and so help build a permanent stable community.[72] The German missionaries in Cameroons were particularly successful in establishing an extensive schools system, and training in developing farms and small businesses.[73]

The most ambitious single missionary effort took place in the Congo,[74] where Leopold had complete control of the country; he wanted the co-operation of the Church in its civilizing, provided it could be done through Belgian missionaries, and provided he had control of their work. There were many aspects of the missions here which reflected the prejudices of the Europeans of the time, yet despite them the genuine missionary spirit also thrived and the seed was planted. The question of the relationship between mission and colonialization or imperialism was always there, of course; it could not be otherwise. Where dominant and nominally Christian powers colonized, Christian missioners, no matter how pure their motives, would benefit overtly or covertly from the fact because their services to the people were appreciated by the colonizers, not necessarily for the right reason. Yet on the whole they were and remained missionaries first and last; 'even though ... indebted to the spirit of the time, they remained loyal to their true mission, the preaching of the Gospel'. They were 'able to preserve the independence of evangelization and "the natives" were quite capable of differentiating between colonialism and mission activity.'[75]

10 The moves to end the transatlantic slave trade

The abolitionist movement was fed from many sources and has a
long history. Duns Scotus (*c.* 1265–1308) was the first to cast doubt
on the Aristotelian and Roman traditions concerning the acceptance of slavery; and legislation of King Alfonso the Wise in Spain
in 1265, based on the experience of slavery obtained by Spaniards
during the wars with the Muslims when both sides used prisoners
of war as slaves, spoke of slavery as the most vile thing that exists.
The Dominican theologian de Soto, and the Archbishop of
Mexico, Alonso de Montufar, objected to the African slave trade on
theological and spiritual grounds. The objectors were not numerous enough initially to counter the vested interests who knew well
how to exploit the traditional attitudes to thwart any change,[76] but
a pattern of opposition to these interests continued to develop. We
have noted[77] that the protests of the priests working in Africa had
brought condemnations of the slave trade from Paul II in 1462,
Urban VIII in 1639 and Benedict XIV in 1744, and also of Sandoval
and others in Brazil and Spanish Latin America. There were
several papal and conciliar condemnations of the enslavement of
American Indians, notably the bull of Paul III, *Sublimis Deus* of
1537, and in the eighteenth century 'an increasing number of
influential philosophers and religious leaders began to challenge
the institution'.[78]

They numbered among them leaders of the Enlightenment, the
political philosopher Montesquieu, and radical Protestants, especially Quakers who had engaged in the slave trade in the USA and
were reacting strongly against it; the growing interest in foreign
missions highlighted the evils of slavery and recruited popular
support for abolition. The Protestant Churches had not much
concerned themselves with such missions in the first two or three
centuries of their existence; now towards the end of the eighteenth
the piety of both Lutherans and Calvinists turned towards this
apostolate. In England the Baptists and Congregationalists were
active, the latter founding the London Missionary Society in 1792
with India as its special concern. Anglican missionary activity also
flourished.

The religious sentiment went along with the economic wisdom of
the times. Smith in his *The Wealth of Nations* dismissed slavery as
outdated and, unable to compete with free labour. The arrogance
of the slave owners told against them also. The British West Indian
planters had become accustomed to bringing their domestic slaves
to England, and this gave the abolitionists a chance to challenge the

institution at law. In 1772 Lord Mansfield, in a famous decision, declared that there was no such thing as slavery in England. Similar decisions were made in Portugal and France. Slavery, it was said, was incompatible with the tradition of freedom of these countries.[79]

As machinery was increasingly able to perform the hard and unpleasant physical labour which had previously provided civilized societies with their reason for supporting slavery, and as economists argued that the institution was inefficient anyway, it was increasingly apparent that any secular justification for this cruel institution was disappearing; yet the plantation owners in Brazil and in the southern states of North America did not agree and it took the terrible carnage and conflict of the Civil War on that continent 1861 to 1865 to finally bring about the beginning of the end of slavery as the basis of a modern society. Most of the states of the newly independent North America had kept slavery out of their territories; it was the tenacity of the slave states that prevented the freedom to all promised by the Declaration of Independence from becoming a reality.

The international tide continued to move against them. In 1778 an anti-slavery society, *Les Amis de Noirs* was founded in France with support from British Quakers, and the Abbé Grégoire, Lafayette and Mirabeau were active in the Assemblies urging abolition. Pressure from the coloureds in Saint-Domingue led to abolition of slavery in French colonies in 1793 and 1794, though in another testimony to the tenacity of the institution, Napoleon reversed this in 1802. A Society for the Abolition of the Slave Trade had been formed in London in 1788, because this was the weakest point in the slavery cycle and the trade was increasingly being seen as evil. With the political mood of the time moving against the West Indies sugar interests the abolitionists' path was further smoothed.[80] Slavery was outlawed by the Danes in 1802, the slave trade by the British Parliament in 1807 and by the United States Congress in 1808. But the African Slave Trade went on because it was so much easier to conduct, and so much more profitable than any other. It had to be internationally suppressed before other more legitimate trade, which England was interested in, could develop.[81] Her efforts towards abolishing the slave trade were then commercial and self interested as well as philanthropic.

Between the end of the Napoleonic wars in 1815 and 1842, most of the other nations of Europe were persuaded to legislate for the suppression of the trade. Legislation was one thing, enforcement in practice was another, and Britain therefore campaigned to have other countries accept her right to have her warships arrest slavers on the high seas, whatever flag they flew; there were important issues of national sovereignty involved here, and the United States and France never conceded this. With the Brazilian and Cuban slave-based sugar industries expanding to supply the markets that the dying British and French Caribbean sugar industries could no longer supply, the trade in slaves not only did not decline: far from it; it increased, with the result that more slaves crossed the Atlantic in the 1840s than had done before abolition;[82] it would not cease until the defeat of the South in the American Civil War finally convinced the remaining outposts of plantation slavery that their industries and the trade which supplied them were doomed. It took rather longer to persuade the Brazilian and Cuban plantation owners that the game was up. Though the secular world, religion and philanthropy, together with sound economic reasons, were all at one in condemning the trade and slavery with it, it was not they which finally defeated it, but the success of the North in the American Civil War.

The war, it is true, was not primarily about slavery but about saving the Union, yet it was the question of slavery in the new states of the Union which threatened that unity. In a fundamental sense then the war was about slavery. However, it was the threat that black slavery posed to free white labour which recruited the North in opposition to it; in defending those rights, white labour was defending a dignity which its Christian European background had given it. It was able to do this because, in a system of representative democracy, which was also an inheritance from the same background, it had the vote, and that vote its democratically-elected government had to respect. The idealistic abolitionists were a force also, but they would not have mobilized a nation alone. It took the threat which black slavery posed for the standards of free white labour to do that. The Civil War in America, which led to the final struggle with the inhuman institution of black slavery and its trade, will be discussed below.

13

The age of revolutions: the seventeenth to the nineteenth centuries

1 Revolutions, political

(i) Britain 1642–49 and 1688[1]

The first successful rejection of absolutism came in England where the Stuarts, James I (1603–1625) and Charles I (1625–49), clashed with Parliament over the latter's understanding of its privileges and what it regarded as the Romanizing of the Church of England. Parliament had come to represent the most powerful political, social and economic forces in the realm and its fundamental conflict with the king was on political power and financial matters; theological issues were secondary. The conflict resulted in civil war 1642–46 which ended in the king's defeat, and in 1648 when he fared no better. Cromwell dominated Parliament and in 1649 ensured Charles's execution.

Cromwell as Protector (1653–58) was resented. Parliament did not function effectively and the twelve military governors enforced a Puritan regime: his son Richard who succeeded him proved to be incompetent and General Monck therefore took control, providing for a freely elected Convention Parliament which asked Charles II (1660–85) to reclaim the throne – which he did. But his co-operation with Louis XIV and his apparent intention of restoring Catholicism to England led the Whigs, nonconformists, merchants and aristocrats to rebel; they won power briefly (1678–81) after alleging a Popish plot and ostensibly protecting the monarch from it.

* The notes and references for Chapter 13 are to be found on p. 411

Concerned lest the situation develop into another civil war, the country opted for Charles, the rebel leaders were exiled and the King kept his crown. His brother James II (1685–88), who succeeded him did not; he openly professed his Roman Catholicism and ignored the laws against them and when the birth of a son promised another Catholic king the Tories and Whigs united in inviting James's eldest daughter Mary, and her husband William of Orange, to claim the throne, an invitation they accepted. The country rallied to this arrangement, and the last of the Stuarts left for exile in France in 1688.

This, the 'Glorious Revolution' was that celebrated by John Locke (1632–1704) in his *Two Treatises of Civil Government* published in 1690. The ideas in it had been worked out before the revolution but, confirmed by the events of 1688, they achieved great impact not only in England but elsewhere. Much of what he says was founded in the mainstream Western social and political theory as mediated by the medieval scholastics. His account of pre-political society is that it is normally peaceful, in contrast to Hobbes's state of war; but since in that society not all obey the natural law given us by God and discoverable by reason, men enter into a social contract and form a political State, retaining full control over life, liberty and property in so doing. The State, however, has no positive role, no obligation to make its citizens wiser, or wealthier; punishing crime and preserving the rights of the citizens is its job. As a final resort against a despotic government which does not recognize these natural rights, the citizen has the right to rebel. If the holder of power neglects or abandons his responsibilities under the social contract then the government is dissolved and can be removed.[2]

To Frenchmen who were labouring under the crushing weight of absolutism, such ideas were attractive, and Locke and his philosophy generally were held in high regard. With Isaac Newton's scientific theories, and to a lesser extent the philosophical ideas of Lord Bolingbroke, of whom Voltaire (1694–1778) was a pupil, they formed a core of rationalistic philosophy which influenced French thought in the early stages of the Enlightenment. Voltaire, who had spent 1725–29 in England, was responsible for publicizing these developments in France, and Montesquieu's *Spirit of the Laws* (1648) suggested that the division and balance of the powers of judiciary, legislature and executive was the secret of England's liberty. In fact it was not strictly accurate in this, but essentially that balance did exist. Though the theory is as old as Plato, the clear formalization of the distinction has rightly had considerable influence on political philosophy since.[3]

Locke's liberty was only meaningful for some. Complete toleration was only for the Anglicans. Protestant dissenters, and still more the Catholics, had their civil liberties curtailed. The Whigs dominated national politics, controlling the House of Lords directly and the Commons indirectly through the system of 'pocket boroughs' which were in their gift or control, while the Tories ruled the shires through their representation among the Justices of the Peace. Social concern was minimal. There was little popular education, and town and national government was unresponsive to the needs of people at large. Even so large-minded a man as Burke saw no need for reform; the settlement of 1688 was perfect.

Locke's doctrine of property 'is directly intelligible today if it is taken as the classic doctrine of "the spirit of capitalism"'.[4] To say that public happiness consists in the protection and freeing of the acquisitive instinct is saying that it is right to accumulate as much wealth as one pleases, and that he who does so is absolute lord of that wealth; Locke says nothing of the duties of its proper use. Its economic implications therefore were not revolutionary but reactionary, as were the political. There were 92 county and 417 borough members in the House of Commons in the mid-eighteenth century. The county members were mainly elected by the Forty shilling freeholders, but open voting meant that the landowners knew who voted for whom, and so could ensure that the members elected represented the country gentlemen who would see that the interests of those same landowners were well protected in Parliament. Half of the boroughs were controlled by wealthy patrons, great landowners or peers, and merchants, lawyers, shipowners, and army and navy officers. A seat in the Commons was a good investment for anyone who had a stake in the system.

That the poor did not have such a stake goes without saying. After the Treaty of Utrecht (1713) when wealth increased enormously, the gulf in England between the rich and the poor, the small upper class and the miserable proletariat, became wider than it had been before, and it had been wide enough then: craftsmen and the artisans toiled long hours and could live well above subsistence level when trade was good, but bad times, and the increasing changes in industrial organization, put them at risk. Below them the hordes of casual labourers had no security or standing at all, while in the countryside the mass of agricultural labourers were always hovering at subsistence level and were increasingly threatened in that by the growing practice of enclosure of the common land on which they depended. The suffering of the poor was compounded by the cruel and incompetent way in which the Poor Laws were too often administered; punishments for crimes against property were harsh in the extreme; by 1740, children could be hanged for stealing a handkerchief worth one shilling. In the lean years the suffering of the proletariat became unendurable; in the countryside food riots erupted, the mob burned and looted and indulged in mindless violence. No wonder the rich feared them. Their outbursts were met by militia savagery, hangings and transportations.[5] The influence of class interests had 'never been more nakedly revealed in political action' than in the Glorious Revolution[6] and its aftermath. The social order now depended on the union of landlords and businessmen, and the rights of property were absolute. It was on top of the tradition of misery which was the life of the poor in the seventeenth and eighteenth century that were piled the miseries of the developing Industrial Revolution, palpable by 1780, and the combination of the two in a world of growing wealth was what made Marx and Engels' analysis of the evils of capitalism so persuasive and so helped bring about another revolution, once thought by many to have been equally glorious.

(ii) America 1776–81[7]

James I chartered the Virginia company in 1606, providing for a central governing board appointed by the king, and a group of settlers was established at Fort James on 24 May 1607. Initially they hoped to get rich quick, for example by finding gold, but it was the discovery of a cash crop, tobacco, marketable in England, which assured their long-term future. Then in 1616 indentured labour employed by absentee landlords in England ended; after seven years those who had worked for the company could become tenant farmers and later own their land outright. Finally in 1619 a legislative assembly, elected by manhood suffrage, was established to administer the settlement, which was also placed under English Common Law. When in 1624 it became a Crown Colony, Charles I permitted the local assembly, the House of Burgesses, to continue.[8] It was on these foundations, a hardworking settler community, culturally united by common origins in Christian Europe, winning its living from the natural resources to hand, and administering its own affairs through an elected assembly and common law, that secured in the colonies, and later the USA, a stable democratic system.

The American Revolution was a very reluctant one which only incubated as a result of several years of misunderstanding, and sharp differences of opinion on understandings, during the arguments and negotiations which everyone was still assuming would lead to settlement. The immediate cause of the misunderstandings lay in the manner in which George III's government went about trying to get a unified contribution from the colonies towards the cost of their defence, which had recently increased considerably because of Indian risings and threats from the French. There were other issues at stake but this was the crux.

On his accession in 1760, the King had done away with the developing cabinet form of government in England and sought to reimpose personal rule through favourites. By 1770 Lord North was nominally Prime Minister but it was the King who ruled. It was a system which resulted in greater rigidity and limited the flexibility of response needed to cope with the volatile situation in America. There was there no American nationalism or separatism as such in 1775, colonists were 'not only content, but proud to be part of the British imperium'.[9] They wanted to keep their constitutional rights as Englishmen in America as they had existed at the end of the Seven Years' War in 1763, the king and Parliament in London controlling foreign affairs, war and peace, and overseas trade, while the colonial assemblies taxed the communities, appointed officials, raised troops, commissioned officers and controlled the land system, the schools and churches. They were freer than their fellow countrymen of the same social rank in England, freer in fact than ordinary citizens in any country in the world in running their own affairs.

However, when the King and his ministers sought to impose new taxes without consultation, a radical opposition emerged, led by Samuel Adams of Boston. There were radicals active in England also, angered at the unrepresentative nature of Parliament and the corruption that was a consequence of it, and they possessed in Tom Paine a propagandist of genius, who at a crucial moment was to sway the colonists towards revolt. In 1770 British troops fired on a mob in Boston, leaving three dead; this helped spark four further years of protest and disorder, which culminated in the raid on the ships in Boston harbour in 1774. For the King this was the last straw, and Parliament, against the advice of many who had a better understanding of the situation, passed the Coercive Acts. The response was the Continental Congress which met at Philadelphia on 5 September 1774.

Since there was no demand for independence at the time, it had a difficult task in deciding how to proceed. It was not seeking total rupture but something like Dominion status. It might have worked had the King and his ministers been able to see what was at stake:

but they could not. Further ill-considered action by London led to Massachusetts becoming effectively independent in October 1774 when its Assembly met at Concord in defiance of General Gage's orders. The winter was spent in preparing for war and the first shots were fired when troops, marching on Concord on Gage's orders, clashed with the Minutemen at Lexington on 19 April 1775.

Yet it was nearly ten months before the final break came. The step involved was one that needed much hard thought. No European colony had broken with the mother country before; republicanism was an unknown quantity in a world dominated by monarchy; the ties with England and its tradition of freedom were strong. The attempts to find a settlement went on and the battle of Bunker Hill (16 June 1775) was actually fought while they were still in progress. As it was, further legislation of 22 December forbade all trade and dealing with the rebellious colonies at about the same time as Tom Paine's *Common Sense* was published in America. The pamphlet cleared minds and strengthened resolve, presenting as it did the case for independence in compelling terms: George III was a tyrant who had violated the compact with his people; reconciliation was not possible on any basis, and only full independence would meet their need.

The Virginia Convention, enraged by the news that George III intended to use German mercenaries to quell the rebellion, took the lead in May 1776, instructing its delegates to the Continental Congress to declare independence; accordingly on 7 June such a resolution was moved, and a committee consisting of Thomas Jefferson, John Adams, Benjamin Franklin, Roger Sherman, and Robert Livingston was set up to prepare a document, with Jefferson being given the task of drafting it. Locke's second *Treatise* probably influenced him in the task, though he claimed not to have consulted it or any other document. He may have been literally correct in this, for the ideas the Declaration contained were not so much those of one author but of a whole political culture which America inherited from the Christian Middle Ages, mediated through the English practice where circumstances had combined to ensure that the structures of representative government and constitutionalism had survived, despite their corruption and abuse by the men of property and their allies. The Declaration of Independence, issued on 4 July 1776, made clear that its basis was the West European tradition on which it was based – belief in certain natural rights, and therefore natural law, which is in harmony with the law of God the creator of all mankind.

We hold these truths to be self-evident, that all men are created equal, that they are endowed by their Creator with certain inalienable rights, that among these are life, liberty and the pursuit of happiness.[10]

The War of Independence came to an end for practical purposes with the defeat of Cornwallis at Yorktown on 19 October 1781, though a definitive peace treaty had to wait until 3 February 1783. It was a triumph of a citizen army against a professional one, but it would not have succeeded without the might of the French navy in its support.

One of the many remarkable things about the Revolution is that, having succeeded by violence, it went on to institute government under the law without any intervening period of chaos. Beginning with the freedom that Englishmen in America had been more successful in preserving than had their fellow-countrymen in England, they wanted to preserve that freedom and the institutions on which it was based. They were not out to create something new but to conserve something of proven value. As John Dickinson put it in the Federal Convention, 'experience must be our only guide; reason may mislead us'.[11]

The leaders of the American Revolution and those who wrote the state and federal constitutions were mainly university graduates. George Mason and Thomas Jefferson, James Madison, John Adams, James Bowdoin, John Dickinson, knew the classical political theorists, and also had experience of government, local conventions, colonial assemblies, the Continental congress. For them liberty was liberty under law, and representative government was limited by the natural law as were all governments. The first Bill of Rights, Virginia's of 12 June 1776, contained elements of Magna Carta of 1215, namely the right to jury trial and to liberty unless deprived of it by law or judgement of one's peers. Others were taken from the Petition of Right against Charles I, that a man not be compelled to give evidence against himself, and that the military be subject to the civil power. Such rights were defensible from natural law, which Blackstone, the best-known English jurist and legal writer, defined as it had been defined by the medievals, drawing on both pagan and Christian insights, 'as coeval with mankind, dictated by God himself, superior in obligation to any other, no human laws are of any validity if contrary to this'.[12] Such a concept of natural law, as we have seen, evolved in the Western tradition from the time of Sophocles, through Aristotle, Plato, the Stoics and finally through Roman jurisprudence, as the foundation on which human law must be based.

This basic affirmation separates the American experiment from that of laicist, Jacobin Europe after the French Revolution.[13] What lies behind the idea of the consent of the governed is the idea hammered out in the emerging polity of Christian medieval Europe via England, that the king is under the law and the constitutional monarch cannot rule his people by other laws than such as they assent to, or place upon them any imposition without their consent. The Bill of Rights likewise was based on the natural law. Man has certain rights and responsibilities as man before he is a citizen. Since these are not created by a government they cannot be taken away by it. Their source is human nature and human history, ultimately the God who is the creator of nature and the master of history. This approach enables limits to be set to the exercise of political and social authority and, unlike the French Bill of Rights, it is based on a historical tradition, through the English common law. It is the product of the Christian Middle Ages, and its understanding of natural law and its implications, not that of the Enlightenment.[14]

That Deism – the creed which admits of a creating God but denies a divine revelation, a providence, God's care for and intervention in the affairs of man – had some influence in America at the time there is no doubt; several of the revolutionary leaders were Deists, notably Benjamin Franklin.[15] But the moral sense which pervaded the new Republic, and which underpinned the virtues which were seen as essential for a healthy republicanism, was Christian. 'That free government rested on a definite moral basis, a virtuous people' was one point on which men of all political views converged. 'Religion helped put the order in ordered liberty, especially by emphasizing the dependence of public morality on private virtue.'[16] De Tocqueville sensed the American Republic's founders' belief in the religious basis of society as indispensable for republican institutions. The numerous religious sects differed on many things but

> all sects preach the same moral law in the name of God ... religion must be regarded as the first of their political institutions ... Christian moral teaching was so generally accepted that no one ventured to challenge it'.[17]

(iii) France 1789

The French Revolution[18] differed from its American and British counterparts in that it was much more social as well as political than they were; it was populist from its inception, though like all effective populism it was ultimately controlled by the few rather than the many, despite its periods of democratic excess. A long-standing grievance was the taxation system; since 1439, when the nobles agreed to grant the king a perpetual tax to which they did not contribute, the mass of the people bore the whole weight of taxation; as de Tocqueville pointed out, inability to resist rather than ability to pay was the criterion for being asked to pay taxes.[19] Not only did Louis XIV's constant wars cause his people immense suffering, but that suffering was increased by his rapacity in taxing the lower classes among the third estate to pay for them: there were sporadic rebellions caused by these injustices, all crushed with great severity. Boulonnais, Béarn, Bordeaux, Brittany, and Paris were among places affected in the period 1662 to 1709. Twelve hundred men taken after the rising in Boulonnais were either broken on the wheel or hanged. The trees along the roads were strung with the bodies of the rebels captured after the defeat in Brittany.[20]

Until periodic famine disappeared in about 1740, acute suffering and starvation were a part of life and a constant spur to rebellions of desperation. Missioners told Vincent de Paul of hordes of peasants, 'searching like pigs for roots of the earth'. Three-quarters of peasants lacked the 25 to 40 acres of land which would have guaranteed a modest livelihood for a family and the reserves to tide them over hard times. On the edge of famine in the good years, in the bad they became destitute and starved; the result was that every twenty five years or so generations were decimated. Then from about 1740 to 1775 there was a period of prosperity, and between 1715 and 1789 the population increased from 18 to 26 million. When the prosperity broke in 1776, those who had for thirty years been free of the terrible insecurities that previous generations knew were not prepared to face the same fate with equanimity.

The failure of the harvest of 1788 primed the rebellion in the country areas, while within the towns the tensions between the various interest groups threatened violence. The capitalist international merchant guilds were on the whole prosperous, the master craftsmen and their few apprentices and journeymen were less so, and were trapped now by changing methods of production and the shrinking of the market for their products; they were also at loggerheads as all sought to maintain their own basic standards. The wealthier members of the third estate prospered, but they were discontented because of their exclusion from the political process. The second estate wanted more political power. Peasants, urban workers, aristocrats, merchants, the bourgeoisie, the sophisticated clientele of the salons, the thinkers and writers of the

Enlightenment were increasingly united against the old regime.

The three 'estates',[21] were firstly the 130,000 or so members of the clergy in a Gallicanized church. The bishops were usually from noble families, the clerical academics came mainly from the wealthy bourgeois, and the parish priests and curates from the less wealthy bourgeois and the peasantry. They were not taxed but, as we have seen, gave grants at five-yearly intervals. Altogether the Church controlled some 10 per cent of the land and was responsible for most of the education and the social work of the time. The second estate consisted of some 400,000 nobles who controlled some 25 per cent of the land. There was a nobility of the sword which had no direct power but the most favoured were close to the King. The nobility of the robe were commoners ennobled for their service to the King as bureaucrats and officials. They had a tradition of loyalty to the Crown though by the late eighteenth century it was being strained by events.

The rest of the population, some 24 million souls, comprised the third estate. The rich bourgeoisie possessed something like 20 per cent of the land and controlled major commerce and industry; the minor bourgeoisie were the smaller master craftsmen, retail tradesmen and the lower ranks of the bureaucracy. It was this section of the population above all who were responsible for stoking the Revolution once it had been sparked by the nobility. Behind them were the industrial wage workers, guildsmen who were never going to own their own shop, the general labourers, and domestic servants – a proletariat which was always hovering on the subsistence line. As events were to prove, many of the clergy also were in sympathy with the third estate.

The overwhelming majority of that estate were peasants. Collectively they owned some 40 per cent of the land, there being great differences in fortune between the various groups among them. At the one end of the scale, there were those with leased property of up to 400 acres, and at the other there were those with 20 acres or less; the latter could support their families in good years but in bad went into debt or starved. Below them were those who owned small plots and little livestock; they were usually the largest group in the village and they depended on wage work to gain a livelihood; they were also employed by the textile trades as cheap labour. They were then even more exposed to misery in hard times. Finally there were the paupers and vagabonds.

It was the calling of the Estates General in 1789, for the first time since 1614, which opened the gates to revolution. The background was the failure by Louis XVI to get necessary fiscal reforms through, and he thought that by calling the Estates General and introducing through it a few moderate reforms the old system would be consolidated. There was no indication that this was not the view of the first and second estates; and since each estate cast only one collective vote, the first and second voting together could keep the huge masses of the third estate in their place. The latter would not accept this and with the support of the majority of the curés secured the approval of voting by heads and some of the clergy also joined the third estate in resisting the King's attempt to close the meeting on 23 June.[22] The storming of the Bastille on 14 July by the people of Paris, led by a mainly bourgeois mob, was followed by a mass insurrection in the countryside, and the Assembly conceded everything the former third estate asked of it. In October it was the mob who swayed events; with the King being reluctant to accept the Assembly's decisions, a hungry crowd, most of them women, raided bread stores and then marched on to Versailles. Thereafter the King and the royal family were virtually prisoners in the Tuileries palace in Paris.

Towards the Revolution, the prelates as a whole were in principle opposed from the beginning. While the parish clergy soon had reason to regret their support for it. Once in train, that Revolution began to take an anti-clerical and anti-religious turn, led by a nucleus of extreme liberals. On 2 November it decreed that the Church should surrender her lands and the clergy would be paid by the state; it ignored the fact that the properties concerned supported not only the clergy but most of the educational and social welfare of the country. The Civil Constitution of the Clergy of July 1790, which made the Church effectively a department of State, was a much more serious measure: the offices of priest and bishops were made elective, and parishes and dioceses were reorganized according to State plan; every aspect of Church life was now subject to secular authority, which was specifically anti-Church for the most part, and in some degree anti-Christian and anti-God. Pius VI did not react until April 1791, when he gave the only response possible: he condemned it.[23]

The French church then had been divided in the face of the Revolution. It was first of all a Gallican church, very much more under the control of the French Crown than of Rome. French bishops were overwhelmingly from aristocratic families; many of the sees were wealthy, as were many religious houses, and many of the latter had very few members. A minority of the parochial clergy were affluent through pluralism and the possession of rich benefices, while the majority lived modestly on scarcely adequate stipends; many were in real poverty. But it was a complacent church rather than a corrupt one; its degeneracy was exaggerated;[24] unfortunately because of its Gallicanism, it had become totally identified by its enemies with a completely discredited regime. Its worst enemies had been its Most Christian kings who controlled it for their own purposes.

The Civil Constitution introduced new and more terrible tensions into the Church. Exiles could identify with the Prussian, Russian, Austrian, Dutch and British alliance against the Revolution: so, most inadvisedly, did Pius VI. The Revolution itself was constantly changing in emphasis if not in general direction and in 1793 it turned into a reign of terror under the Committee of Public Safety, which in its turn was overthrown in 1794 when it became clear that under it no one was safe; the Directory came to power in 1795, with Napoleon emerging as dictator in 1799. Pius VI's opposition to the Revolution led eventually to the seizure of the Papal States in 1798 and to his imprisonment; he died at Valence on 29 August 1799.[25]

He had made provision for the election of a successor in Venice under Austrian protection, and Pius VII was chosen in 1800. Since in 1797, when Bishop of Imola under Napoleon's rule, he had declared that there was no contradiction between Christianity and democracy, he seemed to be the man to deal with Napoleon. For his part the First Consul had been convinced by the resistance of the peasants of the Vendée that the struggle between the Church and the French revolutionary State was counterproductive; he was therefore ready to enter into a Concordat with the Church and he did so. None the less, there were limits to Pius VII's readiness to placate him, and the Pope's refusal to ally himself with the French in the blockade of Britain led once more in 1809 to the occupation of the Papal States and the imprisonment of the Pope, who was consequently unable to exercise his office for several years.[26] Unlike his predecessor, however, he survived his experience as a prisoner of Napoleon and he was to return to Rome in triumph after Napoleon's defeat.

The writings of Jean-Jacques Rousseau (1712–88) best highlight the total conflict between the values of the Revolution and those of the traditional view of human life and society. Rousseau died before the Revolution started, but he had pointed the way to it. In his *Discourse on the Inequality of Man* (1758) he considers man's primitive state, seeing him as asocial but at the same time not warring with his neighbour. He is naturally good; there is no natural perversity in him. Experience, however, teaches him the need of civil society and then political society which he establishes through a social contract – only to find that it binds him in fetters, surrendering the poor to the power of the rich. The simplicity and goodness of the primitive man is contrasted with the evils of civilization. That does not mean that man can go back to primitive society. The need is for reform and a better social order which is to be secured through the better understanding of the social contract and of the General Will of which he treated in *Discourse on Political Economy* (1758). This will is directed to the common good; it is the voice of the people, the will of God, and all particular wills must conform to it. The decisions of a popular assembly do not necessarily express this will. There is a more important law that man must obey and the General Will is to discern this.[27]

The *Social Contract* (1762) expatiates on the contract idea as basic to society and it also says more about the General Will. Rousseau ponders the paradox that, though man is born free he is everywhere in chains, and sets out to establish what is required in order to free him from those chains while giving him the security which society and the State alone can give him. The answer he finds is in making the General Will predominate because in it sovereignty lies, and it is the people who are sovereign. But what precisely is the General Will? Is it the sovereign people legislating, the popular vote in the assembly? Not necessarily, because there is a distinction between the General Will and the will of all. The latter can mistake what the common good requires; in order therefore that a General Will which discerns the true common good may appear, particular interests in the State must be eliminated, and each citizen is then free to think his own thoughts, make his own decisions.[28] When such particular influences are removed then the majority in the assembly expresses the General Will. Those who oppose that Will can then be compelled by the whole body to accept it; they must be forced to be free.

Rousseau's citizen body was conceived as an enlightened one, sharing the Enlightenment's rejection of the past, of the independent organizations within the State, such as guilds and the Church. There is only the State, established by the social contract, the General Will of the citizens as legislator, and the enlightened citizens themselves; given that all are enlightened then the General Will and the will of the majority are one. The theory was adapted to encourage the destruction of the corrupt and unjust old regime. But it also encouraged the rankest individualism – and there was no common law as there was in Locke's England which in theory could

[handwritten: see footnote on how Marxism used this]

limit its effects,[29] There was only the individual and the General Will. It was a recipe for democratic totalitarianism, a dictatorship of the elite,[30] and in due time that totalitarianism appeared. On the positive side, however, the Revolution restored once more to European thought the idea that people have a right to choose their form of government and their rulers. The American Revolution had recently given testimony to that fact, but the small group of colonial states it represented was hardly as yet a serious contender in terms of cultural influence on the Western world. France, however, was such an influence – the democratic idea was back and would come into its own in the twentieth century.

2 Revolutions, industrial and social

(i) The Enlightenment and laissez faire

The industrial revolution gathered pace during the second half of the eighteenth century, which was the period also of the French Enlightenment and of the foundation of the modern science of economics.[31] As we have seen, the Western tradition from the time of the Greeks had philosophized about the *oikonomia*, the problem of ordering the household's work and finances.[32] In Roman law as in medieval times, the household under the headship of the father was the basic cell of social life, and the higher organizations of society were regarded as analogous to it; the city state, the lord of the manor or the king were responsible for the welfare of those communities and in return were entitled to their loyalty.

The Greeks knew the necessity of the market and exchange, and the economy of the Roman Empire was large and complex; commercial, industrial and financial institutions existed, and they worked for profit in the market-place, but a true market economy, a society whose economy was driven and which constantly renewed itself internally in response to market forces, did not. Aristotle saw that money and exchange were essential to the life of the community. A man should be able to sell what he had grown or made, and so make some profit in order to live decently according to the standards of his time; he also distinguished between value in use and value in exchange, money being the accepted medium of exchange. But he did not envision profit-making as a social good in itself, guiding the development of the economy in the direction of making the best use of resources. He looked to the State to keep acquisitiveness under control. Economics and economic behaviour outside the general framework of general rights and duties was unthinkable; social science was a field of applied ethics. Medieval Europe did experience self-sustaining economic growth driven by the merchant and manufacturer, but no one considered that the market was of itself a moral force.

The states of Europe adopted during the sixteenth and seventeenth centuries an economic policy which has come to be called mercantilism.[33] That wealth could be increased by human policy was being increasingly realized, the mercantilist saying that the way to do it was by the government discouraging imports and encouraging exports – the difference would have to be paid for in bullion, so swelling the nations coffers and making it wealthier. Others however disagreed; they advocated free trade, saw that wealth lay not in bullion but in production and commerce and said that the economic process was self regulating and perpetuating. Others identified capital as a separate factor of production and the income from it as profit; it had to be lent or invested to earn that profit. Overall the idea of the unrestrained market economy was taking hold and since this economic liberalism, as it came to be called, developed at the time and as the result of the influence of the Enlightenment which was oriented against received wisdom in any form, it won the argument.

Voltaire and the French Encyclopedists best sum up the spirit of the eighteenth century Enlightenment, but it was European-culture wide and its core convictions were provided by Newton's scientific discoveries and John Locke's philosophy. Collectively the men of the Enlightenment were neither atheists nor materialists but Deists – a creed that was elaborated earlier in the century by some British writers; they believed in God but not in revealed religion or a teaching Church. One group among them spoke as though God had created a world and then left it to proceed on its way according to natural laws which were modelled on those of the new mechanistic conception of the cosmic system,[34] and it is this strand in Deism which had most effect on a group of the enlightened who originally called themselves economists, but later became known as 'physiocrats'. The name is derived from the Greek and means 'nature's rule'; they saw nature in the sense of physical reality as superior to man and his works.

Their founder was one François Quesnay (1694–1774), physician to Louis XV but also devoted to economic studies; he argued that human society was ruled by natural laws which could never be altered by kings and princes. All men should be free to follow their self-interest in enjoying the benefits of property – a freedom consistent with the freedom of others to follow their self-interest. It

Deistic basis of "laissez faire economics"

is said he was once asked by the Dauphin what he would do if he were king and he is reported to have said 'do nothing' – *laissez faire, laissez passer*. This natural law had nothing to do with perennial moral values perceived by right reason. Seeing that the heavenly bodies moved but were not impelled by any external agent or authority, but from a power within themselves, so human life and affairs operated in a similar manner; the benevolent Maker designed men to live in harmony with one another and he gave them the faculties which would enable them to do so. It is from this Deistic philosophy that the methods of economics were derived.[35] There is an order in society and in man, an inner impulse to universal harmony. Any interference with it from earthly authority in his affairs is destructive of this harmony.[36]

If Deism, via the French physiocrats, provided modern economics with its philosophy, it was the Scotsman Adam Smith (1723–90) who gave that economics its basic text with his *An Enquiry into the Causes and the Nature of the Wealth of Nations*, first published in 1776. As famous as the *laissez faire, laissez passer* of the physiocrats was Smith's 'invisible hand' which guides the individual, seeking his own interest in the employment of his capital, to satisfy at the same time the needs of society.[37] A man of wide interests and culture, Smith was by no means a spokesman for the newly-emerging industrial interests in England. He was, for example, well aware of their tendency to combine against the common good, and of the need for justice, even for generosity to the wage earner. Yet there was in his tract all that was necessary, by selective quotation, to justify excesses by those who wished to justify them. The next generation of economists after Smith were less optimistic than he had been, and Thomas Carlyle dubbed it the 'dismal science' because it always seemed to give reasons why the human lot could not be improved.

By the first quarter of the nineteenth century, industrialization had demonstrated beyond doubt that the problems of production which had baffled man in the past had been overcome. It had shown that he had it in his power, in theory, to produce enough, and more than enough, to meet mankind's economic needs in full, given time; but it had created severe social problems in its tumultuous early progress. It need not have done. It was not necessary that the release of man's power to create wealth through industrialization should have produced the industrial pattern and cruelties that it did. They came about because industrial employers on the whole refused to consider the human implications of seeking the maximum profit at all costs and to the exclusion of all other considerations. They knew that their total freedom to do as they liked with their own was in accordance with the natural law that God had put in things. They were in good conscience, they told themselves. They sowed the wind and humanity reaped the whirlwind of Marxism and the horrors it brought with it.

(ii) Britain and the Industrial Revolution[38]

The conditions which predisposed England to become the workshop of the world were many and interrelated. The Glorious Revolution gave complete freedom of action to the propertied. The growing wealth of Empire and the strength of the banking system were disposing causes. The talents of her people were equal to the task of developing the techniques and industries that the demand for mass-produced goods required. The raw materials – coal, iron and steel – which would make the machines, which would make those goods, were at hand. Improved transport and communications systems would facilitate their access to markets with an efficiency hitherto unknown. The enclosure of the common lands and the development of scientific agriculture increased food supplies and made it possible to feed the population in the growing towns. The growth of population and the displacement of the rural workers by the enclosures provided the labour the new industries needed, and an expanding population meant more consumers as well as producers.

The Lancashire cotton industry produced goods which were in wide demand internationally, more cheaply and of a better quality than anything else available, and the market for them was almost limitless under free trade. The industry also had in it a greater potential for producing social injustice, because production was little impeded by any mechanism for the protection of the workers; it had no tradition of industrial production or of guild organization, and most of its employees were women or children. The expansion of the metal trades and of the potteries in the Midlands responded to the mass demand for their products, while coal and iron ore reserves were ample and ready to be exploited as mechanization and steam power were harnessed to the new forms of production and communications. The adult male workers were as much at the mercy of their employers as the women and children. Aristocrats as well as the bourgeois were active investors, and banking and financial services such as the stock exchange developed to enable them to do this.

James Kay, James Hargreaves and Richard Arkwright improved

weaving and spinning methods for the cotton industry in the period after 1733 which led directly to the factory system. James Watt had by 1769 so improved the efficiency of the steam engine that it became practicable to apply it more generally, and Matthew Boulton, an entrepreneur from the metal-working town of Birmingham, undertook to manufacture the engines, and in so doing founded the modern engineering industry. Factories need not be scattered in the hills where the water power was. By 1790 steam power was at work in an increasing number of trades; the industrial city, with its factories, housing and its regimented work-force had arrived, and it changed attitudes and habits as few other changes in the human habitat have done.

Communications were being improved. A series of great canal and road engineers emerged to build up a network of both from the middle of the eighteenth century. The first effective steam locomotive, Stephenson's 'Rocket' (1829), was to introduce a railway boom, or a series of them, which gave a further impulse to England's economic development. Supplies were more reliable and cheaper; dispatch of output was easier, and deliveries faster, cheaper and safer. Steam power also improved the opportunities for travel for everyman who previously was confined to his own immediate locality.

Population was almost doubled in England, from 6.7 million to 12 million between 1760 and 1821,[39] and the workforce for the new industries was there. The growth of the towns and the industrial workforce changed what had been the pattern of human settlement since the beginning of man's history. Urban areas gradually began to employ, and house, more than did the rural, and the concentration of workers in towns induced a new sense of solidarity among those who manned the new industries; communications, by railway as well as by road, the use of the telegraph, and cheaper printing meant they could keep in contact with other workers elsewhere. The way was open for those who wished to tap the anger of the workers in the interest of new causes to do so.

(iii) Social problems of industrialization

To those who saw in the changes only the optimistic possibilities adumbrated by Adam Smith, the unleashing of man's power to create wealth without let or hindrance, was an unalloyed good. But the facts told otherwise for the factory employees in general in the first three-quarters of a century of the revolution, and the reaction, soon to become a violent socialist reaction, set in very early. The exercise of power by employers lacking any sense of social responsibility, the specialization of labour in factory conditions which alienated the worker from his work and, worse still, imposed upon women and children conditions of appalling cruelty, built up a seething mass of resentment. The loss of security in industries that were notorious for their booms and slumps, the unhealthy conditions of work, of housing and of living of the wage earners, the lack of any effective social provision, the great gap between the poverty of the many and the growing riches of the few, the overall reality of oppression to which the poor were subject, all provided ripe conditions for social unrest and many were prepared to exploit them. Among them was Karl Marx, whose powerful mind and revolutionary determination were in time to focus that unrest most effectively.

By the late eighteenth century there existed in England a recognizable new industrial capitalist class which took its place alongside the older monied groups, the landed aristocrats and gentry, the bankers and merchants, the builders of Empire, the men of property from the great professions and older branches of trade, industry and commerce. Many of the new capitalists had started as small masters working alongside their men, though this was becoming less and less common. Capital and labour had already become well separated at the initial stages. Among the new captains of industry there were men of culture and sensitivity, and there were not lacking individuals who from the start treated their employees well. Robert Owen (1771–1858),[40] son of a Welsh shopkeeper who had progressed from apprentice to cotton magnate, had by his innate ability made his New Lanark Mills in Scotland a profitable undertaking, while a developed moral sense made them a model of their kind. He paid his 2000 employees, 500 of them pauper children, good wages, maintained in slack times; he also worked them for reasonable hours, provided sickness and old age insurance, good housing and cheap food supplies, educational and recreational facilities. Owen however was an exception which helped prove the rule; the majority of the new capitalist class were men whose

one aim was money. Men and things were only tools for the attainment of this single object ... power made them tyrannical, hard ... sometimes cruel.[41]

The social problems of the early part of the industrial revolution were compounded by those caused by the enclosing of the land. It was a movement that had been going on since the Middle Ages, but it speeded up considerably from about 1780 as rising population made corn-growing more profitable and pressure for more efficient methods of production increased.[42] The problem was that the enclosures were carried out with the interests of the landowners only in mind, as Arthur Young, one of the Agriculture Commissioners who had initially supported the movement, later recognized. Enclosure of common land and consolidation of the open field system meant that the peasants who had lived on it and worked it under that system received very little consideration in the reorganization; only the freeholders were secure.[43] Young showed that, had proper consideration been given to those displaced, provision could have been made for their support from the plentiful unused or waste land; there were several schemes where this had been done successfully.[44] As it was, pauperism in the rural areas increased by leaps and bounds with a consequent increase in unrest, often violent.

The outbreak of the French Revolution in 1789 and England's involvement in war with France in 1792 exacerbated the situation. Farmers prospered as the price of corn rose but inflation further impoverished the displaced rural workers. In industry many trades were adversely affected by war conditions and discharged their workers, or were able to reduce wages and impose conditions of work which were resented, while mechanization was replacing workers in many of the older crafts, especially in textiles. To those suffering unemployment, inflation was a further blow. Politically, the Revolution raised fears in England; it seemed that some of the traditional radicals might follow the French example and turn to insurrection. Corresponding Societies were banned, Habeas Corpus suspended and a Sedition Act passed. A new wave of industrial unrest in 1798 lead to the Combination Acts of 1799, under which any association of workers was held to be a conspiracy. These acts were 'the first signs of the rising class struggle, of a new age of conflict which marked the nineteenth century'.[45]

Though marginally better off than their rural counterparts, the industrial poor were wretched none the less.

> It was impossible for most of them to live a life of more than bare subsistence and the natural disasters of their personal lives – unemployment, sickness, death of a breadwinner – left families in utter destitution. The only answer for unemployment and poverty was the workhouse.[46]

There were riots and machine wreckings in the North and Midlands and reaction was savage; 17 men were executed at York in 1813 and many more were transported.[47] The peace of 1815 brought no immediate respite as the economic dislocation caused by readjustment to the new conditions was accompanied by a bad harvest in 1816. Displaced handloom weavers were denied court protection and their strikes were broken by the military.

The predicament of the new industrial working class, without protection against sickness, unemployment or accident, living in insanitary conditions, their old skills constantly threatened by machine methods which required children and women rather than adult men, was desperate. Denied what redress the law formerly offered them, and denied also the right to form their own associations, they were entirely at the mercy of employers; in work they had neither security nor the right to dispute wages and conditions, however unjust, and at the same time they were frequently obliged to spend their meagre wages in stores run by employers who then cheated them without pity.[48] The scenes such as those in Mr Diggs's tommy shop depicted by Disraeli in *Sybil* were, the author tells us, drawn from life.

(iv) Social protest and social reform in Britain

The discontent kept alive the hopes of reform, despite the oppressive legislation of the 1790s, and the reaction of the powers that were was often violent. A crowd which gathered to hear a political address in St Peter's Fields, Manchester, in 1819 was charged by the local yeomanry, eleven of the listeners being killed and hundreds injured. New acts to control the unrest included muzzling the radical press. The first sign of relief came accidentally with the 1824 toleration of trade unions. Liberal ideology, on which it was based, said there would be no harm in such legislation because workers did not really want unions. But the responses showed otherwise; they were then allowed to exist for purposes of negotiating wages and conditions, but they were on the edge of legality; any effective action to protect their members was punished.

There was more hope of political reform since it was being demanded by the new middle classes in the burgeoning cities, as well as the old-time radicals. Among the latter there were heirs of John Wilkes, Tom Paine and the American and French Revolutions, urging manhood suffrage, which was also labour's aim. Labour's support for the radicals meant that the reform was now a mass movement, capable of putting real pressure on government. In 1832 a Reform Bill was accordingly passed; it only added 286,000 voters to an existing roll of 366,000[49] but a moderate middle-class reform had been achieved against massive vested opposition, and it had been achieved peacefully; further pressure it was hoped would yield further gains. Yet the labour movement meanwhile had gained little or nothing. Robert Owen's attempt to rally it through the Grand National Consolidated Union flourished for a while, claiming to organize some 500,000 workers. It soon disintegrated, though some of its constituent unions survived and made their contribution to that development of a stable nucleus of trade unions concentrating on purely industrial gains. The more politically inclined found in the Chartists the means of continuing the struggle.

The Charter was drawn up in 1838 by William Lovett and Francis Place – the former a cabinet maker and founder of the London Working Men's Association, and the latter a tailor well known for his radical views and activities. It sought universal manhood suffrage, annual general elections, the secret ballot, equal electoral districts, abolition of property qualifications and payment for MPs. But the difficult economic conditions of 1837 to 1842 caused great distress among the industrial workers in the north; this, and the displacement of skilled adult male workers by the unskilled, gave rise to more radical demands. The message was spread by torch-light processions and meetings. A massive petition with hundreds of thousands of signatures was presented to Parliament as the climax of the campaign in the spring of 1839.

In July the Charter was rejected. It was the high-water mark of the movement. There were riots, strikes and some local insurrec-tions but no concerted attempt to challenge the authorities. Marx, resident in England from 1848, held hopes that the cause was still alive; it was the only working-class movement in the country with which he identified and as it became more fragmented he supported Ernest Jones, who had ideas of the class war akin to his own; but it was a lost cause. The class war had few supporters, the majority 'preferred to defend the cause within the capitalist system'.[50] The revolutionary pressure was on the decline. Many of the middle-class Chartists found another more practical cause in the Anti-Corn Law League which between 1842 and 1846 campaigned for the repeal of the protective tariffs for corn. It taught them the importance of political pressure groups and how to organize them. By the 1850s the system had also begun to return sufficient benefits to enough skilled workers in regular employ-ment, and to operatives in expanding industries, to remove the worst of the social discontents, and the Chartist cause was in total decline. But it eventually conquered; manhood suffrage, the secret ballot, equal electoral districts, abolition of property qualifications and payment for MPs were introduced by degrees.

The improvement in the lot of the wage earners has given rise to the dispute between what has come to be known as the optimist and the pessimist point of view among economic historians. It will probably roll on yet a while; in the meantime it would seem safe to say that between 1780 and 1820, on average standards of living probably fell, that between 1820 and 1850 they on average probably rose, but by the 1850's and 1860's there is no doubt that the optimists have it; improvement was real and substantial.[51] Though agriculture lagged and there were still whole areas of industry and urbanized living in industrial areas which inflicted gross injustice on many, it was apparent that there was more hope for the future than before.

The past remained with it just the same. The most damning indictment of the liberal capitalist regime in the early years of the Industrial Revolution was not its injustices to the adult male worker, but to the women and children who supplied between two- thirds and three-quarters of the employees in the textile trades in the period of its great expansion; many of the children were under fourteen years old, and lucky to earn a halfpenny an hour for up to sixteen hours a day;[52] they were therefore essential to the wealth-creating process in what was the main engine of the initial stages of the industrial revolution. Child labour in itself was a well-established institution before industrialization, and there was toleration on the part of parents as well as masters of much that was cruel and unfeeling. The ignorance and grinding poverty of the former and the greediness of the latter ensured that. The system became increasingly cruel in the process of industrialization in that many of the child workers were taken from poorhouses and were therefore without even a minimum of parental care. Whether the children were from workhouses or from the homes of the poor, they were systematically exploited as the adjuncts of machines to create industrial wealth on an unexampled scale.[53]

The mass of employers refused to accept the evidence that the complete freedom they enjoyed in their mines and factories produced injustices, and they ignored all attempts to allow restrictions on their liberty. The adult workers meanwhile, male and female, were supposed to be able to look after themselves and make satisfactory contracts with their employers; but having no right to organize for their own protection, and lacking any protection in law, they were disadvantaged in negotiation in every way. In those circumstances there could be no fair bargaining.

The scandal of the treatment of children had led to the attempt to introduce legislation for their protection in 1802. An Act, Peel's

Act, was indeed passed but since it lacked sanctions it was a dead letter from the start; it could be, and was, simply ignored. In 1816 Parliament investigated the way it was working and found that manufacturers opposed it on three grounds. The first was the sacredness of freedom of contract, the second that the long hours and strict discipline were favourable to the moral formation of the young people concerned, teaching subordination, industriousness and regularity of life, and finally that the conditions of work were not in fact harmful on medical grounds; they had doctors who were prepared to testify so.[54] But public opinion was gradually being roused by the evidence of injustice, with the result that further legislation was provided in 1819; but since it too did not provide means of enforcement or sanctions it remained a dead letter.

In the aftermath of the 1832 Reform Bill the question of effective legislation to protect the young came up. Antony Ashley Cooper (1801–85), eldest son of the Earl of Shaftesbury and an outstanding Christian, was among those who led the campaign that resulted in the passing of the first effective act in 1833. It forbade the employment of children until they were nine years old, and limited the under-thirteens to eight hours a day; above all it provided inspectors to ensure enforcement.

The 1833 Act was a landmark, embodying as it did the important principle that the liberal capitalists could be curbed by law when acting against the common good, and it was followed by other legislation which gradually tackled the other abuses of child and female labour. The adult male, however, was supposed to be able to look after himself, though he was rarely able to deal with his employer as an equal, individually or collectively. As the century ended the hours and conditions of work even of the best paid still left much to be desired, while below them were the unorganized masses and the sweated labour whose working conditions were appalling and whose life was one of misery and semi-starvation. Their turn was not to come for a good many years.[55]

The example of men like Robert Owen, and the evidence that legislation for the protection of workers did not cause economic disaster, reveal that it was not the process of industrialization itself which caused the social problem, but the ruthless way that selfish employers acted. Polite society meanwhile was easily convinced by the Enlightenment and the idea of *laissez faire* that absolute freedom for the men of property was a positive social good. The truth was that the social upheaval that modern industrialization was bound to cause required the maximum care for the prevention of needless suffering; it was the tragedy of the process as it occurred in England between 1780 and the 1830s that the public philosophy of the time was so grossly regardless of the needs of the wage earners and the poor. Reform continued slowly and often was a mixed blessing. The Poor Law of 1834 revealed the lack of humanity that was typical of the liberal cast of mind. So harsh were its provisions that in some parts of the country they were ignored as being unworkable. On the positive side, it did establish the principle that the community, through the State, was prepared to take action to try and relieve the destitution of the unemployed.

The first steps towards public provision for education for children were taken in the 1830s, though no national legislation was passed until 1870 and even then the voluntary societies were heavily relied on.[56] Effective public health legislation was slow in coming; not until 1875 was a comprehensive and effective Public Health Act passed covering sanitation and water supply in towns. These practical changes forced by reality were accompanied by a rethinking of some of the basic tenets of liberalism. John Stuart Mill, son of James Mill, was educated by his father in the utilitarianism which synchronized well with the liberal capitalism of the early nineteenth century, but Mill junior gradually abandoned its narrower perspectives. His *Principles of Political Economy* revealed the science in a more humane light; he shifted the emphasis in economic thinking from the production of wealth to its distribution, showing that the distribution of the wealth produced is not so strictly governed by immutable laws as theorists alleged. Society has the final say on the matter.[57] Economists might claim that the worker deserved a particular wage but they could not say that some abstract mathematical law supported their judgement.

Though he was by no means a socialist, there was much else about Mill's theories which went a long way to meeting the objections of socialism, such as the taxation of rents and inheritances and the encouragement of workers' co-operatives. His greater sensitivity to the ethical and human problems of economic organization, his gradualism, pragmatism, and avoidance of radical solutions well suited the changing mood and need of the times. However, he had the limitations of his liberal background. He saw no reason for the existence of trade unions, whereas in fact it was the absorption of the energies of the industrial labour movement in this form of action which steadied the social system when it was under threat, enabled a more positive trade unionism to develop, and laid the basis for that effective voice for the labour movement in politics which helped to stabilize British politics at testing times and to eradicate many of the defects of an economy nurtured by liberal capitalism.

A 'new model unionism' made its appearance from the 1840s, composed of craft unions, formed by the more highly paid workers, their organizations were better financed and their policies more mature. They pursued limited industrial aims through whatever collective action in defence of wages and conditions was legal.[58] One of the achievements of the movement was to make the political power of the workers felt. Already that power had been increased by the Disraeli Government's Parliamentary Reform Act of 1867 which had given the vote to the more prosperous urban workers. Further legislation in 1871 (Gladstone) and 1875 and 1876 (Disraeli) secured the legal status of trade unions[59] and their right to bargain for their members, though judge-made law continued to cause problems. The election of two miners for mining constituencies in 1874 marked the first entrance of workers into Parliament. Liberal–labour alliances resulted in more following them, while Conservatives saw the political value of supporting trade union interests at crucial times – witness Disraeli's legislation. Neither alliance however was satisfactory. By degrees an alternative was worked out. The ad hoc Labour Representation Committee of 1900 founded as a result of an initiative by the Trades Union Congress to increase labour representation in Parliament, marked the beginnings of a Labour Party with which the unions could work.[60]

The political consciousness which led to that move was stimulated by the growing tendency among Conservatives to question the point of the working-class alliances, and there was a felt need for means of making the needs of labour known politically. The TUC's establishment of the Labour Representation Committee was stimulated more powerfully still by a decision of the House of Lords in the Taff Vale Railway case, a decision which presented the trade unions with the possibility that their funds were under threat for every unauthorized decision of their officials. The movement roused itself to action for the general election of 1906, and 29 LRC candidates were among the 53 Labour members of Parliament returned – the others decided to stay in alliance with the Liberals or Conservatives, but the LRC members were a strong foundation for a new political force in British politics.

By the closing years of the nineteenth century, therefore, some of the worst excesses of liberal capitalism had been curbed in the country that had felt its first impact, but there were considerable problems still to be faced as severe industrial unrest in the London dock workers' strike of 1889 and in the mining areas in the 1890s reveal. These were the result of a 'new' new unionism, and this time it was labour in the trades which were not craft-based which was the spearhead.

The extent to which poverty and poor living conditions still affected so many, mainly the unskilled workers, is shown by many sources. For example, ten thousand Manchester men offered themselves as volunteers during the South African war in 1899, and 80 per cent were rejected outright on physical grounds, although Army standards had been lowered; only 10 per cent were finally accepted.[61] The studies of the living standards of people in particular cities made by Charles Booth, Seebohm Rowntree, A. L. Bowley and A. R. Burnett Hurst revealed how society was failing them; in York, for example, Rowntree's study showed that 40 per cent of wage earners and their families were living below the minimum standard for physical well-being.[62] It is not surprising that an underlying discontent affected British industrial relations down to the beginning of the 1914 war, especially in industries where the problems of casual labour, or particularly intransigent employers, poisoned them. In 1911 a new wave of strikes which affected the mining, shipping, dock and railway industries was particularly significant in registering a new desperation in these sectors; the response to them showed that the more imaginative and humane leaders of public opinion were recognizing that more positive measures were needed to deal with the situation.[63]

9/24/02

3 Revolutions, industrial and social: continental Europe[64] and the USA

(i) Belgium

Belgium,[65] part of the Dutch Netherlands in 1815 which became a sovereign nation after the revolution of 1830, was the second European country to industrialize extensively. The region had long been the home of industry and trade; as we have seen, its woollen industry had been one of the great centres of production in medieval Europe; there were metal-working centres there also, at Hainault, Dinant, Namur and Liège, while coal had been mined in the Mons area from the seventeenth century.

The French had occupied the country from 1790–1815 and it was in this period that Belgium first began to develop industrially, but it was after it achieved independence under the Liberal regime of 1830 that it began to take off; the Belgians adopted a constitu-

tion which combined the most liberal features of those of France,
England and America, and economic liberalism was part of that
inheritance. In 1834 the State took the initiative in developing a
railway system, basically complete by the 1850s. The iron and steel
industries expanded – as did the coal industry, which by the 1840s
was the biggest on the Continent.[66]

The revolution of 1830 was very much a revolution of the rich
liberals. Only 55,000 of the citizens of the new state were
enfranchized and it was not thought necessary to counter the
social ills of growing industrialism. By 1846 it was clear they were
widespread, but the revolutions of 1848 passed Belgium by. There
was sporadic unrest in the 1860s and stirrings in 1867 as a rash of
strikes followed on an economic crisis, and thereafter the situation
was unsettled; the depression of the 1870s and 1880s, which hit
industrialized Belgium particularly badly, forced the issue: strikes
threatened to bring about revolution and it took the army two
weeks to restore order. A full-scale enquiry into labour conditions
was instituted and a programme of social legislation was begun, but
it took a general strike and further social upheaval to compel
parliament to broaden the electoral base in 1893; real political
influence was at last in the hands of the wage earners, and their
needs received fuller attention from the legislature.[67]

(ii) France[68]

The industrial revolution came slowly to France, its effects being
spread over the century following on the defeat of Napoleon in
1815. Before the Revolution France had had Europe's strongest
economy; a country of some 26 million people, its industries
famous for their luxury goods, a brilliant and inventive intellectual
community, generally productive agriculture and a state-developed
network of roads and canals. Napoleon encouraged the modern-
ization of industry but the revolutionary wars, the high cost of raw
materials, low wages and generally conservative attitudes discouraged innovation.

In 1815 peace returned under a constitutional monarchy –
although only 80,000 of the people had the vote. Many of those
who supported Louis XVIII (1814–1824) had not accepted the
democratic implications of the Revolution, and they gradually
gained more and more influence until Charles X (1824–30) in
1830 attempted to restore the old order by a *coup d'état*. In this he
was not successful, the Liberals organized an effective peaceful
opposition, and a more acceptable monarch was persuaded to take

Charles X's place. So was instituted the July or Liberal monarchy of Louis Philippe (1830– 48).

Liberal did not meant democratic: it ruled in favour of the middle and upper middle classes, who were determined to do as well as they could out of the *laissez faire* mentality it embraced and which was not troubled by a social conscience. Industrialization proceeded slowly but perceptibly. Roads and canals were improved and railways were built. The iron industry grew steadily with the de Wendels and Le Creusot works expanding particularly rapidly. Iron production increased four-fold between 1820 and 1850 until it was second only to Britain's in Europe. The silk industry was mechanized, although most wool-weaving and linen-making were in the hands of village crafts. It was cotton which led the way to industrialization in manufactures.

The 1820s and 1830s saw the first great growth of socialist theorizing. The poor harvests of 1845 to 1847 hit the urban working classes badly and industrial depression added to their suffering and unrest. Nor were the prosperous and politically powerful middle classes happy with the regime in 1848 and they joined the opposition to bring it down, but unity of purpose between the industrial workers and the middle classes did not last long. Initially this unity secured manhood suffrage and the establishment of the national workshops; but these in practice simply became a vast makework scheme for anyone unemployed and this, together with the general air of social radicalism of the time, produced its reaction. Elections for the constituent assembly resulted in a moderate conservative majority while a rebellion by the workers in June 1848 was crushed by the army; Napoleon III became President in December and by 1852 he felt strong enough in control to proclaim himself Emperor.

The Empire retained the forms of a republic: its power rested on the army, but it also had the support of the mass of the people. The Empire fostered economic liberalism, and enjoyed a period of unprecedented material prosperity which helped ensure its stability. The urban working class and the peasants shared to some extent in the prosperity, and the Emperor sought to head off their politicization by promoting and funding self-help schemes of social welfare. Vast programmes of public works were also put in hand. But the urban and increasingly industrialized workers were being denied any real participation in the decision-making processes. The imperial concept was misconceived anyway, and as Napoleon's misjudgments began to weaken the regime from 1860s the end was nigh; the defeat in the disastrous Franco-Prussian War brought it about.

Hostilities had opened on 19 July 1870. General McMahon's army was soon defeated and it, and the Emperor, surrendered at Sedan on 2 September; by 27 October only Paris and a Republican provisional government of national defence under Gambetta carried on the fight, defying Bismarck's request for surrender for four months until forced to concede defeat on 21 January. A National Assembly which was to arrange the peace terms was elected in March, and Adolphe Thiers its President and later head of government negotiated a treaty which was signed on 10 May 1871, the terms including the loss of Alsace and part of Lorraine as well as a five billion francs indemnity. Paris and the Republicans refused to accept either government or peace treaty, and since the working classes and the lower middle class were also angered by the Assembly's decision to end the wartime moratorium on rents and interest payments, those interested in starting a revolution had an easy task. The Paris Commune which was declared on 27 March was revolutionary, not Marxist or proletarian, but mainly bourgeois. It was also short-lived. Government forces laid siege to the city on 30 March and there followed a week of extremely bitter fighting, in which Paris suffered more damage than the Germans had inflicted on it; when finally the Government troops forced their way into the capital on 21 May there were scenes of terrible brutality. In retreating, the communards murdered their hostages and in retaliation the troops took no prisoners. Many famous buildings were destroyed by fire and the courts martial which sat after the victory to try the prisoners, though they passed few death sentences, sent many to the penal colonies.

> Thiers had won a notable victory in the class war ... an assembly of monarchists ... had provoked and then put to fire and sword the people of Paris.'[69]

The Assembly wanted a monarchy, but division among the aspirants denied it to them. Thiers then chose Republicanism because it divided the country least, but it was provided in a form that was adapted to the return of the monarchy in due time, the constitution empowering the Senate and Chamber of Deputies to choose a successor to the President at the end of his seven-year period of office. The deputies were chosen by manhood suffrage, and since a substantial majority of the enfranchised were peasants and conservative in their politics, such was the nature of the administration.

The Third Republic remained unstable: in the period down to 1914, the average cabinet survived for less than nine months. Initially the Republicans dominated the Chamber of Deputies, the Monarchists the Senate, and though the Senate went Republican in 1878, the Monarchist and other anti-Republicans still maintained their no-compromise attitude. An attempt by anti-Republicans to put forward General Boulanger as a dictator in 1888 failed because the General baulked at the crucial moment, but it revealed the strains on the Republic. The Panama Canal scandal, and the Dreyfus affair which followed in the 1890s, further weakened it.

The conflict between the Monarchists and the strongly liberal Republicans obscured the social problem because the increasing urban working class had no influence on political structures. The Monarchists were paternalistic in their understanding of how to meet the needs of the workers and did not consider that they required political power of their own. The Republicans for their part had consistently refused to recognize and press for the workers' demands – and from the Republicans alone could the workers expect any support in the matter. The result was that by the early 1890s the working class had deserted the Republican left[70] and it increasingly held the French political system in contempt, preferring to espouse violent remedies, syndicalism and Marxism as an answer to its problems.

Finally the tension between Church and State posed a challenge to a stable and just political order. Napoleon III had strengthened his alliance with the Church to prop up his regime, and as the Republicans grew in strength they sought their revenge by severing links between the church and State, in particular excluding the latter from education. Too many French Catholics were supporters of monarchy and of extreme right-wing opposition to the Republic on grounds that had no connection with theology and the Church's true role in politics, and everything to do with their own political prejudices. It was an attitude which the international Church, for the good of the church in France, sought to change; we shall see below how Rome went about this. In the meantime, political and social unity suffered from these conflicts too.

The French economy had gradually become more industrialized after the revolution of 1848, the application of steam power multiplying fourfold by 1870, and the discovery of the Bessemer steel-making process in the 1860s enabled steel to be mass-produced cheaply from inferior ores, so transforming the industry. The loss in 1871 of Alsace and part of Lorraine was a considerable setback, but the economy gradually recovered in the 1880s and in the 1890s new technology had enabled home iron resources to be developed. The Industrial Revolution was finally in place. With the consolidation of the Republic, then, and growing industrialization, the modern French State had taken shape. But it had grave defects. Monarchical, anti-democratic and extreme conservative views were still powerful and the French church was still too identified with them, while the Republican refusal to recognize the needs of the working class further severely undermined its stability; the way in which the bourgeoisie had garnered the fruits of the Revolution at the expense of the mass of the people was remarkable among the states of Europe.[71] It was not a socially or politically healthy society.

French utopian socialism flourished in the nineteenth century. Saint-Simon (1760–1825), veteran of the American War of Independence and of the French Revolution, put forward his proposals for the reorganization of society in a series of books from 1817, advocating socially responsible big business, with equality of opportunity and abolition of privileges. Villeneuve Bargemont, Prefect of the Département du Nord, the richest industrial region in France, revealed the social costs of liberal capitalist industrialization; half of the population in the Lille area were indigents. Fourier, Buchez and Le Blanc were advancing their various radical answers to the growing problems of the 1830s and 1840s under the July monarchy.

The Second Empire had not fulfilled any of the hopes of labour; its approach to the social problem, of which it was not unaware, was in general paternalist, though trade union activities were legalized in 1864. The reaction against the Paris commune of 1871, however, hardened attitudes and it was 1884 before full freedom of association was offered to the French workers. Meanwhile Marxism and Syndicalism became increasingly attractive; the latter sought to organize all workers in one big union and then bring the State to its knees by a general strike. Any form of co-operation with employers or State was scorned by it and its eventual aim was total workers' control. A National Federation of Syndicates was formed in 1886 and had close Marxist affiliations until 1894 when the Marxists withdrew after a dispute. The *Confédération Générale du Travail*, the C G T, which embraced a syndicalist policy to the full, emerged in 1895 and became the dominant form of French unionism.

(iii) Germany[72]

Under Napoleon the 300 German states and statelets were reduced to 39, Austria and Prussia being the leading members, and this pattern was confirmed in being as the German Confederation at the Congress of Vienna in 1815. Prussia took the lead in beginning to unify Germany in 1819 by establishing a customs union which gradually removed the number of tariff walls hindering economic development, and it was on the framework thus established that political unification was grafted. Industrialization initially came slowly. As late as 1850 it was very limited, with only 5 per cent of the workforce engaged in modern manufacturing industry. It was the building of railways that made the difference. After the Prussian State became involved in 1842 the expansion began, and by 1849 there were 3000 miles in use in Germany and 1000 miles in Austria. 'It was railways' Treitschke boasted, 'which first dragged the nation from its economic stagnation.'[73]

Though the overall development of a modern economy was limited in the 1840's, the home grown critics of the evils of liberal capitalism were eloquent in warning of the dangers to which its growth laid Germany open; they included Adam Muller (1779–1829) and Franz von Baader (1765–1841). Meanwhile the revolutionary mood of 1848 led to the Frankfurt Congress of that year which was the result of liberal political pressures within the states of the Confederation, sparked by news of the Revolution in France.[74] Nothing came of it; it wasted so much time in endless debates that by April 1849 William IV of Prussia had the initiative again, crushing the liberals there and by degrees everywhere else also, while the Hapsburgs restored their power with the help of the Russians.

German unification was the work of Prussian leadership. William I (1861–92) had no sympathy with liberalism; he was a divine-right absolutist, and with the help of his Chancellor, Otto von Bismarck (1815–98), he was able to rule very much as he pleased. By overriding constitutionally correct attempts to restrain him, Bismarck got the increased military expenditure he wanted in 1862–63, then secured swift, efficient victories in wars with Denmark (1864), with Austria (1866) and with France (1870–71). The patriotic fervour these victories aroused guaranteed that, though it was freely elected on manhood suffrage of citizens over 25 years old, the Reichstag could be manipulated by the Chancellor to his purposes. Germany was effectively a military autocracy ruled by the Emperor and increasingly dominated by Bismarck.

All this did not restrain economic development. With the railways already spurring it from the 1840's, the customs union expanded, and a modern financial and banking system emerged; so too did the great steel companies, the electrical engineering industry, and the chemical industries, the cartels, and a German international policy of overseas expansion. There was a corresponding growth in the major industrial centres, and a growing population – from 35.1 million in 1840 to 64.9 million in 1910; 40 million in cities, with far more of them in towns over 100,000 than in the smaller ones.[75] The Ruhr and Roer coal fields and those of Silesia were progressively exploited from the 1850s. In iron and steel production the country had a great potential, but until 1860s it lagged. The acquisition of Alsace-Lorraine in 1871, the higher tariffs on British imports in 1880, and the introduction of the Thomas and Gilchrist steel manufacturing process in the 1880s changed that, and by the 1890s Germany had taken the lead as Europe's iron and steel producer.

The chemicals, electrical machinery, and shipbuilding industries grew rapidly. Of the textile trades, the traditional ones such as linen slowly adapted from the late 1840s, and the woollen industry similarly modernized from the 1850s. The cotton industry, of little importance before 1850, expanded and the occupation of Alsace in 1871, where the French cotton industry was centred, further strengthened it. With industry came industrial unrest and social- ism. Social concern for the workers was shown by sections of German industry, in a paternalistic but effective way, at an early stage. But as the impact of industrialization gathered pace from the 1860s more independent workers' associations emerged and they were subject to other influences. The workers in the modern- izing textile and iron industries of Prussia, Bavaria, Saxony and Baden were offered help by the liberals in Berlin, Frankfurt, and Breslau in organizing cultural associations, and radicals at Leipzig in 1862[76] arranged a German Workers' Congress, enlisting the aid of Ferdinand Lassalle, who already had a reputation as a radical.

Some 600 delegates duly assembled on 23 May 1863 to form the German Workers' party, forerunner of the Social Democratic Party. Though Lassalle himself died in 1864, the impression his efforts had made on the movement in Germany were formative and lasting. In particular he convinced it that the workers must by their own efforts gain power in the State through universal suffrage. Auguste Bebel and Wilhelm Liebnicht later formed a rival Social Democratic Labour Party in 1859 but the two came together at Gotha in 1875, their aims being to establish a Socialist society, to reject the iron law of wages and to end exploitation.

The success of the socialists was enough to make Bismarck fear their challenge, and in time he would accept it. Before that however he launched an attack on the Catholic Church, the *Kulturkampf*.[77] His reasons for his actions were several. Foremost among them was the growing political power of the Church typi- fied in the appearance of a Catholic political party, the Centre

Party, in 1870, which had been formed because of the fear of a group of Catholics that they and their co-religionists were in danger of being isolated in a Protestant empire, and that the growing anti-clericalism of Progressives and Liberals was also a threat to them. German Catholics had always been suspicious of national unity under Prussian leadership, given the nature of the Prussian State, and this suspicion in time increased. The formation of the party[78] was the initiative of a group of laymen who were convinced that the only way to protect the Church was to have a confessional party in the Reichstag. Bismarck for his part thought an attack on the Church would meet with international approval and so he allowed and encouraged legislation to be passed in 1872–75 which seriously interfered with her internal affairs, but this simply made Catholics rally to the Church's cause and ensured more votes for the party.

While this struggle with the Church was going on, the political strength of the Social Democrats was growing. Their success in the elections of 1878 so alarmed Bismarck that he found an excuse to ban the party by manipulating the parliamentary and electoral system and playing on the fears of socialism. The law was in force until 1890. At the same time he realized that doing something for the workers was good politics since it would reduce the attractions of socialism. Altruistic motives were there at hand also; the example of Disraeli with his 'one nation' Conservatism; the promptings of the 'socialists of the chair', academics stressing Christian charity and justice. The result was the first social insurance legislation of the modern State; against sickness in 1883, with employers contributing two-thirds and employees one-third of the costs; against industrial accidents in 1884 with employers bearing the cost, and against old age and incapacity in 1889 with the costs met by employers, employees and the Reich.[79] A code of factory legislation governing conditions of work was also laid down, and labour exchanges were set up to help workers find jobs. There was no unemployment insurance on a national scale but many municipalities provided it, and they, and private agencies, made provision for housing, public works, and help for migratory workers. No country had a better system of social legislation than Germany before 1914.

It did not immediately impress the socialists, however. With the Erfurt programme of 1891, and under the leadership of Karl Kautsky, the SLP abandoned Lassalleanism and embraced the Marxist class struggle and its prophecies concerning the downfall of capitalism.[80] On the other hand Eduard Bernstein, who had been a close collaborator of Marx and Engels, and whose stay in England from 1888 to 1901 convinced him that Marx's predictions were in error, thought otherwise; the increasing misery of the proletariat, the predicted disappearance of the middle class and the imminent collapse of capitalism were contrary to observable fact. To Bernstein, socialism became simply a movement towards co-operative production and the workers' need to organize to work for reform and democracy.

In 1891 total membership of German unions was only 334,400. In that year the legislation curbing them was relaxed and by 1913 the number they organized had increased tenfold to 3.37 million. The socialist Free Trade Unionists were most numerous with 2.8 million, next were the Christian Trade Unionists with 343,000. They usually united on wage issues and they were allied with parties in the Reichstag.[81] There were great strikes in the Ruhr coalfields (1872 and 1889), and by the steel workers (1905), the dockers in Hamburg (1897) and textile trades in Saxony (1903). The main opposition to the unions came from the major employers in the heavy industries, men like Krupp, the armament manufacturer, Kirdorf, head of the coal and steel cartels of the Rhineland, and Baron Stumm, styled 'king of the Saar'. By contrast there were those like Ernst Abbe, head of Zeiss at Jena who handed over his plant to the workers, while the smaller firms in the lighter industries recognized the value of collective bargaining and the trade unions that made it possible.

(iv) Italy

Italy,[82] like Germany, only emerged as a unified state in the nineteenth century, largely also as a result of ideas and movements set in train by Napoleon or in reaction to them. Here in Italy the Papacy had to grapple with the implications of liberalism and nationalism, first within the Papal States while it ruled them, then when it felt unsure of its independence surrounded by the new national state of Italy. But only much later in the century than Belgium, France and Germany did Italy feel the impact of industrialization. Of the nine states of Italy in 1815, Lombardy and Venetia were part of the Hapsburg empire, and Parma, Modena, Lucca and Tuscany were ruled by relatives of the Emperor. In northern Italy only Piedmont-Sardinia was ruled by an Italian house, that of Savoy. The Papal States in central Italy were politically allies of the Hapsburgs and the Two Sicilies were bound to Austria by treaty. Nationalists rebelled first in Naples and

Piedmont in 1820 but failed, as they did again in 1830, because they did not have the support of the mass of the people.

However, with the 1830s more coherent movements emerged. Guiseppe Mazzini, founder in 1832 of the Young Italy movement dedicated to the cause of Italian unity, sought a democratic republic: others preferred a constitutional monarchy of Piedmont-Sardinia, and a third group looked for a federation of states with the Pope as president. Pope Pius IX, elected in 1846, initially made concessions which endeared him to the nationalists. However, when it became clear that nothing less than full constitutional government of the Papal States, which deprived the Papacy of real political control of them, would satisfy the nationalists, he drew back; he would not for example countenance the use of papal troops against Austria. The murder of his Prime Minister Pellegrini, and the behaviour of the Chamber of Deputies afterwards, finally disillusioned him.[83] Mazzini and Garibaldi's short-lived Roman Republic was abolished by the French, who intervened in 1849 and restored Pius IX to Rome. The search for unity went on thereafter with it becoming plain that the best agency for this would be Piedmont-Sardinia. Cavour, Prime Minister of that state from 1852 dedicated himself to achieving this and by 1860 four states had declared for union, while Garibaldi's Redshirts had reclaimed Naples. By the time that the French forces had been withdrawn from Rome during the Franco–Prussian war, Victor Emmanuel was able in 1871 to enter into Rome in triumph and make it the capital of a united Italy. The Pope, refusing to accept the loss of states, became 'the prisoner in the Vatican'.

Before 1860, Italy was not as a nation well equipped to enter the industrial age; only the north possessed any real tradition which would enable her to do so. She was deficient in basic raw materials, coal and iron; what iron there was in Sardinia, Elba and Val d'Aosta could not be worked competitively with the rest of Europe. She lacked adequate technical skills in her workforce save in the north and she had little capital to invest, while the values of the old regime did not encourage innovation, and speculation was distrusted. Such industry as there was, was linked with agriculture, its workforce being part time; so in quarrying and mining the workers were more connected with agriculture than industry; textile workers were mainly women who also were part-timers on the land; even in 1880 it is calculated that only 20 per cent of the adults in industry were males, and the potential labour force was reluctant to break this pattern of living on the land and using industrial occupations for seasonal or occasional work.

Piedmont was the main woollen centre and silk was manufactured throughout Italy, though concentrated in Piedmont and in
Lombardy. Sulphur was produced in Sicily and was a major export.
Cavour encouraged the construction of railways, the Alpine
tunnels, and the establishment of the steamship connection
between Genoa and the USA; he also negotiated commercial
treaties with other countries. The Milan, Turin, Genoa triangle in
the north was the Italian industrial heartland. Here there were
rivers for hydroelectricity, transport was easier and markets nearer;
these added to the region's long industrial, commercial and financial tradition made it more adaptable to the new needs.

Though overall the Italian economy was ill equipped to modernize, the industrial, financial and commercial tradition of the north
made it ready for it[84] and by the 1880's modern industry was developing there. Pirelli had built his first factory in Milan in 1872 and
the textile industries of Legnano, Vicenza and Biella were helped
by the tariff changes of 1878. Elsewhere, the machinery, steel and
armaments industries grew where hydroelectric power was obtain-
able. In 1883 the Italian Edison Company set up a generating plant
and Milan had electricity for lighting and industrial use. Italian
motor vehicle manufacture began at Turin in 1895, and in 1899
the Fiat company was founded.

Political patterns generally hindered economic development
overall. Each of the states had lived under different legal and fiscal
systems and there was a lack of a national sense of identity and
coherence. The demand for Italian unity had been led by the intel-
lectuals and the middle class. Only 500,000 people had the vote in
the 1870s and the greatest beneficiaries of the *risorgimento* were
unwilling to pay for it, putting the main burden of taxes on the
poor.[85] Seventy-five per cent of the people were peasants or agricultural labourers, most of them living in poverty and oppression.
Illiteracy and political alienation were also problems. Though few
had taken part actively in the *risorgimento*, the many had had their
hopes raised by it, only to find them quickly dashed by the reality.
The new political system was weak. The nobility tended to ignore
it, leaving it to the middle classes. The electorate was increased to
about three million in 1882 and in 1912 adult manhood suffrage
increased this further to eight million.[86] This opened up new possibilities of popular participation but the unfortunate inheritance of
the system meant that Mussolini and his Fascists would be the
immediate beneficiaries.

There was little effective political organization in the nineteenth
century. There were no parties, but cliques which formed around

particular politicians, and coalitions of such cliques formed governments; the desire to control the State for their benefit and that of their clients, rather than to make it serve the national interest, was the operative principle. The discontent of the poor, and of the workers generally, made itself felt through support given to the anarchism of Bakunin and the Marxism of Labriola, while the sheer desperation of the agricultural workers needed no theory to spur them to action. Some workers were organized from the 1860s but the first attempt to organize a Chamber of Labour in Milan in 1874 resulted in the trial of its leaders and in the same year Bakunin had led a rising at Bologna which failed. By 1886 fear of socialism was so great that the right of association, implicit in the constitution, was specifically removed. The Sicilian poor were the real revolutionaries of the 1890s.[87] There was violence, attacks on town halls and customs houses. Convinced there was a socialist uprising, the Government used the army to quell the rioters and in one incident 92 peasants and 1 soldier were killed. Giolitti's government fell and Crispi's took its place. Blind to the economic causes of the trouble, he saw the unrest simply as a socialist plot and imposed martial law on Sicily. The unrest continued.

There were reports of people eating grass, dying of hunger, of municipal granaries stormed, of the financial system failing and payment in kind being used, of peasants occupying land on the great estates. Riots in Rome in January 1898 led to the proclamation of a state of siege and troops being stationed at street corners. In May the troops fired on an unarmed mob in Milan after two policemen had been killed in rioting. There were eighty deaths and the street fighting went on for days. Railway workers and civil servants were put under military discipline so that disobedience could be more easily dealt with. Universities were closed and chambers of labour, village banks, associations of all kinds, including some 3000 Catholic groups and organizations, were dissolved. Newspapers were suspended; the Catholic *Observer* of Milan was suppressed and its editor arrested. Marxism meanwhile was enjoying a vogue among city workers acting

> as tonic on the decadent liberalism of the 1890s and a purgative which eventually destroyed the outmoded radicalism and republicanism of the left.[88]

(v) The United States of America[89]

The United States had none of the gross inequalities of the old world; above all it embodied freedom because it was out of the struggle for freedom that it emerged. It had its blind side; the native Indian population and the enslaved blacks were not to have its benefits, but even these appalling injustices cannot obscure the great positive achievements of the new nation in terms of freedom generally, and the contribution its success here had on the whole democratic movement in the modern world. The franchise was gradually extended once independence had been achieved until all adult males had the right to vote, and all thirteen states adopted constitutions which embodied bills of rights for their people. By the period 1820 to 1850 it was clear that democracy and republicanism did work, and a world which still thought in terms of plutocracy and monarchy took notice of writers like de Tocqueville who told them about it. Foreign travellers were impressed with the lack of poverty in comparison with Europe, and with the opportunities for the worker it offered.

The movement to open up the unexplored West began in the 1840s as the settlers pressed on from Ohio into Indiana and Illinois. Canal, road and rail construction had eased the way in the 1820s and 1830s, and into a country that was still vastly underpopulated came in the 1840s some 1.5 million immigrants.[90] By 1850 the population of the USA was 23 million. The cities expanded steadily and urbanization and industrialization went hand in hand; textiles had adopted the factory system, but steam power came more slowly because of the difficulties facing the iron and steel industries. Not until the 1860s was iron produced in the quantity needed for modern industry, and the engineering industry lagged accordingly. However, metal-based industries connected with agriculture flourished; McCormick's first patent dates from the 1830s.[91]

In the 1850s most manufacturing in the USA was done in shop or household, the proprietor, his family and assistants the workforce; factories, wage earners, machine power were the exception, not the rule. The Civil War (1861–65) helped to change that. Congress financed railways to the tune of 100 million dollars, and in ten years 20,000 miles of track were laid. More coal, iron, steel, cotton and wool were produced during the war years than ever before and the number of northern manufacturers increased by 80 per cent.[92] The first oil well gushed in 1859, and the war made the industry. The war also brought benefits to the farmer, though less than to the industrialist. The Homestead Act of 1862 had offered land to the small farmer, and enough did escape the clutches of the speculators to help many of those for whose benefit it was intended. Demand for its products resulted in agricultural production doubling between 1865 and 1875. The new railroads solved the problems of transport, although the individual farmer was a hostage to fortune when harder times came. The urban workers were less fortunate. Inflation during the war eroded wage increases, and the return of a million ex-servicemen, plus the continued heavy immigration during the 1860s, made the post-war prospect bleak. The contrast with the new wealth of the war-rich, the profiteers, the shady politicians and carpetbaggers, began to inject a note of bitterness into social and industrial relations.

The labour movement had developed slowly. The carpenters' strike in Philadelphia in 1827 and the Mechanics' Union which resulted from it, organizing fifteen other trades, marked its beginning. There was a national labour convention, representing several unions, in 1834,[93] and more strikes in the north-east in the period 1833 to 1837, but the law of conspiracy made effective action difficult until 1842, when a famous case decided that trade unions were legal. Labour groups also turned to politics, starting their own parties or allying with others, and though the economic collapse of 1837 weakened the movement, some states passed useful factory legislation and many industries introduced the ten-hour day.[94]

The Civil War gave the labour movement a distinct impetus; the question of the liberation of the slaves could not but raise questions about the dignity of labour, and the economic side-effects of war already detailed roused instincts of self-defence that encouraged unionism. Local unions proliferated and ten national organizations were set up in the 1860s, including the powerful railwaymen's unions; there were 32 national organizations by 1870 and every large town had its trades association, workers' press and library.

There were attempts also to provide organizations for all workers, one of which was the Knights of Labour, established in 1869. It fought for the 8-hour day and workers' compensation and also favoured semi-socialist measures such as public ownership of public utilities. Secretive at first, it realized that this led to misunderstandings and decided to work openly; as it did so it became clear that there were two opposed factions in the movement, those who wanted direct action in industry to improve the standard of living by aggressive strikes and those who wanted political action only. It did win one great strike against Jay Gould's Missouri Pacific railroad in 1885 but thereafter it fell apart. None the less many of the unions it nurtured survived; it also ensured by its impact that the labour problem was firmly before the public.

The appearance of the union movement and the claim to have the right to challenge employers on wages and conditions soon produced a powerful reaction, and the whole force of the law was brought to bear to support the *status quo*. Courts began actively to interfere with the labour movement. Injunctions were used from 1888 on the grounds of conspiracy in restraint of trade,[95] arrests made and trials without jury held, troops were sent to run the trains. Gould lured the workers into another more violent strike in 1886, and this time he won. The pattern of violence in labour–management relations that had now developed was capable of being exploited by outside interests, most notably the anarchists. In Chicago on 3 May a clash between strikers and the militia left two workers dead, and the local anarchists called a protest meeting in the Haymarket on the next day. Someone – it was never discovered who – threw a bomb into a group of policemen moving to break up the meeting, killing seven of them. In August eight anarchists were sentenced to hang and four of them were executed.[96] The violence at the big Carnegie works at Homestead was more significant in terms of the actual violence generated by industrial conflict alone, planned as it was on both sides in a real class spirit. Henry Frick, president of the company, felt there was no place for the unions in his works and he sought a showdown with them, employing 300 Pinkerton guards for the purpose. The struggle lasted five months and ended in defeat for the workers; again an anarchist intervened, attempting to kill Frick.[97] The Pullman strike raised the stakes further.

Pullman workers were an elite created by paternalism. The workers occupied a model town south of Chicago, paying an agreed rent for their homes, and they were also sold fuel, food, water and services. They were therefore totally dependent on their jobs not only for their wages but for their living standards generally, and when in 1893 and 1894 their wages were cut by from 25 to 33 per cent while the prices charged by the company for housing and services were maintained, they struck, and more than 100,000 other workers came out in sympathy in what was the greatest strike the country had seen. Three thousand police, five thousand strike breakers sworn in as deputy marshals and given firearms, and six thousand federal and state troops were brought in. The injunction was used to keep mails running although the strikers had agreed to provide the necessary manpower. By the strike's end, thirty of the strikers had been killed, sixty injured and more than seven hundred arrested.[98]

In its bitterness and intensity the industrial conflict of these years possessed more than a suggestion of the class war, with the State weighing in for the employers. If businessmen combined to further their own purposes this was in accordance with natural law, but if labour did the same it was conspiracy. Monopoly was good business, but the closed shop for trade unionists was un-American. The government had a responsibility to aid business and protect its interests, but if it did the same for labour that was socialism. That business should influence politics was common sense, but that labour should was un-American. Those who owned property had a natural right to a fair return on it – but all that labour could demand was the going market price. Hence appeals to protect or develop property interests was reasonable, but if the same was invoked in labour's favour, then this was unreasonable.[99]

The major social conflict in America in the nineteenth century was, however, not the conflict between capital and labour, bitter though that was. It was the conflict over the rights of the black slaves which led to the Civil War 1861–1865. Though not directly a war about slavery but about the preservation of the Union, yet it was the dispute about whether slavery should spread throughout that Union, or be confined in some way, which was challenging that ideal; the more fundamental cause of the war, then, lay in the slavery issue.

The incongruity of demanding 'life, liberty and the pursuit of happiness' for themselves while denying basic human rights to slaves was apparent to Americans from the start, but it was only in the states in which the number of slaves was negligible that the institution was outlawed. In the deep South, where there was a conviction that slavery was necessary for the prosperity of the community, it went on as before; it was agreed it was an evil but it was a necessary evil. When in the nineteenth century new states began to be formed as the nation expanded westward, the question of whether slavery was to be accepted by them became crucial.

Since 1787 it had been agreed that north of the Mason–Dixon line[100] and the Ohio river there should be no slavery, but when Missouri sought recognition as a state, this agreement was challenged because most of it lay north of that line. A compromise (the Missouri Compromise) was therefore reached in 1819. Missouri was allowed to keep its slaves on the understanding that henceforth everyone who was on United States territory above the line 36.30°N. would be free.[101] This compromise held until the 1840s, but the basic conflict of rights among the states had not been resolved; it had only been postponed. When it was proposed that Santa Anna, the Mexican President, should cede California to the USA, Congressman David Wilmot suggested that it also should be a slave-free state. The Southerners were angered at this and the Congress was so bitterly divided that it was impossible to agree on the admission of any more states to the Union. Then came the dispute over the Kansas–Nebraska bill in 1854, which embraced not only the slave issue but that of deciding where the transcontinental railway would run.

Senator Douglas, having interests in the latter, and wanting the logjam of principle on slavery broken, made a proposal which would take the onus of the decision on slavery off Congress's shoulders and place it on those of the states by allowing them to decide it for themselves by 'popular sovereignty'. It was accepted reluctantly and after bitter debates, but the matter was not to rest there, for the situation was then confounded by the Dred Scott decision of the Supreme Court which ruled in 1857 that the Missouri Compromise had been, and was, unconstitutional. Slavery could not be kept out of any state according to this ruling; it followed the flag.

It was against this background that Abraham Lincoln (1809–65) slowly emerged as the defender of freedom against slavery, but it was a slow emergence. As a farm boy born in Kentucky and brought up in Indiana, he had had no contact with slavery; he encountered it first, and rejected it, during a trading sally down the Mississippi in 1828. As a lawyer entering politics in the 1830s, however, he was not moved by the abolitionists to oppose slavery initially, and until the early 1850s his attitude was that of a 'free soiler'. He recognized the Southern states' constitutional right to their 'peculiar institution' but disputed the right to spread that institution to free territories where he knew it would undermine the position of the white workers and the dignity of labour generally. In every recorded speech from 1854 to 1861 he repeated the warning of the danger of slavery becoming national and that if it did, free America was doomed.[102]

He was not an abolitionist at the time because he did not think that this was practical politics, but when he had to face the issue his deep conviction that slavery was morally wrong broke through. In 1854 he denounced it as a monstrous injustice, being 'founded on the selfishness of man's nature, opposition to it on his love of justice'. This same moral objection was made apparent in his Quincy speech of 13 October 1858 when he reflected that the conflict was between those who

> think slavery is wrong and those who do not. The Republican party think it is wrong ... a moral, social and political wrong.[103]

Yet it was not the moral evil of slavery he stressed in terms of practical politics, but the fact that slavery was in danger of becoming national and so threatening freedom. His opening speech of the 1858 election campaign on 16 June summed it up:

I do not expect the Union to be dissolved – I do not expect the house to fall, but I do expect it to cease to be divided. It will become all one thing or the other. Either the opponents of slavery will arrest the spread of it ... or its advocates will push it forward, till it shall become alike lawful in all the States.[104]

It was this issue, that the Union would have to be all slave or all free, that led to war. So determined was the South to keep its peculiar institution that it was prepared to secede if it was challenged, but while Lincoln would give to the South its rights under the Constitution, he insisted that that same Constitution as he saw it forbade it to secede. As the war proceeded, the real issue, the rights and wrongs of slavery, became clearer, and Lincoln let the matter slowly mature. He had made a covenant with God to free the slaves when the time was ripe. In September 1862, when McClellan's success in thwarting Lee in his attempt to win a conclusive victory against the North was foiled at Antietam, this time had come. Thereafter there was no danger of foreign recognition of the rebels' cause, and Lincoln's Presidency, and his freedom to announce emancipation, was secure. On 22 September, five days after Antietam, he therefore told his cabinet of the covenant with God and that he now intended to make it good,[105] issuing on 1 January 1863 the Preliminary Emancipation Proclamation, that all slaves in any area under Southern control were freed.

Though initially it freed no slaves, because the South ignored it, and the loyal border states which had not seceded were excluded from its provisions, the Proclamation made the war into a crusade for freedom; victory for the North would mean the end of slavery, as it did. By the passing of the thirteenth amendment to the Constitution in 1865, Congress outlawed slavery throughout the Union. The tragic death by assassination of Lincoln on 14 April 1865 prevented his overseeing reconstruction; it was left to others who proceeded in a spirit of vengeance towards the whites and exploitation of the blacks which has poisoned race relations in the United States down to today. But nothing can deflect the glory of the achievement of Lincoln and the North. Their stand ensured that black slavery could have no place in a modern Western democratic state. Many other forms of what is effectively slavery survived and survive throughout the world today, but the evil of mass black slavery, and the trade it bred, the disgrace of the Western Nations for over three centuries, was no more.

14

Social movements of the nineteenth century and the Church to 1878

1 Socialism and anarchism

(i) Before Marx

As a movement, socialism[1] emerged in the wake of the Industrial Revolution in Europe and it is Europe which provided it with its classic thinkers. It was a reaction to the excesses of individualism as they were evidenced during that Revolution, an individualism most marked in the use, and abuse, of private ownership of productive goods in industry. Generally those who called themselves socialists insisted that the goods which society produces as a whole belong to society as a whole and they should be divided equally among all, and the social ownership of productive goods is necessary so that this should be done.

The rejection of private property then is central to most forms of socialist belief, and this is an idea which, in one form or another, had advocates long before the Industrial Revolution. It was commended by Plato, at least for the guardians of his republic,[2] and though private property was approved by the Scriptures, most of the Fathers, as we have seen, regarded it as a result of the Fall of man, with property in common as more fitting, though in a fallen world they never advocated property in common for the mass of men. It was the ideal of the monk, but for the rest, private property was a natural right. In the Middle Ages, the conviction that Christ and the apostles had renounced private property surfaced, for example, among the Spiritual Franciscans.

Some members of the socialist movement of the eighteenth and nineteenth centuries were strong in their advocacy of the social ownership of the means of production; it now became for some the object of planned practical action. On the other hand some of those who are seen as part of that movement were prepared to see some form of private ownership of productive goods continue. There was also an anarchic strain in some extreme socialist thinking, and it led to mindless violence. As modern socialist thought developed, therefore, it presented a wide range of views: if there was a unifying idea of the movement as a whole it was that the ethos of atomistic individualism in capitalist society should cede to one in which society took more responsibility for seeing justice done to its weaker members. It was solidarity, seen in purely secular terms, that it sought, with a general – though not exclusive – tendency towards the social ownership of the means of production.

The Frenchman François Noël Babeuf (1760–97), who during the French Revolution supported those insisting on the abolition of private property and advocating class war, can be seen as the founder of modern socialism. Not content with the direction the Revolution was going, he plotted to overthrow the Directory and establish communism, but his plans were discovered and he was executed. A co-founder was William Godwin (1756–1836), an Englishman and an anarchist. He claimed that anarchic individualism would make private property superfluous. Believing in human perfectibility, and that man always responds to the truth, he argued that he must always be completely free of the State, of law and of binding obligations; since man was perfect this would mean that the total freedom he had would be exercised for the common good. Private property would not be necessary. Each would have what he needed and only what he needed, and would never treat others with injustice.

Claude Henri de Rouvroy, Count de Saint-Simon (1760–1825) was a horse of a different colour. He had fought in the American Revolutionary war, then abandoned his title and identified with the French Revolution. Insofar as his ideas on the problems of industrialization have a central core and coherence it lies in the need to organize the industrialists. They are to be given a place in society equal to their worth, replacing those older social groups which hinder the process of industrialization. Monarchy should be an industrial monarchy, the king being the first industrialist. However, on the question of private property Saint-Simon was most

Saint - Simon

unsocialist. The fundamental law in each country was to be that which establishes private property,[3] but the owners must work, fulfilling the social obligations of their state rather than enjoying a life of ease.

Saint-Simon therefore allowed of private property, and indeed big business, but ordered society for the good of the masses. It was his disciples who after his death introduced socialism into their creed. Reasoning that humanity was moving towards a harmonious future, they saw that it was ill equipped for this future if *laissez faire* principles prevailed. The worker in fact is exploited and a revolution is needed to put an end to that exploitation, one which would abolish inherited wealth, and in time personal wealth of all kinds, in favour of community ownership. The Saint-Simonians, therefore, pointed the way to State socialism. At the same time, there was no egalitarianism in their creed. On the contrary, they believed there was a natural inequality among men, hierarchy being their ideal.

Charles Fourier (1772–1837), a draper who had started his own business which failed during the Revolution, became a clerical worker, and while earning his living in this way came to despise the dishonesty which was a daily part of commerce. Following Rousseau, he reasoned that the problems of human life and human nature come from man having wandered too far from nature's ways. Nature is in harmony, as the order of the universe demonstrates; man too must return to nature, to a condition in which natural passions and impulses have free play. Society was to be organized in 'phalanxes', that is, self-sufficient groups of approximately 1800 persons, and each such 'phalanx' was to possess one square league of land, preferably in a pleasant situation, a valley with a broad river and fertile land. The law of passionate attraction was to rule in these phalanxes; work, relations between the sexes, everything was to be determined by this sentiment. No one was to work too hard and all labour was to be pleasant. Private property remained, but each was to receive minimum subsistence for work done and the surplus was to be divided between labour, capital and talent. But all members were to be prosperous, even those comparatively the poorest, so there was socialism of a kind. He also saw how disorganized and wasteful unrestrained individualism was and highlighted the value of producer co-operatives. Despite the oddity of his theories, some were found ready to try to put them into practice. More than 30 phalanxes were set up in the USA in the following decades, although none lasted for more than five or six years.

Robert Owen (1771–1858), to whom reference has already been made,[4] stands out among the founders of socialism in being a successful and wealthy manufacturer. The son of a Welsh saddler and ironmonger, he started to work as a shop assistant when only nine years old and moved to London a year later; by the time he was nineteen he was manager of a cotton mill in Manchester and in 1797 he and his partners bought the New Lanark Mills in Scotland. The conditions at the mills were as bad as anywhere, the adults being thieves, drunkards and blackguards, the children recruited from the workhouses of Glasgow and Edinburgh at an early age. Owen immediately started to improve matters. He stopped the recruitment of the very young children, and saw that the older ones had some schooling. He also helped the adults to recover their self-respect. His system was paternalistic and autocratic, but it was based on a genuine regard for human dignity and rights and contrasted so remarkably with the conditions elsewhere that the mills became a centre of pilgrimage for all who were interested in these matters. He operated the mill profitably, indeed the way he treated his workers helped him in this. They worked harder and better because they were happier.

However, after his success and fame with New Lanark, Owen became more and more an impractical dreamer and an intolerant declaimer on all matters and sundry, imagining that he had discovered the whole secret of life and happiness. His industrial schemes became more bizarre; he bypassed the question of private property with his suggestion for self-supporting State-financed villages of co-operation – his 'parallelograms' – as an answer to the problem of unemployment, a sort of scaled-down and more sensibly described Fourierist phalanx. He was in no doubt that these villages would work and reshape the world, but his own involvement with schemes such as the New Harmony in Indiana did not justify his faith. The last practically bankrupted him and he spent his final days in poverty.

Louis Blanc (1811–82) was a Frenchman, a journalist and author who published a book on *The Organization of Labour* in 1840. He stressed more than others had done before him that the State was to be the means of establishing a new order; political action was necessary if social reform was to be achieved. He also argued that the right to work is the fundamental right; the State should finance and set up social workshops where all who could offer guarantees of morality could work. Wages were to be equal and the workshops, after the first year, were to be self-governing; the profits of the operation were to be divided equally each year, one-third for the workers and the other two-thirds for various forms of assistance to others. The social workshops were to welcome capitalists who wished to join them, getting interest on their capital, but otherwise only being paid what they earned by work. Those who chose to stay outside the system would eventually be unable to survive the competition of the workshops, he argued. Blanc was a member of the Provisional government of 1848 which set up national workshops, but these were only an attempt to provide an instant answer to the problem of unemployment. They bore no relationship to Blanc's scheme.

Pierre-Joseph Proudhon (1809–65) was, unlike most of those who wrote about socialism, a true son of the people; born of a peasant family, finding work as a printer's compositor and educating himself by the books that he came across in course of his work. His *Qu'est ce que la propriété* is his best known work, and his answer to the question was that property is theft, although what he meant by property here was the sum total of the abuses that may spring from it, not property itself. Proudhon was the supreme individualist; the only authority he recognized was that which sustained the family; 'socialism' based on his theories would have embraced private property and rejected regimentation of any kind.

(ii) Marxism [5]

In 1847 the Communist League asked two young writers, Karl Marx and Friedrich Engels, to provide for them a statement of their creed; the result was *The Communist Manifesto* (1848) which first gave the socialist movement a coherent philosophy and sense of direction. Marx (1818–83) had studied variously jurisprudence, history, philosophy and political economy at Bonn and Berlin Universities from 1835. In 1843 he went to Paris, where he met and formed a life-long friendship with Engels (1820–95), an industrialist whose generosity later supported Marx during difficult times; he always regarded Engels' contribution to the development of their joint form of socialist theory as equal to his. In 1849 Marx was expelled from Prussia and returned to Paris, from which he was expelled also in the same year, passing to London where he spent the rest of his life.

Marx–Engelism regarded its predecessors in the movement as Utopian, a title which the brief review of some of their theories reveals was not unreasonable. Marx and Engels set out to put socialist thinking on a sound theoretical basis, one that would free it of the Utopian patronage of middle or upper-class sympathizers and recruit the energies of the proletariat in its cause and as the vanguard of the necessary socialist revolution. As it was, their philosophy was not laid out systematically in any one work but scattered over many, written at different times and mostly in response to evolving events, but three main strands are detectable in it – a philosophy of dialectical materialism, an economics or political economics based on the labour theory of value and of the surplus value it created, and thirdly, a theory of the State and revolution.

The *Manifesto* foretold the collapse of capitalism but did not prove its case, nor did *The Critique of Political Economy* (1859) though the preface contains the fullest statement of the theory of historical materialism. Of *Capital*, which deals only with economics, Marx published one volume in his lifetime, in 1867, while the others were edited by Engels and came out in 1885 and 1894. He wrote many pamphlets and shorter works of importance, for example the *Thesis on Feuerbach* (1845), *The Poverty of Philosophy* (1847), *The Class Struggle in France* (1848) and *The Civil War in France* (1871). The best account of Marx's general position is given in fact in Engels's *AntiDuhring* which was published in 1877 and for which Marx provided the chapter on political economy.

As to the philosophy itself, its method was derived from Hegel who reasoned that infinite spirit manifests itself successively in different forms of political organization which come into conflict with other forms or would be forms in a dialectical process, thesis meeting antithesis and a synthesis resulting which preserves what is good in both. But whereas for Hegel it was spirit that was so manifesting itself, for Marx it was matter.

> The mode of production of the material means of existence conditions the whole process of social, political and intellectual life. It is not the consciousness of men that determines their existence but on the contrary, it is their social existence which determines their consciousness[6]

The labour theory of value was taken from the classical economist David Ricardo, who advanced the crude proposition, based on Locke, that the value of a commodity depended on the amount of labour time necessary for its production. Ricardo also taught that the most labour could expect from its daily toil was mere subsistence. Marx put these together and argued that the difference between the subsistence wage the labourer received and the value of what he had produced by his labour was a surplus value which was rightly his, since only labour creates value. The theory is crucial to the whole of Marx's analysis although it was erroneous, since it is utility which governs value in the marketplace, as the medieval

scholastic thinkers had concluded, and provided it is a genuinely
free market working in a moral framework the theory is moral as
well as economic truth. The latter the modern science of economics has confirmed, though it has not yet caught up with the need to
ensure the right moral framework for its operation.

This labour theory of value was the keystone of Marxist economics
and at the heart of its supposed scientific socialism. From it he
deduces the laws of capitalist accumulation, of the concentration of
capital, and of increasing misery which results in the system's self-
destruction. Some Marxists will stress that he appreciated capitalism's
achievements – he did, only to predict its fall with great relish.[7]

> One capitalist kills many ... with the constantly diminishing
> numbers of magnates of capitalism ... grows the mass of misery,
> oppression, degradation ... [and] the revolt of the working class
> ... centralization of the means of production and the socializa-
> tion of labour reach a point where they become incompatible ...
> the knell of capitalist private property sounds ... the expropria-
> tors are expropriated

But as the Industrial Revolution consolidated, the facts stubbornly
refused to confirm Marx's pretentious theory. There was no sign
that the predictions based on it were being borne out. Capitalism
was not collapsing, the growth of companies with limited liability,
the increasing number of investors, the development of the stock
market and of professional management meant that the system
could adjust to the changing conditions. The defects of its liberal
capitalist origins mark the welfare capitalism of today, but the
market or the free economy has proved to be the only one which
can meet the needs of the people.

Dialectical materialism therefore tells us that it is economic
forces which determine the course of history and the labour theory
of value is recruited to demonstrate that capitalism is doomed to
destruction. The class struggle charts the course of the destruction
and reveals what the role of the State is before and after the revolution. Of the class struggle itself, the opening words of the first
section of the *Manifesto* give a dramatic account;

> the history of all the existing societies in the history of the world
> is the history of the class struggle ... Freeman and slave, patri-
> cian and plebian, lord and serf, guildmaster and journeyman

were openly or covertly engaged in an unending conflict.[8] Social
class based on the economic differences between the capitalist
and the non-capitalist in society determines basic attitudes and

leads inevitably to conflict until private property is no more. The *Manifesto* asserts that when the proletariat comes to power there will be no more need for the State. The existing State must be captured by the proletariat and destroyed, but this in the first stage might involve alliance with the bourgeois in conflict with the old regime.[9] Indeed Marx seems at times to have contemplated the possibility of peaceful reforms achieving the aim; certainly his disciples divided into two schools, the first believing that a peaceful transformation of society was possible, the second – the Communist option – that violence was necessary.

Concerning the organization which would replace the bourgeois State, there was little real guidance. The *Critique of the Gotha Programme* (1875) speaks of a transition stage, 'the dictatorship of the proletariat', when the latter would coerce the bourgeoisie. For the rest Marx seemed to have thought that, with the transference of the means of production to the proletariat and the establishment of a planned economy, the State would disappear.[10] Precisely what sort of a society would then emerge he did not say, beyond asserting that it would be one governed by the principle 'from each according to his ability, to each according to his needs'.[11] Marx out-Utopia'd the Utopians at the end.

His predictions have not been borne out by events; his understanding of man, of human society and the motives and institutions which make it work was stunted and inadequate, and the attempt to build a major civilization on them was, we can now see, doomed from the start. Yet his powerful exposure of the defects of raw and unrepentant liberal capitalism served to counter the misleadingly optimistic illusions of those who saw it as the perfect economic form. His stress on economic factors in human life, though exaggerated, made an important contribution to sociology, while his economics enabled him to demonstrate that boom and slump, and concentration of capital, were inevitable in liberal capitalist economies. His theory of surplus value was too extreme and its basis was unsound, but exploitation of the worker was a fact of liberal capitalism and the theory concentrated attention on that fact, which the apologists of that capitalism ignored. Labour was not being given its due, while profits, commodities and things were considered of more value than the common humanity of the worker. Whereas the accepted view was of the positive aspects of economic freedom, he gave the negative their place, showing the evil of its excesses. Division of labour could stunt human lives by reducing work to a repetitive drudge, and the effect of ruthless exploitation for the sake of profit was unjust of its nature. For liberal capitalism's contempt for the worker, humanity has paid a terrible price; it was the conviction that Marx's reasoning bred in would-be revolutionaries reflecting on its injustices which gave us Soviet Communism and all that it has meant in adding to the turmoil and human suffering of the current century. Those who sowed the wind, left humanity to reap the whirlwind.

(iii) The Communist International

The *Manifesto* of 1848 had ended with a clarion call to the workers of the world to unite, because the authors were convinced that the capitalist system was on the brink of collapse; but the failure of the revolutions of that year proved them wrong; Marx accepted that victory was still some way off and sought by his writing, and also by organizing some kind of association, to further the cause. It was not until 1864 that the opportunity to form such an association came his way. Several factors had combined to heighten the sense of international solidarity among workers and radicals at that time; Garibaldi and Mazzini were heroes of the British trade unionists, and Lincoln's abolition of slavery made them strong supporters of the North in the American Civil War; English and French workers also supported the Poles in their insurrection in 1863. A huge meeting organized by the unions in 1863 impressed Marx no end[12] and there seemed to be a new-found solidarity and self-confidence among the workers generally. A meeting was accordingly called in London in September 1864 to consider proposals for the setting up of an International Association of Working Men (IAWM) to foster the interests of the workers in all countries, and some 2000 attended it. Marx drew up the constitution adopted at the second Congress in Geneva in 1865.

There were four more successful meetings of the IAWM down to 1869 and they filled the powers that were throughout Europe with alarm. In fact, since it was mainly a trade union body, it showed itself more interested in reformism than revolution, despite Marx's influence on it. However, the involvement of some of its leaders in the Paris Commune of 1871 made it appear more sinister than it was, and gave the alarmists credibility. Many had heard little of the International until that time; now it was condemned on all sides for its apparent participation in the rising, particularly when Marx's *The Civil War in France* claimed much more involvement in it than the facts warranted.[13]

The truth was that the International was divided on practically every matter of importance – the split between Marx and the anarchist Mikhail Bakunin being the most important one. Bakunin was a Russian of noble birth, expelled from Germany in 1848 for his

Bakunin

participation in the revolution there; he later lived in Switzerland and Italy. He was against State power in principle. Every facet of existing society had to be destroyed. Marx, on the contrary, saw that the new society would arise out of the old and that there was continuity between them. Bakunin also objected to the way the International was organized, and Marx, being convinced that he was out to take it over, secured his exclusion from the Congress of 1872.[14] The First International had petered out by 1876.

Meanwhile socialism, and social democracy, had developed on a national basis and it continued to do so after the International's failure. In Germany it did so between 1863 and 1875. In France it came rather later but in the 1890s there were five French socialist parties. Britain's contributions were, with the exception of Hyndman's, less influenced by Marxism than their Continental counterparts. The Second International was formed in 1889 and was based on Marxist principles, the class struggle, proletarian action, and the socialization of the means of production, though delegates from social democratic and other non-Marxist traditions were involved also. Only the anarchists were specifically excluded from membership.

The changing nature of industrial capitalism, as some of its worst excesses were moderated, strengthened the hand of those who had always seen it as more practicable to work with the system and gain practical improvements, rather than to look to its immediate collapse or destruction. This was not likely anyway, but the Marxist pretence kept alive the suspicions of the powers of Europe that the International was a challenge to the social order. In the meantime, Eduard Bernstein's revisionism threatened the whole structure of Marxist theory and practice. Bernstein (1850–1932), the journalist son of a railwayman, was exiled from Germany in 1888, went to London and returned home in 1901. His experience of the developed capitalism he saw at work in England convinced him of Marx's error. Capitalism was not about to collapse: it had stabilized; and the working class was not revolutionary: they were angry with many aspects of the system, but were prepared to fight for their rights within it. There was no surer way of disturbing the calm of the Marxist faithful than by embracing Bernstein's revisionism, but he had the truth of it, not Marx.

(iv) Pius IX and Communism

Pius IX said little on this subject, but what he said was extremely shrewd and prescient. He referred to the the pernicious doctrines

of Socialism and Communism which were contrary to the laws of
God and Man. They amounted to an attempt to abolish law,
government and property and society itself. Such theories exploit
concepts of liberty and equality to excite continuous agitation by
the workers; they advocate the abolition of property, and, by
undermining the law, human and divine, they subvert the entire
social order. The needs of the poor must be met, and the Church
has always taken the lead in the works of charity. Justice is needed
too and chiefs of State are warned that they must use their power
properly for justice and clemency. Christ's law defends the true
liberty and equality of all men, and Christ himself will judge all in
justice, and reward them according to their works. As for socialism
and Communism, these will not bring equality and justice but, by
going against nature, will bring new disasters.[15]

(v) Anarchism

The anarchists, since they hated all forms of social organization,
were not in any position to initiate or co-operate in either practical
democratic reform or any planned revolution. Their attempt to
remain allied with, and even to control the labour movement, was
the result of their hope that the overpowering anger of that movement would spark a spontaneous revolution that would enable
them to put their ideas into practice. The facts were against them
as they were against Marxism: the latter had nowhere been able to
do more than supply the extreme members of the labour movement with the conviction that revolution was coming. The refusal
of the British trade union and labour movement as a whole to
adopt Marxism, and Bernstein's conviction – based on his knowledge of the British experience – that it was unsound in theory,
accurately reflected the instincts and the political traditions of the
workers of Western Europe generally. Yet Marxism took root, not
in an advanced industrial society with its over-mature capitalism
ready to experience the final struggle between the workers and
their oppressors, but in a comparatively primitive Russia trying to
modernize its social and political system. Further, though there
was in the West a Marxist Workers' International and other
elements of Communist influence on labour organizations' the
socialist movement as a whole was factionalized and at odds, especially on the issue of anarchism, and the anarchists themselves
were at odds on both strategy and tactics in the class war. It was all
less of a threat to the social order than it appeared to be at the
time, but the powers that were can be forgiven for mistaking its

threats of cataclysmic violence for a real will and the real means to produce it. When it came in Russia it did so in conditions that Marx did not predict, and as a result of causes he had not considered, and his theories and their almost total silence on what should replace liberal capitalism were wholly inadequate to the task with which the supporters of those theories were faced. Stalinism was the eventual result – and the epitaph of Marxism.

The frustrated anarchists increasingly identified with the more irresponsible and extreme elements among the socially discontented throughout Europe and the USA and were able to cause enough damage and spread enough panic to give credibility to the fears of those who were convinced that something like a concerted threat to the established order was being mounted. The philosophy of anarchism took root because many individuals felt helpless in the face of oppression, mass poverty and the callousness of the wealthy and were disinclined to commit themselves to the slow unspectacular work of gradualist social and political reform. The short cut of immediate violent action, however irrational and short sighted, appealed to them and 'The Deed' – some isolated and violent act, such as assassination or bomb-throwing, to show contempt for the existing order and hurry the revolution along – became their philosophy and plan of action.

The perpetrators of such deeds chose some existing conflict with the potential for generating violence as an occasion for them and in so doing multiplying their power to disrupt things. Their intervention in the strike in Chicago in April 1886 for an eight-hour day already referred to was a case in point. Violence, the use of strike breakers and armed Pinkerton detectives had already produced counter-violence, and at a meeting they called in support of the strikers on 4 May someone unknown threw a bomb into a group of police who were trying to break it up, killing seven of them. It was now easy to link strikers and anarchists as being in league and enemies of the State. Eight of the anarchists involved were sentenced to hang in August 1886; there was no direct evidence to connect any of the eight with the bomb-throwing, yet four of them were hanged. One of those whose sentences were commuted because of their youth blew himself up on the night before the executions, writing in his own blood 'long live anarchy' before he died.[16]

There was also an anarchist attempt to assassinate Henry Frick during the Homestead strike; the assassin alone planned it, but the result was that the strikers were blamed. Anarchists were also active in France in the 1890s. August Vaillant, who threw a bomb into the Chamber of Deputies in session on 9 December 1893, was caught and executed. On 24 June 1894 the French President, Sadi Carnot, was assassinated in revenge. The death of the President provoked a vigorous reaction by the French government; it also caused the anarchist movement to think again as it realized that French workers had no real sympathy with its violence. When the CGT (the General Confederation of Labour) was formed in 1895 the anarchists increasingly opted for trade unionism and they brought with them their penchant for direct action, providing the union with its philosophy of the general strike to bring down the State.

The anarchists continued to be active elsewhere also. In Spain the Prime Minister was a victim in 1897, the King in Italy in 1900, in the USA President McKinley in 1901, and a second Spanish Premier in 1912. In Russia Alexander II was assassinated in 1881 and an attempt was made to murder Alexander III in 1887. In Russia also in 1905 there came at last the spontaneous revolution for which the anarchists had hoped, though it was to develop in a manner they had not imagined. Instead of a new freedom, the Russian people experienced totalitarianism that surpassed the previous repressions of the Czars.

2 Nationalism, liberalism and the Church

(i) Italy and the Papal States[17]

The final defeat of Napoleon in 1815 resulted in a restoration of monarchy in Europe; political liberalism was for the moment moribund, but economic liberalism was alive and well. When the Pope, Pius VII (1800–1823), who had been imprisoned by Napoleon, returned to Rome in 1815 the Papal States had not been fully restored to him, and Europe was in such confusion that it was difficult to know with whom to deal as he set about the task of rebuilding on that continent a Church devastated by revolution and wars. In South America at the same time she seemed to be on the point of being evicted from many of the former colonies, along with Spanish power.

The Pope's first priority was to foster the spiritual and moral life of the faithful, but to do this he needed to secure his position in Rome. The recent history of the Papacy had confirmed once again that it could not discharge its duty to the international Church without political independence – and that at the time meant the Papal States. However, the desire of Italian nationalists for a unified State was also valid. How to reconcile these two apparently irreconcilable aims was not apparent in the early nineteenth century; not till 1929 was the problem resolved. Of the States, the Romagna (Bologna, Ferrara and Ravenna), two hundred miles from Rome and looking towards Milan, were the most controversial. They provided the majority of the papal revenue and were a barrier against further incursions of Austrian power, but they were traditionally hostile to papal control. Under Cardinal Consalvi the administration was improved; none the less not even he, who was an open-minded moderate,[18] could conceive of the Pope being a constitutional monarch sharing power. With the accession of Leo XII (1823–9) the more modern Papal State that had been emerging was checked.

After Pius VIII's (1829–30) short reign came that of Gregory XVI (1831–46), who was no friend of liberalism.[19] Minor adjustments in the governance of the Papal States he allowed, but elected assemblies and a council of laymen were vetoed and Austrian troops were called on to repress disorders when they were denied: thereafter a spirit of rebellion reigned throughout the pontificate. The Abbé Lammenais, who was convinced that the Church should support democratic movements, did not find the French bishops supportive on the matter and decided in 1831 to appeal to Rome. There Gregory XVI received his request for approval of his programme without showing any displeasure, but when a formal response to it was made in *Mirari Vos* (1832), it was condemnatory: the State could not be indifferent in matters of religion; liberty of conscience as it was being advocated was an absurd idea; liberty of the press, and the separation of Church and State were unthinkable.[20]

By the time of his death in June 1846, Gregory XVI's Roman policies had proved so unsuccessful and thoroughly unpopular that it was clear a change was needed. What it should be, the cardinals were undecided. In the event they elected Pius IX, a man who had a reputation for sympathy with the liberal political position and with the nationalists.[21] He did make considerable concessions. He gave Rome an elected municipal government, a wide measure of liberty of the press and in March 1848 a constitution for the Papal States with an elective assembly having the power of veto. Yet it was impossible to separate the temporal and spiritual elements in his power as sovereign of the Papal States, as events quickly proved. Though, as an Italian, he was supportive of nationalism and suspicious of Austria, he could not encourage or formally approve war against the latter, a Catholic State and people, by the Papal States. His Premier was murdered by volunteers who had been fighting the Austrians, and when Pius's enemies gloated over this he became thoroughly disenchanted with the liberal and nationalist cause, fleeing to Gaeta in November 1848. A republic was now proclaimed in Rome and it took French intervention in February 1849 to restore him to power. In 1860 he lost all the Papal States but Rome and its immediate surroundings to the Nationalists, being saved again by French arms. In 1870 the French withdrew and Rome finally became the capital of united Italy, with the Pope 'the prisoner in the Vatican'.

Pius IX's experience in dealing with the Italian State after 1860 confirmed him in his attitude to it. Italian liberalism interpreted the idea of a free Church in a free State to mean that it could interfere as it liked in the affairs of the Church. It insisted on its consent to the investing of bishops and priests with their temporalities, which gave it a stranglehold on such appointments, while its persecution of religious orders and its policy of secularization was second only in its severity to that of Bismarck's *Kulturkampf* in Germany. It was the experience of liberalism in these contexts which confirmed Pius IX in opposition to it.

(ii) The Syllabus of Errors

Matters came to a head with the publication of the encyclical *Quanta Cura*, and its accompanying *Syllabus Errorum* in 1864.[22] Its condemnations of the defects of liberalism had been contained in a previous document *Iamdudum Cernimus* of March 1861, which protested against the application of the anti-clerical laws of Piedmont to the whole of Italy; these laws, for example, suppressed monasteries and convents, and denied the sacramental view of marriage and the value of religious education. If that was what progress, liberalism and modern civilization meant then the Church would have nothing to do with it. Those who read the *Syllabus*, or heard or read brief snatches from it without knowing the context and background, interpreted it according to their own understanding. The average Englishman or American was outraged; given that both were strongly Protestant in their traditions, and therefore inclined to be if anything less than well-disposed to the Catholic and particularly the papal approach to any matter, and being as ignorant of the conditions on the Continent as the Pope and his advisers were of the conditions existing in theirs, they could hardly be otherwise.

It was to be expected that the document should take exception to those who denied the divinity of Christ, or the existence of God, or who supported Communism and pantheism. Other propositions condemned – that the Catholic Church should no longer be established by law, that the right of freedom of speech should be absolute, that the Church has no right to use force in any circumstances, and that it would be better off without temporal power – undermined traditional teaching, which was culturally conditioned, and which could and did change in time, although Pius IX preferred that it should remain unaltered in his day. It jarred on those who at the time lived in countries where these things no longer happened, as it jars on us today, that these things were said so harshly. The Papacy, however, had not had time since the restoration to develop the world-wide network of sources of information which it needed if it was to judge situations accurately on a world-wide basis. Knowledge of other forms of political liberalism in the USA and the United Kingdom would have shown that the Church and liberalism could live together. But on the basis of its experience on the Continent of Europe, its attitudes were not unreasonable.

Pius IX had still seven more years to reign when the city of Rome was finally seized by King Emmanuel's forces on 19 September 1870. The Law of Guarantees, introduced in Italy on 1 November, the Pope would not accept, refusing in particular its generous financial provisions, despite the problems he was having in finding the means to fulfil the obligations of the Holy See. The problem of political independence was temporarily solved by the status of 'honorary sovereignty' the Papacy now possessed, giving it the same immunity from Italian law as other States had. The need for international recognition and acceptance of the new Italian State ensured that the Papacy itself would not be harassed, but the protection for the Church in Italy was inadequate; as noted, it did not really have freedom from State interference.

In the bitterly anti-clerical legislation introduced in 1867, which sectarian elements forced on the King and the rest of the administration, liberalism was revealed as anti-Church and even anti-Christian.[23] Previously, Catholic deputies had been allowed to take the oath of loyalty to the State with the proviso 'saving the divine and ecclesiastical law'. Now the Pope issued in 1871 the brief *Non expedit*, declaring it was not fitting that Catholics take part in political elections.[24] It did not apply to administrative elections or to other forms of political activity; it was aimed at ensuring that the Italian State received no formal approval from Catholics until the Roman question was solved.

3 The Catholic Social Movement[25]

The primary concern of the Papacy after the restoration of 1815
therefore was to recruit the essential spiritual and organizational
resources of the Church in order to revitalize her after the assault
of Gallicanism, the Enlightenment and the French Revolution.
Italy's was still an agricultural economy, while neither France nor
Germany, countries which had large Catholic populations, were
experiencing industrialization on a scale which threatened to
destabilize society; since it was only the experience of such deeper
effects on larger Catholic communities which would give the
Church, nationally and internationally, some idea of how to react
to them, it is not surprising that coherent policies on the moral
issues involved took time to work out. From the middle of the
century this changed; these matters were pressing and answers to
them were sought. It was the experience of national churches,
those of France and Germany in particular, but also Belgium's,
England's and that of the United States, upon which Leo XIII drew
when addressing the moral issues raised by liberal capitalism in
Rerum Novarum (1891).

(i) France

There was sufficient impact of industrialization in France from the
1820s in regions such as Lille to give an edge to questionings about
the social problems the process produced, and the social
conscience of some was challenged by them. Under the restoration
monarchy (1815–30) devout conservatives were moved by the
sense of *noblesse oblige* to address the matter. The Society of St
Joseph, for example, founded in 1822, trained young people,
provided decent lodgings for them and organized friendly societies which enabled them to draw benefits: paternalistic it may
have been, but in their time such organizations were of great value.
Others were concerned to attack the problems at root. The aristocrat Alban de Villeneuve Bargemont (1784–1850), Prefect of the
Département du Nord, the heart of French industry, drew up a
report for the government in 1829 on the poverty and destitution
which were the defects of English-style *laissez faire* and urged that
the government face the problem of needed social reform.[26]

Under the July monarchy (1830–48), Armand de Melun
(1807–77) was active in organizing charitable work for the poor,
and became the accepted spokesman of those at the bottom of the
social scale who had no vote. He and Villeneuve Bargemont were

responsible for bringing to the notice of the Chamber of Deputies that the social problem – the need to improve the condition of the working classes – was the major issue of the time. Their practical work in organizing workers and helping them led to their being suspected by the police of encouraging subversive activity.[27] Frédéric Ozanam (1813–53) founded the St Vincent de Paul Society, whose local conferences actively sought out the poorest and did what it could to provide them with the necessities of life.[28] He also saw that it was necessary to try to improve social condition. In lectures at the University of Lyons in 1838 he denounced the evils which produced them – economic liberalism which used men as things, an economic system which left wages to the law of supply and demand, injustice in relations between employer and employed for which charity was no substitute, the lack of free organizations for workers, and finally the inadequate State action in social matters. Another outstanding figure was François Ledruille (1797–1860). Born poor, and a worker himself before studying for the priesthood, he became known as 'the workers' priest'. The action of such men meant that the 1848 revolution was unique in not being anti-clerical; the armed workers acclaimed Christ, the priests and Pius IX.

Many Catholics of the right, however, after initially supporting the revolution of 23 February 1848, turned against it as part of a general trend once the Provisional Government became more radical, with the result that the people of Paris rebelled on 22 June 1848. The army was turned on them, as we have seen, and they were defeated. That Paris revolution was part of the 'year of revolutions' which affected Austria, Italy, Germany and Prussia; it was not the work of a few revolutionaries but was symptomatic of the strains that industrialization, and demand for reform, were putting on what was still an old-regime mentality among the rulers of Europe; it was one that Marx was convinced would follow the violent course he predicted.

Under the Second Republic (1848–51), de Melun was able to interest the Provisional Government in assistance for the poor, and legislation on public health, pension schemes, mutual aid societies, education, hospitals, medical services and outdoor relief was passed. President Napoleon continued this concern for the social problem, and the support he received from the workers in consequence helped him to victory in the plebiscite which elected him Emperor in December 1852. By 1869 there were 6,000 Friendly Societies for workers with 900,000 members.[29] Yet most of the families who were helped were those of artisans rather than the

marginalized ordinary labourers. Nor was there any encouragement of leadership towards self-betterment by the workers
themselves. One exception was Maurice Maignen's[30] *Cercle des
Jeunes Ouvriers,* founded in Paris in 1864, which allowed self-
determination for its members along the lines of Kolping's organizations in Germany. Nor was there any encouragement or
opening for them on the most important issue of all: some access
to independent political representation of the interests of the
industrialized urban workers.

The Franco–Prussian War (1870–71) caused a further bout of
soul-searching by conservative Catholics. In particular two aristocratic army officers, Count Albert de Mun (1841–1914) and Count
René de la Tour du Pin (1834–1925) were brought face to face
with the social injustices that existed in French society, and set out
to tackle them. Taking the advice of Maignen, they established
working-men's clubs in Paris and then in other cities; they did
good work but did not organize many industrial workers nor did
they give any responsibility to the members of the clubs. De Mun
was elected a Deputy in 1876 and was a persistent supporter of
social reform, pressing in particular for shorter working hours.

Du Pin went further: what he had seen of the effects of liberal
capitalism on the worker and society convinced him that a new
social order, the corporatist, should replace it. It was an idea which
was particularly connected with the Austrian, Karl von Vogelsang.[31]
Corporatism was inspired by the medieval guild, in which both
employer and employee were organized, and sought to establish a
form of industrial and political organization which did the same,
though it was not suggested that the guilds could be revived; it was
the ideal of co-operation between employer and employed which
the supporters of the idea sought to see at work in industry.

The attractions of corporatism are a little hard for us to understand today because any attempt to explain the idea in theory
raises more questions than it answers, while those of practical
application are even more numerous. The medieval commercial
and craft guilds were a product of very different conditions, when
the basic unit of commercial and industrial production and distribution was the small shop with master, apprentices and
journeymen; it was the most effective of form of economic organization of its time. Wherever that sort of economic organization
survived – and it survived until the eighteenth century in France –
the guilds made sense, but under the impact of capitalism and
mechanization the basis on which they had been established was
no more.

The supporters of corporatism suggested that it should begin at unit level, and involve the workers and their employers in each plant being organized in a corporation which ran it in a manner which allowed full participation for the workers. Based as it was on the Léon Harmel (1829–1915) factory at Val des Bois near Rheims, which was run as a family on a copartnership basis, any capitalist firm could have adopted this scheme had it been interested in doing so; reference to guilds only confused the issue. Harmel's principle was that what was to be done for the workers must also be done by them, and they were given as much responsibility as possible. The right of association in free trade unions was not recognized in France until 1884, but Works Councils were established and were responsible for monitoring relations between workers and the Harmel management, and they could and did discuss pay, discipline, workers' demands, disputes between them and supervisors, as well as being concerned with making work easier and more profitable. For their time they marked a considerable advance.[32]

At the local level then such a model was practicable enough, given the will to make it work. But corporatism went much further than this. There were to be regional and national-level corporations to deal with religious and moral matters, and those of public interest as well as their own industrial/commercial or agricultural concerns.[33] This structure was to provide the basis for a new political order, people of the same occupational group electing delegates for each region, they in their turn providing a platform and a mandate for delegates to a National Assembly. Nothing was said about the executive branch of government; it was assumed that constitutional monarchy was its natural complement.

So much for the very considerable conservative contribution to the Catholic social movement made by France. The liberal contribution began with Lammenais who, in 1822, while still a royalist, had denounced the evils of industrialization. The foundation in 1830 of *L'Avenir*, the Catholic Liberal weekly, gave him and like-minded collaborators wider audiences. Charles de Coux for example (1787–1864), who became the first Professor of Political Economy at Louvain, was aware of the class confrontation in industry and advocated the workers' right of association and also legislation for the limitation of hours.[34] He and the Abbé, later bishop, Philippe Gerbet (1798–1864), had inspired Frédéric Ozanam, founder of the St Vincent de Paul Society. Initially a Royalist, Ozanam showed himself a democrat and a liberal in cooperating with Abbé Maret (1805–84) in the founding of *L'Ère*

Nouvelle after the revolution of 1848. He had already urged that they abandon the kings and statesmen of 1815 and go to the people.[35] Now with Lacordaire, De Coux and Sainte-Foi, he kept up the plea for action to relieve the needs of the industrial workers, urging their fellow Catholics to co-operate with the 1848 revolution and make a specifically Christian contribution. By the beginning of 1849 it was under suspicion as becoming too radical, subscriptions fell away, bishops disapproved of it and penalized priests who supported it, and by March it had to cease publication.

There was also in French social Catholicism a strain of Christian socialism of which Philippe Buchez (1796–1865) was the key figure. A customs official under the first Napoleon, he left government service after the restoration, was a founder member of the Carbonari, a French secret society dedicated to radical political and religious ideals and in 1822 was in danger of execution for his part in a failed insurrection. He avoided this fate and abandoned revolution, qualified as a doctor, became a Saint-Simonian and abandoned that when it became a religion. Finally, deciding that Catholic teaching had the right understanding of man as a social being, he declared for it, though he never became a practising Christian.

He was deeply conscious of the class divide in Europe – the propertied who owned the instruments of labour, and the workers who were entirely at their mercy since they were not allowed to combine for their own protection.[36] Democratic, profit-sharing co-operatives were the answer, with the workers gradually controlling capital and replacing the employers. He had considerable success in attracting supporters, including the Archbishop of Paris, Denise-Auguste Affre. A group of workers published a journal which supported his ideas although it went far beyond Buchez in its attacks on capitalism. Another strain in Catholic socialism stemmed from Fourier's theories: so Hippolyte de la Morvonnais (1802–53), who abandoned the phalanx in favour of a Christian commune, one of which he founded near his home at Guildo in Brittany in 1848. During the Second Republic priests appeared among the ranks of the Christian socialists, but they were not popular with the bishops.

(ii) Germany

The political background to the Catholic social movement in Germany was more helpful to its coherent development than was the case in France. The effect of the revolutionary wars on

Germany was to facilitate moves towards national unity, and the manner in which this happened united the German Catholic Church, and linked it strongly to Rome. The proposal for a Febronian national episcopacy under the prince-bishops, for example, was rejected at the Congress of Vienna in 1815 because the governments did not want a return to the old regime, preferring an agreement with the Holy See, distant and apparently weak. This went well with the growing ultramontane sentiment in Germany, and the resultant ecclesiastical reorganization encouraged a close alliance between the people's church and the Papacy.[37] German Catholics were concentrated in Bavaria in the south, Silesia in the east and Westphalia in the west; they were a minority in Germany, minus Austria, but a powerful minority with considerable political influence.[38] The secular and étatist ethos of the nineteenth century clashed with the all-inclusive claims of the Church, and in particular with her view of the State as at the service of the moral order and not an end in itself. Her traditional teaching was that man has rights and freedoms which come before the claims of the State. The form of State is immaterial as long as the moral order is respected by it.

The gradual emergence of Prussia as the leader of the move to German unity was held in suspicion by Catholics precisely because the Prussian view of the power of the State and its nature did not respect the moral order as the Church understood it, and this tension served to give her a greater sense of unity. So too did the increasing nationalism within Germany; the Church's international nature made her wary of a too-exclusive understanding of the virtue of patriotism. The inherent tension was to come to a head in 1866 to 1870 with the formation of the Catholic Centre Party.

Joseph von Goerres, a former radical and supporter of the French Revolution, was Professor of History at Munich and in a pamphlet *Athanasius* protested against the imprisoning of the Archbishop of Munich in 1827 by the Prussian State, calling for political equality for Catholics.[39] The 'Goerres circle' (1837–48) of like-minded Catholics grew up around him, but it had no effective political action open to it at the time beyond supporting the bishops in stimulating their people to defend their rights and religious liberties and to widen the scope of their interests.[40]

Franz von Baader (1785–1841) had worked in England as a mining engineer in 1792–1796 and then, becoming aware of the social problems of industrialization, launched the first German Catholic challenge to liberal capitalism, denying Adam Smith's assumption that the common good is served by each seeking his

own individual self-interest. Being sympathetic to Lammenais, his
views on Church policies were not well received by his fellow
Catholics in Germany,[41] nor did he until much later receive credit
for his contributions to the debate on the social question, which
were very considerable. His *Evolution and Evolutionism* of 1834,
prepared for the Bavarian government, was very perceptive on
problems and their solutions. Liberty, he said, must not mean one
man using another as a chattel, property must be socially responsible according to the law of God, and since liberal capitalism has
produced a proletariat it should not be surprised that it had led to
the demand for the right to form associations. He did not call for
revolutionary change but for sensible reform by restricting the
absolute freedom of the capitalist. In his *Property and the Propertyless*
(1835) he stressed again the need to give the worker the legal right
to form associations for his own protection in countering the
strength of the employers. Failure to do this would lead to revolution. The social deaconry of the priest, as a mediator between the
propertied and the propertyless, was also advocated; this social
deaconry did in fact develop with great effectiveness in Germany.

It was one such priest, Adolph Kolping (1813–65) who took the
first steps towards developing a practical labour movement within
the Church there. Born of poor parents and working as a shoe-
maker before he studied for the priesthood, he was ordained in
1845, and he dedicated his life to establishing Young Catholic
Workingmen's societies for the craftsmen who travelled from city
to city to find work. The centres provided lodgings and food, social
and recreational facilities, and vocational training; courses for
masters were also provided. They were open to and used by non-
Catholics as well as Catholics, the socialist leader Auguste Bebel,
for example, giving testimony to the value of his membership.[42]
When Kolping died in 1865 there were some 400 branches of what
was a growing movement; though it dealt with only a tiny number
of workers proportionately, and that in old craft rather than the
new industry, his approach to his work, involving the men in
decision-making in particular, possessed important lessons for
others.

The most powerful influence on the Catholic social movement
in Germany however, was Wilhelm Emmanuel von Ketteler
(1811–77). Born of the deeply religious minor landed aristocracy
of Münsterland, his life reflected its sober Catholic realism so that
he was never in danger of being swayed by the fashions of the
moment, romantic or reactionary. The Westphalian church had
been blessed in the previous century with an outstanding bishop,

von Feurstenberg, substitute for the absentee prince-bishop, and enjoyed a progressive cultural and social life combined with a sound Catholic piety; his influence goes far to account for Ketteler's outstanding qualities as priest and bishop.[43]

After his studies in history and government at the Universities of Göttingen, Heidelberg, Munich and Berlin Ketteler entered the Prussian civil service, but resigned at the time of the conflict with the Church over the marriage laws in 1837, studied for the priesthood, was ordained in 1844 and spent most of his time as a country pastor until appointed Bishop of Mainz in 1850. He therefore had little experience of modern industry and its problems before his parishioners elected him to the Frankfurt Convention called by the expectant liberal forces in Germany in 1848. At the National Catholic assembly in the same year, he stressed the importance of overcoming the inequalities of wealth and the need for the Church to address the matter, and he was invited to give the Advent sermons in the cathedral at Mainz under the title of 'Great social questions of our time'.[44] He identified liberalism as the main problem, liberalism which was the result of deism, the Enlightenment and the French Revolution. Its idea of freedom was atomistic; society was a collection of individuals indifferent or opposed to each other, combining only to limit the freedoms of another; it understood private property as being sacred. This, and the stress on the need for individuals to look after their own needs, instead of seeing human freedom and dignity in the context of God's will, law, love and Providence, has produced the Communist reaction, the essential mark of which he found in the abolition of private property. Proudhon's observation 'property is theft' has truth if applied to liberal capitalist private property with no social responsibilities. Against this he balanced St Thomas Aquinas's teaching that ownership of property absolutely belongs to God alone, for it is his world, but that man has a conditional ownership, a stewardship which implies that the use of that property should be for the benefit of all.

The industrialization of the Main–Rhine region where Ketteler's diocese was, was not extensive in the 1850s and 1860s and his concern with his ordinary pastoral duties meant that he had less time to give to the social question. Yet he kept up his interest[45] and in 1864 he published *The Labour Problem and Christianity* in which he accepted Lassalle's version of liberalism's iron law of wages, adapted from Ricardo, which demonstrated that the worker's wages always hover at a level which provides him with mere subsistence, and when the supply of labour exceeds demand, wages drop to below that level.

The answer to the social problem, he judged at this time, lay in
the establishment of worker–producer co-operatives which would
distribute profits to the workers. Finance was to be provided by the
Church through voluntary levies that Christians would impose on
themselves, State financing being considered coercive, and purely
voluntary co-operatives organized within industry insufficient.
Finding that the idea of such Church-financed co-operatives met
with no response, he accepted a year later that State finance would
have to be used.[46] Ketteler was thinking his way through the social
problem and formulating answers to it. Worker co-operatives,
perfectly practicable and good though they were and are in themselves, were of course no complete answer. Realism, practicality,
was always the mark of his mind, not attachment to theory for its
own sake. As industrialization progressed over the next twenty
years, and the full scale of the revolution that it was causing
became clear, so did its potential and its problems. The German
Catholic social movement under Ketteler's guidance was able to
respond to it more than adequately.

In a sermon to workers in 1869 he urged them to become part
of the trade union movement, while warning of some of the possible dangers of such involvement; and he also urged government to
undertake social policies that would favour the worker. He saw that
things were changing in this direction, judged that they could be
for the good if proper policies were put into practice, and began to
work out those policies. His report to the German bishops for their
meeting in 1869, with the Vatican Council preparations in the
offing and the Franco–Prussian conflict threatening, showed the
same realism. It assumed that the factory system and modern
industrial organization was here to stay and saw its positive values,
such as the greater productivity which it made possible. The task
was to see that the workers had protection and a share in the benefits of the system. The policies of enlightened employers were
reviewed and issues on which legislation was needed were identified, including regulations concerning children's and women's
labour, working conditions, hours of work, accident insurance,
Sunday rest and the recognition of workers' associations. State
action was, in other words, needed to resolve the labour question,
along with that of the Church and industry itself. He was particularly insistent that the Church should encourage workers'
associations and protective measures and that the clergy should
support the laity in this.

Politically, as we have seen, meanwhile, that laity had been galva-
nized into action in the wake of Prussia's defeat of Austria in 1866.

Alarmed at hearing the leader of the National Liberals speak of a 'Protestant empire' and knowing their anti-clericalism and that of the Liberals, a group of laymen decided in June 1870 that the formation of a party of their own was called for, and set out her policy. This included protection of the rights of the Church, especially her schools, sacramental marriage, the harmonizing of the interests of capital with those of landowners and of both with the interests of labour and a solid middle class. It supported all attempts to solve the social problem which worked within the law, and was to work for the elimination of the evils which threatened to bring about the moral and physical ruin of the workers.[47] The party was duly formed, and in the elections of March 1871 it received 18.4 per cent of the total vote, its 63 Reichstag seats making it the third-ranking party.

There had been dispute within the Church about the formation of such a party, but events confirmed the wisdom of the move, despite its existence adding to Bismarck's anti-Catholic bias. The definition of papal infallibility at the Vatican Council in July 1870, following on the *Syllabus* of 1864, had roused the ire of the Liberals and Progressives, and Bismarck decided that the Centre Party was a State within a State, while its democratic and social policies, and its support of the Poles, disturbed him. It therefore seemed good to him to curb this Church; in so doing he could isolate France, currently the Papacy's protector, so pleasing Russia and Italy who were at odds with the Vatican. The result was the culture struggle, the *Kulturkampf* (1871–79), which resulted in the expulsion of the Jesuits and interference with Catholic education and marriage laws, but which overall failed to achieve its object. Quite the contrary, its main long term result was to strengthen the Church and Centre Party.[48]

This was the background to the development of the Catholic labour movement which was centred on Aachen and Essen in the Cologne diocese, where Catholics were numerous among both employers and workers.[49] Organized by three priests, Eduard Cronenburg, Johannes Laaf and Hermann Litzinger, that movement was flourishing by 1875 but then suffered setbacks under the double impact of the world recession and the effects of the *Kulturkampf.* The Centre Party was not at first keen on developing a labour or social policy, but in 1877 Count von Galen introduced into the Reichstag the first attempt at wide-ranging social legislation based on Ketteler's 1869 proposals.[50] Thereafter Bismarck's Socialist Law of 1878 made it impossible to encourage labour organization; until 1890 reform relied once again on employer initiative.

Developments in Mönchengladbach where Franz Brandts, a Catholic employer, had his factory[51] then began to exert their influence. Like Léon Harmel, with whom he was in close contact, he held that the aim should be to work for the worker's welfare, but doing so by and with the workers, never without, and certainly never despite, them. In 1880 he formed an association for Catholic industrialists, the *Arbeiterwohl* to improve the workers' conditions. The editor of the organization's magazine, Fr Franz Hitze, had recently completed his doctorate in Rome on corporatism, of which he had been an advocate, and he was to go on to be Professor of Social Ethics in the Catholic theology faculty at Münster. Contact with industry and industrialists, labour and capital, weaned him of corporatism; his editorial policy turned out to be one of endorsing capitalism while calling for better treatment of its workers.[52] Events were to prove this a turning point in the development of social Catholicism, making possible the sidetracking of any grandiose schemes for rebuilding industry, and even the political system, from the bottom up as corporatism evolved. This made the task of reform practicable. One implication was that Christian trade unions should be encouraged.

Corporatism however still had its hold on some. In 1883 there was a conference of those interested in the labour question assembled at Haid Castle in Bavaria, the home of Prince Karl zu Löwenstein, President of the Central Committee of German Catholic Organizations in that year. Löwenstein hoped to make von Vogelsang's corporatism the basis of guidelines for a social policy for the Church but the meeting was split on the matter. Obligatory guilds, corporative organization for industry, were approved, but Hitze was among those who secured the acceptance of the wage contract between employer and worker, and so established that the existing industrial system was acceptable in principle. As it was, the Centre Party leader would have nothing to do with the Haid programme, because he saw it would split the organization. After the repeal of the Socialist law the Church was free to organize more effectively in the social field. Hitze now became the spokesman for the Centre Party on labour matters and the Catholic trade union movement proper developed.

(iii) Belgium

The political background to the Belgian Catholic social movement was unusual in that here Catholics had united with Liberals to overthrow Dutch rule in 1830, and afterwards reached a compromise with them,[53] showing that some forms of liberalism were compatible with Catholicism on a practical level, and Rome accepted that. Unfortunately Belgian liberalism embraced the economic doctrines and attitudes of liberal capitalism at its crudest, and a social conscience amongst the Catholic bourgeoisie which was strong enough to challenge this was lacking; nor was there an aristocracy whose *noblesse oblige* led individuals to concern themselves with the social question. Villeneuve de Bargemont, Albert de Mun and de la Tour du Pin in France were aristocrats, and Ketteler, who was the main influence on the social conscience of the German Church, was of the minor aristocracy. Belgium was a bourgeois nation and the Belgian workers seem to have tolerated their conditions very readily until mid-century. The import of English goods in the 1820s had undermined textile manufacture, and secondary rural employment and the potato crop failures of the 1840s added to the general suffering.[54]

There were however a few outstanding individuals who were vocal in their criticism of the situation. One was Edouard Ducepétiaux (1794–1868) a wealthy industrialist, who had studied law at Liège and Ghent and was a convinced democrat and liberal who possessed a growing awareness of the social problem. He took part in the 1830 revolution and then became Inspector General of Prisons and Charitable Institutions in 1831, a post he held for thirty years. It was one which gave him ample scope to inform his masters of the social conditions of the people through his official reports; he also went beyond them, publishing for example in 1843 two volumes on the condition of young workers and the means to improve it, warning of the danger of social revolution if nothing was done to ameliorate the lot of their kind.[55] His own remedy was that a corporatist structure for industry should be introduced, but at the same time he proposed practical first steps, beginning with effective legislation governing child labour, including provision of an inspectorate.

Another who concerned himself with the problems was Adolphe Bartels (1802–62) a journalist who had participated in the independence movement. He published in 1842 an *Essay on the Organization of Labour* which stressed the need for social as well as political reform. Lammenais and Louis Blanc were among those with whom he was in contact. He argued that political power obtained by peaceful means was the workers' only way forward since the current rulers had no intention of surrendering their power. The Belgian church's role at this time was one of encouraging the traditional works of charity or paternalistic concern, most prominent of which was the St Vincent de Paul Society and its 422 regional conferences. Though these were not intended to encourage social activism, they brought the comfortable middle class into direct contact with the suffering poor and could only help to stimulate their social consciousness and the need for justice as well as charity. Also significant were the associations such as that of St Francis Xavier and St Joseph. As part of the effort they provided some social, educational and recreation facilities as well as savings clubs and poor relief. Their drawback was that they touched mainly the non-industrial workers in smaller towns and they were markedly paternalist.

From the 1860s Belgian Catholicism generally was undergoing changes, some of them painful. The union with the Liberals was increasingly under strain because of the growing anti-clericalism of the latter, and the result of the 1857 elections was a shock: the slogan 'down with the priests' won the Liberals 70 seats; the Catholics held only 38. One reaction was the foundation by some of the younger generation of a new journal *L'Universel*.[56] The leader of the group, which had the support of Ducepétiaux among others, was Prosper de Hauville, a journalist who had been Professor of Natural Law at Ghent until the Liberals had deprived him of the chair. Since their programme included universal suffrage and legal recognition of trade unions they aroused controversy, particularly at the Catholic Congresses at Malines in 1863 and 1864, and that helped concentrate minds on the need for fundamental reforms. But it was to take the violence of 1886 to stimulate real action on the matter.

The scene had been set by the sufferings of the workers which had become increasingly severe in the world-wide recession after 1873, a slump from which the country only made a slow and uneven recovery.[57] Anarchists called a meeting in Liège in March 1886, commemorating the anniversary of the Paris Commune, and this provided the spark for the tinder. The strikes which followed the meeting led to disorder and insurrection and it took the army two weeks to quell it. The experience sobered and frightened the members of respectable society, revealing as it did the suppressed violence which the legacy of injustice and suffering had stored up, and they realized that they had to do something about it.

Belgian Catholics were already aware of what was being done by their co-religionists elsewhere, especially in Germany, and the congresses at Liège in 1886, 1887 and 1890 on the social problem brought it more fully into prominence. At first the corporatists were in the ascendant at these congresses, but gradually what can be called the Christian Democrat tendency asserted itself, a combination of belief in necessary State intervention with essential social legislation, but leaving the maximum initiative to employers, trade unions and co-operative organizations. This was to be accompanied by a wider franchise, electoral reform and workers in parliament.[58] The excesses of the Liberals had produced a reaction at the polls in 1884 and put the Catholic party in power, where it remained for 25 years: it now had a chance to do something about social reform. The conservatives were still in a majority within it and it had to move cautiously, but social policies now became the priority none the less. The result was that Belgian social legislation during this period bears comparison with that in any other country.

(iv) Italy

In Italy, which as a modern State dates from 1870, the Catholic social movement's growth was hindered politically by the Roman question. An interesting glimpse of Roman thinking on a key issue at mid-century is provided in the findings of a commission appointed by Pius IX to look into the economic organization of the Papal States after the revolutions of 1848: it led to encouragement being given by the Pope in 1852 to the formation of religious associations of employers and workers according to industry or trade, with voluntary occupational organizations developing out of them and having representation on the government of the City of Rome; it was a form of corporatism.[59]

Regarding their relationship with the new Italian State, Catholics were subject to the *Non Expedit* of 1871 which meant no participation in national elections. By implication therefore, there could be no involvement in party politics, which were concerned with fighting elections and forming governments. To provide some focus and stimulus for acceptable Catholic social commitment the *Opera Dei Congressi* was formed. Below the national level there were diocesan and parish committees, 4000 of the latter by the late 1890s, and to these committees other associations, confraternities and local election committees were affiliated.[60] Rural credit unions, five hundred of them, were organized through the ODC, and about the same number of mutual aid societies for agrarian and industrial workers; from the latter, unions later developed. The ODCs and their satellites were regarded by the State as a source of subversion and after the Milan disturbances of 1898 many were forced to disband.

Yet the intransigence of the Church regarding the Italian State and of the Italian Liberals regarding the Church was already begin-

ning to look outdated. Bakunin's anarchism was giving way to a
socialism of the Marxist variety, adapted to a mainly agrarian
people, and was making inroads among the poor. As real industrialization in the Turin, Genoa, Milan region took off in the 1890s,
both Liberals and Catholics had to cope with Marxism's increasing
appeal here and in the rural areas. Socialists preached revolution,
the class war and the abolition of private property; the Catholics
stressed social harmony and respect for the law, while within the
ODC, the Christian Democrats, Giuseppe Toniolo, Romulo Murri
and Luigi Sturzo, urged their programme of social reform. The
ODC was suspended in 1904[61] but the second section lived on,
being renamed the *Economic and Social Union*: its purpose was
education in the ethical principles of economic order and the
organization of appropriate associations for this purpose.
Catholics were allowed to participate in the national elections in
1904 and Don Sturzo was energetically but prudently urging the
establishment of Christian social democracy.[62]

(v) The United States of America

In 1790, when the first American bishop, John Carroll, was conse-
crated, there were but 35,000 Catholics in the United States out of
a total population of 3.9 million[63] and they were concentrated
mainly in Maryland, Pennsylvania and Kentucky. Catholicism
remained very much a minority religion until immigration from
Europe increased between 1820 and 1850 when there were nearly
one million new arrivals, predominantly Irish Catholics. By 1850
Catholics numbered 1.6 million out of a population of 23 million,
or approximately 1 in 14, by 1900 12 million out of 78 million, or
more than 1 in 6.[64]

The characteristics of a rapidly expanding Catholic population
before the Civil War were that it was conscious of being a despised
proletariat, a consciousness kept alive by the nativist and Know-
Nothing movements,[65] and the result was that the local churches
developed a defensive mentality and with it a considerable degree
of internal unity and organization. By 1867 the number of charitable organizations, hospitals, journals, newspapers and societies of
all kinds generated by the Catholic community filled nine closely
printed pages of the *National Catholic Almanac*. The Church's
contribution to the solution of the social problems of society took
the form of succouring the successive waves of immigrants which
looked to it for spiritual and material help.

> It might be maintained that the Catholic Church was ... one of the most effective of agencies for democracy and Americanization. Representing as it did a vast cross section of the American people ... it could ignore class, section and race ... the Church of the newcomers ... regarded as aliens ... it could give them not only spiritual refuge but social security[66]

The major social upheaval in America in the nineteenth century was the Civil War and the slavery problem which led to it. Since most of the burgeoning Catholic population was at the bottom end of the social scale and had settled in the North, their passive sympathies went with the growing Northern opposition to the institution, though there was also fear of the effect of freed blacks on the labour market; the Southern Catholics for their part went mainly with the pro-slavery opinion. The bishops did not declare on the matter; so those from North and South continued to meet in, for example, the Provincial Councils of Baltimore and Cincinnati, which straddled Northern and Southern Territories[67] and were both able to address their flocks on the conflict.

Both opinions, pro and anti-slavery, were able to appeal to the tradition of Catholic moral theology which, while encouraging freedom by lawful means as the ideal, and insisting on the proper treatment of slaves, did not oppose the institution of slavery as such, on the grounds that it seemed permanently embedded in human society. Had those Christians who supported the institution been able to rethink from first principles in the light of the changing practicalities, they would perhaps have seen that the centuries-old hope of ending this sad state of affairs was upon them. How difficult it was for good men and women to do this was shown by Abraham Lincoln's experience. Though he was not a practising Christian, the virtues he possessed were compatible with Christian belief and he seemed in many ways to be walking example of all Ten Commandments and the beatitudes. Yet we have seen that although he was instinctively opposed to the institution from the first time he came into contact with it, because of his respect for honest free labour, its apparent impregnability prevented him openly seeking to challenge it. Moved in conscience to give his fellow countrymen the lead for its abolition as the conflict went on, it was only when military success put the victory of the Northern cause beyond doubt that he dared to give it. Moral considerations alone would not suffice. Politics being the art of the possible, the abolition had to be seen to be in the national interest before he could announce it. After Antietam that moment came.

The social problems of industrialization under economic liberalism did not begin seriously to affect the USA until the last decades of the century. There had been some trade union militancy in the 1820s and 1830s as we have noted, but the recession of 1837 and the legal restrictions on union activity thereafter curbed that growth. From the 1850s to 1877 the Molly Maguires[68] were active among the more than a quarter of a million Irish immigrants and their families in the Pennsylvania coalfields; they were a secret society, not a union, born of conditions of near-slavery in which their employers held them, and their savage violence testifies to the bitterness this had bred in them; it took the execution of twenty of their leaders to curb them.

What there was of a union movement sought to achieve its aims through political means until the 1860s, when the vast increase in industrial production demanded by the war produced problems as well as opportunities for labour and led to a revival of interest in its organization in industry. After the war America's industrial potential continued to develop until by the end of the century it was challenging to be the world's leading industrial power. The labour movement really dates from this period, and as the Church had been involved with the social needs of her predominantly immigrant and working class members, from the beginning, she was involved with their problems at work which was, for most, unskilled labour in the new factories, workshops, mines and their related services. Increasing numbers of them found themselves involved in the labour organizations that sprang up to try to give some protection against unscrupulous employers when no other protection was available to them. Given the lawless conditions that often existed, the question of participation in secret societies was a real one.

It was not always as clear however what exactly constituted a secret society in the technical sense. In the confused and brutal world of developing industrialism under the purest *laissez faire*, some labour organizations operated secretly as the only way to survive against unscrupulous employers who sought to destroy any such sign of independence among the workers. Should membership of them be denied to Catholics? It was clear that the Molly Maguires were a secret society plotting against the State because their acts of arson and murder were crimes, but could secrecy be reconciled with honest trade unionism?

The question arose over the Knights of Labour, the most significant manifestation of the growing ability of labour to organize. A union for skilled and unskilled workers alike, and the first major development in the American industrial labour movement, it had been founded in 1869 and grew slowly but unspectacularly, but fear of presenting too open a target for employers who denied the workers' right to associate for their own defence led to it remaining a secret society. Whether they were a secret society in an anti-social or anti-Church sense was disputed. It was a matter of some importance. Two-thirds of its 750,000 members in the middle 1880s were Catholics, and one of them, Terence Powderly, was its Grand Master.[69]

There were those in the American church who suspected the Knights, but it was not until they opened branches in Canada in 1881 that the question came to a head. As in the United States there was a high proportion of Catholics among its members there; the Archbishop of Toronto did not think they called for any condemnation and he made none, but Archbishop Taschereau of Quebec not only objected but went so far as to secure a condemnation of them from Rome, and in 1884 proceeded to attempt enforcement of it. In the United States the Bishop of Portland and Maine supported Taschereau but the majority of his colleagues, persuaded by Powderly and Cardinal Gibbons, were either undecided or more inclined to be in favour of the union.

Taschereau asked Rome to make its condemnation universal, whereon Gibbons' Committee on Secret Societies was asked to look into the activities of the Knights in the United States, and the result was a strong defence of the organization.[70] Gibbons, in Rome in 1887 to receive the Cardinal's hat, presented a letter in defence of the Knights, written in conjunction with Bishops Keane and Ireland, and having the backing of Cardinal Manning in England. It secured from Rome the assurance that Catholics could indeed belong to law-abiding labour organizations.[71] Gibbons' argument concerning the matter had been practical. There was no evidence that the organization was anti-social and, since the American church was predominantly a working-class church, to condemn the Knights would be to run the risk of the church losing their loyalty. The acceptance of the organization meant the Church formally approved of trade unionism and it has been noted that not only the Catholic Church benefited. The American Federation of Labour which later brought the industrial labour movement to maturity and secured it a firm place in the scheme of things was much influenced by its Catholic members.[72]

(vi) Britain

In 1912 there were 2.3 million Catholics in England, Wales and Scotland out of a population of 40.8 million, a proportion then of

some 1 in 20.[73] In England they were mainly in the urban areas of
London, the Midlands and Lancashire; in Scotland they were
concentrated overwhelmingly in Edinburgh and Glasgow. Catholic
emancipation had come only in 1829, the restoration of the hierarchy in 1850, and while the faith had never died out, it was the
Irish influx from the 1840s which in both countries provided the
Church with a popular base once more. It also ensured that it
would be working-class in the main; there were landowning families among those which had kept the faith through penal times,
and there were wealthy converts and a small Catholic professional
class, but there was very little of a Catholic middle-class generally.

Even more than in the United States, absorbing and providing
pastoral care for this growing Church, so many of whose members
were of the poorest, was in itself of major social importance, the
more especially since a great deal of emphasis was placed on providing schools for Catholic children at a time when much of the cost of
so doing had to be borne by the Catholic community in whole or in
large part. One of Cardinal Manning's first acts after his consecration as Archbishop of Westminster in 1865 was to turn down a
proposal for building a cathedral until something had been done
for the education of the poor children[74] and his appeal to the
wealthier members of his flock was successful in getting the fund-
raising off to a good start. Some State financial support for denominational schools had been provided since 1842 but when in 1870 an
education Bill threatened to deprive them of this assistance, the
demise of all denominational schools seemed only a matter of time.
Manning fought for the Catholic sector with the remarkable result
that although 1000 denominational schools did disappear, not one
of them was Catholic; equally remarkable was the fact that the
hundreds of new ones that had had to be built were mainly financed
out of the offerings of the poor themselves.[75] Not until 1902 were
denominational schools financed, as were those run by the local
boards, from the rates.

Manning had been interested in the social problems of poverty
among the rural poor when he was an Anglican clergyman in the
1840s, and this sympathy with them and with the urban and industrial poor grew with the years rather than diminished. His province
when he was Catholic Archbishop of Westminster embraced the
whole London area, including Dockland, and provided full scope
for these sympathies. Speaking at the Leeds Mechanics' Institute in
1874, he argued that there was a contradiction between the accumulation of wealth that was a mark of the times and the moral
conditions that extreme poverty imposed on the working classes:

unregulated conditions of labour make of men beasts of burden and destroy family life, with their debilitating drain on the energies and humanity of parents and children.[76] He was concerned not with politics but with the Gospel demands of love and justice, and he was ready to offer his services, even in the bitterest of conflicts, if he could do good for others. This was most dramatically shown in the dock strike in 1889, when he was 81 years old and just three years before his death.

The dockers as a whole were one of those groups of unskilled and casual workers who still had to benefit appreciably from the rewards that industrialization was already returning to some of their fellows in skilled or more sheltered trades. Manning understood[77] from his observations that one of the cruelties of the system was the effect of the recurrent slumps on those who found it hard to eke out a living even when work was available more or less regularly. When it was not, they had no savings or other resources of their own and there was precious little help from elsewhere for themselves and their families; in consequence their lives were lives of recurrent desperation. This was particularly the case during the recession of 1873, whose after-effects were felt until the 1890s, and the country was intermittently disturbed by labour disputes of increasing bitterness.

Tillett, the dockers' leader, had written to Manning in March 1888 about the difficulties he was up against in his work; the union that he led was a fledgling and weak organization that had crept into existence in 1887 and it was always in difficulties given the nature of the industry. Manning was encouraging in reply, and in the meantime in 1888 and 1889 the gasworkers in London pressed for and got concessions from their employers, so encouraging the dockers there to put forward their case.[78] Their demand, made on 13 August 1889, was for an increase from 4 or 5 pence an hour to 6 pence, plus a better bonus arrangement. It was a gamble that paid off because the better-paid stevedores' societies, aristocrats of the dock workers, decided to support them; various other labour and socialist organizations also came to their help and considerable public sympathy was shown for their case. In the April of 1889 Charles Booth's *Life and Labour of the People in London* had exposed the squalor of dock life, which had consequently been widely commented on in the press generally, and this no doubt accounts at least in part for the sympathetic hearing the dockers got for their case.

By 28 August the mood of the strikers was changing somewhat as they picketed en masse to prevent men even more desperate than they, the lowest rank of the casual workers who hung around the docks, from taking their places and their jobs; the threat of violence was now in the air. So it went on until, on 4 September, a few employers conceded the dockers' demands. But still the majority held out. Manning, who was kept closely in touch with events though a journalist on the Radical paper the *Star*, had approached the President of the London Chamber of Commerce on 1 September asking him to take an initiative in finding a way out, but got no response. On 5 September the Cardinal himself tried to get the employers interested in acting, but to no avail. On the 6th, however, the Lord Mayor did assemble a committee of conciliation of which the Cardinal was a member, and this body arranged an agreement which gave the dockers their 6 pence an hour from 1 March 1890.

Reluctantly, on 7 September, the dock directors accepted this, but the dockers now would not, since some had already secured the increase and all were adamant they would have it immediately. After further futile meetings on the 8th and 9th, Manning said he was willing to deal with the strike leaders on the matter and he was delegated so to do. On 10 September therefore he set out in the company of one official to go to the East End and meet in a schoolroom with the strikers. The meeting was tense and suspicious at first and Manning proposed 4 November as a compromise date for the increases to become effective. At first this was rejected but Manning's honesty and earnestness convinced the majority that this was the best settlement available and that continuance of the strike would only impose needless suffering on their families and the country. Manning's influence over the strikers and their leaders, many of whom were Catholics, was notable, as was his shrewdness, tact and charm in dealing with both sides.[79] On September 14 the negotiations were successfully concluded. The Pope, and Cardinal Newman, sent congratulations. The Press generally acclaimed him and the *Daily Telegraph* noted that his achievement would change the way his fellows regarded Catholics.[80]

The final tribute to Manning from the ordinary people of his time came after his death on 14 January 1892. The body lay in state from Saturday the 16th to Tuesday the 19th and *The Times*, which had always been at odds with Manning, could scarcely credit the crowds that came to pay their respects. On the Sunday they were estimated at 100,000, and even more came on the Monday. Traffic in Victoria was brought to a halt. On the Thursday, the four miles from the Brompton Oratory, where the requiem was said, to the cemetery at Kensal Green, was lined all the way with mourners despite the London fog; at the church, a mile along Ladbroke Grove, and at Notting Hill the pavements were overflowing and every vantage point packed; at the Harrow Road the crush was so great that the procession was halted and the police had to clear a way through. There had been no greater spontaneous outpouring of respect and love for a public figure in London in recent years. The vast majority who came to the lying in state and the funeral were ordinary Catholics and of course, many of them the Irish immigrants for whom he had done so much. But there were also English people of every walk of life and of every shade of belief, as *The Times* noted on 15 and 22 January.

4 International conferences/schools of social Catholics

(i) Fribourg 1885

In 1885, a group of social Catholics met at Fribourg in Switzerland under the auspices of the bishop of that city, Mgr Mermillod.[81] They were mainly representative of the Austrian (von Vogelsang's), or French (de la Tour du Pin's) corporatist school; the latter was present, as was Kuefstein of the Vogelsang's group. From Italy there was Medalago Albani, and from Germany, zu Löwenstein. Gaspar Descurtins, a Swiss politician with working-class origins, a rarity at the time, was present at the gathering. Louvain was also represented.

George Helleputte had been responsible for introducing building guilds on a major project at Louvain in 1887 and this seemed to some to represent the beginnings of something on the right lines, a project with masters and men working together; they did not however pretend that these would be applicable where industrial relations were adversarial. They realized that in order to restructure industry as they wished, they would need adequate State legislation on, for example, hours of work. It also thought that the Harmel model of industrial relations was not applicable in companies owned by shareholders and run by professional managers. But if shareholders can own, why cannot those who actually do the work? why cannot workers form companies and borrow money to run them? The union could not come up with conclusion on this or any of the other practical problems posed by the theory of corporatism.

The union did provide for Leo XIII, at his request in 1888, an account of their deliberations on the dignity of labour, on property and market speculation. Reports were also made on the minimum wage and on credit and interest; one on the corporative organization of society, an earlier elaboration, was made probably by de la Tour du Pin. One thing was clear from their deliberations, and this was that they were opposed to economic liberalism, whose defects had not been overcome by its maturing, and they saw legislation as essential to prevent the brutal labour policies of which it was capable.

(ii) The Liège Congresses 1886, 1887 and 1890

Belgium had been shocked by the violence and the extent of the industrial unrest in the spring of 1886, which was part of a pattern that had been developing since the 1870's. All across the capitalist world outbreaks were occurring in the economically disturbed years following on 1873; Marx's predictions of capitalist collapse seemed to many be upon them. Liège became the centre of an active social Catholicism which stressed that the paternalistic and 'do nothing' approach to labour and the social problem was not sufficient, so conflicting with the views of Woeste, the leader of the Catholic party.[82]

Among those who attended the first conference were de Mun, Mgr Mermillod, Léon Harmel, and the Bishop of Nottingham Edward Bagshawe, author of *Mercy and Justice to the Poor, the true Political Economy*. Harmel's thinking developed as the times required; he abandoned the opposition to government regulation of labour conditions that he had once shared with Charles Perin and he saw that, good though the arrangements at Val des Bois were, they were not the whole answer: workers' associations, true independent trade unions were also needed, which put him in opposition to his paternalistic colleagues as they well recognized. The pilgrimages to Rome that he organized take on a new significance in the light of this; he was not simply a paternalist wanting to bask, with his followers, in the light of the Pope's approval, but was ready to do or accept whatever the situation demanded to overcome the social problem. De Mun and de la Tour du Pin were also realizing that a new approach was needed but they were not prepared to go this way. At the third Congress in 1890, the main debates were on the question of State intervention, and whether workers and employers should have separate or joint organizations, and the general trend of opinion was in favour of both. There was also a general mood of support for government regulation of working hours and Sunday labour, and also provision of insurance as proposed in Germany and Austria; the social insurance schemes in Germany were also welcomed.

(iii) The Angers school

Those who were opposed to State intervention to solve the social question held their meetings in Angers with the approval and support of its bishop, Mgr Freppel. They included the Belgian disciples of Charles Perin whose views were liberal economic tempered by paternalism,[83] and they drew their main strength from an association of law professors at Angers, Lyon and Lille, and from the disciples of Le Play, a man of extreme conservative views;[84] generally this school had corporatist leanings. Mgr Freppel himself was very assertive, expressly opposed to any government action which would limit the employers' and workers' freedom of action concerning wages and conditions agreements, and regarded the Liège proposals as socialist recommendations. On the other hand Georg von Hertling, a Professor of Philosophy at Munich University and also of the liberal school of social Catholicism, argued the impossibility of replacing industrial capitalism with a theoretically desirable corporatism. Like Hitze, he had been impressed by the more practical proposals of the Mönchengladbach group.

15

A summary of the social witness and teaching of the Church *c.* 1500 to 1878

1 Introduction

The significance of the Church's social witness and teaching in this period is necessarily more limited than in those we have previously examined, that of the Middle Ages particularly. With the break-up of Christendom the Church lost that central position in the affairs of Western Europe which she had possessed since the days of the Christian Roman Empire. The Reformation and its consequences meant that many countries were now lost to it in whole or in part, while the Papacy and the international Church were deprived of much of their influence as the Catholic monarchies sought to maximize their control of ecclesiastical organization and life in their kingdoms. The Church also lost in large part that strong influence in the universities of Europe which had marked the medieval period. Founded as they were in answer to her educational needs, they had played a key role in the development of her theology and canon law and in the intellectual and political development of the times as they educated generations of laymen who found employment in the service of the State. Her bishops and clergy were now formed to meet the demands of the post-Reformation period – which meant the education of priests in seminaries and a concentration on the essentials of her teaching and discipline in the face of sectarian conflict and the task of rebuilding Church unity which had been shattered by that Reformation and its consequences; the faithful had to be rallied as

* The notes references for Chapter 15 are to be found on p. 418

they faced the problems of maintaining fidelity to Catholic truth and life in circumstances which were rarely easy.

The image of a fortress Church can be exaggerated; it has a certain truth, though she was a fortress in many ways divided against herself because of the attitude of the Catholic monarchs which conflicted with the Papacy's role as universal shepherd. The combined assault on it by those monarchs in the late eighteenth century seemed at one time to threaten its continued existence and though the French Revolution ended the threat from the Bourbons, Napoleon's imprisonment of two popes seemed to threaten it again. When the first of them, Pius VI, died in captivity in 1799 it really did appear to some as if the end of the Papacy had arrived, but the dying Pope had made provision for a conclave in Venice to elect a successor, Pius VII, who was to see the defeat of Napoleon and preside over a Church purified and strengthened by the terrors of the Revolution.

Where the Papacy had been able to take an initiative in new fields, as for example in the reform of the Church's missionary work throughout the world with the foundation of the Congregation for the Propagation of the Faith in 1622, it had shown that it could still powerfully exert its influence in a positive manner. Now, after 1814, it did the same – dedicating itself to the improvement of the spiritual and moral life of the Church and rebuilding and extending her essential structures. The emphasis was necessarily on the internal and organizational needs of the Church, and success here revived her missionary spirit, revealed in the revival of the foreign missions, and a powerful and significant revival it turned out to be. Progress in the older Europe was slower and more cautious, and moved little beyond the traditional concerns as the after-effects of the Enlightenment and revolution still exerted themselves. Little attention could be given immediately to the new social, economic and political problems that were facing what was still the heart of the international Church. Regional, local and personal initiatives in these matters, however, were taken, and showed that there were among her pastors and people at every level, and in every aspect of her service, those who were aware of their responsibilities to a changing society. Scattered and often divided on the policies to be pursued, their influence was, more often than not, marginal and it was not until the Papacy emerged from the shadows after the First Vatican Council that the necessary lead towards more concerted action was given – but when it did so it, it was on the basis of what those individuals had achieved that Rome was able to proceed.

2 The Church and the social order

The initiative of individuals therefore was the most vital element in her social witness and the teaching on which it was based until the time of Leo XIII. The continuance of the urbanization process and economic development in Europe throughout the sixteenth and seventeenth centuries, and the breakdown of the feudal and medieval social system that it entailed, increased the freedom of the rural and urban dwellers but left them with a less assured place in society than they had previously had. The process had started in the late Middle Ages. They had not come to terms with it and the size of the problem was magnified in the early modern world. In the central Middle Ages the poorest peasant had the benefit, limited enough, of the protection by custom of at least subsistence needs, and in the smaller medieval towns the active life of the Church's guilds and charities, and the community spirit engendered by her universal presence, had made it easier to respond to local needs. Inevitably the weakening of the positive influence of the Church in the wake of the Reformation, and the rebuilding of ecclesiastical life that was her first priority after it, meant that she was less able to influence effectively the new social, political and economic developments.

On the Continent, her role as dispenser of charitable aid continued during the sixteenth and seventeenth centuries though it could only be a palliative in terms of the overall problems of the poor. The more organized way in which St Vincent de Paul was able to tackle the task, given his extensive contacts among the rich and the powerful, was a pointer to that more comprehensive national approach which was needed but which the Church had neither the mandate nor the means to provide. In her missionary work in the New World however she was responsible for all education and also for charitable provision for the sick and the poor. For the protection and well-being of Indians and the black slaves it was her priests, religious and confraternities which were the most active.

Meanwhile the increasing social impact of the industrial revolution on society in nineteenth-century Europe generally from after the end of the Napoleonic wars produced problems of a scale and a nature which were unique in man's history. There had been urban civilizations of great wealth and complexity before but the economic base of society had remained agricultural. By the first half of the nineteenth century the town in Britain had become the main centre of economic activity; industrialization ensured that soon more people lived in urban than country areas; this was going to become increasingly the pattern in the nations of Europe. In the countries where the Church's presence remained strong, in France particularly, there were active private social charity initiatives to meet the growing needs, and individuals were becoming aware that more than charitable action was needed; the result was that the 1848 revolution had the distinction of being the only one in that country's modern history which was not anti-clerical. The tensions in French society, however, were bitterly reflected in the Church and she could not build on this early positive success, so that one of Leo XIII's first problems was how to get the Catholics of France to see the positive side of republicanism and take their full part in making it work.

In Germany, industrialization came more slowly, but from about mid-century it was having an impact on the Catholic community and under the guidance of Bishop Ketteler a strong Catholic social movement developed. In Belgium there was a slower awakening. However, from the 1860s there were significant initiatives although it took the insurrectionary unrest of the 1880s to ram home the urgency of the problems and produce real reforms. In Italy progress was even slower and in the United Kingdom and the USA it was to be the eve of *Rerum Novarum* before marked reactions to the growing problems were to be registered in the Church.

3 The Church and the political order

The tendency to political absolutism which was evident in Europe from the sixteenth century was dictated partly by reaction against the growing political and social instability from the middle of the fifteenth century; a strong national monarchy to ensure the peace and to guide the State to prosperity became the preference of the most influential social forces of the time. It was commended by some political philosophers who had experienced the results of rebellion and were convinced that absolutism, and the divine right that seemed best to support it, was the only sure way to political order. The mainstream political theorists among the neo-scholastics who developed the Catholic tradition in these matters in the sixteenth and seventeenth centuries were prepared to accept absolute monarchy if the political tradition of the country evolved that way; but that absolutism had to be conditioned by the divine and natural laws which, in that tradition, implied and made explicit the right to rebellion when the king acted so unjustly towards his subjects that the good of the State, the common good, was seriously undermined. They were then very conditional absolutists. The divine right and the absolute monarch were in principle suspect. That political power comes from God, but through the agency of the people, represented the main stream of the tradition on the matter. The insistence that there is, in certain circumstances, a right to rebel against a ruler whose actions indicate he is not ruling for the common good, is in fact a denial by implication of absolutism, including the absolutism of the divine-right monarchy.

It was this medieval conviction, of the ultimate right of the people to rebel against an unjust ruler whose actions threatened the very existence of the commonwealth, which was appealed to by the British settlers in America in their quarrel with the mother country. John Locke may have been their proximate authority for this, but it was on that tradition, much of which was embodied in the British constitution, that Locke drew. Respect for law, and the belief in the moral responsibility of each before God, were the bedrock of the representative principle which was embedded in the political traditions and structures, although in seventeenth-century England it justified the rule of a plutocracy rather than democracy. In the USA, on the other hand, the founding fathers were able to draw on the inherited tradition of true representative government, and they established the first working democracy in the modern world.

The relations between State and Church in the absolute monarchies revealed the uneasiness that existed between the international Church and such political systems. Christian monarchs were proud of their titles but were adamant that they would have the maximum control over the Church in their territories that they could wrest from a weakened Papacy. Ironically it was the French Revolution which, by bringing royal absolutism to an end, saved the Church from the threat that this control might become, for all practical purposes, almost total. Popular belief identifies the Catholic Church with the role of staunch positive supporter of royal absolutism, but the truth is that her work has always suffered more than it gained by identification of the two; had she had a free choice in the matter the international Church would not have accepted a yoke which she had fought so fiercely to throw off in the eleventh century, but in countries such as France and Spain she was in no position entirely to prevent kings having their way. It was certainly too easy for bishops and clergy generally therefore to accept this *fait accompli* as part of the divine order, making a virtue of necessity, but the tradition of the Church, one which has reasserted itself since the collapse of the old regime, is that Gelasian theory which respects the autonomy of the secular order and in return expects it to respect hers. What however is true is that, while the absolute Catholic kings, aristocrats, and the rich and powerful political forces of the right wing were at best doubtfully true friends of the Church, they were less her absolute enemies were than the secular and atheistic forces which lay behind much political liberalism, republicanism and totalitarian democracy, and still more socialism. Not unnaturally then, in the imperfect world of political choices which any social organization had to make, she found herself more likely to regard the monarchs and right-wing politicians as the lesser of two evils.

The discovery of the new world, the break-up of Christendom, and the religious wars of the sixteenth and seventeenth centuries faced the Church's theologians and philosophers with new moral problems in the field of international relations. They responded by showing that the proper understanding of natural law included a true international law, not limited to Christian lands but applying to all states, covering for example the proper treatment of ambassadors, the freedom of trade and respect for commercial treaties, and the right of war to punish transgression. Each nation realizes it is not isolated nor wholly independent, and that sympathy of mind will grow as peoples get to know one another. Each then has an interest in the preservation of order not only within their own borders but throughout the world. The rights of nations, and the human rights of the more undeveloped nations and peoples which the Europeans came into contact with in the new world, were to be respected. These peoples must not be deprived of their possessions or their liberty. All mankind is one and all men have the right to enjoy these things.

Questions of democracy and nationalism were raised by the French Revolution. Democracy itself was not the problem: popular sovereignty, the right of the people to chose their form of State and rulers was justified by the tradition, but all forms of State and systems of government had to work within the context of divine and natural law. Democracy as evidenced in the French Revolution, however, was totally laic and secular, and in the extremes anti-Christian and anti-God, and terrible injustices were perpetrated in its name. It was totalitarian in tendency and this was the Church's quarrel with it. Only when it got rid of its totalitarianism could she accept democracy.

The situation in Europe after the defeat of Napoleon was complicated by the relics of Gallicanism which made the alliance

of State and absolute monarchy part of the God-ordained nature of
things. Too many French Catholics found it impossible to accept
the validity in theory, still less the practical reality, of popular sovereignty as the Church understood it. Opposition to everything the
Revolution stood for was their attitude, an attitude which the
Church's social teaching did not justify, as Leo XIII was to point
out to them. Before him, however, they were too easily allowed to
maintain their illusion, to the long-term detriment of the Church,
and the people's true good. The problems of latent totalitarianism,
which the democratic forms and theories of the French Revolution
encouraged, remained, and that they were real is testified by the
history of the twentieth century. It is precisely because
Marxist–Leninism and Italian and German Fascism were able to
exploit the volatility of the politically unstable European working
classes, enraged by the harshness of political and economic liberalism, that true and thoroughgoing totalitarianism, sustained by
ideologues of the right and the left, settled on Europe in Nazism
and Stalinism in our day.

A form of nationalism which is based on true patriotism, love of
one's native or adopted land, is in itself a sound sentiment.
Patriotism is in principle implied in Christian belief. In itself it
bears no overtones of anything which is contrary to the solidarity
of all people in the Fatherhood of God but rather witnesses to the
variety of peoples which share in that solidarity. To love the nation
and the people into which I am born is then a way of thanking God
for that diversity and rejoicing in it. As such it is not only compatible with Christian belief but demanded by it. However, some forms
of nationalism by contrast stress the virtues, real or imagined, of a
particular nation-state, to the detriment of other nations or
peoples; in this it is a perversion of patriotism; it turns love of
country and nation into a denial of solidarity.

The idea of the innate superiority of one people, race or nation
over others takes many forms and has many titles. An imperialism
which encourages the belief in the manifest destiny of one race or
nation to rule others whether they like it or not, is one. Racialism,
the misuse of eugenics in order to prove an illusory innate difference between peoples which marks one race as intrinsically
superior to others is a particularly virulent form of the illusion.
Marxism transferred the illusion to one social class, the proletariat;
the working out of the economic logic of capitalism which elimi-
nates the enemies of that class will bring them into their kingdom.
Liberal capitalism transferred it to the bourgeoisie. Those not of
this class were condemned as shiftless and wastrels: inferior people.

If only they worked hard enough they too could join the comfortable rich.

The Italian nationalism of the early nineteenth century was in principle benign, but from the point of view of the Papacy it was problematic even in this form; when it was linked with anti-clericalism and secularism – to the point of atheism in some of its supporters – it was of course anathema. The positions of the benign nationalist and those of the Papacy were in conflict because it was impossible to see how the rights of each could be reconciled with that of the other; it was finally resolved in 1929 when circumstances had changed completely from those which existed a hundred years previously. The position of the Papacy was determined primarily by spiritual, theological and ecclesiastical considerations, not political. Christ had promised that his Church would last to the end of time, and that Church had been compelled by the experience of nearly two thousand years to conclude that only by being independent of any worldly authority in spiritual and moral matters could she discharge Christ's mandate – to preach the Gospel to all men. She must be politically sovereign because unless she was, Christ's Church was Caesar's servant. She was prepared by obey secular authority on secular matters, but on those which affected her duty to teach in his name she must enjoy political independence, and the possession of the Papal States as they had existed historically had enabled her to do that. No pope of the time could imagine being secure against secular influence in the Church's affairs in any other way.

The desire of the Italian nationalists for a united nation with the whole of the peninsula under the rule of a legitimate national State was in itself valid. This seemed to require the abolition of the Papal States and the reduction of the Papacy to the Diocese of Rome with its bishop directly subject to the new national authority, and this the latter could not of course accept; the Bishop of Rome was also head of an international Church and could not be subject to a temporal monarch. But it was not only the principle of the absorption by a national State of the Church which was a problem. The nature of the proposed Italian State was also. It was one which embraced the principles of continental political liberalism which saw the Church as an anachronism to be curbed, and if possible eliminated, or at least rendered completely ineffective. That liberalism intended to deny the international Church any of her traditional rights in the guidance of her people; her personnel were to be subject to the State as never before and her sacramental theology and spiritual life generally were to be reconstructed on any lines it chose to impose; in its most extreme form it was not only anti-clerical and anti-ecclesial, it was anti-religious and atheistic. Only when it became plain that the Italian State had abandoned these attitudes, or at least that it was not concerned to pursue policies based on them in practice, was any compromise with the Church possible.

4 International law and international relations

The solidarity of all men that the common Fatherhood of God implied had always encouraged the Church to think in terms of one morality and law governing all nations and of the idea of one international community under a unified government of nations. St Augustine had developed the idea of a society of nations, and the role of the Papacy in union with the Franks in the formation of Christendom was a practical attempt to see Church and State working together to establish a new Christian order. The Holy Roman Empire, the successor of Charlemagne's, revived under the Ottonians in the tenth century, sought to continue this tradition, with the Church's role becoming increasingly central in Christendom; Dante in the fourteenth century looked to a world State governed by a political authority in extension of the Roman imperial ideal.

The neo-scholastic theologians of the sixteenth century, in the wake of the break-up of Christendom and the division of Europe during the Reformation, stressed the idea of a society of independent nations, whatever their cultural origins or theological traditions, and on this basis sought to establish some principles of international law.[1] The most significant of the theologians in question were Francisco de Vitoria (1483–1546), Dominic de Soto (1494–1560), and Francisco Suarez (1548–1617). De Vitoria was Professor of Theology at the University of Salamanca (1526–46) and his lectures De Indis and De Jure Belli give him claim to be the founder of modern international law.[2] De Soto was Professor of Theology at Salamanca in 1532–56 and imperial theologian at the Council of Trent. His work De Justitia et Jure went through twenty-eight editions between 1553 and 1600. Suarez was Professor of theology at Coimbra from 1597–1615 and his Tractatus de Legibus ac de Deo Legislatore (1612) and Defensio Fidei (1613) contain his writings on international law and politics and had immense influence.[3]

These theologians were concerned with the moral issues raised by Spanish imperialism and particularly by dealings with the

Indian tribes and peoples in the Indies. The settlers in these lands were very interested in having the indigenous population serve them, as slaves if necessary, and used familiar arguments to show this was morally justifiable. De Vitoria however reasoned that there was an international law, not limited to Christian lands, but applying to all states without reference to geography, creed or race; under it the rights of Indians were equal to those of the Europeans, so they were entitled to equal justice. Suarez took up the idea of the law of nations and showed that it implied a certain unity among peoples, not only physical but also in some sense political and moral. Though individual states are perfect communities, nevertheless each is also a member of a community of nations and each is in some way dependent on the other; they therefore need the introduction of a common law to govern them. The most prominent figure in the development of modern international law was the Dutchman Hugo Grotius who published his great work *De Jure Belli et Pacis* in 1625, but the neo-scholastics were his forerunners.

5 *Economics*

The medieval scholastics who dealt with the moral issues raised by the growing capitalism and market economy of the fourteenth and fifteenth centuries based their teaching on first-hand knowledge of how markets worked and absorbed the essential economic theory that lay behind them; their findings were the basis of the analytic work of the later classical economists including Adam Smith. Bernardino of Siena and Antoninus of Florence in the fifteenth century were the most outstanding thinkers and writers on economics of their time; in the sixteenth and seventeenth centuries Molina (1535–1600), Lessius (1554–1623) and de Lugo (1583–1660), in their treatises on justice and law, made the most considerable contributions.[4] On economic institutions, as for example the theory of property, the pivotal concern was their compatibility with the public or common good. Fiscal policy they were interested in not in terms of economic analysis but of the justice, for example, of taxation, whether and when it might be imposed, by whom, on whom and for what purposes and to what extent. They also made some sociological analysis of the nature of taxation. Although theirs was a primarily ethical approach, they had to consider the economic realities to which it applied and it is within their systems of moral theology and law that economics as a study begins to have a separate existence, an autonomy as a science. More than any other group the neo-scholastics can claim to have been the founders of scientific economics. Their analytical tools and their concepts were more serviceable, more accurate than much later work, and nineteenth-century economics would have developed more surely had they been established on the foundations these men had laid.

Their applied economics were guided by the concept of the public good. It was explained in terms of the satisfaction of the economic wants of individuals insofar as their right reason, a natural law concept, revealed those wants to them. We have learned to distinguish between wants and needs; with right reason as their guide the distinction was implicit; a reasonable approach to wants avoided the threat that economic goods would become an end in themselves. Their practical understanding of public or common good is the same, technique aside, as that of modern welfare economics.[5] The unjust in economic policy and business practice was what was contrary to the public welfare or common good.

Their pure economics – economic analysis rightly so called – was related to this common good factor. Value resulted from wants and their satisfaction, not a new approach in principle since it was implicit in Aristotle's value in use and value in exchange, but they developed this idea into an incipient subjective or utility theory of exchange value. Molina established that though cost was a factor in establishing the exchange price, it was not its cause. Utility was the source or cause of value, and this utility was not inherent in the goods themselves but summed up the uses to which the individuals contemplating purchase thought they were applicable, and the importance they saw in those uses. Although they did not resolve the paradox of value, they saw that utility value lay not in terms of abstract goods, but goods relative to their abundance or scarcity, the utility of goods available in the particular circumstances. Finally they teased out all the factors which determined price.[6] They did not go a step further and produce the schedule of demand and supply, but the elements of it were there and the nine-teenth-century developments simply put the final touches to their work. Nor did they identify just price with normal competitive price, but with any competitive price that the market produced; it was just to pay such a price. If this led to gains by merchants, they were justified, and if they suffered losses because they were incompetent or unlucky, that too was justified, as long as the gain or loss resulted from the unhampered working of the market – that is to say, a market unhindered by price-fixing or monopoly. They were thinking in terms of ethical justification of freely-working competition, but in so doing they made a valuable contribution to economic analysis. It was an approval of gaining in any legitimate way. It was not an approval of profit-hunting in itself;[7] the common good remained the framework of their thinking. However, they were familiar with the facts of rising capitalism and were ready to learn from it wherever it developed in a morally sound manner; theirs was an analysis based on observation of the working economy. Lessius was familiar with the Antwerp exchange and Molina questioned businessmen about their methods; his subsequent writings were monographs examining the economic conditions of the times.

Their understanding of money was strictly metallist as was that of Aristotle and Adam Smith. They saw the debilitating effect of coin debasement on prices and so evolved a quantity theory of money; they dealt with questions of foreign exchange, international bullion movements and credit in a manner which compared favourably with much later analysis. No integrated theory of distribution emerged, however, as they did not apply their insights regarding demand and supply to the income formation process, while the rent of land and the cost of labour were not considered as analytic problems because the practical conditions had not crystallized these issues. Nor did the considerable attention given to the relief of the poor, unemployment and mendicancy produce any notable analytic insights. On profits and interest, however, they did make contributions. The risk effort theory of business profit was due to them, and de Lugo, following on a Thomistic insight, described business profits as a kind of wage for social service.[8] They also worked out a theory of interest.

This was connected with the question of usury, which continued to be a matter of controversy in the early modern world. The charging of interest on loans to compensate the lender for his risk or trouble in lending was gradually accepted in medieval times, as we have seen, as the concept of money as capital was becoming clearer. The gradual appearance of a genuine money market throughout Europe as its economy grew and expanded offered to all who had capital the possibility of earning a morally acceptable interest on it, on the principle that in justice anyone may ask and pay the current price for anything in a free market; the suspicion that interest in general was usurious was thus finally laid to rest. It was the absence of such a market, which established a rate of interest that was socially acceptable, that made it essential, in earlier times, for each loan or type of loan to be assessed separately by canonists or theologians. This in its turn led to the complexities of determining what conditions justified interest charges.

A consensus had been developing among moralists from the fifteenth century that, in any region where opportunities for investment were frequent, it might reasonably be assumed that anyone who had money to lend at what was accepted as the going rate of interest might charge such interest. The social acceptance of that rate, registered by the general approval of the authorities, removed that fear of injustice in such transactions which lay behind the usury legislation and this was accepted by Benedict XIV in his encyclical *Vix Pervenit* on the subject in 1745, though he recommended that, for a clear conscience and defence against misunderstanding, any such money-lending contract entered into should preferably register what profit was expected from it and if it was a contract of *mutuum*, they should make sure an extrinsic title to it existed.[9]

The theory of interest which can be garnered from the literature generated by the usury controversy is centred on the prevalence of business profit; it is this which leads to a rate of interest above zero. St Antoninus of Florence had noted that though money, the means of exchange, might in itself be sterile, capital was not because it was a condition for embarking on business, and Molina and others, while insisting that money itself was not productive, not a factor of production, were of the same opinion, but they accepted that capital – the merchant's tool[10] – was productive. This raises the question of the dispute over interest which is supposed to have taken place between the scholastics and their opponents in the sixteenth and seventeenth centuries. The truth is that, in terms of economic analysis, there was no such dispute.[11] The Protestant moralists and the lay lawyers differed among themselves on usury and interest and used scholastic arguments in stating those differences. The context was the one described, the increasing importance of the money market and its function in establishing a fair rate of interest. Thus the debate over the *mutuum* was gradually stilled.

Given the importance of defending the poor against the exactions of the loan shark, while at the same time allowing business loans at interest, the scholastic contribution to the handling of this problem over the centuries was of major importance morally, and, in terms of economic analysis, resulted in major contributions to the development of the modern science of economics.

The fundamental moral principle here is that financial power of any kind, like economic power of any kind, must be exercised in a way which helps, not hinders, the common good. Where personal loans for consumption purposes to people in desperate need are concerned, usury in the sense of interest of any kind is still sinful. Penal rates of interest, in banking, commercial or industrial practice, any abuses of the power of capital in a manner which destabilizes economies, business practices which enable small groups to exploit specialized technical and financial knowledge in anti-social ways, excessive desire for quick profits in speculative markets, or the exaggerated expectations that all can make easy money which fuels reckless and unsustainable booms, pervert the proper use of wealth and markets and undermine the social order and are in that sense usurious. Money, interest, capital, markets, are economic tools or mechanisms which are only good if they serve the common good.

6 Papal social teaching

The publication in 1891 of Leo XIII's encyclical *Rerum Novarum* inaugurated the modern Papacy's practice of issuing at intervals what have come to be called social encyclicals, documents concerned with current problems of social ethics. Leo did not initiate the practice of issuing encyclicals; they had a history going back to the early Church and had become the accepted form for papal pronouncements on doctrinal or moral matters since 1587 when Sixtus V reorganized the work of the Holy See. Various popes, as we have seen, responded to problems presented by the treatment of Indians in the new world, and also black slavery there and in Africa, and, after Benedict XIV (1740–58) began the practice of issuing encyclicals systematically to help preserve the faith and where necessary confirm the moral teaching of the Church, several dealt with social issues and the moral problems raised by them.

Those which were issued between 1740 and 1891 have recently been examined in a general study by Michael Schuck.[12] The author is somewhat disingenuous in suggesting that the corpus of 77 such encyclicals issued before 1878 are in any way comparable in their importance and impact to those which have followed. The Industrial Revolution and its consequences, which still affect every aspect of the everyday lives of the whole of mankind, produced for the first time nations whose people were overwhelmingly urbanized in modern cities in economies dominated by capitalism, the factory and the machine, and the wealth they have created. It has been a revolution which has brought much suffering to mankind. It has also offered to it, for the first time in its history, the oppor-

tunity of providing for the material needs of all. It has not realized
this goal, but it is within its grasp if the political will is there. The
Revolution is still unfinished and it still holds out almost endless
potentialities for mankind; it is limited only by the genius and
imagination of man, the ultimate resource. The series of encyclicals beginning with that of Leo XIII have since been issued in
response to the changing situation of society over the years in the
course of this Revolution, and they bear an importance for the life
of the Church and of mankind which far outweigh any published
before 1891.

That there was a social teaching in those issued between 1740
and that date is true none the less and Schuck's analysis of it is
essential to a fuller understanding of the evolution of the modern
teaching. On the ethics of civil society, pre-political society, the
atomization of it which resulted from the ideas of the
Enlightenment and the impact of the French Revolution with its
attack on all intermediary institutions between citizen and State,
the popes emphasized the Christian belief in the essential social
nature of man, centring it on a territorial communitarianism, the
self and society as nurtured by a specific geographical region and
its religious and moral customs. Being embedded in such a
community gives the person a sense of identity and purpose which
is defined by the functions and obligation he or she has in that
community. They include special non-voluntary obligations, their
duties to family, friends, the parish, the neighbourhood and their
country, and these precede private choice. It is a vision of an inter-
dependent social order which stresses the continuities of life and
their role as sources of obligations and responsibility. The family is
central to it: the perpetual nature of marriage vows, the authority
of the husband over his wife and children, the parental responsibility for the rearing and education of children. The source of
morality is in God's will transmitted through the Scriptures, the
Church's tradition and her pastors helping to form a tightly knit
community.[13]

The teaching on political ethics is mainly given in the context of
the infringement of the Church's rights by the Bourbon monarchs
of France, Spain, Naples, Sicily and Parma over the matter of the
explusion of the Society of Jesus from their realms, the conflicts
with Austria and Hungary over Febronianism and Josephism and
then with the French Revolution and its aftermath. The attack,
which stemmed from liberalism, on the Church's institutions of
charity and education, on religious orders and on the Christian
idea of marriage had also to be countered. The central concept of

political ethics stressed is that of the divine origin of all legitimate State authority. This teaching places on those who exercise it the obligation of using that authority in accordance with God's law, failing which they will suffer eternal punishment. The citizen is bound to obedience to such a just political order; only its disregard of the law of God can justify opposition to its laws. The respect for the State because of its origin is reflected in the Church's desire to work with it in care for the people, though the two institutions are separate and independent and have their own specific ends. On some matters their jurisdictions overlap, on marriage and education for example, and here agreement must be reached in the light of the obligations and rights of both institutions. On political freedom, this is seen as based on the law of God which protects true liberty; freedom should not be used as a pretext for wrong-doing. Human rights likewise stem not from individual will and that of the State but from divine law also; that law gives each one rights which others must respect.[14]

Regarding the economy and the ethics of its functioning, the market economy is morally acceptable and Christians are free to invest money, own property, engage in trade and commerce, make loans and contracts, in the service of the needs of individuals and the community. The immoral business practices of entrepreneurs, exorbitant profits, fraud, Sunday labour and usury, are condemned, as is the socialist attack on private property. On the relations between rich and poor, the alleviation of the sufferings of the latter is on occasion said to be left to the charity of the well-to-do, and on occasion the need for justice is stressed. The Church has a special duty to the poor, and the State is to be guided by the Church's teaching on its duty in this matter, especially through the support of intermediate institutions.

Notes and references

Abbreviations used in the notes

CAH	Cambridge Ancient History
CEHE	Cambridge Economic History of Europe
CELA	Cambridge Encylopedia of Latin America
CHLA	Cambridge History of Latin America
CMH	Cambridge Medieval History
CHMPT	Cambridge History of Medieval Political Thought
NCMH	New Cambridge Modern History

Introduction

1. The terms 'social doctrine', 'social teaching' and 'Catholic social ethics' are used interchangeably in what follows. Ethics strictly is a philosophical science and morality a theological, though in practice the terms 'theological ethics' and 'moral philosophy' are also widely used.
2. John XXIII, *Mater et Magistra*, 1961 (219). The figures in parenthesis refer to the paragraph numbers of the text. Except where otherwise indicated, the editions of the encyclicals used are from Claudia Carlen, *The Papal Encyclicals* (Ann Arbor, 1991). There are seven volumes. The first two are numbered; the five containing the texts are not; they cover the periods 1740–1878, 1878–1903, 1903–39, 1939–58 and 1958–81.
3. John Paul II, Address to the Second Meeting of the Council of Latin American Bishops (CELAM) at Puebla, 1979, in *Puebla: Evangelization at Present and in the Future of Latin America* (London, 1980), p. 7.
4. John Paul II, *Redemptor Hominis*, 1980 (37–8).
5. *Puebla*, p. 7.
6. *Mater et Magistra* (218–22).
7. John Paul II, *Sollicitudo Rei Socialis*, 1987 (41) J. Michael Miller (ed)

The Encyclicals of John Paul II (Huntingdon Ind. 1996).

8. *Sollicitudo Rei Socialis* (1).
9. John Paul II, *Laborem Exercens*, 1981 (3), and Congregation for the Doctrine of the Faith, *Libertatis Conscientia*, 1986 (72) in A. T. Hennelly (ed.) *Liberation Theology: A Documentary History* (New York, 1990), pp. 461ff.
10. *Sollicitudo Rei Socialis* (1).
11. *Libertatis Conscientia* (72).
12. *Sollicitudo Rei Socialis* (41).
13. Pius IX, *Quadragesimo Anno* (137).
14. Second Vatican Council, *Gaudium et Spes*, 'Pastoral Constitution on the Church in the Modern World' (41), in Austin Flannery, *Vatican Council II: The Conciliar and Post Conciliar Documents* (Wilmington, Delaware, 1975), pp. 903ff.
15. *Gaudium et Spes* (76).
16. *Gaudium et Spes* (43).
17. *Octogesimo Adveniens* (CTS London 1971).
18. *Libertatis Conscientia* (72).
19. *Libertatis Conscientia* (80).
20. *Gaudium et Spes* (75).

1 The Old Testament

1. John Bright *A History Of Israel* (London, 1980); 'A History of Israel' in Raymond Brown et al. (eds.), *The New Jerome Biblical Commentary* (London, 1992); B. W. Anderson, *Understanding the Old Testament* (Prentice Hall, 1986); O. Eissfeldt, *The Old Testament: An Introduction* (New York, 1965).
2. Bright, *History of Israel*, pp. 162ff. and 177ff.; W. Eichrodt, *Theology of the Old Testament* (London, 1978), Vol. 1, pp. 306ff.; G. von Rad, *Old Testament Theology* (London, 1975), Vol. 1, pp. 327ff. and J. L. McKenzie, *The World of the Judges* (Englewood Cliffs, NJ, 1966).
3. Eichrodt, *Theology*, Vol. 1, pp. 232ff., 250ff.
4. Eichrodt, *Theology*, Vol. 1, pp. 270ff.; R. Otto, *The Idea of the Holy* (Oxford, 1950).
5. Bright, *History*, pp. 118ff. and J. L. McKenzie, *The Two Edged Sword* (London, 1956), pp. 45ff.
6. W. de Burgh, *The Legacy of the Ancient World* (London, 1967), p. 322, n. 1.
7. Eichrodt, *Theology*, Vol. 1, p. 75; D. Winton Thomas, *Documents from Old Testament Times* (Edinburgh, 1958), pp. 27ff.
8. Eichrodt, *Theology*, Vol. 2, pp. 232ff. and 242ff.
9. There is no single word in Hebrew which expresses our idea of justice as primarily a legal concept, but the root word, righteousness, refers to a quality founded in law and can include that

concept, though righteousness is also much more than that. See 'Righteousness', J. L. McKenzie, *Dictionary of the Bible* (London, 1965); Christopher J. H. Wright, *Living as the People of God* (Leicester, 1983), ch. 6.

10. Wright, *Living*, p. 143.
11. Roland de Vaux, *Ancient Israel: Its Life and Institutions* (London, 1980), p. 94.
12. de Vaux, *Ancient Israel*, p. 99.
13. R. Davidson, *The Old Testament* (London, 1975), p. 25; W. Zimmerli, *The Old Testament and the World* (London, 1976), p. 9, similarly underlines that the exodus was an act of salvation which is centred not on man's liberation in itself but on the power of God in freeing his people.
14. Brown et al. (eds.), *New Jerome Biblical Commentary*, p. 1232.
15. Russell Kirk, *The Roots of American Order* (La Salle, Ill., 1974), pp. 19–20.
16. de Vaux, *Ancient Israel*, p. 177.
17. Bright, *History*, p. 244; de Vaux, *Ancient Israel*, p. 73.
18. de Vaux, *Ancient Israel*, p. 74.
19. de Vaux, *Ancient Israel*, p. 76.
20. de Vaux, *Ancient Israel*, pp. 78ff.
21. de Vaux, *Ancient Israel*, p 170; J. L. McKenzie, 'Loans', *Dictionary of the Bible*; T. Divine, *Interest: An Historical and Analytic Study in Economics and Modern Ethics* (Milwaukee, 1959), pp. 6ff.
22. Wealth usually means the possession of a large disposable income, property the physical ownership of land and buildings, or the physical possession of anything valuable, paintings for example. In fact they largely overlap; the wealthy are the property owners and vice versa.
23. Eichrodt, *Theology*, Vol. 2, p. 120.
24. Eichrodt, *Theology*, Vol. 2, p. 321.
25. P. Grelot, *Man and Wife in Scripture* (London, 1964), p. 29.
26. de Vaux, *Ancient Israel*, p. 40.
27. de Vaux, *Ancient Israel*, p. 40.
28. J. L. McKenzie, *The Two Edged Sword*, p. 95.
29. Orlando Patterson, *Freedom in the Making of Western Culture* (London, 1991), p. x.
30. de Vaux, *Ancient Israel*, p. 89.

2 The New Testament

1. Second Vatican Council, *Dei Verbum*, 'Dogmatic Constitution on Divine Revelation' (19), in Austin Flannery, *Vatican Council II: The Conciliar and Post Conciliar Documents* (Wilmington, Delaware, 1975), pp. 750ff; Xavier Léon-Dufour, *Dictionary of the New Testament*

(London, 1980), pp. 77ff.

2. R. Schnackenburg, *The Moral Teaching of the New Testament* (London, 1964), pp. 110ff.; W. Schrage, *Ethics of the New Testament* (Edinburgh, 1988), pp. 98ff., 107ff., 229ff., 235ff.; G. Theissen, *Social Reality and the Early Christians* (Edinburgh, 1992), pp. 60ff., 115ff., 321ff.

3. Schnackenburg, *Moral Teaching*, pp. 54ff.; Schrage, *Ethics*, pp. 88ff.; George Strecker, *The Sermon on the Mount* (Edinburgh, 1988).

4. R. Schnackenburg, *God's Rule in God's Kingdom* (London, 1963), pp. 41ff.

5. Eschatology is derived from the Greek *eschata*, meaning the last things, the divine act which marks the end of history. On earth the kingdom has come in Christ's person and grows mysteriously in the hearts of those who accept it and become members of his Church. Between its inauguration, and its consummation in the judgement at the end of time, the Gospel has to be preached and lived in holiness. It is a time of hope and joy and its consummation is to be desired, not feared.

6. Léon Dufour, *Dictionary*, pp. 48ff and 63ff; Schrage, *Ethics*, pp. 107ff; W. R. Farmer, *Maccabees, Zealots and Josephus* (New York, 1958); S. G. B. Brandon, *Jesus and the Zealots* (Manchester, 1967).

7. R. Bauckham, *Bible in Politics* (London, 1989), pp. 74ff.

8. Léon Dufour, *Dictionary*, pp. 51f., 90.

9. A. Harnack, *The Expansion of Christianity in the First Three Centuries* (London, 1904), Vol. 1, p. 184.

10. Schnackenburg, *Moral Teaching*, pp. 110ff.; Schrage, *Ethics*, pp. 107ff., 235ff.; Bauckham, *Bible in Politics*, pp. 79ff., 84ff., 142ff.; J. L. McKenzie, *The Power and the Wisdom* (London, 1965), ch. 12.

11. Bauckham, *Bible in Politics*, pp. 79ff.

12. Bauckham, *Bible in Politics*, pp. 85ff.

13. Schnackenburg, *Moral Teaching*, pp. 121ff.; Schrage, *Ethics*, pp. 98ff. and 229ff.; Bauckham, *Bible in Politics*, pp. 73ff.; L. H. Marshall, *The Challenge of New Testament Ethics* (London, 1967), pp. 161ff., 174ff.

14. Michael Grant, *St. Peter* (London, 1994), p. 56, quoting Strabo the geographer.

15. In theory all work was respected in the Roman world; the tradition of early Rome and its independent peasant class which formed the backbone of its legions ensured that. But the growth of a ruling aristocracy and the slave population degraded physical labour even of free men. See below, footnote 21.

16. Schnackenburg, *Moral Teaching*, pp. 132ff.; Schrage, *Ethics*, pp. 92ff.; B. Witherington, *Women and the Genesis of Christianity* (Cambridge, 1990), pp. 237ff.; 'Divorce', in *Dictionary of Catholic Theology* (London, 1967), Vol. 2.

17. Witherington, *Women and the Genesis*, pp. 163ff., also his *Women in the Earliest Churches* (Cambridge, 1988); Florence Gillman, *Women who Knew Paul* (Collegeville, Minnesota, 1991).

18. Peter Brown, *Body and Society: Men, Women and Sexual Renunciation in*

Early Christianity (London, 1988), p. 52.

19. Witherington, *Women and the Genesis*, pp. 166 and 172.
20. Karl Adam, *The Spirit of Catholicism* (London, 1959), pp. 130ff.
21. R. Macmullen, *Roman Social Relations* (New Haven, 1974), p. 114, notes the 'verbal kicks delivered indiscriminately to the whole body of the *vulgus*' by Horace, Martial, Juvenal, Seneca, Tacitus and other Latin authors. Cicero refers to 'craftsmen, petty shopkeepers, and all that filth of the cities'. That manual work coarsened body, soul and manners was the belief of polite society. Working with one's hands for a living was sordid. The mass of workers who kept the machinery of civilized living operating, and still more the common soldiers and labourers, were beneath notice. Free labour was despised; no free-born man could accept the mastery of another implied by the wage contract. 'The very wages of a labourer' said Cicero, are 'the badges of slavery' (*De Officiis* I, 150; MacMullen, p. 115). The petty traders were despised because it was believed that all lied about their wares; only a wealthy trader, who could retire to his country estate, was respected. Only the rich man could be trusted to be honest. The slave could never overcome his servile background, and the poor man was by nature a liar and a cheat. Poverty was degrading, ugly; the view of respectable people was that those without money deserve to be held in contempt. By contrast Christianity from the first welcomed the poor, the freedman and the slave, and it took root in the urban areas throughout the Empire where the poor congregated. So in Alexandria the oldest Christian church was among the docks, by the wharves. Through Christianity they were given a status they previously lacked; the Greek word for poor for example meant cringing, begging W. de Burgh *The Legacy of the Ancient World* London 1967 p. 325 n.1..

3 The social witness of the early Church

1. H. Chadwick, *The Early Church* (Harmondsworth, 1971), pp. 27ff.
2. W. H. Frend, *The Rise of Christianity* (London, 1984), p. 86; A. Harnack, *The Expansion of Christianity in the First Three Centuries* (London, 1904); J. Daniélou and H. Marrou, *The Christian Centuries*, Vol. 1, *The First Six Hundred Years* (London, 1984); H. Jedin and J. Dolan (eds.), *Handbook of Church History* Vol. 1, *From the Apostolic Community to Constantine* (London, 1968) and Vol. 2, *The Imperial Church from Constantine to the Early Middle Ages* (London, 1980); F. F. Bruce, *The Spreading Flame* (Exeter, 1978).
3. Orlando Patterson, *Freedom in the Making of Western Culture* (London, 1991), p. 293. See Frend, *Rise*, pp. 126ff and 178ff.
4. L. Duchesne, *The Early History of the Church, from its Foundation to the End of the Third Century* (London, 1909), p. 34.

5. Harnack, *Expansion*, Vol. 1. p. 261.

6. M. P. Charlesworth, *The Roman Empire* (Oxford, 1968); Michael Grant, *The World of Rome* (London, 1964) and *The Climax of Rome* (London, 1968); A. H. M. Jones, *The Decline of the Ancient World* (London, 1961).

7. Rarely was an emperor deified in his lifetime; it was the Senate which decided the matter after his death. If deification was decreed, the emperor joined the list of state gods as did Caesar, Augustus, Vespasian and Hadrian, for example. Only emperors whose views and attitudes were abnormal deified themselves; so Caligula and Domitian. See Charlesworth, *The Roman Empire*, pp. 94ff.

8. Jedin and Dolan, *Handbook*, Vol. 1, p. 134.

9. M. I. Finley, *The Ancient Economy* (Cambridge, 1964), p. 55; H. Daniel Rops, *The Church of the Apostles and Martyrs* (London, 1960), p. 128.

10. Finley *Ancient Economy*, F. Oertel 'The Economic Life of the Empire', Ch 5 of Vol 12 *CAH* (Cambridge 1939), R. Duncan Jones, *The Economy of the Roman Empire* (Cambridge, 1984); M. I. Rostovtzeff, *The Social and Economic History of the Roman Empire* (Oxford, 1957).

11. Daniel Rops, *The Church*, p. 129.

12. R. MacMullen, *Roman Social Relations* (New Haven, 1974), p. 88. The rich as a whole were a minute number of the population, the senators and equites together accounted for little more than one tenth of one per cent of it. Money was the key to entrance to this elite for outsiders. Those enriched by the commerce and trade of the Empire, many of them freedmen, were welcome as members.

13. Daniel Rops, *The Church*, p. 136.

14. As to the numbers of slaves in round terms by the second century AD, Galen's figures, that there were about as many slaves as there were free male citizens, some 22 per cent of the population, cannot be improved on (Jones, *Economy*, p. 273).

15. J. H. Uhlhorn, *Christian Charity in the Ancient Church* (Edinburgh, 1883); J. Cadoux, *The Early Church and the World* (Edinburgh, 1923); Stephen Benko and J. O'Rourke, *Early Church History: The Roman Empire as the Setting of Primitive Christianity* (London, 1972); W. A. Meeks, *The First Urban Christians* (New Haven, 1984); R. M. Grant, *Early Christianity and Society* (London, 1978).

16. P. Allard, *Ten Lectures on the Martyrs* (London, 1907), p. 155.

17. Jedin and Dolan, *Handbook*, Vol. 1, p. 169, Frend *Rise*, p. 179.

18. Meeks, *The First Urban Christians*, p. 73.

19. Danielou and Marrou, *Christian Centuries*, Vol. 1, p. 117.

20. Frend, *Rise*, p. 173.

21. Among the ancients, 'both Plato and Aristotle had found in reason the real man . . . both failed to reach an adequate concept of personality' because of their difficulties over the problem of the union of soul and body. Augustine was the first to attain such an adequate concept. 'Being a believer in the doctrine of the word made flesh'

he could not accept that the body was irrelevant to man's true self-hood. de Burgh, *The Legacy of the Ancient World*, p. 374.

22. The reasons for Constantine's action, the nature of his conversion and the effect of the Empire's acceptance of the Church and Christianity have long been causes of controversy. Chs. 30 and 31 of Jedin and Dolan, Vol. 1, provide a good summary of them.

23. H. Chadwick, *Early Church*, p. 56.

24. Jedin and Dolan, *Handbook*, Vol. 1, p. 311.

25. Harnack, *Expansion* VAI pp. 190ff

26. W. H. Lecky, *A History of Western Morals from Augustus to Charlemagne* (London, 1911), Vol. 2, p. 78.

27. R. Margotta, *An Illustrated History of Medicine* (London, 1967), p. 102.

28. Harnack, *Expansion*, Vol. 1, pp. 264ff. Tatian mentions the excellence of Christian moral doctrines as the reason for his conversion. The Acts of the Christian Martyrs reveal the effect of their courage on spectators to their suffering. Cyprian attests to the influence of the moral power of the new faith in convincing him of its truth.

29. Harnack, *Expansion*, Vol. 1, pp. 260f.

30. Jedin and Dolan, *Handbook*, Vol. 1, p. 309.

31. Frend, *Rise*, p. 570. The growing wealth 'was generously applied to the philanthropic work started by the Church' *CMH*, Vol. 1. *The Christian Empire and the Foundation of the Teutonic Kingdoms (Cambridge 1911)* p. 591.

32. *CMH*, Vol 1, pp. 566, 593. See also A. Dopsch, *The Economic and Social Foundations of European Civilisation* (London, 1937), pp. 245 and 250ff.

33. 'Hospitals, History of', *New Catholic Encyclopedia*, Vol. 7. See also Daniélou and Marrou, *Christian Centuries*, pp. 327ff; Jedin and Dolan, *Handbook*, Vol. 2, pp. 409ff.; I. Giordani *The Social Message of the Early Church Fathers* (Boston, 1977), ch. 12; Uhlhorn, *Christian Charity*, ch. 4; W. Chadwick, *The Church, the State and the Poor* (London, 1909), pp. 52ff. and L. I. Conrad et al., *The Western Medical Tradition* (Cambridge, 1995), pp. 77ff.

34. Jedin and Dolan, *Handbook*, Vol. 1, p. 309.

35. Margotta, *History of Medicine*, p. 102.

36. Dopsch, *Foundations*, pp. 249.

37. Conrad, *Medical Tradition*, p. 78; Jedin and Dolan, *Handbook*, Vol. 2, p. 411.

38. Lecky, *Western Morals*, Vol. 2, pp. 22ff. Augustine had a theoretical problem in that he did not see that one could decide exactly when the soul entered the fetus, but 'his fundamental rejection of the ending of pregnancy at any time was unambiguous'. Jedin and Dolan, *Handbook*, Vol. 2, p. 400.

39. Samuel Dill, *Roman Society from Nero to Marcus Aurelius* (London, 1905), pp. 234ff.

40. E. Troeltsch, *The Social Teaching of the Christian Churches* (London, 1931), Vol. 1, pp. 123ff.

41. *Apol.* 43.1–2, Daniélou and Marrou, *Christian Centuries*, p. 173.

42. Daniélou and Marrou, *Christian Centuries*, p. 179; Cadoux, *Early Church*, p. 446.
43. Harnack, *Expansion*, Vol. 1, p. 219.
44. L. J. Swift, *The Early Fathers on War and Military Service* (Wilmington, Del., 1983), pp. 26ff.
45. Cadoux, *Early Church*, p. 275.
46. *Apol.* 37.4 and 42.2–3; Swift, *Military Service*, p. 38.
47. Cadoux, *Early Church*, p. 277.
48. *On Goodness and Patience* 14, *On Morality* 2, and *To Demetrianos* 3 and 17. Swift, *Military Service*, pp. 48f.
49. The *Divine Institutes*, 6.20.15–17 and 1.1.13, *On the Death of Persecutors* 52.4; Swift, *Military Service*, pp. 62 and 67.
50. Allard, *Ten Lectures*, p. 171.
51. *Letter to Polycarp* 1–5. F. X. Murphy, *Moral Teaching in the Primitive Church* (Tenbury Wells, 1968), p. 71.
52. Harnack, *Expansion*, Vol. 1, p. 210; Jedin and Dolan, *Handbook*, Vol. 2, pp. 403ff.
53. Lecky, *Western Morals*, Vol. 2, p. 66.
54. *Homily on Ecclesiastes*. Peter Phan, *Social Thought: The Message of the Fathers of the Church* (Wilmington, Del., 1984), p. 128.
55. G. M. de Ste. Croix, in 'Early Christian attitudes to property and slavery', *Studies in Church History*, Vol. 12 (Oxford, 1975), countering what he saw as the exaggerations of some Christian apologists, asserts that 'I have not been able to find in any early Christian writer anything like a demand for the abandonment of slavery or even for a general freeing of existing slaves' (p. 21). Imagining he would was just as naive as the exaggeration he is criticizing.
56. Allard, *Ten Lectures*, pp. 172ff.
57. Frend, *Rise*, p. 420.
58. Uhlhorn, *Christian Charity*, p. 107.
59. Uhlhorn, *Christian Charity*, p. 351. George Ovitt 'The Cultural Context of Western Technology: early Christian attitudes towards manual labour', in Allen J. Frantzen and D. Moffat (eds.), *The Work of Work: Servitude, Slavery and Labour in Medieval England* (Glasgow, 1994), pp. 78ff, traces the importance of labour as a means of developing the spiritual self, as a theme of the Scriptures and the monastic writers.
60. Uhlhorn, *Christian Charity*, pp. 353ff.; Ovitt, 'Cultural Context', pp. 78ff.
61. Chadwick, *Early Church*, p. 69. J. Danielou, *The Ministry of Women in the Early Church* (London, 1961).
62. Brown, *Body and Society*, p. 60.
63. Brown, *Body and Society*, pp. 263ff., 279f., 298f., and 369ff.
64. Daniel Rops, *The Church*, Vol. 1, pp. 368ff., Frend, *Rise*, p. 291.
65. Augustine, *Literal Commentary on Genesis* XI.42. Ambrose, *On Paradise* XII.56. Elizabeth A. Clark, *Women in the Early Church* (Wilmington, Del., 1983), pp. 40f.

66.   Clark, *Women*, p. 15. Of the five chapters in her book which trace the Fathers' teaching on the matter, only the first is concerned with the weaknesses and lure of women; the other four deal with their virtues.

67.   Clark, *Women*, p. 205.

68.   *Miscellanies* III.6.49; Clark, *Women*, p. 52.

69.   *Miscellanies* III.12.79; Clark, *Women*, p. 54.

70.   Troeltsch, p. 130. Lecky observed that Christianity regarded all forms of sexual relationships other than lifelong and monogamous marriage as immoral, however difficult the doctrine was in practice, and added presciently that since no other ethical teaching has been so dominated by theological principle as that on marriage, none would be so deeply affected by its decay, *Western Morals*, Vol. 2, p. 351.

71.   Daniel Rops, *The Church*, pp. 129, 130 and 232ff.

72.   Daniélou and Marrou, *Christian Centuries*, pp. 175f.; Jedin and Dolan, *Handbook*, Vol. 2, pp. 394ff.

73.   Duchesne, *Early History*, p. 73.

74.   G. H. Sabine and T. L. Thorson, *A History of Political Theory*, (Hinsdale, Ill., 1973), p. 190.

4 The social teaching of the Fathers of the Church

1.   Brian E. Daley, *The World of the Fathers* (Wilmington, Del., 1980); F. L. Cross, *Early Christian Fathers* (London, 1960); B. Ramsey, *Beginning to Read the Fathers* (New York, 1985); Joannes Quasten, *Patrology* (Westminster, Md., 1992 (4 vols.)).

2.   F. X. Murphy, *Moral Teaching in the Primitive Church* (Tenbury Wells, 1968), pp. 33ff.

3.   Murphy, *Moral Teaching*, pp. 73ff.

4.   Peter Phan, *Social Thought: The Message of the Fathers of the Church* (Wilmington, Delaware, 1984), pp. 55ff.

5.   Phan, *Social Thought*, pp. 71ff.

6.   Phan, *Social Thought*, pp. 102ff.

7.   A. Meredith, *The Cappadocians* (London, 1995).

8.   Phan, *Social Thought*, pp. 112ff.

9.   Phan, *Social Thought*, pp. 135ff.

10.   Phan, *Social Thought*, pp. 167ff.

11.   Phan, *Social Thought*, pp. 260ff.

12.   Roman civil law, *jus civile*, was applicable only to Roman citizens and was based on the twelve tables, composed *c.* 450 BC. As the Empire spread it became desirable also to have a law which could apply to all peoples who lived under its rule. This, the law of the peoples or nations, *jus gentium*, was derived from those common elements which the lawyers saw were in the law codes of people subject to

Rome, and in 242 BC a praetor was appointed to deal with is law. The mass of cases and legislation continued to grow and the need to codify them grew accordingly. The jurists or philosophers of law emerged spontaneously, from about 100 BC, to meet the need, then gradually, from the second century AD, speculative elements, notably natural law theory, were introduced to aid this task. So Celsus and Gaius for example – but it was Ulpian (*c.* 170–228) who was mainly responsible for securing this concept its place in Roman jurisprudence. See de Burgh, *Legacy of the Ancient World* (London, 1967), pp. 236, 263 and 300ff.

13. Sophists such as Hippias (481–411 BC) based moral duty upon an unwritten natural law. Socrates (469–399) saw human nature and its ethical values as constant. Plato's (427–347) phrase 'according to nature' indicated the conformity of things to the ideal type; the four cardinal virtues of prudence, justice, fortitude and temperance delineating man's natural moral sense. Aristotle (384–322) distinguished between two forms of justice, conventional and 'natural, which is the same everywhere'. de Burgh, *Legacy*, pp. 163ff. See R. Charles with D. Maclaren, *The Social Teaching of Vatican II* (San Francisco, 1982), pp. 66ff.

14. *Republic* III.2. Sabine and Thorson, *History of Political Theory* (Hinsdale, Ill., 1973), p. 161. Stoicism stressed the power of the human will, the importance of freedom and the reality of God's providence; despite the difficulties and problems of life, the good man could overcome. It succeeded because, like Christianity, it was a philosophy of suffering. It failed because ultimately it was a philosophy of despair. de Burgh, *Legacy*, p. 342, n. 2.

15 R. W. and A. J. Carlyle, *A History of Medieval Political Theory in the West*, (6 Vols London 1903–1936) Vol. 1, *The Roman Lawyers of the Second Century to the Political Writers of the Ninth* (London, 1903)', pp. 37, 74, 103. Cicero and Seneca were the two Roman writers the Fathers drew on most frequently. Cicero (104 BC to 43 BC), the greatest of Roman orators, was active in politics; incurring the enmity of Mark Antony, he was executed. His speeches and letters, and other writings, are important resources for our knowledge of his times, and his books *de Legibus* and *de Re Publica* made Greek thought and Roman history available and intelligible to future generations. Seneca (4 BC to AD 65) was a rhetorician, philosopher and writer, tutor to the young Nero and his advisor as Emperor until his attempts to restrain his master's excesses led to his dismissal. The suspicion of treachery which was held against him by Nero led to his committing suicide. His letters reveal the nobility of the Stoic ideal and his thought seemed to many Christians to be so near to theirs that at one time he was wrongly thought by some to have been a convert. T. Stockton, *Cicero: A Political Biography* (London, 1970); M. T. Griffin, *Seneca: A Philosopher in Politics* (Oxford, 1976).

16. Man's reasoning on moral matters is prone to error so that divine

positive (revealed) moral law, is necessary to give certain guidance (St Thomas Aquinas, *Summa Theologiae*, Ia IIae, Q. 99 'Of the precepts of the old law', Art. 2 ad 2.

17. Origen *Contra Celsum*, v.40. R. W. and A. J. Carlyle, *Political Theory*, Vol. 1, p. 104.

18. Tertullian, *De Corona* v and vi; Lactantius, *Div. Instit.* iii.8; St Ambrose, *Ep.* lxxiii.10; St Augustine, *Contra Faustum* xix.2; St Isidore, *Etymol.* v.4. R. W. and A. J. Carlyle, *Political Theory*, Vol. 1, pp. 104ff.

19. 'Those whose condition is such that their function is the use of their bodies and nothing better can be expected of them, those I say are slaves by nature', *Politics*, 1.5.

20. *De Legibus* i.10.28 – 12.33; *De Officiis* i.13.41; *De Republica* iii.24–5. R. W. and A. J. Carlyle, *Political Theory*, Vol. 1, pp. 8 and 11.

21. Seneca, *Ep.* v.6 and *Ep.* xix.2, and Ulpian, *Dig.* 1.17.32 and 1.1.4. R. W. and A. J. Carlyle, *Political Theory*, Vol. 1, pp. 22 and 47f.

22. Ambrose, *Ep.* lxiii.112; *Enarr. in Psalm* cxxiv.3. R. W. and A. J. Carlyle, *Political Theory*, Vol. 1, p. 121.

23. St Augustine, *De Civitate Dei* xix.16; St Gregory, *Ep.* iv.23. R. W. and A. J. Carlyle, *Political Theory*, Vol. 1, p. 123.

24. Homily on Ecclesiastes, Phan, *Social Thought*, p. 128.

25. *De Rep.* i.7.12. R. W. and A. J. Carlyle, *Political Theory*, Vol. 1, p. 14.

26. *De Rep.* i.26. 41 and 42. R. W. and A. J. Carlyle, *Political Theory*, Vol. 1, p. 15.

27. *De Off.* i.17.54, *De Rep.* ii.1.1–3, and iii.13. R. W. and A. J. Carlyle, *Political Theory*, Vol. 1, p. 14.

28. R. W. and A. J. Carlyle, *Political Theory*, Vol. 1, p. 70.

29. Irenaeus, *Adv. Haer.* v.24; Justin Martyr, *First Apology* 17. R. W. and A. J. Carlyle, *Political Theory*, Vol. 1, p. 129.

30. *De Civitate Dei* xix. 13 and 15; *Against Faustus* xxii.27; *The Good of Marriage* 7. Phan, *Social Thought*, p. 195.

31. St Augustine, *De Civitate Dei* xix.7 and 13; *On the Free Choice of the Will* 1.6; *Letter* 130.13. Phan, *Social Thought*, p. 195.

32. St Augustine, *De Civitate Dei* xix.15; *De Doctrina Christiana* ii.23; St Gregory, *Exp. Mor. in Job* xxi.15. R. W. and A. J. Carlyle, *Political Theory*, Vol. 1, pp. 126f.

33. Ambrose, *De Officiis* i.28; *Ep.* xl.2. R. W. and A. J. Carlyle, *Political Theory*, Vol. 1, p. 162.

34. Augustine, *De Civitate Dei* v.19 and 21. R. W. and A. J. Carlyle, *Political Theory*, Vol. 1, pp. 151 and 167f.

35. H. Deane, *The Social and Political Ideals of St Augustine* (New York, 1967), p. 117.

36. St Isidore, *Etym.* xv.2, ix.3, 4; *Sententiae* iii.47–52. R. W. and A. J. Carlyle, *Political Theory*, vol. 1, pp. 172–3. St Isidore of Seville (*c.* 560–636) was bishop of that city and an encyclopaedist, famed for his learning in science, history and theology.

37. Jedin and Dolan, *Handbook*, Vol. 1, *From the Apostolic Community to Constantine* pp. 418ff. Vol. 2, *The Imperial Church from Constantine to*

Notes and references 385

The Early Middle Ages pp. 136ff. and Frend, *Rise*, pp. 488ff., 534ff., 653ff.; Peter Brown, *Augustine of Hippo* (London, 1967), pp. 233ff.

38. 'When Augustine became Bishop of Hippo . . . he set about . . . conciliation . . . but fanatics committed barbarous outrages on Catholic clergy and churches . . . Such disorders demanded the intervention of the secular power.' J. B. Bury, *The History of the Later Roman Empire* Vol. 1 (London, 1958), p. 380.

39. *Enarr. in Ps.* xxxvii and *Ep.* xxi.4. R. W. and A. J. Carlyle, *Political Theory*, Vol. 1, p. 180.

40. Frend, *Rise*, pp. 624f.; R. W. and A. J. Carlyle, *Political Theory*, Vol. 1, p. 183.

41. Gelasius, *Tractatus* iv.11; *Ep.* xii.2. R. W. and A. J. Carlyle, *Political Theory*, Vol. 1, pp. 190f.; Jedin and Dolan, *Handbook*, Vol. 2, pp. 616ff.; Frend, *Rise*, pp. 810ff.

42. A. H. M. Jones, *The Later Roman Empire* (Oxford, 1964), Vol. 2, pp. 769f.

43. C. Avila, *Ownership: Early Christian Teaching* (London, 1983), p. 24.

44. *Cambridge Economic History of Europe*, Vol. 1 *The Agrarian Economy of The Middle Ages* (Cambridge, 1966), pp. 256ff.; Jones, *Later Roman Empire*, Vol. 2, pp. 796ff.

45. *CEHE* Vol. 1, pp. 116ff.

46. 'The land tax had trebled in living memory by 350, taking more than a quarter of the farmer's produce. It was inflexible and thoroughly ill distributed.' P. Brown, *The World of Late Antiquity* (London, 1974), p. 36.

47. Jedin and Dolan, *Handbook*, Vol. 2, pp. 401ff.

48. Jones, *Later Roman Empire*, Vol. 2, pp. 811f.

49. Jones, *Later Roman Empire*, Vol. 2, p. 810.

50. Jones, *Later Roman Empire*, Vol. 2, p. 811; Avila, *Ownership*, pp. 29ff.

51. Alan Watson, *The Law of the Ancient Romans* (Dallas, 1970), p. 3, quoted in Avila, *Ownership*, p. 15.

52. Fritz Schulz, *Classical Roman Law* (Oxford, 1954), p. 339; Avila, *Ownership*, p. 19.

53. W. W. Buckland and Peter Stein, *A Textbook of Roman Law* (Cambridge, 1966), p. 188; Avila, *Ownership*, p. 19.

54. Jones, *Later Roman Empire*, Vol 2. pp. 714, 857ff., 1040.

55. *CAH*, Vol. 12, p. 244.

56. *The Tutor*, 2.12.120. Phan, *Social Thought*, p. 67.

57. *The Stromata* 3.6. Phan, *Social Thought*, p. 70.

58. *Quis Dives Salvetur?* 13. Phan, *Social Thought*, p. 73.

59. *Quis Dives Salvetur?* 16, 17. Phan, *Social Thought*, pp. 75f.

60. Avila, *Ownership*, pp. 48f.

61. Homily on 'I will pull down my barns' 1. Phan, *Social Thought*, p. 114.

62. Homily on 'I will pull down my barns' 4, 7. Phan, *Social Thought*, p. 117.

63. *Homily on Psalm 14.* Avila, *Ownership*, p. 56.

64. Frend, *Rise*, pp. 749ff.

65. Bury, *Later Roman Empire*, Vol. 1, p. 139.
66. *Homily* II.4 'On Lazarus'. Phan, *Social Thought*, p. 137.
67. *Homily* LXVI.3. Phan, *Social Thought*, p. 144.
68. *Homily* XII.3. Phan, *Social Thought*, p. 158.
69. *Homily* XII.4. Phan, *Social Thought*, pp. 159f.
70. *In Inscriptionem Altaris*, Avila, *Ownership*, p. 88.
71. *De Nabuthe* 1, 2, 11, 53, 55. *Ep.* 2.11. Phan, *Social Thought*, pp. 167ff., 180ff.
72. *On the Duties of the Clergy* I.28. 136. 137. Phan, *Social Thought*, p. 178.
73. *Didache*, iv.8; *Epistle of Barnabas* xix.8; St Justin, *First Apology* xiv; St Cyprian, *De Op. et Elem.* 25. R. W. and A. J. Carlyle, *Political Theory*, Vol. 1, pp. 132ff.
74. I. Giordani, *The Social Message of the Early Church Fathers* (Paterson, NJ, 1944), Ch. 12 'Solidarity'.
75. Augustine, *Ep.* clvii.iv, and Jerome *Ep.* cxxx.14. R. W. and A. J. Carlyle, *Political Theory*, Vol. 1, p. 135.
76. Ambrose, *De Nabuthe* ii, *Hom.* 8.22, *De Off.* i.28. Phan, *Social Thought*, pp. 162f. R. W. and A. J. Carlyle, *Political Theory*, Vol. 1, p. 136.
77. St Ambrose, *Commentary on Ps.cxviii.*8, 22. Seneca *Ep.* xiv.2. R. W. and A. J. Carlyle, *Political Theory*, Vol. 1, pp. 24 and 137.
78. R. W. and A. J. Carlyle, *Political Theory*, Vol. 1, pp. 52f.
79. Avila, *Ownership*, p. 153.
80. John Gilchrist, *The Church and Economic Activity in the Middle Ages* (New York, 1969), p. 51.
81. Ch. 3, above. p. 66ft. 41.
82. *Apol.* 39. J. Cadoux, *The Early Church and the World.* Edinburgh 1923 p. 313.
83. Irenaeus IV xxx. el, Clement, *Paed.* III.xi.78f., Cadoux, *Early Church*, p. 446.
84. *Summa Theologiae*, IIa IIae, Q. 77, art. 4, quoting Augustine's commentary on Psalm 70. For ease of reference to the Summa I have throughout used the three-volume American edition of the then current English version translated by the Fathers of the English Dominican Province, published New York, 1947.
85. Cadoux, *Early Church*, p. 446. *see above* p. 66
86. Lactantius, *Divine Institutes* 6.18. Phan, *Social Thought*, p. 99; Basil of Caesarea, *Homily on Psalm xv.* Phan, p. 111; Ambrose, *On Tobit*, 2.7, 11. Phan, p. 180; Augustine, *Sermons* 239.4. Phan, p. 228.
87. H. Chadwick, *The Cambridge History of Medieval Political Thought* (Cambridge, 1988), p. 15.
88. *Letter* 188.13; *Homily on Psalm 61.*4. Swift, *Military Service*, p. 94.
89. *On The Duties of the Clergy*, 1.27.129 and 3.3.23. Swift, *Military Service*, p. 98.
90. *Duties*, 1.176; 3.19.110, 116; 1.35.176–7. Swift, *Military Service*, p. 99.
91. *Duties*, 2.7.33; 1.29.139 and 3.14.87. Swift, *Military Service*, p. 100.
92. *Duties*, 1.36.178. Swift, *Military Service*, pp. 101ff.
93. 'Greater love has no man than this, that a man lays down his life for

his friends' (John 15.13) is capable of either a passive or active interpretation, i.e. raising no resistance, or actively defending his friends
and losing his life in the process.

94. *Duties*, 1.36.178. *Discourse on Psalm 118*.15.22. Swift, *Military Service*,
    pp. 102f.
95. *City of God* 15.4; *Letter*, 189.6 and *Letter* 229.2. Swift, *Military Service*,
    pp. 113ff.
96. *City of God* 19.7. Swift, *Military Service*, p. 116.
97. Sermon 302.15. Swift, *Military Service*, p. 123.
98. *On the Lord's Sermon*, 1.20.63–4. Swift, *Military Service*, pp. 124ff.
99. *Against Faustus* 22.75. Swift, *Military Service*, p. 129.
100. *City of God* 4.6; *Questions on the Heptateuch* 6.10. Swift, *Military Service*,
     pp. 134ff.
101. *Letter* 185.2.8. Swift, *Military Service*, p. 138.
102. *Letter* 189.6; *City of God*, 1.4, 5 and 7. Swift, *Military Service*, p. 139.
103. *Against Faustus* 22.75. Swift, *Military Service*, p. 139.
104. *Letter* 185.2.8 and *Commentary on Psalm 124*.7. Swift, *Military Service*, p.
     140.
105. Above, pp. 83 ft 38.

5 The church, society and politics in the early Middle Ages

1. M. Keen, *The Pelican History of Medieval Europe* (Harmondsworth,
   1968), pp. 11ff.; Judith Herrin, *The Formation of Christendom* (Oxford,
   1989); A. H. Bredero, *Christendom and Christianity in the Middle Ages*
   (Grand Rapids, 1994).
2. Philip Hughes, *A History of the Church* (3 Vols) (London, 1979) Vol.
   2, *The Church in the World the Church Created*, p. vii.
3. R. W. Southern, *Western Society and the Church in the Middle Ages*
   (Harmondsworth, 1972), p. 1.
4. 'Christianity' in *International Encyclopedia of the Social Sciences* (New
   York, 1968), Vol. 2.
5. J. H. Mundy, *Europe in the High Middle Ages 1150–1309* (London,
   1973), p. 25. Mundy speaks of the time of the 'Papal Monarchy'
   when the leadership was exercised in the most dramatic fashion, but
   its beginnings were in the papal link with the Franks from the eighth
   century.
6. The date of the conversion and much else about him and his rule
   are open to various interpretations, given the paucity of the records
   of the time; the importance of his leadership of the Franks and its
   consequences, is however not in doubt. See R. Collins, *Early Medieval
   Europe 300–1000* (London, 1991), pp. 104ff.
7. C. W. Previté-Orton, *The Shorter Cambridge Medieval History* Vol. 1, *The
   Later Roman Empire to the Twelfth Century* (Cambridge, 1966), p. 296.
8. F. Stenton, *Anglo-Saxon England* (Oxford, 1975), p. 104, credits him

not only with apostolic zeal but political acumen, his Roman statesman's instinct telling him of the advantages that lay in returning to
Rome a lost province.

9. Previté-Orton, *Shorter Cambridge*, Vol. 1; Collins, *Europe 300–1000*; C.
    W. Hollister, *Medieval Europe: A Short History* (New York, 1994), Part
    1; M. Deanesly, *A History of Early Medieval Europe 476–911* (London,
    1966); J. M. Wallace-Hadrill, *The Barbarian West 400–1000* (Oxford,
    1985).

10. Hollister, *Medieval Europe*, p. 1.

11. S. Clough and R. Rapp, *European Economic History* (London, 1975),
    p. 38.

12. F. Heer, *The Medieval World* (London, 1962), p. 231.

13. Hollister, *Medieval Europe*, p. 1.

14. Kenneth Clark, *Civilization* (Harmondsworth, 1987) p. 30.

15. Wallace-Hadrill, *Barbarian West*; Deanesly, *Medieval Europe*, chs. 2 to 6.

16. Wallace-Hadrill, *The Longhaired Kings* (London, 1962), pp. 163ff.

17. By Bishop Ulfilas (310–81), a Cappadocian who had been taken
    captive in a Gothic raid. Ordained bishop for the Goths by the Arian
    Eusebius in 341, he preached among the Visigoths for three years.
    By 400 all the Goths were Arian Christians.

18. Traced in *The History of the Franks* (Harmondsworth, 1977). Gregory
    was Bishop of Tours, 573–94. He continued work on his *History* until
    the year of his death.

19. Previté-Orton, *Shorter Cambridge*, vol. 1, p. 158.

20. W. Levison, *England and the Continent in the Eighth Century* (Oxford,
    1949), pp. 82f.

21. Wallace-Hadrill, *Longhaired Kings*, p. 244.

22. Jedin and Dolan (eds.), *Handbook of Church History* Vol. 3 *The Church
    in the Age of Feudalism* (London, 1969), pp. 6ff., 26ff. T. F.-X. Noble,
    The Republic of St. Peter: The Birth of the Papal States 635–825
    (Philadelphia, 1984).

23. Timothy Fry (ed.), *The Rule of St. Benedict* (Collegeville, Minn.,
    1980); Christopher Dawson, *The Making of Europe* (London, 1932),
    pp. 189ff.; C. H. Lawrence, *Medieval Monasticism* (London, 1984),
    chs. 1–5.

24. Fry (ed.), *Rule* ch. 3, p. 179.

25. Fry (ed.), *Rule* ch. 48, p. 249.

26. Fry (ed.), *Rule* ch. 59, p. 271.

27. 'Many, like St. Walaric, the founder of St. Valery sur Somme, were
    themselves of peasant origin. Others, though noble by birth, spent
    their whole lives working as peasants, like St. Theodulph, the abbot
    of St. Thierry, near Rheims, whose plough was hung up in the
    church as a relic by the peasants.' Dawson, *Making*, p. 202.

28. K. S. Latourette, *A History of the Expansion of Christianity*, Vol. 2 *A
    Thousand Years of Uncertainty* (London, 1938), p. 356.

29. Fry (ed.), *Rule*, introduction, p. 123.

30. Hastings Rashdall, *Medieval Universities* (ed. Powicke and Emden,

Oxford, 1936), Vol. 1, p. 27.

31. J. M. Clark, *The Abbey of St. Gall* (Cambridge, 1926).

32. Dawson, *Making*, p. 232.

33. Jedin and Dolan, *Handbook*, Vol. 3, chs. 14 and 15; Collins, *Early Medieval Europe*, pp. 260ff and 282ff.; D. Bullough, *The Age of Charlemagne* (London, 1980); H. Fichtenau, *The Carolingian Empire* (Oxford, 1948).

34. Previté-Orton, *Shorter Cambridge*, Vol. 1. p. 309.

35. H. A. L. Fisher, *A History of Europe* (London, Fontana edn, 1960), Vol. 1, pp. 175f.

36. Bullough, *Charlemagne*, pp. 99ff.

37. Rashdall, *Medieval Universities*, Vol. 1, pp. 28ff.

38. Deanesly, *Medieval Europe*, pp. 399f.

39. Previté-Orton, *Shorter Cambridge*, Vol. 1, pp. 323ff.

40. C. Dawson, *Religion and the Rise of Western Culture* (London, 1950), p. 90.

41. Hollister, *Medieval Europe*, pp. 107ff.; Marc Bloch, *Feudal Society* (London, 1971), Vol. 1, *The Growth of Ties of Dependence*. chs. 1 and 2.

42. Previté-Orton, *Shorter Cambridge*, Vol. 1, p. 346.

43. N. Cantor, *Medieval History* (London, 1963), p. 214.

44. Bloch, *Feudal Society*, Vol. 2, *Social Classes and Political Organization*. p. 446.

45. Previté-Orton, *Shorter Cambridge*, p. 432; Bloch, *Feudal Society*, Vol 2, pp. 412ff; Bredero, *Christendom*, pp. 105ff.

46. Previté-Orton, *Shorter Cambridge*, pp. 433f.

47. Hollister, *Medieval Europe*, ch. 12; Hughes, *History*, Vol. 2,. pp. 181ff., 191ff.; Jedin and Dolan, *Handbook*, Vol. 3, chs. 42–44; Colin Morris, *The Papal Monarchy: The Western Church from 1050 to 1250* (Oxford, 1989), pp. 79ff.

48. Previté-Orton, *Shorter Cambridge*, Vol. 1, p. 471.

49. Dawson, *Religion*, p. 143.

50. Jedin and Dolan, *Handbook* Vol. 3, pp. 320ff.

51. C. H. Lawrence, *Medieval Monasticism* (London, 1984) ch. 6; Jedin and Dolan, *Handbook*, Vol. 3, pp. 324ff.

52. See Jedin and Dolan, *Handbook*, Vol. 3, ch. 22 and pp. 198ff; Peter Llewellyn, *Rome in the Dark Ages* (London, 1993), pp. 297ff.

53. Previté-Orton, *Shorter Cambridge*, Vol. 1. p. 457.

6 The Church, society and economics in the early Middle Ages

1. N. J. Pounds, *An Economic History of Medieval Europe* (London, 1994), ch. 2; R. Latouche, *The Birth of the European Economy* (London, 1954); G. Duby, *Early Growth of the European Economy* (London, 1974); *CEHE* Vol. 1, *The Agrarian Economy of the Middle Ages* (Cambridge, 1966),

pp. 180ff and 284ff.

2. H. Green, *Medieval Civilisation in Western Europe* (London, 1971), pp. 35ff., Pounds, *Economic History*, pp. 40ff; *CEHE* Vol. 1, pp. 31ff.
3. Latouche, *Birth*, p. 83.
4. R. Cameron, *A Concise Economic History of the World* (Oxford, 1993), pp. 44ff.; S. B. Clough and R. T. Rapp, *European Economic History* (London, 1975), pp. 46ff.
5. Latouche, *Birth* p. 88.
6. *CEHE*, Vol. 1, p. 45.
7. *CEHE*, Vol. 1, p. 71.
8. *CEHE*, Vol. 1, pp. 72ff.
9. Latouche, *Birth*, p. 177.
10. *CEHE*, Vol. 1, p. 49.
11. Latouche, *Birth*, p. 193.
12. Pounds, *Economic History*, pp. 64ff and 343ff.; Latouche, *Birth*, pp. 152ff.; Duby, *Early Growth*, pp. 101ff.
13. Pounds, *Economic History*, p. 66.
14. Latouche, *Birth*, pp. 88ff.
15. Duby, *Early Growth*, p. 109; Latouche, *Birth*, p. 124.
16. D. Whitelock, *The Beginnings of English Society* (Harmondsworth, 1971), p. 109.
17. E. Mason, *St Wulfstan of Worcester (1008–1095)* (Oxford, 1990), pp. 184f.
18. Duby, *Early Growth*, p. 97; Latouche, *Birth*, p. 153.
19. Duby, *Early Growth*, p. 109.
20. Latouche, *Birth*, p. 155.
21. Latouche, *Birth*, pp. 162f.
22. *CEHE* Vol. 3, *Economic Organization and Policies in the Middle Ages* (Cambridge, 1965), pp. 11f.
23. Cameron, *Concise Economic History*, p. 56; Pounds, *Economic History*, pp. 170, 204.
24. Latouche, *Birth*, p. 289.
25. Latouche, *Birth*, pp. 235ff.; Pounds, *Economic History*, pp. 223ff.; *CEHE*, Vol. 3, pp. 3ff.
26. H. Pirenne, *Economic and Social History of Medieval Europe* (London, 1978), pp. 46ff.; *CEHE* Vol. 3, pp. 16ff.
27. *CEHE*, Vol. 3, p. 10.
28. *CEHE*, Vol. 2, *Trade and Industry in the Middle Ages* (Cambridge, 1987), pp. 316ff.
29. *CEHE*, Vol. 3, pp. 25ff.
30. Cameron, *Concise Economic History*, pp. 51ff, 68ff; Lynn White, in C. Cipolla (ed.), *Fontana Economic History of Europe* Vol. 1, *The Middle Ages* (London, 1973), pp. 143ff; Lynn White, *Medieval Technology and Social Change* (Oxford, 1962); J. Gimpel, *The Medieval Machine* (London, 1988); R. J. Forbes and E. J. Dijksterhuis, *A History of Science and Technology* (Harmondsworth, 1963), vol. 1, ch. 8; Francis and Joseph Gies, *Cathedral, Forge and Watermill: Technology and Invention in the Middle Ages* (New York, 1994).

31. Lynn White, *Technology*, p. 44 and in Cipolla (ed.), *Economic History*, p. 147.
32. Lynn White in Cipolla (ed.), *Economic History*, pp. 149f.
33. Lynn White, *Technology* pp. 75f. and in Cipolla (ed.), *Economic History*, p. 150.
34. Lynn White in Cipolla (ed.), *Economic History*, p. 153; Gies, *Cathedral*, pp. 47f. and 149.
35. Gimpel, *Medieval Machine*, pp. 1ff.
36. *CEHE*, Vol. 2, p. 697.
37. Lynn White, *Technology*, pp. 40f.; Gimpel, *Medieval Machine*, pp. 63f; Gies, *Cathedral*, pp. 62ff. and 80.

7 The Church and society in the central Middle Ages

1. K. Clark, *Civilisation* (Harmondsworth, (1992), p. 38.
2. George Holmes, *Oxford History of Medieval Europe* (Oxford, 1992), p. v; Christopher Brooke, *Europe in the Central Middle Ages 962–1154* (London, 1975); H. Mundy, *Europe in the High Middle Ages 1150–1309* (London, 1973); Colin Morris, *The Papal Monarchy: The Western Church from 1050 to 1250* (Oxford, 1989).
3. Morris, *Papal Monarchy*, p. 1.
4. Enough of the Gothic achievement remains to tell us that 'in sheer bulk of material shifted, in area covered and in space developed, it is evident that the Gothic age was pre-emininent in all cultural epochs known, through recorded history and about the globe'. It was the outcome of religious inspiration 'the origin of the greatest art the world has ever seen'. John Harvey, *The Master Builders* (London, 1971), p. 129. Churches were the industrial work to which the men of the times attached the most importance; society's creation, they were therefore its pride: the expression of man's gratitude to God. David Edwards, *Christian England* (London, 1981), pp. 152–3. See G. Duby, *The Age of the Cathedrals* (London, 1981), pp. 156ff.
5. H. Jedin and J. Dolan (eds.), *Handbook of Church History* Vol. 3, *The Church in an Age of Feudalism*, p. 369; Morris, *Papal Monarchy*, pp. 111f. and 129.
6. Jedin and Dolan (eds.), *Handbook*, Vol. 3, p. 368.
7. Jedin and Dolan (eds.), *Handbook*, Vol. 3, pp. 380f.; Gerd Tellenbach, *The Church in Western Europe from the Tenth to the Early Twelfth Century* (Cambridge, 1993), pp. 222ff., 231ff. 'Henry III and William of England might be careful in selecting their prelates, but Henry thought only of his secular interests.' C. W. Previté-Orton, *The Shorter Cambridge Medieval History:* Vol. 1 *The Later Roman Empire to the Twelfth Century* (Cambridge, 1966), p. 490.
8. Jedin and Dolan (eds.), *Handbook*, Vol. 3, pp. 382f.; Tellenbach,

Church in Western Europe, pp. 242f.; Morris, *Papal Monarchy*, pp. 116f.

9. Jedin and Dolan (eds.), *Handbook*, Vol. 3, p. 385; Morris, *Papal Monarchy*, pp. 121f.

10. J. W. Thompson, *An Economic and Social History of the Middle Ages* (New York, 1928), pp. 660f.

11. M. Chambers et al. *The Western Experience to 1715* (New York, 1979), p. 256.

12. C. W. Previté-Orton, *The Shorter Cambridge*, Vol. 1, p. 501.

13. Jedin and Dolan (eds.), *Handbook*, Vol. 3, pp. 445ff.; Morris, *Papal Monarchy*, pp. 147ff.; H. B. Mayer, *The Crusades* (Oxford, 1972). The *CMH*, vol. 5, *The Victory of the Papacy*, p. 265 and K. Hitti, *The Arabs* (London, 10th edn, 1970), p. 635. Both give as much weight to the political and racial aspects of the origin of the crusade movement as they do to the religious. The tension between East and West went back to the fifth century BC.

14. Mayer, *Crusades*, pp. 30ff.

15. Morris, *Papal Monarchy*, pp. 157ff.

16. N. Tanner, *Decrees of the Ecumenical Councils*, Vol. 1 (London and Georgetown, 1990).

17. R. W. Southern, *Western Society and the Church in the Middle Ages* (Harmondsworth, 1972), pp. 111ff.; Morris, *Papal Monarchy*, pp. 405ff.

18. Southern, *Western Society*, pp. 128ff.

19. John Gilchrist, *The Church and Economic Activity in the Middle Ages* (New York, 1969), pp. 93ff., 101f.; Previté-Orton, *Shorter Cambridge*, Vol. 1, p. 618; Morris, *Papal Monarchy*, pp. 214ff.

20. Southern, *Western Society*, pp. 131f.

21. C. H. Lawrence, *Medieval Monasticism* (London, 1984), pp. 137ff.; Southern, *Western Society*, pp. 241ff.; Morris, *Papal Monarchy*, pp. 74ff.

22. Southern, *Western Society*, p. 249.

23. H. De Ridder-Symoens (ed.), *A History of the University in Europe*, Vol. 1 *Universities in the Middle Ages* (Cambridge, 1994), pp. xix and 35; Hastings Rashdall, *The Universities of Europe in the Middle Ages* (ed. Powicke and Emden, Oxford, 1936); C. Dawson, *Religion and the Rise of Western Culture* (London, 1950), ch. 10.

24. De Ridder-Symoens (ed.), *History of the University*, p. 201.

25. De Ridder-Symoens (ed.), *History of the University*, p. 15f.

26. De Ridder-Symoens (ed.), *History of the University*, p. 82.

27. De Ridder-Symoens (ed.), *History of the University*, pp. 79, 80, 117, 201–2.

28. De Ridder-Symoens (ed.), *History of the University*, pp. 21ff.

29. De Ridder-Symoens (ed.), *History of the University*, p. 32.

30. J. McConica (ed.), *History of Oxford University* (Oxford, 1986), Vol 3 ch. 1.

31. H. Rashdall, writing in *CMH*, Vol. 6, pp. 600ff.

32. D. Knowles, *Evolution of Medieval Thought* (London, 1993), ch. 15.

33. Knowles, *Evolution*, ch. 16.

34. There were aspects of Aristotle's thought which could not be reconciled with Christian belief, for example that the world was eternal and that the human soul died with the body, while neither he nor Plato considered the possibility of a created world. W. de Burgh, *The Legacy of the Ancient World* (London, 1967), p. 456.

35. St Thomas was the son of the Count of Aquino in the State of Naples. He studied at the University of Naples and while there came into contact with the Dominicans, joining them against his family's strong objections. He then studied in Cologne under Albert the Great in 1248 and then in Paris where he also taught from 1252; his teaching was there attacked by conservative theologians from 1269. He died at Fossanova on the way to the Council of Lyons in 1274. He was then about 48 years old.

36. de Burgh, *Legacy*, p. 458; F. C. Copleston, *A History of Philosophy,* Vol. 2 (London, 1950), pp. 313ff.

37. Knowles, *Evolution*, pp. 253f. and pp. 258ff.; Copleston, *History of Philosophy*, Vol. 3, ch. 10; S. Jaki, *Science and Creation* (Edinburgh, 1986); A. C. Crombie, *Styles of Scientific Thinking in the European Tradition* 4 (London, 1994), 3 Vols. Vol 1 pp. 24ff.

38. Lawrence, *Medieval Monasticism*, pp. 146ff.; Southern, *Western Society*, pp. 250ff. and Morris, *Papal Monarchy*, pp. 340ff.

39. Lawrence, *Medieval Monasticism*, p. 149.

40. Southern, *Western Society*, p. 259; J. S. Donnelly, *The Decline of the Cistercian Brotherhood* (London, 1949), pp. 72ff.

41. Southern, *Western Society*, pp. 257ff. On the economic effect of Cistercian monasteries see *CEHE* Vol. 1, pp. 76f; Brooke, *Europe*, pp. 75ff and 94; J. Gimpel, *The Medieval Machine* (London, 1988), pp. 3ff.

42. Lawrence, *Medieval Monasticism*, pp. 161f.

43. Southern, *Western Society*, p. 260.

44. Lawrence, *Medieval Monasticism*, p. 160.

45. N. J. Pounds, *An Economic History of Medieval Europe* (London, 1994), pp. 225ff.; F. Braudel, *Civilisation and Capitalism* (London, 1984), Vol. 3, pp. 93ff., 144ff., 546ff.

46. Pounds, *Economic History*, pp. 72f.; Braudel, *Civilisation*, pp. 108f.

47. M. Postan, *The Medieval Economy and Society* (Harmondsworth, 1972), p. 213.

48. Braudel, *Civilisation*, pp. 111f.

49. Pounds, *Economic History*, pp. 413ff.; Braudel, *Civilisation*, p. 128.

50. Braudel, *Civilisation*, p. 94.

51. Dawson, *Religion*, p. 195.

52. Pounds, *Economic History*, p. 290.

53. Dawson, *Religion*, p. 196.

54. In 1099 in Mainz, and 1106 at Worms. H. Pirenne, *Economic and Social History of Medieval Europe* (London, 1978), p. 182.

55. Pounds, *Economic History*, pp. 290ff.; Postan, *Medieval Economy*, pp, 242ff.

56. E. Troeltsch, *The Social Teaching of the Christian Churches* (London, 1931), vol. 1, p. 255.
57. Lawrence, *Medieval Monasticism*, p. 201.
58. Jedin and Dolan (eds.), *Handbook*, Vol. 4, *The High Middle Ages to the Eve of the Reformation*, pp. 162ff., 208ff., 443ff., Morris, *Papal Monarchy*, pp. 339ff., 442ff., 470ff.; Edward Peters, *Inquisition* (London, 1989).
59. Morris, *Papal Monarchy*, p. 347.
60. Jedin and Dolan (eds.), *Handbook*, Vol. 4, p. 103.
61. Jedin and Dolan (eds.), *Handbook*, Vol. 4, pp. 214ff; Morris, *Papal Monarchy*, pp. 473ff.
62. *CMH* Vol. 6, *The Victory of the Papacy* p. 724.
63. *CMH* Vol. 6, p. 726; H. Kamen, *The Inquisition and Society in Spain in the Sixteenth and Seventeenth Centuries* (Bloomington, Ind., 1985).
64. Dawson, *Religion*, p. 260.
65. Dawson, *Religion*, p. 262.
66. Previté-Orton, *Shorter Cambridge*, Vol. 1, p. 618; Morris, *Papal Monarchy*, pp. 214ff.

8 The Church and society in the late Middle Ages

1. C. W. Hollister, *Medieval Europe: A Short History* (New York, 1994), ch. 15; D. Hay, *Europe in the Fourteenth and the Fifteenth Centuries* (London, 1966); D. Waley, *Later Medieval Europe: from St. Louis to Luther* (London, 1964); B. Tuchman, *A Distant Mirror* (London, 1979).
2. Hollister, *Medieval Europe*, p. 236.
3. H. Jedin and J. Dolan (eds.), *Handbook of Church History* Vol. 4, *From the High Middle Ages to the Renaissance*, pp. 269ff.; C. W. Previté-Orton, *The Shorter Cambridge Medieval History* Vol. 2 *From the Twelfth Century to the Renaissance*, pp. 782ff.; C. T. Wood (ed.), *Philip and Boniface VIII* (London, 1971).
4. They were 'hampered by no scruple save loyalty to their master'. Previté-Orton, *Shorter Cambridge*, Vol. 2, p. 783.
5. The Knights Templar were founded in 1128 to protect pilgrims to the Holy Land. They were the most famous and largest of the Knightly Orders, having some 15,000 members and being possessed of immense wealth: strong among Philip's reasons for wanting their destruction was his desire to despoil them. His deviousness in exploiting the worst aspects of inquisitorial practices in bringing about the downfall of an order whose guilt was always doubtful marks the whole procedure as scandalous. The Church, and Pope Clement V in particular, emerges from the gruesome tale with little credit either. S. Howarth, *Knights Templar* (London, 1982).
6. M. Keen, *The Pelican History of Medieval Europe* (Harmondsworth, 1968), ch. 19; Jedin and Dolan (eds.), *Handbook*, Vol. 4 *The High*

Middle Ages to the Eve of The Reformation, ch. 37–40; G. Mollat, *The Popes at Avignon* (London, 1963); Y. Renouard, *The Avignon Papacy* (London, 1970).

7. R. W. Southern, *Western Society and the Church in the Middle Ages* (Harmondsworth, 1972), pp. 136ff.

8. Keen, *Pelican History*, p. 280.

9. Keen, *Pelican History*, pp. 284ff.; Previté-Orton, *Shorter Cambridge*, Vol. 2, ch. 32; Jedin and Dolan (eds.), *Handbook*, Vol 4, chs. 46, 49, 50; W. Ullmann, *The Origins of the Great Schism* (London, 1948).

10. Previté-Orton, *Shorter Cambridge*, Vol. 2, pp. 958ff; Jedin and Dolan (eds.), *Handbook*, Vol. 4, pp. 423ff.; B. Tierney, *The Foundations of Conciliar Theory*, (Cambridge, 1955); E. R. Jacobs, *Essays on the Conciliar Epoch* (Manchester, 1963).

11. Previté-Orton, *Shorter Cambridge*, Vol. 2, p. 962.

12. Hay, *Europe*, p. 347ff.

13. Jedin and Dolan (eds.), *Handbook*, Vol. 4, chs. 56 and 57.

14. Jedin and Dolan (eds.), *Handbook*, Vol. 4, chs. 47 and 58; Hay, *Europe*, pp. 313ff.; *CMH*, Vol. 7, *Decline of Empire and Papacy*, pp. 796ff.

15. Gordon Leff, *Medieval Thought: Augustine to Ockham* (Harmondsworth, 1950), pp. 258ff. and 296ff.; D. Knowles, *Evolution of Medieval Thought* (London, 1993), chs. 24–28.

16. F. C. Copleston, *A History of Philosophy* Vol. 2 *Medieval Philosophy: Augustine to Scotus* (London, 1950), p. 485.

17. Jedin and Dolan (eds.), *Handbook*, Vol. 4, ch. 43.

18. See below, ch. 9, pp. 187ff.

19. Hollister, *Medieval Europe*, pp. 326ff.; Hay, *Europe*, pp. 126ff.

20. Previté-Orton, *Shorter Cambridge*, Vol. 2, ch. 29; J. Sumption, *The Hundred Years War: Trial by Battle* (London, 1992).

21. L. Mollat and P. Wolff, *Popular Revolutions of the Late Middle Ages* (London, 1973), pp. 123ff.

22. Previté-Orton, *Shorter Cambridge*, Vol. 2, pp. 881ff. and 1035ff.; Mollat and Wolff, *Popular Revolutions*, pp. 161ff.

23. A. Myers, *England in the Late Middle Ages* (Harmondsworth, 1971), pp. 29ff; Mollat and Wolff, *Popular Revolutions*, pp. 184ff; R. B. Dobson, *The Peasants Revolt of 1381* (London, 1983).

24. Previté-Orton, *Shorter Cambridge*, Vol. 2, pp. 868ff; Mollat and Wolff, *Popular Revolutions*, pp. 142ff.; M. V. Clarke, *The Medieval City State* (London, 1926), pp. 73ff.

25. Previté-Orton, *Shorter Cambridge*, Vol. 2, pp. 980ff.; Marina Warner, *Joan of Arc* (London, 1983).

26. Hollister, *Medieval Europe*, ch. 16; Pounds, *Economic History*, pp. 443ff.; Waley, *Later Medieval Europe*, ch. 5; H. A. Miskimmin, *The Economy of Early Renaissance Europe 1300–1460* (Cambridge, 1975); *CEHE*, Vol. 1, *The Agrarian Economy and the Middle Age* ch. 8, Vol. 2, pp. 240ff., 379ff.

27. Tuchman, *Distant Mirror*, p. 24.

28. Pounds, *Economic History*, p. 445; R. Horrox, *The Black Death* (Manchester, 1994).
29. The workers of Florence were to demand that the number of cloths the industry in that city produced should be maintained at 20,000 per annum. A century earlier its output had been 84,000. S. Clough and R. Rapp, *European Economic History* (London, 1975), p. 110.
30. Pounds, *Economic History*, p. 450.
31. Clough and Rapp, *Economic History*, p. 111f.
32. Pounds, *Economic History*, p. 475.

9 Church and politics in the central and late Middle Ages

1. Colin Morris, *The Papal Monarchy* (Oxford, 1989), p. 34; R. W. Southern, *Western Society and the Church in the Middle Ages* (Harmondsworth, 1972), pp. 15ff. and *The Making of the Middle Ages* (London, 1959); *International Encyclopedia of the Social Sciences*, Vol. 2, article on 'Christianity'.
2. C. Dawson, *Religion and the Rise of Western Culture* (London, 1950), pp. 162–3.
3. Morris points out that the idea fostered by some historians concerning the supposed medieval hostility to marriage is in error. It was seen as 'ordained by God in paradise, honoured by the presence of Christ at Cana ... the first established of religious orders' [*Papal Monarchy*] p. 332. See E. Schillebeeckx *Marriage, Secular Reality and Saving Mystery* London 1980 [2 Vols in one] Vol 2.
4. Morris, *Papal Monarchy*, pp. 354ff.; J. Parkes, *The Jews in the Medieval Community* (New York, 1976).
5. Morris, *Papal Monarchy*, p. 319.
6. R. W. and A. J. Carlyle, *A History of Medieval Political Theory in the West*, Vol. 1, *The Roman Lawyers of the Second Century to the Political Writers of the Ninth* (London, 1903), pp. 290ff. J. H. Burns (ed.) *The Cambridge History of Medieval Political Thought* (Cambridge, 1988) notes that there was no systematic and coherent political philosophy before the twelfth century but there were elements of thought about government and society as it was or ought to be (p. 170).
7. R. W. and A. J. Carlyle, *Political Theory*, Vol. 1, pp. 199ff.
8. R. W. and A. J. Carlyle, *Political Theory*, Vol. 1, pp. 231ff.
9. R. W. and A. J. Carlyle, *Political Theory*, Vol. 1, pp. 236ff and 250ff.
10. R. W. and A. J. Carlyle, *Political Theory*, Vol. 3. *Political Theory from the Tenth to the Thirteenth Centuries*, chs. 3, 5, 6 and pp. 182ff.
11. *de Legibus* iii. 9.2. R. W. and A. J. Carlyle, *Political Theory from the Tenth to the Thirteenth Centuries*, Vol. 3, (London, 1915) pp. 36f. 'Bracton's words are an admirable summary of the principle that all authority represents some essential principle of justice and equity, that an unjust authority is no authority.'

12. *de Legibus* iii 9.2 R. W. and A. J. Carlyle, *Political Theory*, Vol. 3, p. 35.

13. Gerbert, later Pope Sylvester II (999–1003), *Epistolae* 107. R. W. and A. J. Carlyle, *Political Theory*, Vol. 3, p. 148.

14. *ad Gebehardum.* R. W. and A. J. Carlyle, *Political Theory*, Vol. 3, p. 167.

15. R. W. and A. J. Carlyle, *Political Theory*, Vol. 3, p. 168. It is Carlyle's demonstration that the social contract implicit in Manegold's words is not an isolated instance but characteristic of the oaths in question which makes it hard to accept the view that 'pactum' here did not mean what it clearly did seem to mean. See *CHMPT*, p. 246.

16. R. W. and A. J. Carlyle, *Political Theory*, Vol. 2, *The Political Theory of the Roman Lawyers and Canonists from the Tenth to the Thirteenth Century*, (London, 1909), p. 248.

17. R. W. and A. J. Carlyle, *Political Theory*, Vol. 4, *The Theories of the Relationship between the Empire and the Papacy from the Tenth to the Thirteenth Centuries*, (London, 1922), p. 391.

18. M. V. Clarke, *Medieval Representation and Consent* (London, 1936); R. W. and A. J. Carlyle, *Political Theory*, Vol. 5, *The Political Theory of the Thirteenth Century* (London. 1928), pp. 128ff. and Vol. 6, *Political Theory from 1330 to 1600*, (London 1936) A. R. Marongiu, *Medieval Parliaments, a Comparative Study* (London, 1968); A. R. Myers, *Parliaments and Estates in Europe to 1789* (London, 1975).

19. Clarke, *Medieval Representation*, p. 278.

20. R. W. and A. J. Carlyle, *Political Theory*, Vol. 5, p. 129. Athenian democracy was in fact an aristocracy which was based on class distinctions. The mass of the producers, mainly slaves, were excluded from political rights and duties. Rome was less restrictive, but lacking a representative system it could only be democratic as a city; under the Empire only the forms of democracy remained. It was the evolution of the principle of representation which 'provided an escape from the dilemma upon either horn of which every ancient state was sooner or later impaled . . . [it] . . . rendered possible the national democratic state'. A. Pollard, *The Evolution of Parliament* (London, 1920), p. 150. Medieval representation initially meant selection by those authorized to select, but it was open to development in the direction of popular election, and it did so develop.

21. Myers, *Parliaments*, p. 23. He goes on (pp. 36ff.) to show that this form of government evolved only in Western Christendom.

22. The development of the towns is what made the medieval representative system possible. The elected representatives of the citizens, through their participation in the estates system of the time, embodied the principle of true representation in that system and so gave it a different character and demonstrated the constitutional significane of the towns and cities. The estates ceased to be a feudal hierarchy based on land tenure only and became a true political community in which nobles and the knights of the shires co-operated with the commons for agreed ends. Dawson, *Religion*, pp. 208f.

23. Marongiu, *Medieval Parliaments*, p. 25.

24. A. L. Poole, *From Doomsday Book to Magna Carta* (Oxford, 1951), p. 468.
25. Poole, *From Doomsday Book*, p. 485.
26. Edwards, *Christian England*, p. 134.
27. Bishop Stubbs's vision of a clear and logically developing pattern of representative government has been questioned by later constitutional historians on good grounds, though such a pattern did emerge eventually. Marongiu, *Medieval Parliaments*, pp. 77ff.
28. Edwards, *Christian England*, p. 154; F. M. Powicke, *The Thirteenth Century* (Oxford, 1962), ch. 4.
29. Pollard, *Evolution*, chs. 8 and 16.
30. *Reg II* 209 col. 759. R. W. and A. J. Carlyle, *Political Theory*, Vol. 5, p. 157.
31. R. W. and A. J. Carlyle, *Political Theory*, Vol. 1, ch. 5.
32. *CHMPT*, pp. 381ff.
33. C. W. Previté-Orton, *The Shorter Cambridge Medieval History*, Vol. 2, p. 682.
34. See *CHMPT*, p. 396.
35. *CHMPT*, p. 382ff.
36. R. W. and A. J. Carlyle, *Political Theory*, Vol. 5, p. 455.
37. Lawrence, *Medieval Monasticism*, p. 84.
38. Lawrence, *Medieval Monasticism*, p. 156.
39. C. H. Lawrence, *The Friars* (London, 1994), p. 82.
40. M. V. Clarke, *Medieval Representation and Consent* (London, 1936), p. 293.
41. Clarke, *Medieval Representation*, p. 294.
42. Clarke, *Medieval Representation*, p. 296.
43. Clarke, *Medieval Representation*, pp. 312f.
44. R. W. and A. J. Carlyle, *Political Theory*, Vol. 5, pp. 10ff., 31ff., 46ff., 67ff., 90ff.; G. H. Sabine and T. L. Thorson, *A History of Political Theory* (Hinsdale, Ill., 1973), pp. 236ff.; F. C. Copleston, *A History of Philosophy* Vol. 2 (London, 1950), ch. 40.
45. *de Regimine Principum* 1.1. R. W. and A. J. Carlyle, *Political Theory*, Vol. 5, pp. 11f.
46. Aquinas, *Summa*, Ia, Q. 96, art. 4, 'Whether in a state of innocence, man would have been master over man.'
47. *de Reg. Princ.* 1.4. Copleston, *History*, Vol. 2, p. 415.
48. *de Reg. Princ.* 1.14. Copleston, *History*, Vol. 2, p. 416.
49. *de Reg. Princ.* 1.15. Copleston, *History*, Vol. 2, p. 415.
50. *Summa*, IIa IIae, Q. 65, art. 1, 'Whether in some cases it may be lawful to maim anyone.'
51. Copleston, *History*, Vol. 2. pp. 406ff.
52. *Summa*, Ia IIae, Q. 90, art. 1, 'Whether law is something pertaining to reason'.
53. *Summa*, Ia IIae, Q. 91, art. 1, 'Whether there is an eternal law'.
54. *Summa*, Ia IIae, Q. 91, art. 2, 'Whether there is in us a natural law'.
55. *Summa*, Ia IIae, Q. 94, art. 2, 'Whether the natural law contains several precepts or only one'.

56. *Summa*, Ia IIae, Q. 91, art. 4, 'Whether there was any need for a divine law', Q. 93, art. 3, 'Whether every law is derived from the eternal law', Q. 95, art. 2, 'Whether every human law is derived from the natural law', and art. 4, 'Whether Isidore's division of human law is appropriate'.
57. *Summa*, Ia IIae, Q. 95, art. 2.
58. *Summa*, Ia IIae, Q. 90, art. 3, 'Whether the reason of any man is competent to make laws', Q. 97, art. 3, 'Whether custom can obtain the force of law', ad 3.
59. *Summa*, IIa IIae, Q. 42, art. 1, 'Whether sedition is a special sin distinct from other sins' and art. 2, 'Whether sedition is a mortal sin', ad 3.
60. *Summa*, Ia IIae, Q. 105, art. 1, 'Whether the Old Testament enjoined fitting precepts concerning rulers'.
61. Sabine and Thorson, *History*, ch. 16; R. W. and A. J. Carlyle, Vol. 6, *Political Theory from 1300 to 1600* (London 1936), pp. 40ff.; H. Jedin and J. Dolan (eds.), *Handbook of Church History* Vol. 4, *From the High Middle Ages to the Reformation* pp. 359ff.; *CHMPT*, pp. 416ff., 558ff.; Copleston, *History*, Vol. 3, *Ockham to Suarez* (London, 1953), ch. 11.
62. R. W. and A. J. Carlyle, *Political Theory*, Vol. 6, pp. 44ff.; Jedin and Dolan (eds.), *Handbook*, Vol. 4, pp. 363ff., Copleston, *History*, vol. 3, ch. 8.
63. Jedin and Dolan (eds.), *Handbook*, Vol. 4, p. 368.
64. R. W. and A. J. Carlyle, *Political Theory*, Vol. 6, p. 218.
65. R. W. and A. J. Carlyle, *Political Theory*, Vol. 6, pp. 128ff.
66. H. Sidgwick, *The Development of European Polity* (London, 1913), pp. 308f.; Bernard Guenee, *States and Rulers in the Later Middle Ages* (Oxford, 1985), pp. 185ff.

10 The Church and economics in the central and late Middle Ages

1. D. Herlihy, 'Church property on the European continent, 701–1200', *Speculum* XXVI (1961), pp. 88ff.
2. John Gilchrist, *The Church and Economic Activity in the Middle Ages* (New York, 1969), p. 34.
3. P. D. Partner, 'Papal finance and the Papal State', *History Today VII* (1957), pp. 766ff. and 'The budget of the Roman Church in the Renaissance period' in E. Jacob (ed.), *Italian Renaissance Studies* (London, 1960), pp. 256ff.
4. P. D. Partner, *The Papal State under Martin V* (London, 1958), p. 193.
5. J. Scarisbrick, 'Clerical taxation in England 1485–1547', *Journal of Ecclesiastical History* (1960), pp. 41ff.
6. J. Gilchrist, *Economic Activity* pp. 41ff.
7. J. Scarisbrick, *Henry VIII* (London, 1968), p. 340.
8. H. Jedin and J. Dolan (eds.), *Handbook of Church History* Vol. 4, *From the High Middle Ages to the Reformation*, p. 372.

9. Council of Constantinople IV.15, quoted in Gilchrist, *Economic Activity*, p. 29.

10. Colin Morris, *The Papal Monarchy: The Western Church from 1050 to 1250* (Oxford, 1989), p. 320.

11. Jedin and Dolan (eds.) *Handbook*, Vol. 5, *Reformation to Counter Reformation*, pp. 7f.

12. L. Pastor, *The History of the Popes from the Close of the Middle Ages*, vol. 11 (London, 1912), p. 166.

13. Gilchrist, *Economic Activity*, pp. 94f.; Partner 'The budget', pp. 256ff.

14. See above, pp 94–5.

15. S. B. Clough and R. T. Rapp, *European Economic History* (London, 1975), p. 113.

16. C. Cipolla (ed.), *The Fontana Economic History of Europe:* Vol. 1 *The Middle Ages* (London, 1973), p. 331 see above, p. 229.

17. *CEHE*, Vol. 2, p. 630.

18. Clough and Rapp, *European Economic History*, pp. 100ff.; Cipolla (ed.), *Economic History*, pp. 319ff and 325ff.; *CEHE*, Vol. 3, *Economic Organization and Policies in the Middle Ages* pp. 444ff.

19. J. W. Baldwin, *The Medieval Theories of the Just Price. Romanists, Canonists and Theologians in the Twelfth and Thirteenth Centuries* (Philadelphia, 1959), p. 59, quoted in Gilchrist, *Economic Activity*, p. 53. See also Odd Langholm *Economics in the Medieval Schools: Wealth, Exchange, Value, Money and Usury according to the Paris Theological Tradition 1200–1350* (New York 1992).

20. Aquinas, *Summa Theologiae*, IIa IIae, Q. 77, art. 4, 'Whether, in trading it is lawful to sell a thing at a higher price than what was paid for it'.

21. Baldwin, *Just Price*, p. 48; Gilchrist, *Economic Activity*, p. 59.

22. *Summa*, IIa IIae, Q. 77, art. 3, 'Whether a seller is bound to state the defects of the things sold', ad 4.

23. *Summa*, IIa IIae, Q. 77, art. 1, 'Whether it is lawful to sell a thing for more than it is worth', ad 1.

24. *Summa*, IIa IIae, Q. 77, art. 2, 'Whether a sale is rendered unlawful through a fault in the thing sold', ad 3.

25. Clough and Rapp, *European Economic History*, p. 92. Concern for preventing monopoly or restraint of trade of any kind was general in medieval times and was a particular target of government. See *CEHE*, Vol. 3, pp. 424ff. The protection of the community and the consumer was usually the aim; when it was applied to labour some used it to deny the rights of collective action.

26. See, p. 211.

27. 'The small farmer is often hard up just before the harvest, or if the crops are bad, or if storm or flood destroy his little possessions, and to time him over hard times he must borrow . . . the rich neighbour who lent would not lend for nothing; so the peasants used him and hated him and when there was a visitation hurried to accuse him.' *CMH*, Vol. 7, p. 744.

28. G. Duby, *Early Growth of the European Economy* (London, 1974), p. 109.

29. 'In order to constitute a "mutuum" all that was required was that one person should deliver something to another by way of loan . . . not necessarily money . . . it could be any *res fungibilis*, e.g. corn . . . the sole duty of the debtor in a contract of mutuum was to repay the exact amount received . . . never to pay interest.' R. Sohm, *The Institutes: A Textbook of the History and System of Roman Private Law* (Oxford, 1907), pp. 372–3. A 'res fungibilis' means a thing consumed in its use, such as corn.   It was clearly unjust to repay not only the loan of corn but also some extra charge beyond that. Money was only a means of exchange in Roman law and as such it was used up in use; it was indistinguishable from any other money of the same value (ibid. p. 304). Interest therefore could not be taken on it.

30. 'By interest is meant a certain percentage on capital payable by way of compensation for the use of the capital.' This required a verbal contract of 'stipulatio' by which A promises to pay B an agreed sum in interest per month, e.g. 1 per cent, or 12 per cent per annum (Sohm, *The Institutes*, pp. 382f.).

31. Gilchrist, *Economic Activity*, p. 63.

32. Gilchrist, *Economic Activity*, p. 64.

33. Gilchrist, *Economic Activity*, p. 65.

34. Gilchrist, *Economic Activity*, p. 69.

35. Gilchrist, *Economic Activity*, p. 70, quoting M. Pacant 'St Bernardin de Sienne et l'usure', *Le Moyen Age* LXIX (1963), pp. 743ff.

36. Gilchrist, *Economic Activity*, p. 115.

37. *CEHE*, Vol 3,. *Economic Organizations and Policies in the Middle Ages* p. 561; Gilchrist, *Economic Activity*, p. 15.

38. Jaques Bernard, *Trade and Finance in the Middle Ages 900–1500* in Cipolla (ed) *Economic History* pp. 309ff.

39. In *The Protestant Ethic and the Spirit of Capitalism* (ed. T. Parsons, London, 1955, Preface by A. Giddens). It was first published as a two part article in 1904–5 and republished in a revised version in 1920. Its thesis has not gone unchallenged over the years. See Giddens' Introduction, pp. xxiiiff.

40. F. Braudel, *Civilisation and Capitalism 15th–18th Centuries* (London, 1984), Vol. 2, p. 402. Without making a direct attack on historical materialism, Weber among others 'attacked it in its own stronghold . . . capitalism is in great measure the result of a religious spirit'. R. W. Green (ed.) *Protestantism and Capitalism* (Boston, 1959), p. 62.

41. *The Protestant Ethic*, p. 170. That ethic is no great gift to mankind. It suggests a malevolent materialism rather than the spirit of the New Testament. It imprisons man in an iron cage (p. 181). Wesley was one of the witnesses on whom Weber relied, but Wesley foresaw the dangers to the Church through Puritanism. He did not however see the cosmic extent of those dangers – 'a world so dominated by moneymaking that its whole organization is determined by that one great aim'. Green, *Protestantism*, p. 19.

42. *The Protestant Ethic*, p. 91.

43. See above pp. 148ff, 196f and 229.

44. On a study of the economic activities of Catholics in one part of Germany, Baden, in 1895 and one which has been challenged as inaccurate anyway (*Protestant Ethic*, Introduction, p. xxiv); Weber concludes that 'the religious ethos of the West in the middle ages' dominated by Catholic belief, rendered it incapable of concentrated moneymaking, the cause lying in 'the permanent intrinsic character' of that belief (p. 40).

45. J. A. Schumpeter, *History of Economic Analysis* (London, 1963), pp. 80–81f.

46. Braudel, *Civilisation*, Vol. 2, p. 402.

47. *CHMPT*, pp. 621ff.; W. J. Macdonald, *The Social Value of Property According to St. Thomas Aquinas* (Washington DC, 1939).

48. *Summa*, Ia IIae, Q. 98, art. 1, 'Whether in the state of innocence, generation existed', ad 3.

49. *Summa*, IIa IIae, Q. 66, art. 1, 'Whether it is natural for a man to possess external things'.

50. *Summa*, IIa IIae, Q. 66, art. 2, 'Whether it is lawful for a man to possess things as his own'.

51. *Summa*, IIa IIae, Q. 66, art. 2. See Q. 57, art. 3, 'Whether the right of nations is the same as natural right'.

52. *Summa*, a Iae, Q. 105, art. 2, 'Whether the judicial precepts (i.e. of the Old Law) were suitably framed as to the relations of one man with another'.

53. *Summa*, IIa IIae, Q. 57, art. 2, 'Whether right is fittingly divided into natural right and positive right.'

54. *Summa*, IIa IIae, Q. 57, art. 3, 'Whether the right of nations is the same as the natural right'.

55. *Summa*, IIa IIae, Q. 66, art. 2; Q. 57, art. 2 ad 3.

56. *Summa*, IIa IIae, Q. 32, art. 5, 'Whether almsgiving is a matter of precept', ad 2, quoting St Basil *In Hom. Luc. xii.18*, and IIa IIae, Q. 66. art. 7, 'Whether it is lawful to steal in case of need'.

57. *Summa*, IIa IIae, Q. 117, art. 1, 'Whether liberality is a virtue' and art. 4, 'Whether it belongs to a liberal man chiefly to give', ad 1. and Art. 5 'Whether liberality is a part of justice?'

58. *Summa*, IIa IIae, Q. 117, art. 3, 'Whether the use of money is an act of liberality', ad 1, and Q. 134, 'Of magnificence'.

59. *Summa*, Ia IIae, Q. 105, art. 2, 'Whether the judicial precepts were suitably framed as to the relations of one man to another', ad 3.

60. Aquinas *On Princely Government* 1.15. A. P. D'Entrèves, *Aquinas: Selected Political Writings* (Oxford, 1970).

61. Aristotle, *Politics* 2.5.4, and Aquinas *Summa* IIa IIae, Q. 58, art. 6, 'Whether justice is a general virtue, essentially the same as all virtues.' MacDonald, *Social Value*, pp. 41–2.

62. *Summa*, Ia IIae, Q. 21, art. 1, 'Whether there is justice in God'.

63. *Summa*, IIa IIae, Q. 61, art. 2, 'Whether the mean is to be observed

in the same way in distributive as in commutative justice'.

64. *Summa*, IIa IIae, Q. 61, art. 1, 'Whether the species of justice are suitably assigned; commutative and distributive', ad 3.
65. *Summa*, IIa IIae, Q. 61, art. 1.
66. *Summa*, IIa IIae, Q. 61, art. 2.
67. *Summa*, IIa IIae, Q. 66, art. 8. 'Whether robbery may be committed without sin', ad 3.
68. *Summa*, IIa IIae, Q. 29, art. 3, 'Whether peace is the proper effect of charity', ad 2 and 3.
69. *Summa*, Ia IIae, Q. 105, art. 2, 'Whether the judicial precepts were suitably framed as to the relations of one man to another'.
70. *Summa*, Ia IIae, Q. 100, art. 5, 'Whether the precepts of the decalogue are suitably set forth'.
71. Clough and Rapp, *European Economic History*, pp. 91ff.; Sylvia Thrupp, 'The Guilds', ch. 5 in *CEHE*, Vol. 3; Steve Epstein *Wage Labour and the Guilds of Medieval England* (London, 1991); H. Swanston, *Medieval Artisans: an Urban Class* (Oxford, 1989) and H. Boissonade, *Life and Work in Medieval Europe* (London, 1937).
72. Pounds, *Economic History*, p. 290.
73. For example country victuallers were able to sell at markets in Coventry, Chester, London and York, and Chester imported weavers from Shrewsbury, against the opposition of those already in the town when it wanted to set up a new branch of the trade. E. Lipson, *The Economic History of England* (London, 1947), Vol. 1, p. 439. Guild conservatism has been overstressed; the medieval guilds were not as obstructively monopolist as the physiocrats and early liberal economists charged. Medieval labour was so mobile that if restrictions of membership were overdone, those excluded could easily set up in the suburbs or nearby villages. The guilds encouraged mobility of labour with their certificates of service in a guild acting as passports to employment in other towns. In most lines of consumer goods, guild society stimulated demand, so much so that they were the objects of sumptuary legislation seeking to curb it. Thrupp in *CEHE*, Vol. 3, p. 280.
74. Pounds, *Economic History*, p. 291; M. Postan, *The Medieval Economy and Society*, (Harmondsworth, 1972), p. 242.
75. Epstein, *Wage Labour*, p. 167.
76. Epstein, *Wage Labour*, p. 158.
77. Epstein, *Wage Labour*, pp. 103ff. and 124ff., surveys the details of apprenticeship and the standards of production of the guilds.
78. J. H. Clapham in *CMH*, Vol. 6, *Victory of the Papacy*, 1929, ch. xiv *Commerce and Industry in the Middle Age*. 494.
79. Clough and Rapp, *European Economic History*, p. 93.
80. Boissonade, *Life and Work*, p. 212.
81. Clough and Rapp, *European Economic History*, p. 97.
82. Mortimer Chambers et al. *The Western Experience to 1715* (New York, 1979), p. 272.

83. E. Heimann *History of Economic Doctrines* (New York, 1964), p. 23
84. Schumpeter, *History of Economic Analysis* (1963), p. 95.
85. R. De Roover, *St. Bernardino of Siena and Sant' Antonino of Florence: The Two Great Economic Thinkers of the Middle Ages* (Boston, Mass., 1967).
86. Sombart and Keynes quoted in J. Messner, *Social Ethics* (London, 1965), pp. 818f. See D. Dillard, *The Economics of J. M. Keynes* (London, 1966).
87. Morris, *Papal Monarchy*, p. 321.
88. D. H. Allport, *Ramsden: Story of a Wychwood Village* (Oxford, 1965), p. 8. The monastery was also the nearest centre for culture or learning, spreading not only a knowledge of religion but examples of good husbandry, and of many skills and crafts. S. and B. Webb, *English Local Government* (London, 1927), Vol. 7, pp. 15ff., note the existence of the monasteries, not far short of some 1000 throughout the land, large and small, and their work for the people.
89. Morris, *Papal Monarchy*, p. 321.
90. B. Tierney, *Medieval Poor Law* (Berkeley, 1959), p. 15. See Gilchrist, *Economic Activity*, pp. 76ff.; Morris, *Papal Monarchy*, pp. 320ff.
91. Tierney, *Poor Law*, p. 11.
92. Tierney, *Poor Law*, p. 62 quoting the canonist Joannes Teutonicus.
93. Tierney, *Poor Law*, pp. 106ff.
94. S. and B. Webb, *English Local Government* Vol. 7, p. 6.
95. Tierney, *Poor Law*, p. 109.
96. Morris, *Papal Monarchy* pp. 324f.; Gilchrist, *Economic Activity*, pp. 81ff.; Jedin and Dolan, *Handbook*, Vol. 4, ch. 4; L. Conrad et al., *The Western Medical Tradition* (Cambridge, 1995), pp. 149ff.; M. Clay, *The Medieval Hospitals of England and Wales* (London, 1909); Miri Rubin, *Charity and Community in Medieval Cambridge* (Cambridge, 1987); N. Orme and M. Webster, *The English Hospital 1070–1570* (London, 1995); *International Encyclopedia of the Social Sciences* (New York, 1968), Vol. 10, article on 'Medical care'.
97. Rubin, *Charity*, p. 153.
98. *Encyclopedia of the Social Sciences*, Vol. 10, 'Medical care'.
99. Gilchrist, *Economic Activity*, pp. 83ff.
100. Gilchrist, *Economic Activity*, p. 98.
101. Gilchrist, *Economic Activity*, p. 86.

11 The medieval Church: some social attitudes

1. 'The Position of Women' in C. G. Crump and E. F. Jacob (eds.) *The Legacy of the Middle Ages* (Oxford, 1926). Eileen Power *Medieval Women* (ed. M.M. Postan) Cambridge 1975. Shulamith Shahar, *The Fourth Estate: The History of Women in the Middle Ages* (London, 1983) and D. Baker (ed.) *Medieval Women* (Oxford, 1984); Nancy Partner

(ed.) *Studying Medieval Women: Sex, Gender, Feminism* (Cambridge, Mass., 1994).

2. John Russell writing on 'Population in Europe' in *Fontana Economic History of Europe*, Vol. 1, p. 45.
3. Baker, *Medieval Women*, p. 2.
4. Eileen Power in Crump and Jacob (eds.), *Legacy*, p. 432.
5. Power in Crump and Jacob (eds.), *Legacy*, p. 433.
6. Shahar, *Fourth Estate*, p. 280.
7. Shahar, *Fourth Estate*, p. 269.
8. M. Bloch, *Slavery and Serfdom in the Middle Ages* (London, 1975) and his chapter 6, section 3, 'The decline of slavery' in *CEHE*, Vol. 1. Allen J. Frantzen and Douglas Moffat (eds.) *The Work of Work: Servitude, Slavery and Labour in Medieval England* (Glasgow, 1994); Orlando Patterson, *Freedom in the Making of Western Culture* (London, 1991) and *Slavery and Social Death* (Harvard, 1982); M. I. Finley, *Ancient Slavery and Modern Ideology* (Pelican, 1983).
9. H. S. Klein, *African Slavery in Latin America and the Caribbean* (Oxford, 1986), pp. 8ff.; J. Lockhart and S. B. Schwartz, *Early Latin America* (Cambridge, 1984), pp. 17ff. and 26ff.
10. *CEHE*, Vol. 1, *The Agrarian Economy of the Middle Ages*, p. 247.
11. *CEHE*, Vol. 1, *The Agrarian Economy of the Middle Ages*, p. 249.
12. E. Mason, *St Wulfstan of Worcester (1008–1095)* (Oxford, 1990), pp. 184ff.
13. Martin Rule's edition of Eadmer's *De Vita et Conversatione Anselmi*, in the Rolls series (1884) quoted in J. Brodrick SJ, *A Procession of Saints* (London, 1949), p. 55.
14. As presented in the essay 'How ancient slavery came to an end' in Bloch, *Slavery and Serfdom*; Frantzen and Moffat (eds.) *Work of Work*, pp. 95ff. and 101ff.
15. Frantzen and Moffat (eds.) *Work of Work*, pp. 101ff.
16. R. Cameron, *A Concise Economic History of the World* (Oxford, 1993), p. 55.
17. *The Social Teaching of the Christian Churches* Vol. 1, (London 1931) p. 163; J. H. Uhlhorn, *Christian Charity in the Ancient Church*, (Edinburgh, 1883), p. 35. George Ovitt in his article 'The cultural context of Western Technology: early Christian attitudes towards manual labour' (Frantzen and Moffat (eds.) *Work of Work*) shows how the Christian tradition, especially in the monastic life, encouraged respect for manual work and those who performed it.
18. It was in the building crafts that were engaged in the construction of the cathedrals that the skills of medieval craftsmen were most apparent; see above, p. 134, note 4. G. Duby, *The Age of the Cathedrals* (London, 1981), stresses that the theology of the Middle Ages insisted on the dignity of labour; 'the teaching of the Oxford and Paris masters reproved the disdain shown for manual labour by aristocratic society' (p. 154).
19. *CMH*, Vol. 7, *The Decline of the Emperor and the Papacy*. p. 750.

20.   *CEHE,* Vol. 1, pp. 735ff.; *CMH,* Vol. 7, pp. 737ff.; L. Mollat and P. Wolff, *Popular Revolutions of the Late Middle Ages* (London, 1973).
21.   Mollat and Wolff, *Popular Revolutions,* pp. 25ff. and 123ff.
22.   Mollat and Wolff, *Popular Revolutions,* pp. 184ff. and 204ff.; R. B. Robson, *The Peasants Revolt of 1381* (London, 1983).
23.   Pounds, *Economic History,* pp. 216ff.
24.   S. B. Clough and R. T. Rapp, *European Economic History* (London, 1975), pp. 91ff.; M. Postan, *The Medieval Economy and Society,* (Harmondsworth, 1975), p. 241ff. Sylvia Thrupp, 'The gilds', *CEHE* Vol. 3, *Economic Policies and Organization in the Middle Ages* ch. 5; Steve Epstein, *Wage Labour and Guilds in Medieval Europe* (London, 1991); H. Swanston, *Medieval Artisans: An Urban Class* (Oxford, 1989); H. Boissonade, *Life and Work in Medieval Europe* (London, 1937). Antony Black *Guilds and Civil Society in European Political Thought* London 1984.
25.   Boissonade, *Life and Work,* pp. 206f. and 216ff.
26.   *CEHE,* Vol. 2, *Trade and Industry in the Middle Ages* pp. 638ff. and 652ff. But it is noted that while the guilds were involved with fixing wage rates in the earlier period, they were fair. That they should 'be left free to find their own level and that everyone should be free to strike his own bargain, was abhorrent to the men and women of the thirteenth century'. It was considered that they should be reasonable, varying with supply and demand and changes in money values (p. 642).
27.   Epstein, *Wage Labour,* pp. 159ff. on the Church's successful efforts to establish Sunday rest, and holidays on up to 30 or 40 feast days a year.
28.   Boissonade, *Life and Work,* pp. 220ff. On wages and hours, see Epstein, *Wage Labour,* pp. 149, 189, 215ff., 235.
29.   Boissonade, *Life and Work,* p. 302.
30.   Boissonade, *Life and Work,* p. 308. Swanston in her study of the artisans of York (p. 175) concludes that they were prosperous as never before.
31.   Mollat and Wolff, *Popular Revolutions,* pp. 142ff., 161ff. and 174.
32.   C. Dawson, *Religion and the Rise of Western Culture* (London, 1950), p. 207.
33.   Patterson, *Freedom,* p. 363; C. Morris, *The Discovery of the Individual 1050–1200* (London, 1972); Anthony Black, 'The individual and society', *CHMPT,* ch. 18.
34.   Patterson, *Freedom,* p. 366.
35.   Patterson, *Freedom,* p. 373.
36.   Patterson, *Freedom,* p. 375.
37.   Patterson, *Freedom,* p. 403.
38.   David Edwards, *Christian England* (London, 1981), p. 134.
39.   F. H. Russell, *Just War in the Middle Ages* (Cambridge, 1975), p. 294.
40.   Morris, *Discovery,* pp. 144ff.
41.   *CMH,* Vol. 6 *The Victory of the Papacy,* ch. 24; M. Keen, *Chivalry* (London, 1984), pp. 6ff.
42.   Decretum II.XXIII, Q. 1; J. Eppstein, *The Catholic Tradition of the Law of Nations* (London, 1935), p. 81.

43. Russell, *Just War*, p. 295.
44. Aquinas, *Summa Theologiae*, IIa IIae, Q. 40 'Of War', art. 1, 'Whether it is always sinful to wage war'.
45. *Summa*, IIa IIae, Q. 40, art. 2, 'Whether it is lawful for clerics or bishops to fight' ad 2 and 3.
46. The following is taken from Eppstein, *Catholic Tradition*, pp. 92f. with a few minor changes in wording.
47. Russell, *Just War*, p. 303.
48. Russell, *Just War*, p. 308.

12 The Church, absolutism and imperialism

1. E. N. Williams, *The Ancien Régime in Europe: Government and Society in the Major States 1648–1789*, (Harmondsworth, 1979); William Doyle, *The Old European Order 1600–1800* (Oxford, 1992); Stephen J. Lee, *Aspects of European History* (London, 1992).
2. A. J. P. Taylor, *The Course of German History* (London, 1953), p.13; Lee, *Aspects*, ch. 14.
3. Lee, *Aspects*, ch. 16; *New Cambridge Modern History*, (Cambridge 1970) Vol. 4, *The Decline of Spain and the Thirty Years War* 1609–48/59 (Cambridge, 1970), pp. 352ff. The latter (p. 358) notes that Gustavus Adolphus of Sweden was the last who thought religion and power politics should be allied. Richelieu by contrast thought that State interests alone should count and that 'Catholics as well as Protestants ignored the Pope's solemn protest against the clauses of the peace treaties which were injurious to the Catholic Church'.
4. H. Sidgwick, *The Development of European Polity* (London, 1913), pp. 317ff.
5. Taylor, *German History*, pp. 6ff.; Lee, *Aspects*, ch. 3; W. M. McGovern, *From Luther to Hitler* (London, 1946), pp. 30ff; Quentin Skinner, *The Foundations of Modern Political Thought*, (Cambridge, 1978), 2 Vols 1. *The Renaissance* 2. *The Age of Reformation* Vol. 2, chs. 1–3.
6. Skinner, *Foundations*, Vol. 2, p. 113.
7. McGovern, *Luther to Hitler*, p. 31.
8. Taylor, *German History*, p. 9.
9. The wealth of the Church had been accumulating for over one thousand years. The more earnest of the reformers realized later that 'the active greed of the new possessioners, the laymen who had taken over from the clergy was more disgraceful than the parasitism of those whom they had supplanted'. H. Scarisbrick, *Henry VIII* (London, 1968), p. 523. See W. G. Hoskins, *The Age of Plunder 1500–1547* (London, 1975), ch. 6.
10. Williams, *Ancien Regime*, chs. 5, 6; Lee, *Aspects*, chs 21, 22; *NCMH*, Vol. 5, *The Ascendancy of France 1648–88* (Cambridge, 1961), chs. 1, 2, 6, 10 and Vol. 6, ch. 10; H. Jedin and J. Dolan (eds.) *Handbook of*

Church History Vol. 6, *The Church in the Age of Absolution and Enlightenment*, chs. 1–4 and 20, and Vol. 7, *The Church between Revolution and Restoration* pp. 3ff; H. Daniel Rops, *The Church in the Seventeenth Century* (London, 1963).

11.   Daniel Rops (*Seventeenth Century*, p. 188) identifies Bossuet as the most powerful Christian voice of the age.

12.   Daniel Rops, *Seventeenth Century*, pp. 196ff.; *NCMH*, Vol. 5, pp. 129ff.

13.   Daniel Rops, *Seventeenth Century*, p. 232; *NCMH*, Vol. 6, pp. 326ff.

14.   Daniel Rops, *Seventeenth Century*, ch. 1; Jedin and Dolan, *Handbook*, Vol. 6, pp. 22f. and pp. 80ff.; P. Coste, *The Life and Works of St. Vincent de Paul*, 3 vols. (London, 1934); M. Purcell, *The World of Monsieur Vincent* (London, 1964).

15.   Williams, *Ancien Regime*, pp. 158ff.

16.   Daniel Rops, *Seventeenth Century*, p. 41.

17.   W. J. Callahan and D. Higgs (eds.), *Church and Society in Catholic Europe of the Eighteenth Century* (Cambridge, 1979), p. 3.

18.   Callahan and Higgs, *Church and Society*, p. 5; Doyle, *Old European Order*, pp. 132ff.

19.   Callahan and Higgs, *Church and Society*, p. 21. Doyle argues that the alms, far from being indiscriminate, were carefully handled. Those who administered them were always short of funds and were on the watch for the undeserving. Recipients tended to be those resident in the district whose needs and circumstances were known (p. 130).

20.   Callahan and Higgs, *Church and Society*, pp. 45f.

21.   Philip Hughes, *A Short History of the Catholic Church* (London, 1967), p. 168.

22.   Jedin and Dolan, *Handbook*, Vol. 6, ch. 4 and Daniel Rops, *Seventeenth Century*, ch. 6.

23.   'As was realized at the time in many quarters, the destruction of the Society was only the first objective; the grand assault would be against the church and the Apostolic See . . . the struggle with the Society . . . was therefore a struggle with the Papacy.' L. Pastor, *History of the Popes* Vol. 37, London 1950, p. 310.

24.   W. Bangert, *A History of the Society of Jesus* (St Louis, 1972), pp. 395ff. 413ff.

25.   Daniel Rops, *The Church in the Eighteenth Century*, (London 1950), p. 230f.

26.   Jedin and Dolan, *Handbook*, Vol. 6, pp. 453ff., 469ff.; Daniel Rops, *Eighteenth Century*, pp. 227ff.

27.   Bodin was Professor of Jurisprudence at Toulouse. His *Six Books of the Commonwealth* (1576), elaborated an integrated political philosophy. G. H. Sabine and T. L. Thorson, *A History of Political Theory*, (Hinsdale, Ill., 1973), ch. 21; Skinner, *Foundations*, Vol. 2, p. 284ff. McGovern pp. 56ff.

28.   Skinner, *Foundations*, Vol. 2, p. 298.

29.   Hobbes graduated from Oxford in 1608 and became a tutor to the Cavendish family. Disagreements with the Long Parliament led to

his departure to France in 1640 where he was briefly tutor to the future Charles II. He published *Leviathan: or the Matter, Form and Power of the Commonwealth, Ecclesiastical and Civil* in London in 1651, becoming reconciled to the Commonwealth which had executed Charles I in 1649; he could live under any government which effectively controlled the State. Sabine and Thorson, *History*, pp. 422ff. McGovern, pp. 66ff. F. C. Copleston, *A History of Philosophy* Vol. 5 *Hobbes to Hume* (London, 1959), pp. 1ff. and 32ff.

30. Copleston, *History*, Vol. 5, p. 35.
31. *Summa*, IIa IIae, Q. 42, art. 2, 'Whether sedition is always a mortal sin'. See above, p. 185.
32. Skinner, *Foundations*, Vol. 2, p. 177.
33. Skinner, *Foundations*, Vol. 2, p. 321.
34. J. Brodrick, *Robert Bellarmine* (London, 1929), Vol. 1, p. 224.
35. The right can only be exercised 'once the most careful considerations have been made by an appropriate representative assembly of the whole commonwealth'. Skinner, *Foundations*, Vol. 2, p. 178.
36. Skinner, *Foundations*, Vol. 2, p. 177f.
37. L. S. Stavrianos *The World since 1500* (Englewood Cliffs, 1982), ch. 7, 8; C. R. Boxer, *Portugal's Seagoing Empire* (New York, 1975), and *The Dutch Seaborne Empire* (London, 1965); J. H. Parry, *The Spanish Seagoing Empire* (London, 1975); John Bowle, *The Imperial Achievement: the Rise and Transformation of the British Empire* (Harmondsworth, 1974).
38. Stavrianos, *World*, pp. 103ff.; Lee, *Aspects*, ch. 18.
39. Jedin and Dolan, *Handbook*, Vol. 5, *Reformation to Counter Reformation* (London, 1981), chs. 45, 46, and Vol. 6, *The Church in the Age of Absolutism and Enlightenment* (London, 1981) ch. 15; J. Lloyd Mecham, *State and Church in Latin America* (Chapel Hill, 1966); C. H. Haring, *The Spanish Empire in America* (Oxford, 1947); *Cambridge History of Latin America* Vol. 1, 'Colonial Latin America' (Cambridge, 1978).
40. Parry, *Spanish Seagoing Empire*, p. 152.
41. *Cambridge Encyclopedia of Latin America*, p. 131.
42. H. R. Wagner and H. R. Parish, *The Life and Writings of Bartolomé de las Casas* (Albuquerque, 1967); Stafford Poole, *In Defence of the Indians by Bartolomé de las Casas*, (De Kalb, Ill., 1974); Helen Rand Parish (ed.) *The Only Way: Bartolomé de las Casas* (New York, 1994).
43. Communities are 'never sufficient unto themselves . . . that they do not require some mutual help, society or communication, either to their greater advantage or from moral necessity. . . . They need some law whereby they may be directed and rightly ruled . . . And although this come partly from natural law, yet not sufficiently and for all purposes . . . Therefore it has been possible to introduce some special laws by the customs of the people themselves . . . the things appertaining to this law are very closely related to the natural law and are easily deduced from it . . . so although it [international law] is not an obvious deduction . . . it is . . . in accord with nature

and ought to be accepted by all.' Suarez, *De Legibus ac de Deo Legislatore* Lib. II, Cap. XIX (iv) 9, in J. Eppstein, *The Catholic Tradition of the Law of Nations* (London, 1935).

44. J. F. Maxwell, *Slavery and the Catholic Church* (London, 1975), p. 70.

45. L. Hanke, *Aristotle and American Indians* (London, 1959) and *All Mankind is One* (De Kalb, Ill., 1971).

46. John Hemming, *Red Gold* (London, 1985), p. 344; *CHLA* Vol 2 'Colonial Latin America', pp. 512ff.; J. Lockhart and S. B. Schwartz, *Early Latin America* (Cambridge, 1984), pp. 192f., 196f., 281f.; C. R. Boxer, *The Golden Age of Brazil* (London, 1962), p. 275.

47. Hemming, *Red Gold*, p. 482.

48. Philip Caraman, *Lost Paradise* (London, 1975); *CHLA* Vol. 2, pp. 512ff.; *NCMH*, Vol. 4, pp. 711ff.; W. Bangert, *A History of the Jesuits* (St Louis, 1972), pp. 257ff.

49. Caraman, *Lost Paradise*, pp. 249ff.; Bangert, *Jesuits*, pp. 257f., 350ff.

50. The Governor of Paraguay investigated the reductions and cleared the Society of all the charges against it in their regard. Bangaert, *Jesuits*, p. 354.

51. *CELA*, p. 138.

52. R. Mellafe, *Negro Slavery in Latin America* (London, 1975), p. 128.

53. Jedin and Dolan, *Handbook*, Vol. 6, p. 255; Bangaert, *Jesuits*, p. 256; A. Valtierra, *Peter Claver: Saint of Slaves* (London, 1966).

54. Mellafe, *Negro Slavery*, p. 128.

55. A missioner in Saint Domingue befriended there a remarkable young African slave, the son of an African King, captured in battle and sold into slavery: intelligent and of a noble nature he had the good fortune to possess a master who recognized his qualities and gave him a responsible post on his estate and the missioner helped in his education. The young man is known to history as Toussaint L'Ouverture, the humane leader of the first successful slave rebellion and founder of the State of Haiti. A true Christian gentleman, brave soldier, brilliant commander, and a great statesman, he was betrayed by Napoleon and died in exile in 1803. C. L. R. James, *Black Jacobins* (London, 1938); W. Parkinson, *This Gilded African: Toussaint L'Ouverture* (London, 1980).

56. *CHLA*, Vol. 2, p. 373. Frank Tannenbaum published *Slave and Citizen* in 1947. See also R. Coupland *The British Anti-Slavery Movement* (London, 1933), pp. 26ff. and W. Elkins, *Slavery* (London, 1971), pp. 72ff.

57. *CHLA*, Vol. 2, p. 373.

58. See above, p. 224 and footnote 14.

59. *New Catholic Encyclopedia* Vol. 8, p. 460, quoting H. Priestly, *The Coming of the White Man* (New York, 1929).

60. Mecham, *State and Church*, p. 41.

61. Mecham, *State and Church*, p. 41.

62. M. Meyer and W. Sherman, *The Course of Mexican History* (New York, 1982), p. 193.

63. E. Hobsbawm, *The Age of Empire 1875–1914* (London, 1989); R.

Koebner and H. D. Schmidt, *Imperialism* (Cambridge, 1964); H. Wright (ed.), *The New Imperialism* (Lexington, Mass., 1976); D. K. Fieldhouse, *The Colonial Empires* (London, 1966).

64. W. Woodruff, *The Impact of Western Man* (London, 1966), p. 51.
65. R. Oliver and J. D. Fage, *A Short History of Africa* (London, 1988); T. Pakenham, *The Scramble for Africa 1876–1912* (London, 1991).
66. Jedin and Dolan, *Handbook*, Vol. 7, *The Church between Revolution and Restoration* ch. 11; Vol. 8, *The Church in the Age of Liberalism* (London, 1981), chs. 12, 13; Vol. 9, *The Church in the Industrial Age* (London, 1981), chs. 38, 39; Stephen Neill, *A History of Christian Missions* (Harmondsworth, 1977); K. S. Latourette, *A History of the Expansion of Christianity* (London, 1941–4), Vols. 4, 5 and 6.
67. Jedin and Dolan, *Handbook*, Vol. 5, ch. 47.
68. James Duffy, *Portugal in Africa* (Harmondsworth, 1962), p 40; A. Hastings *The Church in Africa 1450–1950* (Oxford, 1994), p. 73ff.
69. Neill, *Christian Missions*, p. 405.
70. Jedin and Dolan, *Handbook*, Vol. 8, pp. 190f.
71. Hastings, *Church in Africa*, pp. 248ff.
72. Neill, *Christian Missions*, p. 429.
73. Jedin and Dolan, *Handbook*, Vol. 9, p. 547.
74. Hastings, *Church in Africa*, pp. 434ff.
75. Jedin and Dolan, *Handbook*, Vol. 9, p. 557 and n. 153.
76. Maxwell, *Slavery*, pp. 47, 50, 67.
77. Above, p. 261.
78. H. S. Klein, *African Slavery in Latin America and the Caribbean* (Oxford, 1986) p. 243.
79. Klein, *African Slavery*, p. 244.
80. Coupland, *Anti-Slavery Movement* , p. 73.
81. Oliver and Fage, *Short History of Africa*, p. 116.
82. Twice as many as when Wilberforce and Buxton took up the task of abolition. Coupland, *Anti-Slavery Movement*, p. 173.

13 The age of revolutions: the seventeenth to the nineteenth centuries

1. M. Ashley, *The English Civil War* (London, 1992); C. Hill, *The Century of Revolution* (London, 1961).
2. John Locke, *Two Treatises of Government* edited by Peter Laslett (Cambridge, 1960); G. H. Sabine and T. L. Thorson, *A History of Political Theory*, (Hinsdale, Ill., 1973) pp. 483ff; F. C. Copleston, *A History of Philosophy* Vol. 5 *Hobbes to Hume* (London 1959) (London, 1950). ch. 7 W. M. McGovern *From Luther to Hitler*, London 1996, ch. 4.
3. Sabine and Thorson, *History*, pp. 513ff.
4. L. Strauss, *Natural Right and History* (Chicago, 1953), p. 246.

5. Basil Williams, *The Whig Supremacy 1714–1760* (Oxford, 1962), pp. 26ff and 128ff., Dorothy Marshall *Eighteenth Century England*, London 1963, pp. 34ff. Plumb, *England in the Eighteenth Century* (Pelican, 1979), pp. 15ff.

6. C. Dawson, *The Gods of Revolution* (London, 1972), p. 17.

7. M. A. Jones, *The Limits of Liberty: American History 1607–1992* (Oxford, 1995); S. E. Morison, *The Oxford History of the American People* (Oxford, 1965); R. B. Nye and J. E. Morpurgo, *A History of The United States* (2 vols). (Harmondsworth, 1965).

8. Morison, *American People*, pp. 51f.

9. Morison, *American People*, p. 180.

10. R. B. Birley, *Speeches and Documents on American History* (Oxford, 1951), Vol. 1, p. 2.

11. Morison, *American People*, p. 270.

12. Morison, *American People*, p. 272.

13. J. C. Murray, *We Hold These Truths* (New York, 1960), p. 28.

14. Murray, *We Hold These Truths*, p. 38.

15. Russell Kirk, *The Roots of American Order* (La Salle, Ill., 1974), p. 343.

16. C. Rossiter, *Springtime of the Republic* (New York, 1953), pp. 429 and 433.

17. Kirk, *Roots*, pp. 332f.

18. Stephen J. Lee, *Aspects of European History* (London, 1992), ch. 37; E. N. Williams, *The Ancien Régime in Europe* (Harmondsworth, 1979), ch. 8, W. Doyle, *The Oxford History of the French Revolution* (Oxford, 1979)..

19. H. Sidgwick, *The Development of European Polity* (London, 1913), p. 382.

20. Williams, *Ancien Régime*, pp. 217ff.

21. Charles Endress, *History of Europe 1500–1848* (London, 1975), pp. 192ff.; Williams *Ancien Régime*, pp. 200ff.

22. H. Jedin and J. Dolan (eds.) *Handbook of Church History* Vol. 7, *The Church between Revolution and Restoration*, p. 19; E. E. Y. Hales, *The Catholic Church in the Modern World* (New York, 1960) p. 35.

23. Jedin and Dolan, *Handbook*, Vol. 7, p. 27; Hales, *The Catholic Church*, p. 36ff.

24. N. Hampson, *The Social History of the French Revolution* (London, 1963), p. 29.

25. Jedin and Dolan, *Handbook*, Vol. 7, p. 49.

26. Jedin and Dolan, *Handbook*, Vol. 7, p. 73.

27. Copleston, *History*, Vol. 6 *French Enlightenment to Kant*, pp. 71ff.

28. Copleston, *History*, Vol. 6, p. 90.

29. Murray, *We Hold These Truths*, p. 307.

30. J. L. Talmon, *The Origins of Democratic Totalitarianism* (London, 1955), p. 43. 'The idea of a people . . . is restricted to those who identify with the general will', these are given a blank cheque on behalf of the people 'without reference to the people's actual will . . . Rousseau's Legislator . . . shapes the "young nation". His superior wisdom . . . prepares it to do his will.' This involves 'The elimination of men and influences not of the people and not identified with the general will embodied in the social contract. The

Legislator is to create a new type of man ... make man virtuous' (pp. 48f). Rousseau's enlightened liberalism certainly helped prepare the modern mind for nineteenth and twentieth century democratic totalitarianism.

31. E. Heimann, *History of Economic Doctrines* (New York, 1964); R. L. Heilbroner, *The Worldly Philosophers* (New York, 1965); J. A. Schumpeter, *History of Economic Analysis* (London, 1963).

32. Heimann, *Economic Doctrines*, pp. 22ff.

33. Heimann, *Economic Doctrines*, pp. 24ff.; Schumpeter, *Economic Analysis*, ch. 7.

34. Copleston, *History*, Vol. 5, *Hobbes to Hume* (London, 1959), p. 174.

35. Heimann, *Economic Doctrines*, p. 49.

36. Heimann, *Economic Doctrines*, p. 51.

37. Adam Smith, *Enquiry into the Causes and the Nature of the Wealth of Nations* (Cannan edn, New York, 1937), p. 423.

38. D. S. Landes, *The Unbound Prometheus* (Cambridge, 1991); Paul Mantoux, *The Industrial Revolution in the Eighteenth Century* (London, 1964); Phyllis Deane, *The First Industrial Revolution* (Cambridge, 1988); Brian Inglis, *Poverty and the Industrial Revolution* (London, 1972).

39. B. R. Mitchell and P. Deane, *Abstract of British Industrial Statistics* (Cambridge, 1962), pp. 5f.

40. M. Cole, *Robert Owen of New Lanark* (London, 1953); G. D. H. Cole, *Life of Robert Owen* (London, 1965); R. Owen, *New View of Society and Report to the County of Lanark* (ed. V. Gatrell, London, 1970).

41. Mantoux, *Industrial Revolution*, p. 388.

42. Deane, *First Industrial Revolution*, pp. 42ff.

43. H. Friedlander and J. Oser, *Economic History of Modern Europe* (New York, 1953), p. 27ff.

44. Inglis, *Poverty*, pp. 120ff.

45. Steven Watson, *The Age of George III* 1760–1813 (Oxford, 1960), p. 363.

46. Plumb *England in the Eighteenth Century*, p. 151.

47. Watson, *George III*, pp. 570f.

48. D. Thomson, *England in the Nineteenth Century* (Harmondsworth, 1979), p. 38.

49. Thomson, *Nineteenth Century*, p. 74.

50. D. McClellan, *Karl Marx* (London, 1976), p. 260.

51. Deane, *First Industrial Revolution*, p. 268.

52. Deane, *First Industrial Revolution*, p. 97; Inglis, *Poverty*, pp. 138ff.

53. 'Possibly the most important reason for the cotton industry's ability to maintain its profits and hence its rate of investment was that it enjoyed an almost inexhaustible supply of low priced labour. While women and girls and pauper children could be put to work for 12 to 16 hours a day in cotton mills at bare subsistence wages, and while there remained a "reserve army" of domestic handloom weavers prepared to work longer and longer hours for smaller and smaller returns, the cotton industry could always command as much labour

as the demand for its products warranted and wages stayed low. Between about 1820 and 1845 the industry's total output quadrupled but the wages of its operatives barely rose at all.' Deane, *First Industrial Revolution*, p. 100.

54. J. Roach, *Social Reform in England 1780–1880* (London, 1978), pp. 78ff; R. Charles, *Man, Industry and Society* (London, 1964), pp. 68ff.

55. E. L. Woodward, *The Age of Reform* (Oxford, 1958), p. 590.

56. Roach, *Social Reform*, p. 123.

57. Heilbroner, *Wordly Philosophers*, p. 109.

58. Charles, *Man, Industry and Society*, p. 48.

59. S. and B. Webb, *A History of Trade Unionism* (London, 1920), ch. 5; Thomson, *Nineteenth Century*, pp. 147ff.

60. H. Pelling, *A Short History of the Labour Party* (London, 1965), ch. 1; H. Clegg, A. Fox and A. F. Thompson, *History of British Trade Unionism* (Oxford, 1964), Vol. 1, ch. 10.

61. R. Ensor, *England 1870–1914* (Oxford, 1960), p. 513.

62. E. H. Phelps Brown, *The Growth of British Industrial Relations* (London, 1959), p. 25.

63. R. Charles, *The Development of Industrial Relations in Britain 1911–1939* (London, 1973), ch. 1.

64. Landes, *Prometheus*; Friedlander and Oser *Economic History* A. S. Milward and A. B. Saul, *The Economic Development of Continental Europe* 1780–1870 (London, 1979); J. H. Clapham, *The Economic Development of France and Germany, 1815–1914* (Cambridge, 1923);

65. E. Cammaerts, *The Keystone of Europe* (London, 1939); E. H. Kossman, *The Low Countries* (Oxford, 1978).

66. Landes, *Prometheus*, p. 156.

67. Cammaerts, *Keystone*, pp. 181ff.; Kossman, *Low Countries*, pp. 179, 251, 314 and 361ff.

68. A. Cobban, *A History of Modern France* (3 vols. Harmondsworth, 1977); T. Zeldin, *France 1848–1945* (2 vols, Oxford, 1973).

69. Cobban, *Modern France* Vol. 2, p. 215.

70. P. A. Gagnon, *France Since 1789* (London, 1964), p. 254.

71. W. L. Shirer, *The Collapse of the Third Republic*, London 1970, pp. 68–71.

72. K. Pinson, *Modern Germany* (London, 1959); G. Craig, *Germany 1866–1945* (Oxford, 1973).

73. Clapham, *France and Germany*, p. 150.

74. Pinson, *Modern Germany*, p. 81.

75. Clapham, *France and Germany*, p. 279.

76. Pinson, *Modern Germany*, p. 197.

77. Craig, *Germany*, pp. 69ff.

78. J. N. Moody, *Church and Society* (New York, 1953), pp. 446ff.

79. Pinson, *Modern Germany*, p. 246; Craig, *Germany*, pp. 150ff. Pinson (p. 185) notes the parallel between Bismarck's legislation and the social programme of the Centre Party.

80. Pinson, *Modern Germany*, p. 208.

81. Pinson, *Modern Germany*, p. 247.

82. Denis Mack Smith, *Italy: A Modern History* (Ann Arbor, 1969); Christopher Seton Watson, *Italy from Liberalism to Fascism* (London, 1967); S. B. Clough, *An Economic History of Modern Italy* (London, 1964).

83. Hales, *Catholic Church*, pp. 101ff.; Jedin and Dolan, *Handbook*, Vol. 8, The Church in an Age of liberalism pp. 57ff., 83ff.

84. Mack Smith, *Italy*, p. 153.

85. Mack Smith, *Italy*, p. 86.

86. R. Ergang, *Europe Since Waterloo* (London, 1965), p. 236.

87. Mack Smith, *Italy*, pp. 173ff.

88. Mack Smith, *Italy*, p. 190.

89. Jones, *Limits of Liberty*; Morison, *American People*; Nye and Morpurgo, *The Growth of the United States*; also S. Morison and H. S. Commager, *The Growth of the American Republic* (2 vols. Oxford, 1963); H. U. Faulkner, *American Economic History* (London, 1960).

90. Morison, *American People*, p. 480.

91. Faulkner, *American Economic History*, pp. 23f., 212 and 417.

92. Nye and Morpurgo, *The Growth of the United States,* Vol. 2, p. 538.

93. Faulkner, *American Economic History*, p. 302.

94. Nye and Morpurgo, *The Growth of the United States*, Vol. 2, p. 389.

95. M. Josephson, *The Robber Barons* (New York, 1962), p. 367.

96. B. Tuchman, *The Proud Tower* (London, 1991), p. 67.

97. Josephson, *Robber Barons*, p. 371; Tuchman, *Proud Tower,* p. 82.

98. Tuchman, *Proud Tower,* p. 423f.

99. Morison and Commager, *American Republic*, Vol. 2, p. 232.

100. Mason and Dixon surveyed the boundary between Maryland and Pennsylvania in the years 1762 to 1767 in order to settle a dispute between the Calverts and the Penns who were the respective proprietors of the two colonies. It became the boundary between free and slave states.

101. Morison and Commager, *American Republic*, Vol. 1, pp. 619ff.

102. Nye and Morpurgo, *The Growth of the United States* Vol. 2, p. 450.

103. Morison and Commager, *American Republic*, Vol. 1, pp. 654, 657.

104. Morison and Commager, *American Republic*, Vol. 1, pp. 655.

105. Morison and Commager, *American Republic*, Vol. 1, pp. 669.

14 Social movements of the nineteenth century and the Church to 1878

1. A. Gray, *The Socialist Tradition: from Moses to Lenin* (London, 1963); G. Lichtheim, *A Short History of Socialism* (London, 1970); G. D. H. Cole, *A History of Socialist Thought* (7 vols. London, 1953-60).

2. *Republic* Bk IV.3.2

3. Quoted by Gray, *Socialist Tradition*, p. 155.

4. See above, p. 291.
5. R. N. Carew Hunt, *The Theory and Practice of Communism* (Harmondsworth, 1963), foreword by Leonard Shapiro; D. McLellan *Karl Marx* (London, 1977) and *Karl Marx: Selected writings* (Oxford, 1977).
6. Preface to *A Critique of Political Economy*, in Gray, *Socialist Tradition*, p. 303.
7. Capital 1.31 in McLellan, *Marx: Selected Writings*, p. 487.
8. McLellan, *Marx: Selected Writings*, p. 222.
9. Carew Hunt, *Theory and Practice*, p. 98.
10. Carew Hunt, *Theory and Practice*, p. 105.
11. *Critique of the Gotha Programme*, in McLellan, *Marx: Selected Writings*, p. 569.
12. McLellan, *Karl Marx*, ch. 7; Carew Hunt, *Theory and Practice*, chs. 11 and 13.
13. The Commune and Marx's pamphlet 'helped brand the International as the greatest threat to society and civilisation' (McClellan *Karl Marx* p. 401). It was said it had co-operated with Napoleon and Bismarck, it was blamed for the great Chicago fire of 1871 and the French Foreign Minister circulated the governments of Europe asserting that the International was a menace to the established order.
14. Carew Hunt, *Theory and Practice*, p. 139f.
15. *Nostis et Nobiscum* (1849), paras. 6, 18, 21 and 23–5 in Claudia Carlen, *The Papal Encyclicals*, Vol. 1, 1740-1878 (Ann Arbor, 1991), pp. 298ff.
16. Barbara Tuchman, *The Proud Tower*, London p. 68.
17. E. E. Y. Hales, *The Catholic Church in the Modern World* (New York, 1960), pp. 72ff.; H. Jedin and J. Dolan (eds.) *Handbook of Church History* Vol. 7 *The Church between Revolution and Restoration*, pp. 100ff.
18. Jedin and Dolan, *Handbook*, Vol. 7, p. 102.
19. Jedin and Dolan, *Handbook*, Vol. 7, p. 263.
20. Hales, *Catholic Church*, p. 93; Jedin and Dolan, *Handbook*, Vol. 7, p. 286ff.
21. R. Aubert, *The Church in a Secularized Society* (London, 1978), pp. 3ff; Hales, *Catholic Church*, ch. 7; Jedin and Dolan, *Handbook*, Vol. 8, *The Church in the Age of Liberalism*, ch. 4.
22. Hales, *Catholic Church*, ch. 10; Jedin and Dolan, *Handbook*, Vol. 8, pp. 293ff.; Aubert, *Secularized Society*, pp. 39ff.
23. Jedin and Dolan, *Handbook*, Vol. 8, pp. 258ff.
24. Article on the *Non expedit* in the *New Catholic Encyclopedia* (London, 1967), Vol. 10, p. 486.
25. Aubert, *Secularized Society*, ch. 8; Jedin and Dolan, *Handbook*, Vol. 9, *The Church in the Industrial Age*, chs. 12 and 13; W. Charlton, *The Christian Response to Industrial Capitalism* (London, 1966), ch. 5; A. R. Vidler, *A Century of Social Catholicism* (London, 1964); J. N. Moody, *Church and Society* (New York, 1953); Paul Misner, *Social Catholicism*

in *Europe* (London, 1991).

26. Vidler, *Century of Social Catholicism*, p. 10.
27. Vidler, *Century of Social Catholicism*, p. 30.
28. Misner, *Social Catholicism*, p. 59; Moody, *Church and Society*, p. 129.
29. Vidler, *Century of Social Catholicism*, p. 63.
30. Vidler, *Century of Social Catholicism*, p. 67; Misner, *Social Catholicism*, p. 130.
31. Misner, *Social Catholicism*, ch. 9; M. H. Elbow, *French Corporative Theory 1789-1948* (New York, 1953); R. H. Bowen, *German Theories of the Corporate State* (New York, 1947), and A. Diamant, *Austrian Catholics and the First Republic* (Princeton, NJ, 1960).
32. Vidler, *Century of Social Catholicism*, p. 124; Charlton, *Christian Response*, p. 196.
33. Misner, *Social Catholicism*, p. 180.
34. Moody, *Church and Society*, p. 128; Misner, *Social Catholicism* p. 44.
35. Vidler, *Century of Social Catholicism*, p. 37.
36. Vidler, *Century of Social Catholicism*, pp. 13ff.; Misner, *Social Catholicism*, pp. 52ff.
37. Jedin and Dolan, *Handbook*, Vol. 7, p. 140.
38. K. Pinson, *Modern Germany* (London, 1958), p. 173.
39. Pinson, *Modern Germany* p. 178.
40. Moody, *Church and Society*, p. 440.
41. Misner, *Social Catholicism*, pp. 46f.; Moody, *Church and Society*, pp. 393ff.
42. Pinson, *Modern Germany* p. 181; Misner, *Social Catholicism*, pp. 76f.
43. Moody, *Church and Society*, p. 412.
44. Misner, *Social Catholicism*, pp. 136ff. The sermons especially angered Marx. Moody, *Church and Society*, p. 414.
45. Misner, *Social Catholicism*, p. 136.
46. Misner, *Social Catholicism*, p. 140.
47. Pinson, *Modern Germany*, p. 186.
48. Pinson, *Modern Germany*, pp. 187f.
49. Misner, *Social Catholicism*, p. 145.
50. Misner, *Social Catholicism*, p. 146.
51. Misner, *Social Catholicism*, p. 112; Jedin and Dolan, *Handbook*, Vol. 9, p. 222.
52. Misner, *Social Catholicism*, pp. 183ff.
53. Jedin and Dolan, *Handbook*, Vol. 7, pp. 279ff.; Moody, *Church and Society*, pp. 286ff.; Hales, *Catholic Church*, p. 85.
54. Charlton, *Christian Response*, p. 122.
55. Misner, *Social Catholicism*, p. 49.
56. Vidler, *Century of Social Catholicism*, pp. 93f.
57. Misner, *Social Catholicism*, pp. 190ff.; E. H. Kossman, *The Low Countries* (Oxford, 1978), pp. 316ff.
58. Vidler, *Century of Social Catholicism*, pp. 148ff; Misner, *Social Catholicism*, pp. 192ff. Jedin and Dolan, *Handbook*, Vol. 9, p. 111.
59. Misner, *Social Catholicism*, pp. 127f.

60.   Misner, *Social Catholicism*, p. 241.
61.   Jedin and Dolan, *Handbook*, Vol. 9, p. 484.
62.   Misner, *Social Catholicism*, pp. 249ff.
63.   Aubert, *Secularized Society*, p. 254; H. U. Faulkner, *American Economic History* (London, 1960), p. 286.
64.   Jedin and Dolan, *Handbook*, Vol. 9, p. 150.
65.   Jedin and Dolan, *Handbook*, Vol. 8, pp. 131, 136.
66.   H. S. Commager, *The American Mind: an Interpretation of American Thought and Character Since the 1830s* (New Haven, 1950), p. 193, quoted in Aubert, *Secularized Society*, p. 271.
67.   Aubert, *Secularized Society*, p. 256.
68.   Arthur Lewis, *The Molly Maguires* (London, 1964).
69.   Aubert, *Secularized Society*, pp. 260ff.; Charlton, *Christian Response*, pp. 130ff.
70.   H. J. Browne, *The Catholic Church and the Knights of Labour* (Washington, 1949); Tracy Ellis, *The Life of Cardinal Gibbon* (Milwaukee, 1952), Vol. 1.
71.   Jedin and Dolan, *Handbook*, Vol. 9, p. 162f.
72.   Marc Carson, *American Labour and Politics* (Carbondale South, Ill., 1958), p. 284.
73.   Jedin and Dolan, *Handbook*, Vol. 9, p. 135.
74.   Robert Gray, *Cardinal Manning: a Biography* (London, 1985), p. 206.
75.   Gray, *Cardinal Manning*, p. 284.
76.   Gray, *Cardinal Manning*, p. 243.
77.   Gray, *Cardinal Manning*, p. 294.
78.   H. Clegg, A. Fox and A. Thompson, *History of Trade Unionism in Britain* (Oxford, 1964), Vol. 1, pp. 58ff.
79.   Clegg, Fox and Thompson, *History of Trade Unionism*, p. 63.
80.   Gray, *Cardinal Manning*, p. 309.
81.   Misner, *Social Catholicism*, pp. 202ff.; H. Daniel Rops, *A Fight for God* (London, 1963), pp. 141ff.
82.   Misner, *Social Catholicism*, pp. 191ff.; Jedin and Dolan, *Handbook*, Vol. 9, pp. 110f.; Charlton, *Christian Response*, pp. 127f.
83.   Jedin and Dolan, *Handbook*, Vol. 9, pp. 107ff.
84.   Misner, *Social Catholicism*, pp. 208ff.

15 A Summary of the social witness and teaching of the Church, c. 1500 to 1878.

1.   See above, pp. 258.
2.   J. B. Scott, *The Spanish Origins of International Law: de Vitoria and the Law of Nations* (Oxford, 1934). See R. Charles with D. Maclaren, *The Social Teaching of Vatican II* (San Francisco, 1982), pp. 257ff.
3.   H. Wright (ed.) *Francisco Suarez: Addresses in Commemoration of his Contributions to International Law and Politics* (Washington, 1933). J.

Eppstein, *The Catholic Tradition of the Law of Nations* (London, 1935), pp. 262ff.; Copleston, *History of Philosophy*, Vol. 3, *Ockham to Suarez* pp. 391ff.

4.	J. A. Schumpeter, *History of Economic Analysis* (London, 1963), pp. 94ff. B. W. Dempsey *Interest and Usury* (London, 1943) contains a full exposition of the economics of the three.

5.	Schumpeter, *Economic Analysis*, p. 97. Economics was seen by Adam Smith as concerned with the ordered knowledge of the social phenomena affecting the acquisition and use of wealth, an understanding which encouraged later less thoughtful economists to ignore the human element; man, the living garment of divinity becomes in their hands the sackcloth thrown over the goods (J. Messner, *Social Ethics* (London, 1946), p. 747). Professor Alfred Marshall (1842-1924) saw the science as concerned with the procurement and use of the means of material well-being, so humanizing it. Professor Arthur Pigou (1877-1959) who had been Marshall's pupil published in 1920 *The Economics of Welfare* which analysed the distribution and stability of national income and the relation between wealth and welfare. Costs of production he pointed out, are not necessarily paid only by the private producer. In ill, health they fall on the worker who suffers as a result of bad conditions, and on the community at large in damage to the environment. Nor is private profit necessarily a good guide in terms of the common good. Where private costs are too low, the industry may become too large for that good; where they are too high it may be too small for it (Heiman, *History of Economic Doctrines*, p. 207).

6.	Schumpeter, *Economic Analysis*, p. 98.

7.	Schumpeter, *Economic Analysis* p. 99.

8.	Schumpeter, *Economic Analysis*, p. 101.

9.	L. Watt, *Usury* (Oxford, 1965), pp. 21-2. See Claudia Carlen, *The Papal Encyclicals 1740–1878* (Ann Arbour USA, 1991), p. 17. para. 9.

10.	Schumpeter, *Economic Analysis*, p. 105.

11.	Schumpeter, *Economic Analysis*, p. 106.

12.	Michael Schuck, *That They May Be One: The Social Teaching of the Papal Encyclicals 1740-1989* (Washington, DC, 1991).

13.	Schuck, *That They May be One*, pp. 31ff.

14.	Schuck, *That They May be One*, pp. 5ff., 16f.

Index

of political authority's demands
39
in social order 4, 80
socialism and 319
in use of wealth 88, 89, 90, 91,
92, 209–10, 346, 373
Justin Martyr 55, 59, 62, 74, 80,
86–7, 92
*see also Index of Biblical, Classical
and Patristic References*
Justinian I, Roman Emperor 62,
72, 76

Kautsky, Karl 307
Kay, James 289
Keane, Bishop James John 351
Kempe, Margery 164
Kentucky 348
Kerala 267
Ketteler, Wilhelm Emmanuel von
340–2, 343, 345, 361
Keynes, John Maynard 215
Khan, Great 155
kingdom, Christ's 28, 30–1, 32–3,
35, 45
Kirdorf (coal and steel magnate)
308
Knights Hospitaler 218
Knights of Labour 313, 350–1
Knights Templar 160, 192, 235
Know-Nothing movement, USA 348
Kolping, Adolph 336, 340
Korea 268
Krupp, Gustav 308
Kuefstein (corporatist) 355
Kulturkampf 306–7, 332, 343

Laaf, Johannes 343
labour
dignity of 213, 225, 313, 355
division of 197, 291, 325
exchanges 307
feudal dues 122–3, 227
freedom of contract 295, 296
indentured 276
Industrial Revolution problem
2–3, 7–8, 289–311

Middle Ages 226, 228–32
Roman era 84–5
sweated 296
unskilled 220, 226
see also slavery; trade unions;
wage labour; *and under*
children; women
Labour Party, British 298
Labour Representation Committee
298
labour theory of value 215
Labriola (Marxist) 311
Lacordaire, Jean Baptiste Henri
338
Lactantius 67, 74, 92, 95
*see also Index of Biblical, Classical
and Patristic References*
laesio enormis 199
Lafayette, Marquis de 271
laissez faire 264, 288, 296, 301, 320,
334, 350, 356
laity
clergy distinction 170
missionaries 267
and political loyalties 5
Lammenais, Abbé 331, 337, 340,
345
La Morvonnais, de 338
Lancashire 289, 352
land
in Biblical times 18–20, 32, 208
early medieval 112, 116, 120,
122, 123, 128, 131
Church: early church 93–4;
medieval 112, 116, 120, 123,
191, 227, 245
clearance and reclamation,
medieval 123, 128, 133, 146,
148, 168, 191, 225, 232
enclosure of British common
275, 289, 291–2
France, 18th century
distribution 282
as gift of God 18, 19, 208
monastic 123, 146, 227, 245
in Roman Empire 56, 84–5, 90,
94

Moerbeck, William of 144
Molina, Luis de 367–9, 370
Molly Maguires 350
monarchy
    under law 17–18, 110, 111, 171,
        172, 253, 280, 361–2
    medieval concept 104, 110, 111,
        172–3, 280, 362
    Old Testament 11, 15–18, 19, 26
    Papacy challenged by national
        2, 156, 159–60, 161, 246,
        250–2, 283, 284, 358, 359
    Roman emperors and church
        53–5
    see also absolutism; divine right
        theory; resistance; ruler and
        ruled
monasteries
    corruption 116
    early church 69–70
    early medieval 102, 107–8, 123–4
    education 104, 107–8, 134, 141
    feudal rights 146
    Henry VIII suppresses English
        192, 193, 245
    industry 108, 124, 146
    Irish, 6th century 107
    land 123, 146, 227, 245
    nursing 219, 250
    organization 107, 180–1
    and peasant society 102, 107–8,
        123, 124
    persecution in 19th century
        Italy 332
    property 146–7, 192–3, 318
    proprietary churches 191, 192
    scriptoria 104, 109–10
    State draws on resources 7, 107
    in towns 108, 125–6
    welfare provision 216, 217–18,
        220
    women's 219, 222, 250, 268
    work and dignity of labour
        69–70, 107, 226
    see also individual orders
Mönchengladbach group 344, 357
Monck, General George 273

money 126–7, 369, 370–1
Mongolia, Inner 155
Monica, St 71
monopolies, municipal grants of
    199, 211, 212
monopolistic practices 199, 214,
    230, 231
Mons 130, 299
Montesimos, Antonio 257
Montesquieu, Charles de
    Secondat, Baron de 113, 270,
    274
Montpellier 152, 218
Montufar, Alonso de, Archbishop
    of Mexico 270
morality
    Christ's non-legalistic 29
    early church 61, 63, 65, 66
    economic 40–3, 75, 195–206,
        214, 232, 367–71
    Hobbes' theory of 253
    Old Testament link with
        religion and law 13
    Roman decline in 57
    and trust, in market economy
        212
    US, on Christian basis 280
More, St Thomas 153
Moses 11, 14–15, 97
Muller, Adam 305
Mun, Count Albert de 336, 345,
    356
Münsterland 340
Murri, Romulo 348
Muslims
    invasion defeated at Poitiers
        103, 104–5
    learning 141, 144, 152
    in Spain 154, 256, 270
    trade 124–5, 147, 196, 223
Mussolini, Benito 310
mutual aid societies 335, 347
mutuum (loan) 201, 202, 370
mystery religions, Oriental 55

Nabal 20
Naboth's vineyard 18, 19, 90–91

Index of Modern Authors

Index of Biblical, Classical and Patristic References